DRAMATIC EFFECTS
WITH A MOVIE CAMERA

DRAMATIC EFFECTS WITH A MOVIE CAMERA

GAIL SEGAL AND SHERIL ANTONIO

BLOOMSBURY ACADEMIC
LONDON • NEW YORK • OXFORD • NEW DELHI • SYDNEY

BLOOMSBURY ACADEMIC
Bloomsbury Publishing Plc
50 Bedford Square, London, WC1B 3DP, UK
1385 Broadway, New York, NY 10018, USA
29 Earlsfort Terrace, Dublin 2, Ireland

BLOOMSBURY, BLOOMSBURY ACADEMIC and the Diana logo are
trademarks of Bloomsbury Publishing Plc

First published 2021

Cover design by Namkwan Cho
Cover image: *Luxor* (2020) directed by Zeina Durra. Cinematography by Zelmira Gainza.
Film-Clinic Productions. Mohamed Hefzy, Producer.

A catalogue record for this book is available from the British Library.

Library of Congress Cataloging-in-Publication Data
Names: Segal, Gail, 1952- author. | Antonio, Sheril D., 1960- author.
Title: Dramatic effects with a movie camera / Gail Segal and Sheril Antonio.
Description: London : Bloomsbury Academic, 2020. | Includes
bibliographical references, filmography, and index.
Identifiers: LCCN 2020036662 (print) | LCCN 2020036663 (ebook) |
ISBN 9781350099494 (hardcover) | ISBN 9781474285827 (paperback)
| ISBN 9781474285834 (pdf) | ISBN 9781474285841 (epub)
Subjects: LCSH: Cinematography. | Motion pictures—Production and direction.
Classification: LCC TR850 .S35 2020 (print) | LCC TR850 (ebook) | DDC 777—dc23
LC record available at https://lccn.loc.gov/2020036662
LC ebook record available at https://lccn.loc.gov/2020036663

ISBN: HB: 978-1-3500-9949-4
PB: 978-1-4742-8582-7
ePDF: 978-1-4742-8583-4
eBook: 978-1-4742-8584-1

Typeset by Lachina Creative, Inc.
Printed and bound in India

To find out more about our authors and books visit
www.bloomsbury.com and sign up for our newsletters.

Preface

Today, as we proof the layout of our book, a viral pandemic circles the globe, leaving an imprint on every continent, forcing a reckoning. The movie industry has, like other venues for creative expression, taken a major hit. And yet storytellers committed to motion pictures have demonstrated pluck and ingenuity, using what resources they have on hand—even if just a cell phone, a one-room apartment, and a cat—to stage and record drama. Within months of the pandemic's onset, guilds across the world began revising protocols for safe media production so that the "show could go on," and as soon as possible. All the while, demand for visual storytelling content increased, particularly as the parameters of our lives narrowed and the need to be transported became more urgent.

Movies have provided escape, fantasy, inspiration, or adventure, even a chance at love, and the enduring pleasure of catharsis as we see characters navigate life's perils and survive. Some of these characters emerge with new insight. Others manage to transform, serving as an example. Movies have brought the human community with all its variations of race, creed, gender, and culture into our homes, inviting connection at a time when isolation has been our prescription.

Also, at this time, conversations have intensified, worldwide, around the subject of race and identity, and this too has impacted moviemaking, with film industry standards in America and elsewhere called on to become more inclusive, entitling unheard voices and fostering a new wave of stories indigenous to the storyteller. Some beautiful examples of this have emerged recently, too recent for our exploration, and we look forward to opportunities in the future to think and write about their dramatic effects.

We hope by the time this book is available to you that the possibility of seeing images come to life on the big screen in your local cineplex is once again real.

Gail Segal and Sheril Antonio

Acknowledgments

First, we want to acknowledge the many students we have taught over many years in the Graduate and Undergraduate Film Divisions and in Art and Public Policy at New York University. They have kept us in conversation with all that's crucial in the art of making film. A hearty thanks, as well, to NYU's Tisch School of the Arts, which supported our first efforts with grant funding.

We are grateful to Sasie Sealy and Suzanne Nakasian, who assisted with revisions of early drafts, and to early readers Annie Howell, Bette Gordon, and Ed Wilson, whose encouragement proved indispensable. No project from our desk could succeed without the aid of Patti Pearson, Director of Strategic Initiatives at TSOA. Julia Lord of Julia Lord Literary Management offered terrific counsel along the way.

The immense amount of image work required a good deal of assistance. Godofredo Astudillo, Craig Johnson, Brian Hubbard, Lucas Soares, Ajai Vishwanath, and Tim Delaney, filmmakers all, helped to bring the text to life with images. An additional toast of gratitude to Tim Delaney for his good cheer and technical savvy dispensed over many months as we prepared the images for publication.

The last lap in any book project seems to involve the most concerted effort. This was a welcomed collaboration; thanks to our dedicated editor, Renée Villaneuva-Last, and Molly Montanaro of Lachina Creative for assembling so tastefully all the elements into the book's final form.

Special thanks, finally, to the terrific team at Bloomsbury Press, past and present: Lynsey Brough, James Piper, Georgia Kennedy, Amy Jordan, Erin Duffy, and in particular Katie Gallof, who saw the book through to the end.

Contents

48 Chapter four

The moving camera

72 Chapter five

The wide shot and mise en scene

90 Chapter six

The long take

Introduction

Who could have imagined in 1895 when the Lumiere brothers set up a movie camera on the streets of Lyon that moving images would have such magical power? Within a few years, the spell of motion pictures locked step with storytelling to earn cinema the status as one of our most cherished pastimes and common social currencies. Today, scores of online sites and streaming services, movie blogs, and podcasts create a twenty-four hour cycle of movie watching and critique. And now a movie, regardless of its means of distribution, has the capacity to create a community overnight. Any viewer can ante-in with an opinion.

As it turns out, our opinion about a given movie matters, not only for the way it translates into box office tallies or online "hits"—but also as proof of our willingness to enter the world that the filmmaker has conjured. A movie is a contract, of sorts, between the filmmaker's vision and our inclination to enter the story created by it.

The dynamic between a film and its audience is the basis for this writing. The project: to go behind the scenes to the construction of a movie, looking closely at techniques that accumulate to produce the dramatic effects that give cinema its power. Stretching our capacity to analyze a film also educates the talent for making movies. It enlarges the capacity to bring to life on screen a world, albeit magic, that is believable, endowed with sufficient gravity and coherence.

Engaging in critical analysis involves attention to the interaction between dramatic effects and the techniques used in the service of storytelling. This can lead to uncovering patterns of technique, and variations from those patterns, that combine to give a movie its consistent tone and style.

I think cinema, movies, and magic have always been closely associated. The very earliest people who made film were magicians

—Francis Ford Coppola,

Academy of Achievement Interview, 1994

Dramatic effects

The notion of **dramatic effect** refers to the response engendered by what we see and hear on screen. Effects include, but are not limited to, the arousal of suspense, delight, sadness, surprise, anxiety, thrill, fear, or laughter. A scene might even provoke frustration or impatience. The practice of close reading requires awareness of our individual response as we attempt to understand precisely what dramatic effect the filmmaker intends.

Film techniques refer to the means by which a given effect is evoked. These include, but are not limited to: lighting, camera placement, angle, shot size, duration, stasis, movement, hand-held camera movement, steady cam movement, subjective camera, mise en scene, location, set design, costume design, editing, and sound design. The project of this book is the exploration of camera techniques and their effects.

The art of looking closely

Two simple questions allow a viewer to determine a number of particulars about the way a movie, or a scene in a movie, has been made: 1) What dramatic effects are in play? 2) What combination of techniques has been used to create them?

The following still frames are taken from one of the very first films. It is a one-minute movie from one camera position, in one shot (meaning that there are no cuts or in-camera edits). This film was the creation of two brothers, Auguste and Louis Lumiere, in 1897. Despite primitive resources, they were able to exercise a wide range of technical choices: subject and location, camera placement, camera angle, composition, blocking and staging of character(s), and use of light and shadow. The techniques are employed for maximum dramatic effect.

What are the effects? The story is about a small child with one goal: to retrieve her doll. The doll lies at the end of the sidewalk. To complicate the narrative, there is a crevice in the sidewalk between the child and the doll, and she has only just begun to walk, making her gait unsteady. Accompanied by her nursemaid, who hovers behind her, she toddles along in a Sunday dress toward the crevice. Slowly moving over the relatively long stretch of sidewalk, the viewer waits, anticipating, for the better portion of the fifty seconds, as she approaches the break directly in her path. The frame is composed so that the sidewalk creates an off-centered diagonal, stretching corner to corner. The diagonal has become a common tool, often used for deepening the two-dimensional surface of the frame. The sidewalk widens in the foreground as it narrows in the distance. This adds perspective to the composition. Placing the camera at the end of the sidewalk on a diagonal impacts our sense of space but it also works as a way of stretching time. This triggers our apprehension as the child toddles toward us, and toward the sizeable crack in the sidewalk. French filmmaker, Bertrand Tavernier, provides commentary on the DVD and cites it as the first suspense film made. (Figure 0.1)

The angle of the camera is pitched above the child, adding to our sense of her vulnerability. The Lumiere brothers add to the dramatic effect with the presence of a nursemaid. She gives the story a sense of false security. Although she hovers nearby, she does not spare the child her calamity. Through placement and stasis,

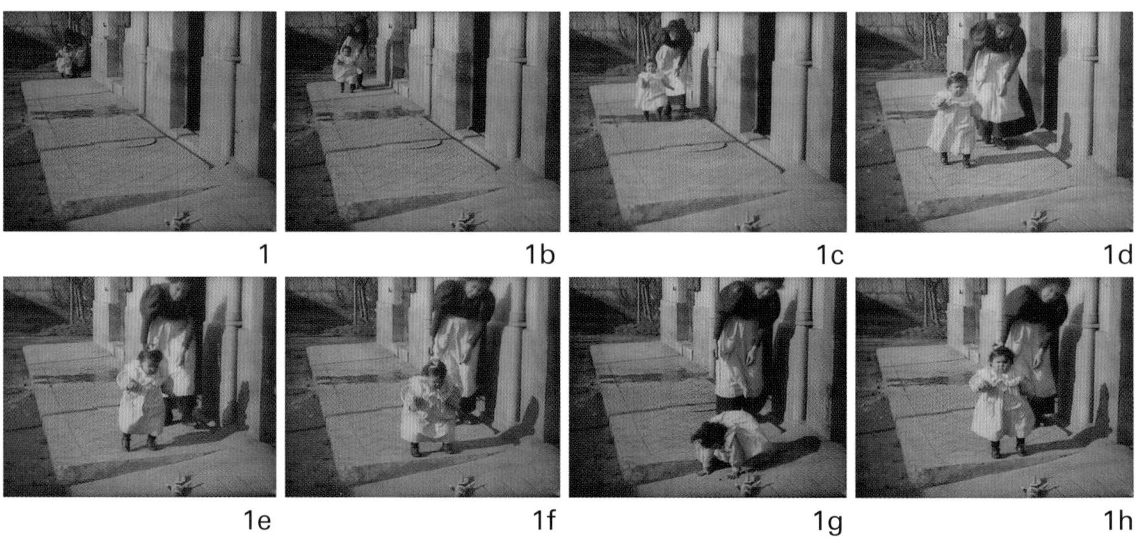

Figure 0.1
Baby's First Steps (1897). *Lumiere Brothers' First Films.* Directors: Auguste and Louis Lumiere. Cinematographers: Auguste and Louis Lumiere.

the camera is also detached, or objective, meaning it does not, through movement or framing, comment or intrude on the action. This contributes to the suspense and comedy. Working backwards, you might say that *suspense* and *humor* are the effects. The techniques employed are just the ones mentioned—static camera, one take (camera work), the break in the sidewalk (location), extending the length of the sidewalk and depth of field through diagonal (camera position and mise en scene), a child learning to walk (camera angle and casting) holding a doll baby (prop), AND the nursemaid (casting, blocking, and staging).

Eventually, with our two questions in mind, we might also discern the filmmaker's overall **strategy**. The strategy in this case might have been to apply technique to enhance suspense, encouraging the viewer to fear the worst, and when the worst happens the viewer still laughs! (We laugh, of course, because it is *not* the worst—the child's overall wellbeing remains intact.)

It's remarkable—the number of techniques manipulated to successfully create the desired dramatic effects in a one-minute movie. While the technical choices available to filmmakers today offer vastly more variation and complexity, certain considerations remain the same. A movie still has the power to incite dramatic effects that occur through the application of particular techniques. Driving this application is an overall strategy that takes into account the story's dramatic elements—character, plot, theme—with consideration, too, for tone and style. The interplay between story and technique conspires to make the movie a *particular* world, with a style tailored to the *particulars* of its story and narrative form. The pages to follow offer a spirited analysis of the impact such interplay can have on a movie's construction.

The Lumiere Brothers' First Films

Practice your critical analysis of technique in additional one-minute films by the Lumiere Brothers. They can be found online along with more information about the Lumiere Brothers and their contribution to cinema.

Devising a strategy for deploying camera technique doesn't diminish or deny the value of choices made on set when surprises or obstacles steer the style of camera coverage in a particular direction. A strategy can be organized around an intuitive camera, as in *Thou Wast Mild and Lovely*, the second feature by director Josephine Decker. The camera seems to make moment-to-moment decisions that unsettle the viewer into a present tense (key word, "tense"), certainly among the desired effects. In Wong Kar-Wai's film, *Fallen Angels*, an abstract of visual imagery is unleashed that requires a degree of playfulness and spontaneity from the cinematography. In each film, however, the idiosyncratic visual imagery gives way to patterns of coverage, which in turn, lead the viewer to trust the filmmaker's authority and the world created.

Each film demonstrates a necessary dynamic between camera and editing. Isolating a given technique presumes that it can be analyzed separate from other techniques. This is false. Of course the choice of shot size implicates shot length (duration). Framing is informed by color palette and set design. Our devotion to and exploration of camera technique will include, from time to time, the interaction of camera with shot duration, shot sequence, blocking and staging, choice of location, mise en scene, color palette, or in some instances, casting. That being said, isolating a given technique also encourages authority in thinking through the specific dramatic effects a filmmaker hopes to achieve. This can be felt as a sure-handedness in visual storytelling.

Implicit in this authority is the search for methods of giving the film world *coherence*, *credibility*, and *authority*. *Coherence* insures that each element in a scene and each scene in the movie belong to one another, that they are part of the same world. *Credibility* asks for a believable world—a condition demanded of even the most fantastic of films, as in Terry Gilliam's *Brazil* or Stanley Kubrick's *2001: A Space Odyssey*. Finally, *authority* refers to a particular kind of fitness that all the best filmmaking requires. Sidney Lumet told a group of graduate directing students that physical fitness was one of the most valuable assets of being a director. But the impact of *The Verdict* stems not only from the director's stamina, but also from commitment to technical choices that demonstrate passion, intuition, dexterity, precision, and stance. This gives the movie its authority.

One last claim about the capacity of technical choices to inform a movie's stance, often felt as "tone." In his essay, *Feeling Into Words*, the poet Seamus Heaney uses the analogy of drawing water from a well to illustrate the meaning of stance.[1] Paraphrasing, he says that "craft," is simply turning the crankshaft: it insures that the bucket can be lowered on the rope and raised from the bottom of the well. For moviemakers this translates into directing actors toward a believable performance, securing a readable image with the camera, recording audible sound, etc. But craft is not enough. To actually get water into the bucket requires more than facility, more than superior craftsmanship. Seamus Heaney calls this, alternatively, "technique," which includes a point of view, a stance toward story content and characters—a way of seeing the world. Even those who have written and directed a short film know the sensation that resembles a rope tightening against the pull of the windlass. This acts as a counter-weight, a gravity that holds the particulars of a movie world in place. The movie then becomes a well of experience that others—the audience—can drink from.

For avid moviegoers wanting a look behind the scenes of moviemaking, you will hopefully find insight into the various ways that choices related to camera work can make us laugh, cry, squirm, shriek, and/or delight. If you happen to be a moviemaker as well as a moviegoer, you know already the burden of divining a water source. This practice of looking closely at the good work of other filmmakers, will, we hope, sharpen the tools you need for drawing that water out of the ground.

Our exploration considers the work of a hundred directors from over twenty-five countries. Even this wide net has not satisfied our thirst as writers given the many filmmakers we admire who are not represented in these pages. This includes significant figures from every decade of film history as well as young directors emerging as we write with movies of original vision and robust technique.

Further practice at close reading

Guido Anselmi, the protagonist of *8½*, is a film director suffering a midlife crisis fueled by a dreadful creative block. In Shot 1, Guido (off-screen) sees his producer (centered) arrive at the spa hotel where Guido has come hoping to revive his spirit. Shot 1b, a reverse shot, reveals their reunion.

Discussion questions

1. In Shot 1, identify the ways that the camera placement echoes decisions made by the Lumiere brothers in *Baby's First Steps*?
2. How does the choice of camera angle inform our understanding of the dynamic between Guido and his producer?
3. How would you describe the camera angle in Shot 1b?
4. In what ways does the camera angle reinforce information provided in Shot 1?
5. Which other techniques are used to enhance our understanding of their relationship?

Notes

1. Seamus Heaney's discussion of stance can be found in the essay, "Feeling Into Words," from his book length collection, *Preoccupations* (1980, Faber and Faber).

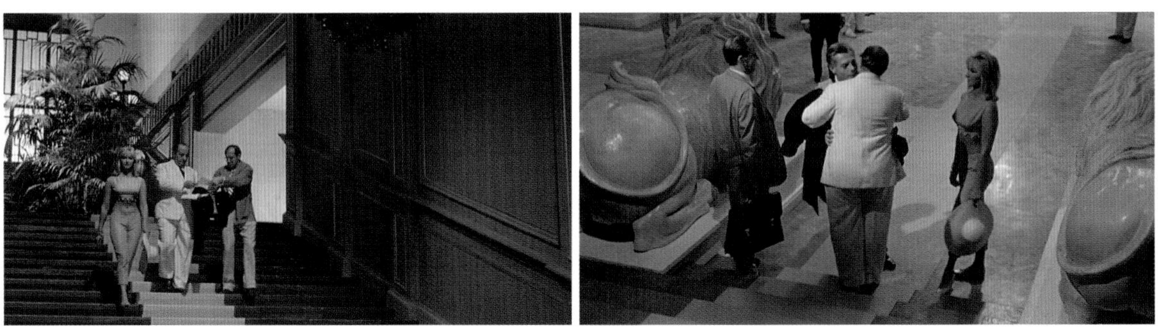

1 1b

Figure 0.2 *8½* (1963). Director: Federico Fellini. Cinematographer: Gianni Di Venanzo.

1

Camerawork

Nearly everyone knows the experience of perusing vacation photographs and discovering an object or figure that went completely unnoticed at the time the picture was taken. The camera, unlike the human eye, resists endearment; it is democratic and detached. It privileges any aspect lit within the border of the frame.

Lighting is, of course, an essential element for capturing an image. Light and shade can be manipulated for creating mood, tone, style, and in the most basic way, emphasis—guiding our attention to a specific portion of the frame. For our purpose, the immediate focus is the **frame**—the border of the image—and the capacity of the camera to corral component parts within that border. In moviemaking, this organization translates into a sequence of shots. Sequencing different shot sizes directs the viewer's attention, enhances story progression, and creates dramatic effects.

The shot

The still frames depicted in Figure 1.1 occur sequentially in Yasujirō Ozu's feature film, *An Autumn Afternoon*. The two shots picture the same room, and yet the camera organizes space to achieve two distinct impressions. In the first image, the wall of windows is prominent and the wooden stool cushioned in red, barely visible. The second image, with different framing, emphasizes the wooden stool. The shift in emphasis highlights the way changes in composition alter perception of the same space, and in so doing, impact story development. This interaction between the placement of objects/subjects within a frame (i.e., the red-cushioned stool) and the border of the frame will drive much of our conversation (Figure 1.1).

The **shot** is the most fundamental unit of filmmaking. **Wide shot**, **medium shot**, and **close-up** describe changes in the size of objects relative to the frame, also implying distance between the viewer and the content of the image. The perceived change in distance is accomplished through changing the camera's position and/or the focal point of the camera lens.

The camera

The corralling of component parts echoes the Latin root of the word *camera*, which means "room" or "enclosure." The movie camera, like the still camera, organizes space.

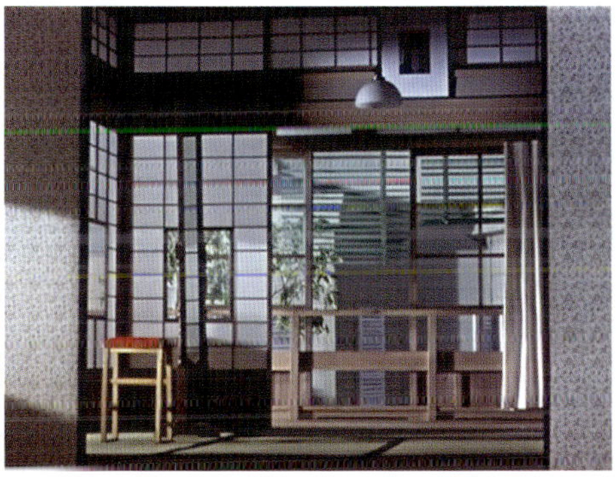

1

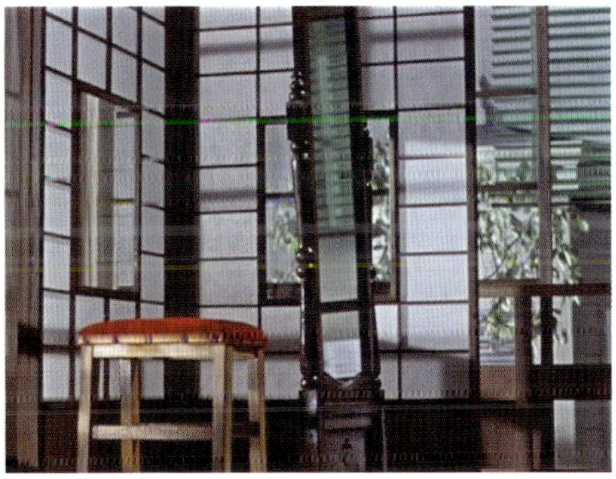

1b

Figure 1.1
An Autumn Afternoon (1962). Director: Ozu Yasujirō. Cinematographer: Yûharu Atsuta.

Variation in shot size

If we could transport ourselves to the occasion of seeing a motion picture for the first time, the sensation of seeing objects change in relative size in correlation with a movie's plot would seem almost miraculous. The still frames from Murnau's 1924 film, *The Last Laugh*, convey something of the ingenuity in manipulating image proximity, from wide shot to medium shot, or medium shot to close-up through the cut, as a way of directing the viewer's eye. In Figure 1.2, the sequence includes an extreme wide shot, the **establishing shot**, which cuts to a medium wide shot of the same action.

Figure 1.3 depicts another sequence from *The Last Laugh*, which includes changing shot sizes. It begins with a wide shot that cuts to a medium shot, ending with a close-up of the same action.

Cinema's pioneering directors maximized this technique, controlling the viewer's story knowledge from moment to moment through changes in proximity and perspective.[1] It was Murnau's film that first startled early audiences with fluid camera movements, introducing another method for adjusting proportion and expanding the means by which distance between viewer and image content might be controlled. **Camera movement** and the **cut** made changes in proximity and perspective inevitable, insuring their use and practice in the future of filmmaking. Today, after over a century of technological advances, altering the relative size of the image persists as a fundamental tool in the language of visual storytelling.

Figure 1.2
The Last Laugh (1924). Director: F.W. Murnau. Cinematographer: Karl Freund.

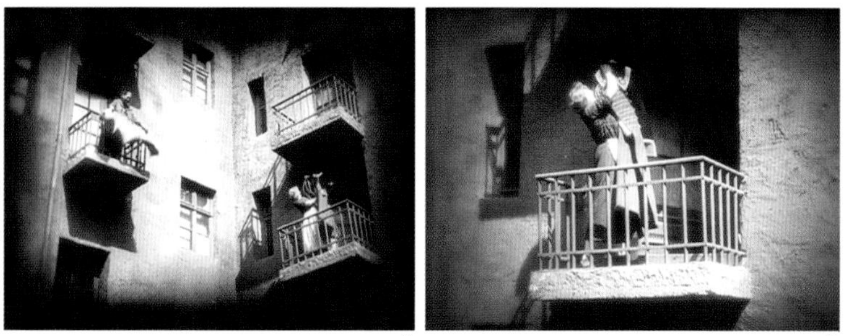

1 2

Figure 1.3
The Last Laugh (1924). Director: F.W. Murnau. Cinematographer: Karl Freund.

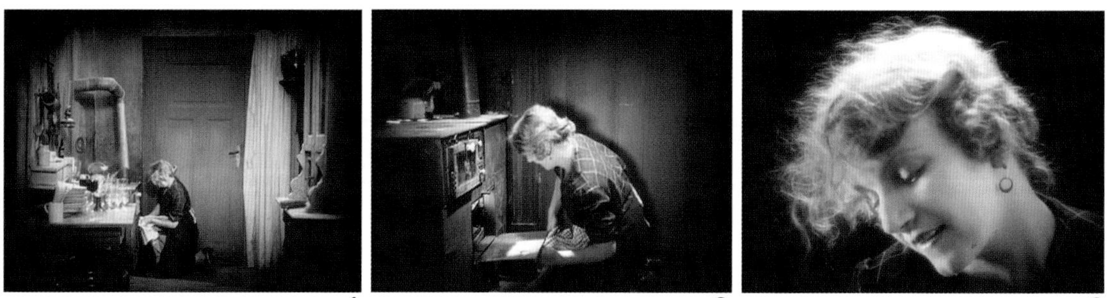

1 2 3

The cinematographer's field is incommensurable. It gives you an unlimited power of creating.

—*Notes on the Cinematographer* by Robert Bresson, 1997. Green Integer.

Organizing space

Variation in shot size is at the heart of the camera strategy in the prologue of *KAOS*, a 1984 feature film by Paolo and Vittorio Taviani. This variation functions to emphasize certain moments in the drama while also providing key story elements not included in the dialogue between characters. The prologue—a self-contained story told in four minutes—is a perfect length for exercising the muscle of close observation. We can easily determine which camera techniques have been used to create which dramatic effects. We can also discern the **pattern of technique** in the overall strategy that gives this short film credible **coherence**.

The first shots of the prologue are close-ups, revealing three men, each in turn, bearded, clothed in sheepskin, and fixed on the sight of what they discover to be a male bird sitting on a nest of warm eggs. Mockingly, they wrench the bird from the nest in the last close-up before an abrupt transition to an **extreme wide shot** that places the men in a vast landscape of boulder and scrub grass, bringing into view two other men who sit near a fire in front of a large umbrella (Shot 12, Figure 1.5).

The next set of shots (Figure 1.6) resume the use of medium close-ups and close-ups. They frame the sport of dangling the bird, as the men, one at a time, throw eggs—treating the bird as their mark. This succession of shots ends with the same extreme wide shot. This use of the wide shot emerges as a pattern in the film, a punctuation or narrative marker in what could be understood as a break between short acts.

The transition from close-up to extreme wide shot reveals the proximity between characters, as well as the characters in relation to the environment. The effect inverts the two examples from the Murnau film where shifts in proportion direct audience attention to a particular aspect of the previous, wider frame, not unlike a detail of a painting pictured in an art book. The wide shots in the *KAOS* prologue work as establishing shots, but the establishing takes place *after* characters are introduced and dramatic action has occurred. Having located the men in a rocky wilderness,

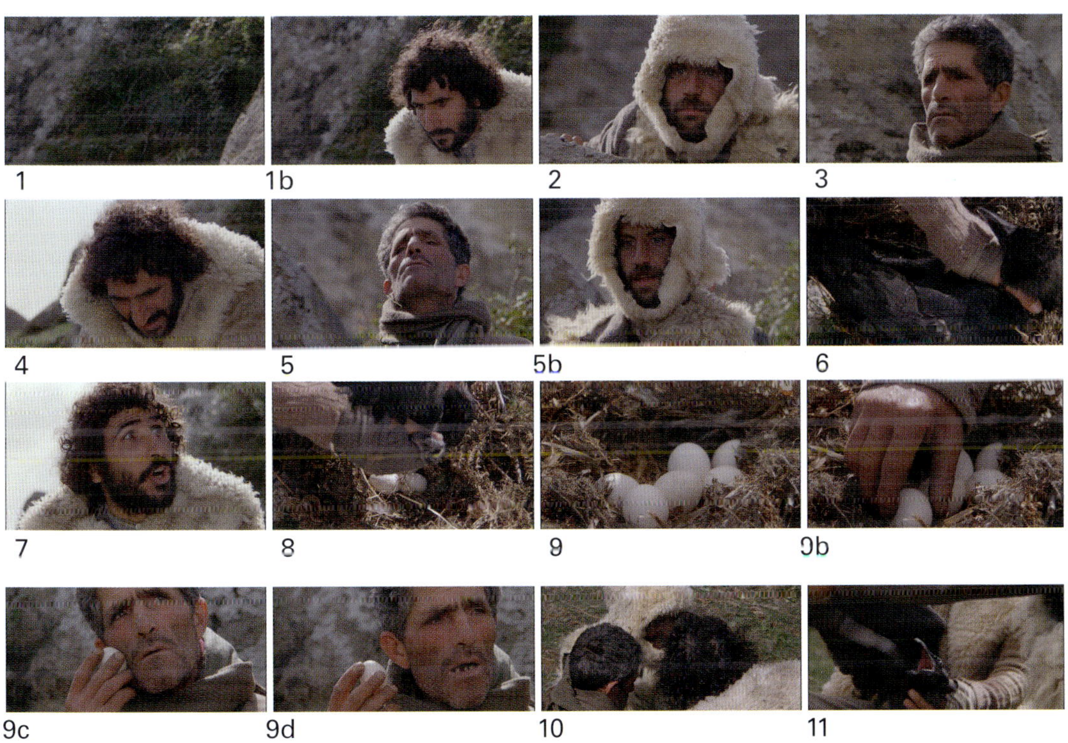

Figure 1.4
KAOS (1984).
Directors:
Paolo and
Vittorio Taviani.
Cinematographer:
Guiseppe Lanci.

the wide shot depicts proportion—suddenly characters that all but filled the frame in close-up are diminished by the comparative size and scale of their surroundings. The story's thematic interest—the tug between artistic impulse and primitive instincts, dominance and freedom—is reinforced by the visual play between close-up and wide shot, even as the wide shot performs its explicit narrative function. The force of male dominance expressed by character behavior, costume, and tight framing converts the men to diminished status when seen against the backdrop of a massive boulder in the wide shot—nature shown having more sovereignty than their base instincts.

The third act features the same range of close-ups and medium close-ups (Figure 1.6). The man seen earlier in the extreme wide shot near the fire intercepts the bird. Without the insertion of wide shots this character would

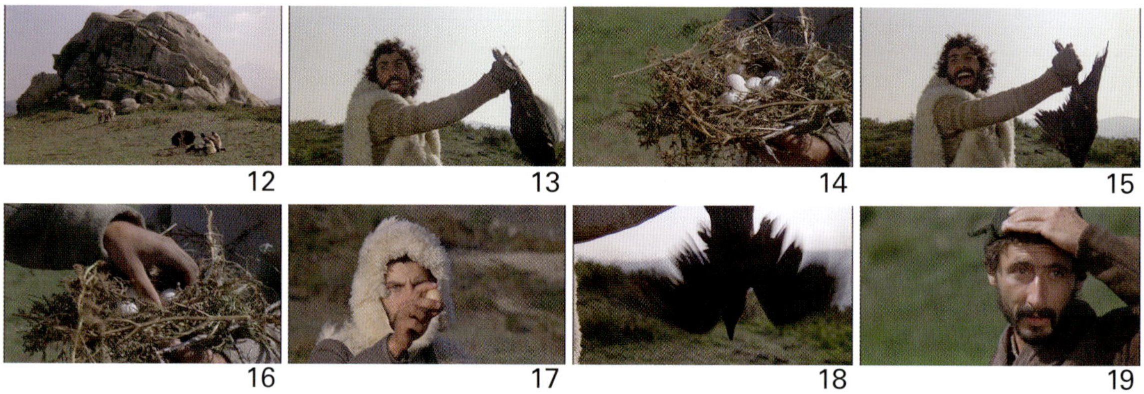

Figure 1.5 *KAOS* (1984). Directors: Paolo and Vittorio Taviani. Cinematographer: Guiseppe Lanci.

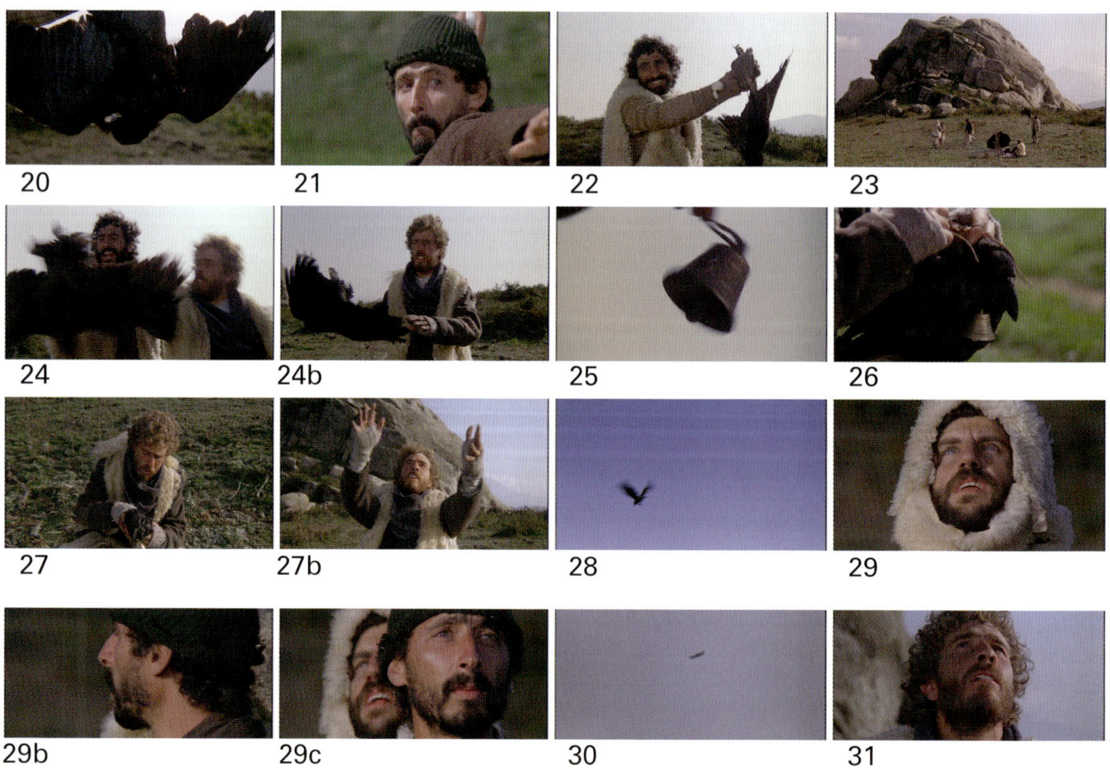

Figure 1.6 *KAOS* (1984). Directors: Paolo and Vittorio Taviani. Cinematographer: Guiseppe Lanci.

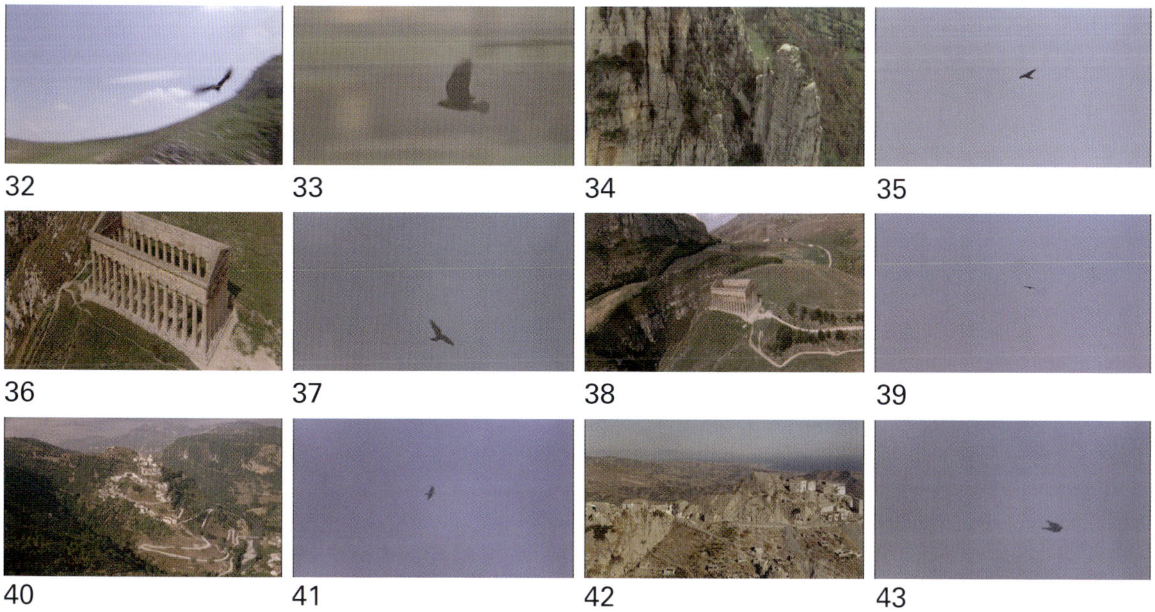

Figure 1.7 *KAOS* (1984). Directors: Paolo Taviania and Vittorio Taviani. Cinematographer: Guiseppe Lanci.

appear to materialize from nowhere. Locating him, and allowing the viewer a sense of relative distances between characters, renders his action plausible. With bird in hand, he ties to its neck a bell. He lifts the bird into the air, "Go!" The bird takes flight. The men look up (a close-up). This is followed by a series of extreme wide shots that alternate between the bird against the sky and the aerial view of the dusty Sicilian landscape. Up to this point, the camera, while varied in its framing (close-ups interposed with extreme wide shots) and angles (several **Dutch tilts**), has been committed to the action occurring within a more or less static frame. With the bird's flight, the camera breaks free to long fluid tracking shots that follow the direction and the height of the ascending bird. Alternating shots of bird in flight and bird's eye view reflect a play between camera movement and the bird's direction. The earlier pattern of punctuating each series of close-ups and medium close-ups with wide shots expands into aerial shots that deliver an ever-increasing distance between camera and ground, as a wider reach of it is seen (Figure 1.7).

In four and a half minutes, a story is told. The sequence includes camera stasis and motion, a diversity of camera height, angle, and level, and shots with a range of relative size that accumulate gracefully. Frames are repeated and graphic construction within frames is also, in some instances, repeated. Wide shots positioned at regular intervals loosen into extreme wide shots of bird in flight, which alternate with landscape vistas representing, literally, the bird's-eye view. The predominantly static camera is liberated into a grand expanse pictured through moving aerial cinematography, freeing the viewer from the ground below.

A case study in shot size and duration: fathers and sons

A comparison of scenes from two debut feature films, *Ordinary People* and *Buffalo 66*, illustrates the dynamic achieved through interaction between shot size and shot duration. Both scenes manage the interplay between technique and story toward evoking the isolation of the main character. And yet, the strategies are vastly different.

The 1980 feature, *Ordinary People*, is a family drama. The mother's favorite son has died in a boating accident. Surviving is his younger brother, Conrad, seventeen, who, pressured by grief and guilt, tries unsuccessfully to take his own life. The movie opens in this aftermath of memory and regret with Conrad having just returned home from the hospital, struggling to maintain balance despite his overly solicitous father and his mother's mask of denial and false cheer. Nearly an hour into the film, Conrad's maternal grandparents come to visit and begin taking family photographs. The camera is passed from grandmother to father as various groupings are made. The father, who constantly tries to warm the chill between his wife and son, insists on taking a picture of the two of them. He fumbles with the camera, prolonging an already tense moment. The wife grows impatient, then she is irritable: "Hand me the camera," she tells him repeatedly. The father persists. Finally Conrad, fueled by his mother's discomfort and his own feelings of rejection, shouts at his father, "Give her the goddamn camera!" Conrad's outburst pierces the façade of false family gaiety, which further isolates him, and leaves the other family members standing around in stunned awkwardness, all but the mother, of course, who offers to make lunch.

The scene begins with a shot of the mother, grandfather, and son widening to include the father, and widening further to the grandmother snapping the photo (Figure 1.8). This is followed by a volley of alternating shots: on one side, family members being photographed, and on the other the bystander(s) and photographer. This volley constitutes the major portion of the scene and culminates in the son shouting at his father. Redford aggravates the tension by having the son turn away from the camera in the two shot with his mother (Shot 15) just before the scene cuts to him in the single close-up that frames his outburst (Shot 17). After this, the son sinks into a chair (the only one seated) and the volley shots repeat, interrupted by cutaways to the son in a medium close-up (Figure 1.9, Shot 19b).

Even before the outburst, certain shots are repeated with enough variation to obscure their repetition. These familiar images make it less obvious that the frames are tightening to extreme close-ups. The opening wide shot leads to medium shots that build to the close-ups and then open out again to medium shots after Conrad's outburst. The shot size corresponds to the story conditions—as tension increases, the shots become tighter and tighter, culminating in close-ups of their faces. The duration of each shot also changes as the scene moves toward its climactic moment. As the shots tighten, the volley between them quickens. This acceleration of pace is a strategy not unlike a car reaching maximum speed before a moment of collision. After the outburst, the pace slows with shots of longer duration and medium focal length appropriate to convey the now-diffused energy of the scene. A volley between two has become a triangle, with the added shot of Conrad alone in the chair, reinforcing the story's theme and plot.

The strategy of shot sequence is not at all conspicuous. Redford and director of photography, John Bailey, work against drawing attention away from story dynamics to technique or style.[2] The camera technique allows the viewer to enter the story world without distraction. Even moments of intense dramatic effect are delivered in a style very much at the service of story.

This differs radically from the camera strategy we see in the scene from Vincent Gallo's first feature film, *Buffalo 66*. Unlike *Ordinary People*, the conspicuousness of camera treatment and shot duration asserts itself from the very beginning of the scene. It asks to be considered both apart from the dramatic action and in relation to it.[3] The effect is like two separate lines of music sung in unison.

The story centers on another ill-favored son, Billy, named for the Buffalo Bills, who is a loser of dramatic proportions. He

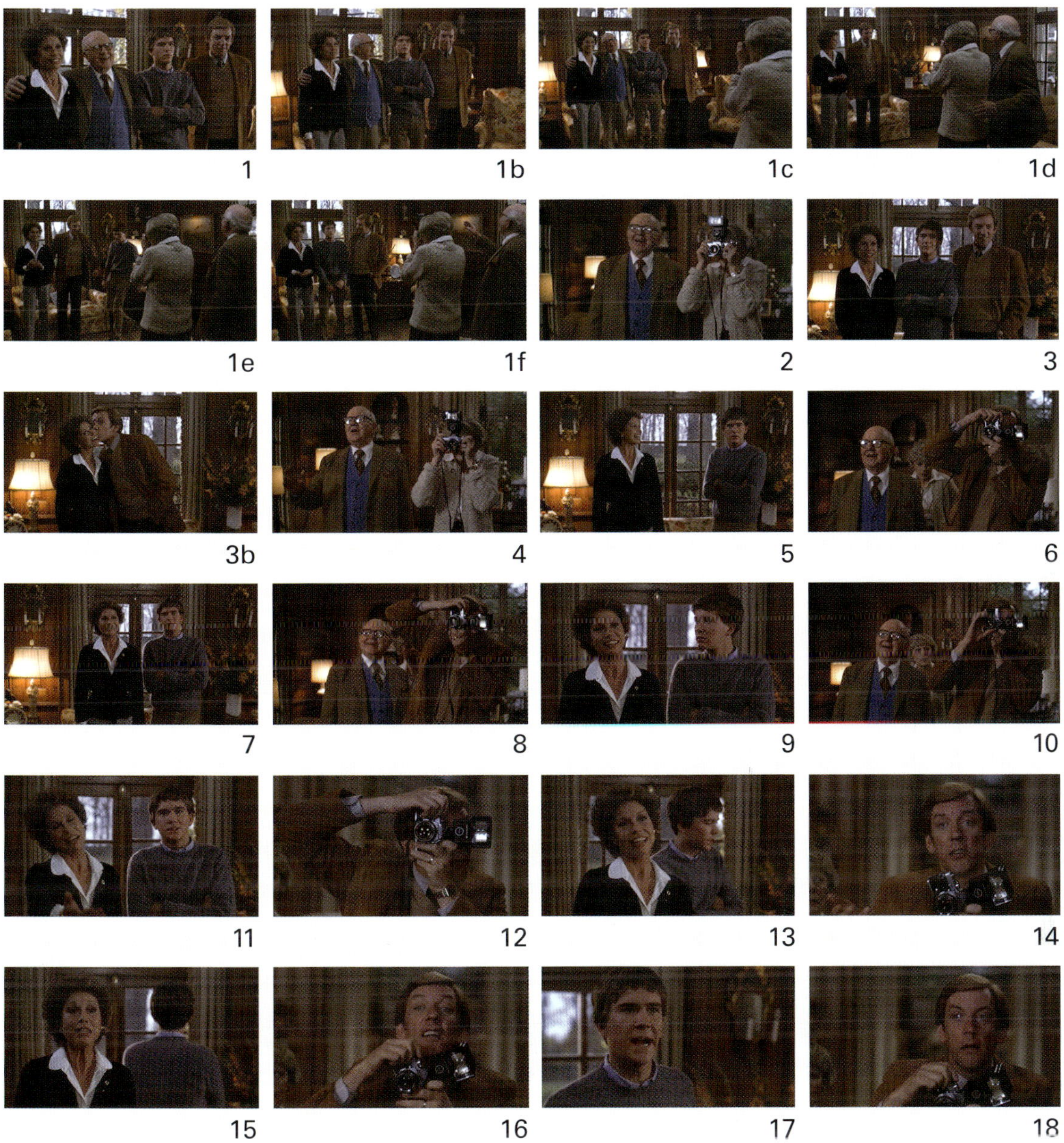

Figure 1.8 *Ordinary People* (1980). Director: Robert Redford. Cinematographer: John Bailey.

Q: What films are you the most happy with and why?

A: I guess *Ordinary People* is the most satisfying for me, and not because it won so many Academy Awards. It represents the kind of film I want to make. It's humanitarian filmmaking. For me, *Ordinary People* was the strongest synthesis of all the filmmaking elements. I was so pleased with what Redford and I were able to do photographically, within the context of not distracting from what the story was about.

—John Bailey, director of photography, in conversation with Dennis Schaeffer and Larry Salvato. *Masters of Light*, 2013. University of California Press.

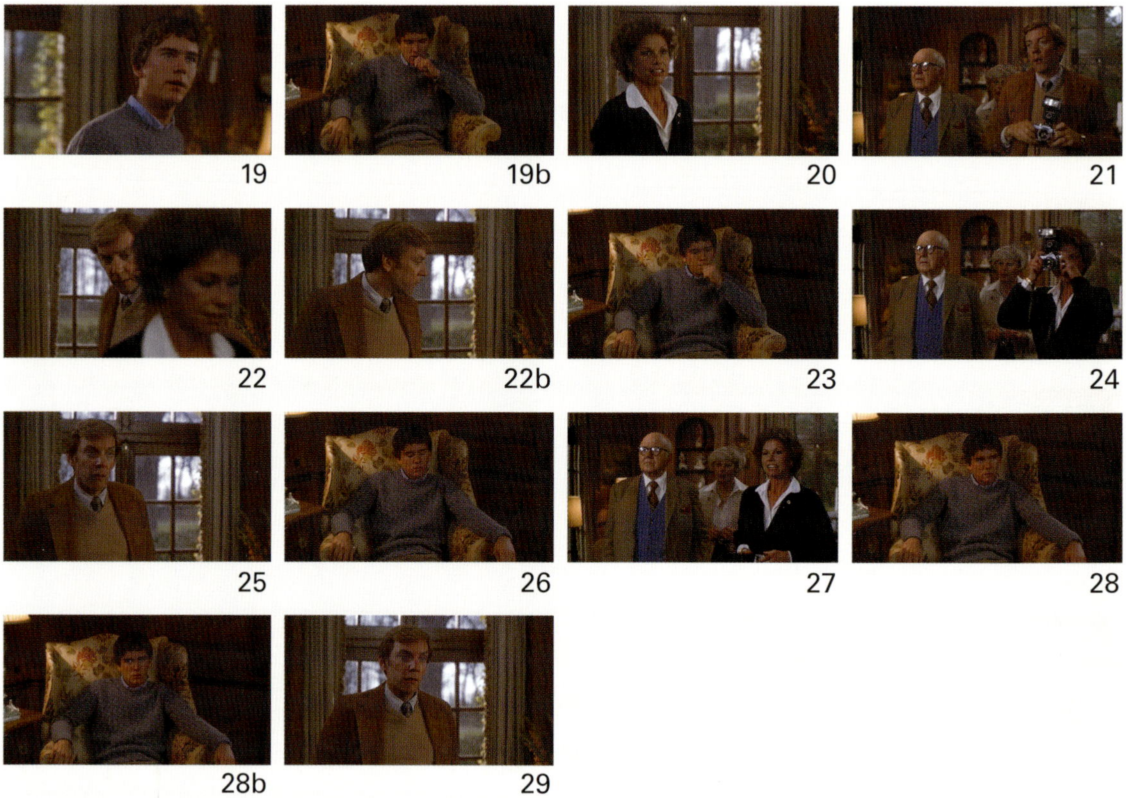

Figure 1.9 *Ordinary People* (1980). Director: Robert Redford. Cinematographer: John Bailey.

has returned home for a visit after serving a five-year prison sentence, though his parents are led to believe that he's been overseas with the CIA. With him, as an emotional bodyguard, is his hostage, Layla, who he has kidnapped from a nearby dance studio, and forced to pose as his wife. From the beginning, the father's disdain for his son is transparent, though, for sure, he likes Layla. The mother, who also likes Layla, can barely bring herself to focus on Billy, what with the Buffalo Bills on TV, polluting all efforts at exchange with constant background static. As in *Ordinary People*, family photographs figure into the narrative—not taking photographs in this instance, but viewing them. Layla asks to see pictures of Billy as a child, and the mother responds by asking her husband, "Where is it?" What they show her is an overstuffed family album that features pictures of the two of them. The father eventually finds the one photograph of Billy as a young boy accompanied by his dog, a dog that was killed by the father, we learn, as punishment for the boy's negligence.

The scene takes place from beginning to end around the family's small dining room table. It is late afternoon. The four characters sit at each of the four sides of the table, with Billy opposite Layla, and the father opposite the mother. By the end of the scene, the mother has left the table to make dinner, and Layla has gone to an adjacent room with the father to hear him sing one of his old lounge tunes at the family piano. Billy sits alone at the table, eyeing the one photograph taken of him as a child.

The dramatic arc of the scene inverts somewhat the progression in *Ordinary People.* Here the scene opens with a strained awkwardness and ends with gaiety. The gaiety, of course, belongs to Layla, along with the mother and father. Billy, alone at the table, has no part in it, other than the way it brings into focus his dislocation and despair.

The camera is self-consciously minimal. There are four basic compositions; each used again and again, comprising the thirteen shots in an eight-minute scene (Figure 1.10). This yields a shot duration of approximately

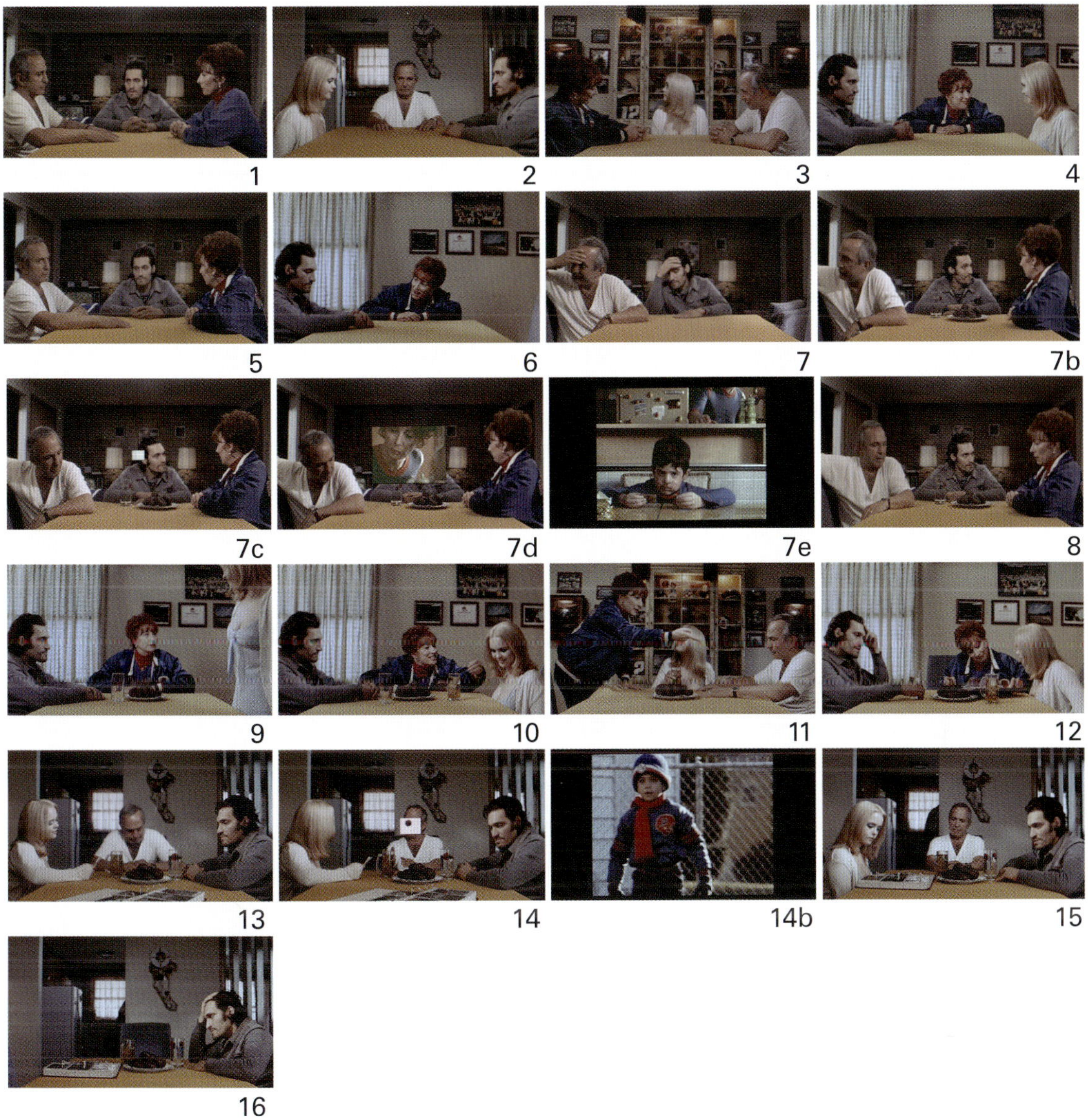

Figure 1.10 *Buffalo 66* (1998). Director: Vincent Gallo. Cinematographer: Lance Acord.

30 seconds, a long time for an image to remain on screen, particularly one with so little character movement or pictorial depth. (By way of contrast, the longest static shot in the scene from *Ordinary People* is about 10 seconds.) The spare number and variety of the compositions intensify the static shots, giving them a fierce, penetrating quality that challenges our comfort as viewers.

Camera placement and the use of cutting underscore the effect. The camera moves around the table counter-clockwise, capturing each of the four compositions in sequence, beginning with an opening "three shot" of Billy at center between his father and mother (Shot 1). After this initial rotation, the four frames alternate for the rest of the scene, not in sequence but erratically, moving occasionally clockwise and then suddenly counter-clockwise from an earlier position. Layla excuses herself to the restroom and the three shot becomes a two shot (Shot 6). This allows the audience to see Billy alone with each parent, a rather telling pair of images. The mother, preoccupied up until this moment with Layla, tries now, as an afterthought, to engage her son. The frame isolating Billy and his father speaks for itself, the first of several grinding interactions between father and son (Shot 7).

Although the camera is static with limited action in each frame, the effect, shot to shot, is spatially disorienting. Gallo combines a number of techniques to achieve this effect. To begin, his camera violates what in film practice is understood as the **180-degree rule**, an imaginary line the camera should remain behind to keep the viewer oriented in space. This violation makes it tough to map a particular environment. While the risk of disorientation is minimized by the fact of one location—the dining room table—the result is still destabilizing. Each shot becomes a fragment of a discontinuous series of shots, a detachment that resonates visually with Billy's emotional predicament.

Added to this, the shots are not motivated, as in *Ordinary People*, by the exchange among characters. Nor is the camera position and angle aligned with a character's point of view. There are also long periods of awkward silence, the absence of dialogue made more noticeable by the grating noise from the TV. The flatness and repetition of frames reinforce the deadness of emotional exchange—a chilling absence of connection between Billy and his parents. By the end of the 12-minute scene, we want desperately to leave the table.

For sure the camera work draws attention to itself.[4] In the most extreme way, an insert the size of a postage stamp will, on two occasions, break into the static three shot over the face of the father before it widens to fill the frame with flashbacks—mini-scenes from Billy's childhood (Shots 8 and 12). This leaves no doubt as to the camera's presence. The repeated still frames and their taxing duration act as commentary on Billy's circumstance—a falsely accused ex-con who lives in a suspended state with no place to physically or emotionally land. Even the applications of the camera strategy cited above create a conspicuous disconnect not unlike that which characterizes Billy who lives in a suspended state with no place to land, physically or emotionally. Too, any impatience we might suffer as a viewer with the fractious state of family affairs *and/or* the technique by which it is given intensifies our gratification when, later in the film, a genuine, human connection is made.

In summary, one can feel the weight given to the choice of shot size in every moment of these two films. This is also true of the prelude from *KAOS*. The influence of shot size on each unfolding narrative is impossible to overstate. The interaction between the two—shot size and story—is explicit and drives our experience of the story unfolding. One can grasp more viscerally this interaction with the simple assignment of creating a photo-roman, a story told in a sequence of still photographs. Challenge yourself by insisting on three different shot sizes: a wide shot, medium shot, and close-up. You will discern quickly the different dramatic effects created by variation in shot size.

Discussion questions

1. How does the camera work in *Buffalo 66* (Figure 1.10) approximate point of view and to what end?
2. Do we initially notice the disruption in the 180-degree rule?
3. What is the effect of the camera calling attention to its movements?

Notes

1. A thorough and provocative evaluation of cinema's capacity to vary image size and distance is found in Rudolf Arnheim's classic text, *Film as Art* (University of California Press, 1957).

2. For further insights from cinematographer John Bailey, see Chapter 3 in the book-length collection of interviews with cinematographers, *Masters of Light* (University of California Press, 2013).
3. David Bordwell explores at length the modes and forms of film narration in *Narration in the Fiction Film* (University of Wisconsin Press, 1985). A distinguishing factor between classical narration (*Ordinary People*) and alternative forms of narration (*Buffalo 66*) is the latter's use of stylistic devices that are more prominent where as the use of style in the classical narrative is limited to the transmission of story information or moving the narrative forward.
4. The visual style of *Buffalo 66* is influenced by Gallo's decision to shoot the film on 35mm reversal stock, which produces a positive image on a transparent surface (rather than the conventional 35mm color negative stock, which is later developed in a lab). Reversal stock creates immense challenges in production, particularly with lighting. In a 2015 interview, Gallo expressed his continued satisfaction with the color saturation, contrast, and modern classic look achieved by shooting on reversal stock. *From the Vaults: Vincent Gallo on Buffalo and Buffalo 66*, March 30, 2015. http://www.dailypublic.com.

2

The static camera

Anchoring the camera and building dramatic action inside the border of the frame represents another basic tool for storytelling in film. We have already seen examples of action in a static frame in the one minute film by the Lumiere Brothers and also as the camera strategy in the scene from *Buffalo 66*.

Elevating the technique to achieve desired dramatic effects requires thoughtful consideration of the size of the shot, blocking and staging, depth of focus, and rhythm of the action. This chapter looks at a variety of applications of the static camera, each of which demonstrates finesse in managing these elements. Emphasis is given to the way the same tool, thoughtfully employed and integrated with narrative, can create vastly different effects.

Staging action in a static frame

Any discussion of storytelling with a static camera will include a consideration of **shot size** (wide, medium, close-up, etc.), **figure movement** (does the movement of characters within the shot occur left to right? right to left? etc.), **image depth** (does the shot have volume, making use of foreground, middleground, or background?), and **rhythm of action** (in what way is time managed within the shot—is it hectic? relaxed? varied?).

The exploration of effects created by the static camera also leads to a discussion of formal properties in film, beginning with a definition of terms. Certain films demonstrate a greater attention to the formal arrangement of elements within the frame. Examples illustrate the way in which repetition, for these films, is central to formal treatment. Such treatment can be used to create graphic parallels among shots, to reinforce character dynamics, and to act as a container for narrative complexities.

The static camera requires that the filmmaker dramatize the narrative within the frame. This not only implicates the environment but also provides an opportunity to stage the talent in relationship to that environment in telling ways. One can block and stage actors against the location to enhance the dramatic effect of the scene. There is no better example of this than a brief moment from a longer scene in Charlie Chaplin's film, *The Gold Rush*. The movie features Chaplin's most memorable on-screen character, the Tramp. The three still frames from the film, depicted in Figure 2.1, occur in a single shot. The camera is fixed, the shot is a **medium wide shot**. The location: a dance hall. The dance hall has volume, though this is eclipsed in the first image by characters crowding the foreground. The Tramp is in the crowd, center frame, his back to the viewer (Shot 1a).

The music starts, dancing begins. The men and women step onto the dance floor, moving into the middleground of the shot. The Tramp is left behind in the foreground. Having characters move toward or away from the camera is one sure way of animating a static shot. Here, Chaplin uses it with great economy to convey narrative meaning. The Tramp's position in the frame (foreground, center), his dark clothing—in combination with the hall's lighting—emphasizes his isolation. It is the interaction between figure movement and image depth that visually isolates the Tramp, reinforcing his status as an outsider.

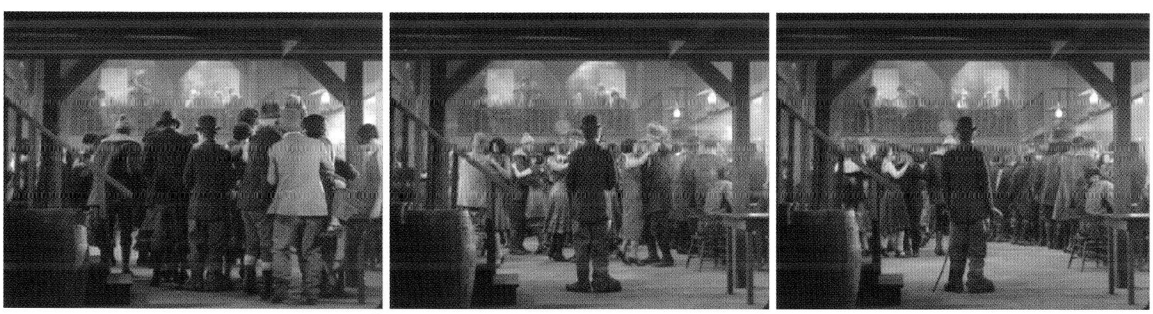

1 2 3

Figure 2.1 *The Gold Rush* (1925). Director: Charlie Chaplin. Cinematographer: Roland Totheroh.

The rhythm of action is relaxed. The camera holds on the isolated Tramp, making drama out of a simple hand gesture—first, right arm at his side, then right hand resting on his hip, and finally, fingers tapping on his hip, conveying his self-conciousness in being left out.

Sixty-five years after the making of *The Gold Rush*, the Finnish screenwriter and director Aki Kaurismaki dramatizes the plight of another loner in *The Match Factory Girl*.

The scene also takes place at a dancehall. Like the Tramp, Iris, the protagonist, is centered in the shot (Figure 2.2, Shot 2). She and the row of women face the camera at a very slight diagonal. Like the Tramp, she is also abandoned in the frame. Kaurismaki substitutes the use of image depth with off-screen space. Additionally, in *The Gold Rush*, Chaplin isolates the Tramp in the foreground. Here, one by one, the women disappear from the frame as they are invited onto the dance floor. Iris is left sitting alone, but for the shadows of couples dancing off-screen, cast on the wall behind her.

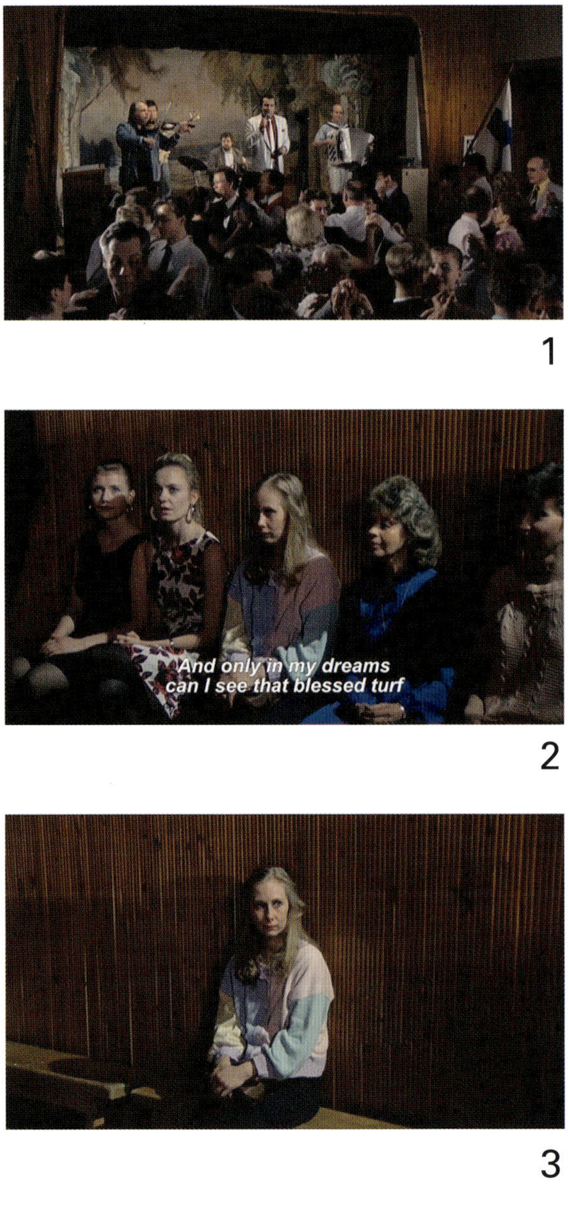

Figure 2.2 *The Match Factory Girl* (1990). Director: Aki Kaurismaki. Cinematographer: Timo Salminen.

Visual humor and off-screen space

Aki Kaurismaki delights audiences with wry visual humor that exploits the static frame. Photographed by Timo Salminen and bathed in golden, Finnish light, his 2002 feature, *The Man Without a Past*, portrays a story told in sequences of predominantly static shots. The presentation of action, staged before a fixed camera, can risk seeming theatrical. But Kaurismaki's commitment to medium shots undermines any sense of theatrical space.

The medium shot situates characters in limited context with well-defined borders. It is also true in this particular film, that the combined force of the static camera with medium shots strengthens our perception that the characters are trapped in a world where the slightest shift in circumstance requires enormous effort. Finally, the medium shot allows the director to manipulate **on-screen** and **off-screen space**. This is handled with precision to create humor and establish an ironic tone.

In the scene referenced by the first nine shots of Figure 2.3, the protagonist, after a beating by local thugs, discovers that amnesia prevents him from remembering even his name. He is cared for by a family of limited means (wife, husband, and their two boys). They regard their meager circumstances—dilapidated dwelling and night shifts at a coal yard two nights a week—as good fortune which adds to the film's ironic tone. The Scandinavian summer light saturates the color in the daylight exteriors, which comprise the nine shots of the scene. (The tenth shot is a transition shot to the next scene). In six of the nine shots, the camera remains static. All three moving shots begin or end as static shots and pan with methodical pace from left to right, following character movement. The framing privileges medium shots. The one wide shot (a man returning home from a day of labor) (Shot 4) functions as an establishing shot, but as in the prologue of *KAOS*, it occurs deep in the scene as a revelation. Once it occurs we understand, finally, the spatial relations between the characters, as well as certain associations within the scene.

The scene opens with a static medium shot of a portly man seated outdoors playing an accordion. Every element within the shot is static, save the limited movement of the man's hands and the accordion. A man of his girth playing an accordion is humorous, regardless

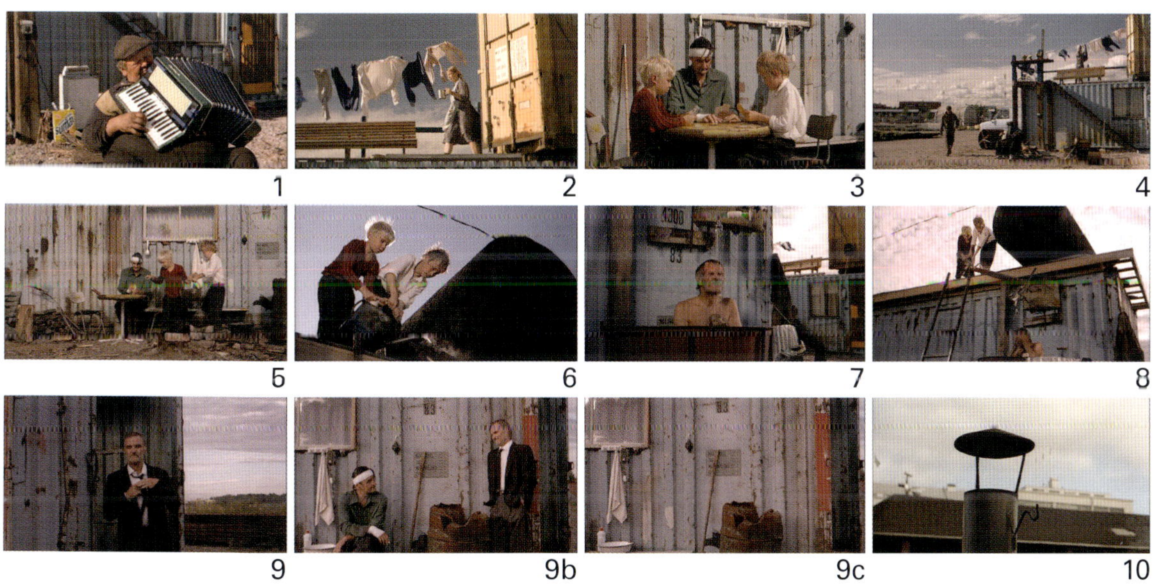

Figure 2.3
A Man Without a Past (2002).
Director: Aki Kaurismaki.
Cinematographer: Timo Salminen.

of shot size. But the medium shot has him bulging out of the frame, rendering legs and arms disproportionately small. The stasis of the shot, in combination with the shot's duration, gives us an opportunity to observe the rundown surroundings, which are staged with formal grace in a repetition of graphic lines and shapes. The bulky roundness of the man's cap, face, limbs, and belly is set against the striation of the building slats, stripes that match the keyboard and the pleated bellows of the accordion. The result, of course, is visual pleasure and comedy.

The first shot and the two shots that follow (the woman watering her plants, a card game between toe-headed boys) are independent tableaus, with humor staged inside the frame. The wide shot of the fourth frame portrays the father's arrival. It locates the accordion player in relation to the woman above him watering the plant. It also preps the four shots that follow.

In the very last shot of the scene (Shot 9), the father appears showered, shaved, and dressed in his finery. The accordion music stops as he adjusts his tie and utters the first spoken words in the scene. "It's Friday night," he says, as the camera pans left (for the third and last time), following him into a static shot with "the man with no past." Once the shot rests, he delivers his second line, "Let's go out to dinner." The two men stand. The "man without a past" follows him out of the frame. We're left to study the frame, empty now of characters or activity, thereby increasing our awareness of off-screen space. The use of visual association continues as the next scene opens with another "watering can"—a whistling teapot (a close-up, static shot) furthering the rhyme. Kaurismaki uses off-screen space once again in *A Man Without a Past*. The shot construction displays the camera's coyness, using framing as a device to withhold aspects of the scene that occur out of view.

A tool for provocation

Humanité, the second feature film by director Bruno Dumont, is, like *The Man Without a Past*, peopled with characters that endure limited possibilities. The camera style reinforces this sense of entrapment. But unlike *The Man Without a Past*, in which confinement within the frame is eased by charming visual humor, *Humanité* shows no interest in levity or wit. The use of static camera serves, instead, the purpose of confrontation. In this film, stasis, working with shot duration and image content, provokes the viewer, insisting on a reaction.

Pharaon is a police detective in a working class town in the North of France. Troubled by a recent crime—the brutal rape and murder of an eleven-year-old girl—he tries to cheer himself with the company of friends (Domino and Joseph). In the scene pictured, comprised of four static shots, Domino and her boyfriend Joseph, meet late one afternoon when Pharaon drops by.

The action between Domino and Joseph occurs in four parts: Domino stands alone facing the window when Joseph arrives; they embrace; they undress; and then they slide onto the floor as the sex act begins. This "love" scene is framed in a wide shot, formally, with its internal frames of window and door. There are only two lines of dialogue, spoken when Joseph first arrives. "What's wrong?" Domino asks, "What's the matter?" Joseph doesn't answer. The camera stasis and camera placement (i.e., distance from subject and angle) steal every ounce of eroticism from the lovemaking. With no dialogue to humanize them, emphasis is given to the mechanics—removing underwear (each takes off his/her own) and finding a workable position (from the sofa to the floor).

The window acts as a frame within the frame in the first shot of the scene, but it is the doorway that becomes the vantage point for Pharoan,

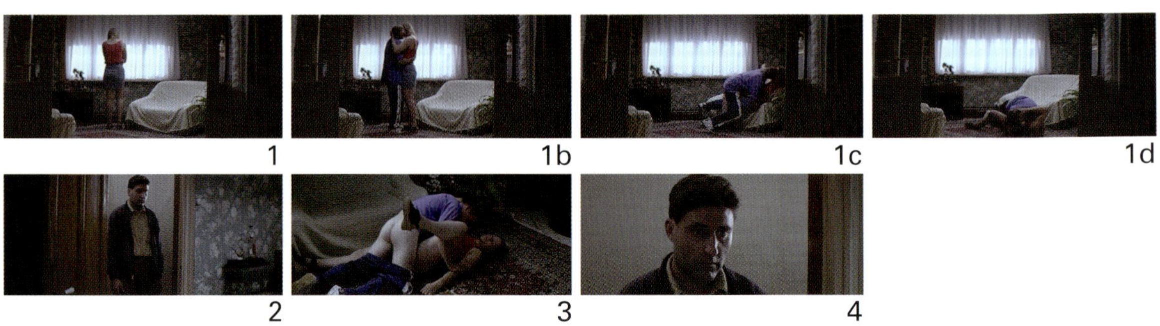

Figure 2.4 *Humanité* (1999). Director: Bruno Dumont. Cinematographer: Yves Cape.

who is both friend and detective. Each of the four static shots asks the viewer to remain alert, if not detached, much like a detective's gaze. When we see Pharaon frozen in the doorway looking down (a medium long shot, also divided by architectural structures), we assume the object of his gaze. The assumption is confirmed with the third shot—a closer, more graphic view of the sex act, from Pharaon's perspective or "**point of view**." It is further confirmed by Domino's reaction: seeing Pharaon, she lifts her head in protest. Committed to finishing what has begun with Joseph, she turns her head away, as Pharaon, and the camera standing in for him, look on. The shot (3) lasts for twenty seconds, during which time we, as viewers, by way of the anchored camera position and shot duration, are bound to this perspective. What was mechanical in the behavior of Joseph and Domino (I am hesitant to call them lovers) seems more functional than passionate. Certainly all romance, affection, or warmth is drained from the act. And then: a close-up of Pharaon, our accomplice in the act of watching (Shot 4).

For the full twenty seconds of the shot, the film insists that we, as viewers, study the face of Pharaon, who, though plagued with horror over the rape crime he discovered that morning, is immobilized by a compulsion to study the act of sex. Even after being "caught," when Domino meets his gaze, his attention is not diverted, nor does he leave. The scene's shot construction, a simple progression of wide shot, medium shot, medium shot, close-up, combines with narrative action and shot duration, to drive our experience as viewers toward greater and greater discomfort. This gives the scene a disturbing complexity.

The nature of this discomfort is worth exploring. It is not the discomfort that comes from story events, as when "bad" things happen to "good" people, or characters compromised in terms of "goodness," are endeared to the viewer, nonetheless. This is the discomfort of our having to look for too long at an image that refuses immersion. By "immersion" I mean the capacity to sink into the world of the film, identifying with character, living through his or her struggle or desire.[1] Any viewer becomes, like Pharoan, a voyeur. Judgment of Pharoan for his intrusive stare will include our fixed attention, as well.

Figure and ground

Few directors have been more committed to the static frame than Yasujirō Ozu. Nearly thirty years before the release of *An Autumn Afternoon* in 1962, Ozu all but abandoned camera movement and dedicated his storytelling to the use of the stationary camera and low camera angle position. A low angle camera placement heightens the separation *between* the various fields: foreground, middle ground, and background; more importantly, it distinguishes figure from background. Consider the shots in Figure 2.5 taken from four different scenes, representing Ozu's collaboration with cinematographer Yûharu Atsuta.[2]

In Ozu's films, scenes are dominated by the interaction between and among characters. In sequences, each shot is composed as a separate unit with an eye toward balanced composition. The handling of empty space and internal framing (a frame within a frame) includes but is in no way limited to visual symmetry. It may be difficult to register from the still frames Ozu's preference for quieting the action within the frame. It is not just the camera that is static, but entire scenes unfold with characters seated in one place or limited in their movement within the environment or range of physical actions. This encourages the viewer to absorb more fully the disquiet between characters or any tension between character and environment. It also serves to give the environment additional narrative weight.

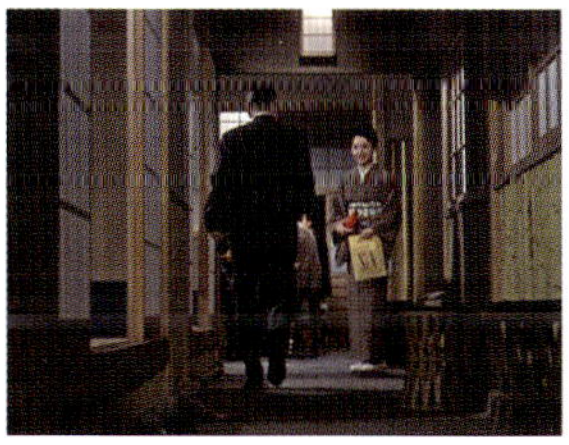
1

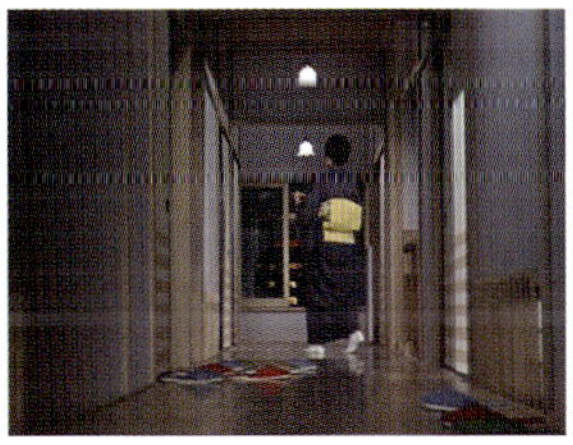
2

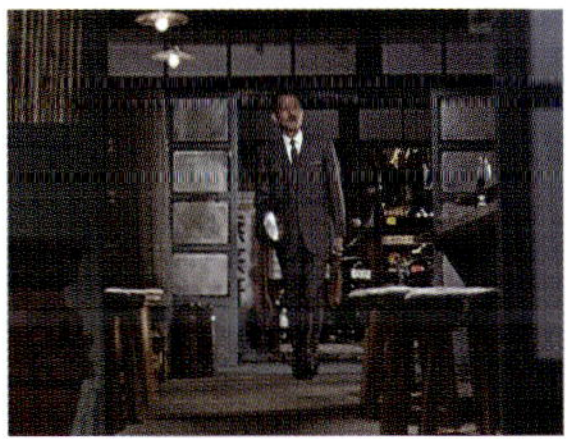
3

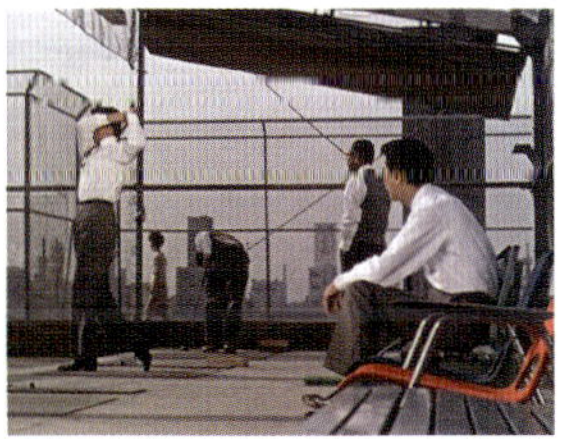
4

Figure 2.5 *An Autumn Afternoon* (1962). Director: Yasujirō Ozu. Cinematographer: Yûharu Atsuta.

Image as punctuation

While character interactions dominate the movies made by Ozu, the films also make use of the occasional static shot without characters, a shot that pictures only environment. This shot will often function as a pause, like a grammatical comma, adding emphasis to the environment, while also encouraging viewer reflection. In film terms, this character-less static shot is often used by Ozu as a **transition shot**.

One such transition shot is the static image of two adjacent windows in Hirayama's office. It occurs at the end of a sequence in which a friend drops by the office to suggest to Hirayama, a widowed father, a prospective husband for his only daughter. As the conversation comes to an end, Hirayama invites his friend to an evening of dinner and drinks. "No, I have tickets to the baseball game. I have to go," his friend says. Hirayama urges; his friend refuses. Hirayama urges again; his friend refuses. This is what is heard while the viewer looks at the image of the office windows.

At first glance, the construction seems symmetrical: a pair of windows, blinds drawn to the same height, and a splash of red adjacent to each window frame. The placement of additional props complicates the symmetry. Particularly noticeable are the two white telephones, one appearing larger than the other. The shot has no obvious or persuasive relevance to the plot. The shot is used as a visual hinge, closing the door on one scene as it opens into another. However, in Ozu's story world, it also has **expressive value**. The image acts as a reminder of Japan's booming sector of business and industry, which will, as the story unfolds, work in opposition to values of family life and home. Ozu will often end a scene with a static shot of the environment. This also acts as punctuation, giving the viewer the opportunity to reflect on the scene's drama before moving the story forward.

The graphic framing of this particular image—symmetrical relations gone slightly awry—also underscores this tension, reflecting a theme that threads throughout the film. In *An Autumn Afternoon* we are persistently prompted (by content of conversation and/or image) to consider the intrusion of modern western habits into the traditional society of Japan in the 1960s, much as the physical structures and props that represent that intrusion appear in this shot.

Emotional intensity with visual restraint

Ozu's commitment to a stationary camera goes hand-in-hand with his interest in compositions that have a painterly, still-life quality. What effect does it have on the viewer, these lovely static shots stripped of camera movement or animated character action within the frame? How does the movie overcome the "fixedness" of each shot to achieve vitality in the storytelling from scene to scene? First, it should be noted that while scenes in an Ozu film may be visually "quiet" he is liberal in adding carefully applied musical score to achieve desired effects. Production design and spatial depth will often be used to enliven the image. The most persuasive dynamism occurs, not so much through exigencies of plot, but in the sincere exchanges between characters.

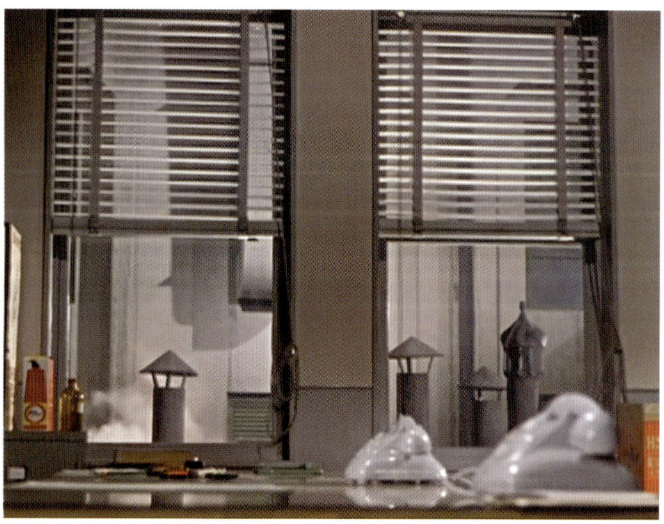

Figure 2.6 *An Autumn Afternoon* (1962). Director: Yasujirō Ozu. Cinematographer: Yûharu Atsuta.

> Your movie should lull people into a place of openness and vulnerability.
>
> —Cary Fukanaga, *Interview* magazine, December 2, 2015

The films are animated by the emotional life of the people who populate the screen—the orderliness of visual imagery is in equal measure to the messiness of human relationship depicted in each story. It may even be true that the formal qualities in the rendering allow the most incidental human muddle greater poignancy. Here is a touching example from deeper into story of *An Autumn Afternoon*.

Hirayama enters the room of his daughter, Michiko, just after she has learned that the young man she fancies is already engaged. Determined to see that she finds a mate, the father insists on introducing her to another prospect. Michiko, reluctant to displease him, agrees. Her disappointment is palpable. Immediately following this exchange, she is framed in a static medium shot with her back to the camera. "Unhappy?" her father asks. The reveal of Michiko's face (Shot 2b) makes all too clear the depth of her sadness. The father is seen in a medium wide shot, encouraging, once more, the "blind date." "If you dislike him, say so," the father says, "but I want you to meet him." Michiko turns back around, making no reply until she is framed again with her back to the camera. (Figure 2.7, Shot 4) "Yes," she responds. Michiko's limited movement in shots of identical staging serves to heighten the effect of the one movement she makes in turning around to face her father. (Figure 2.7, Shot 2b) "Join us for tea," the father insists. Michiko remains silent as her father leaves. (Figure 2.8, Shot 7)

The camera returns to Michiko, framing her, as before, from behind in a medium shot. (Shot 8) It is here that stasis and consistent shot construction

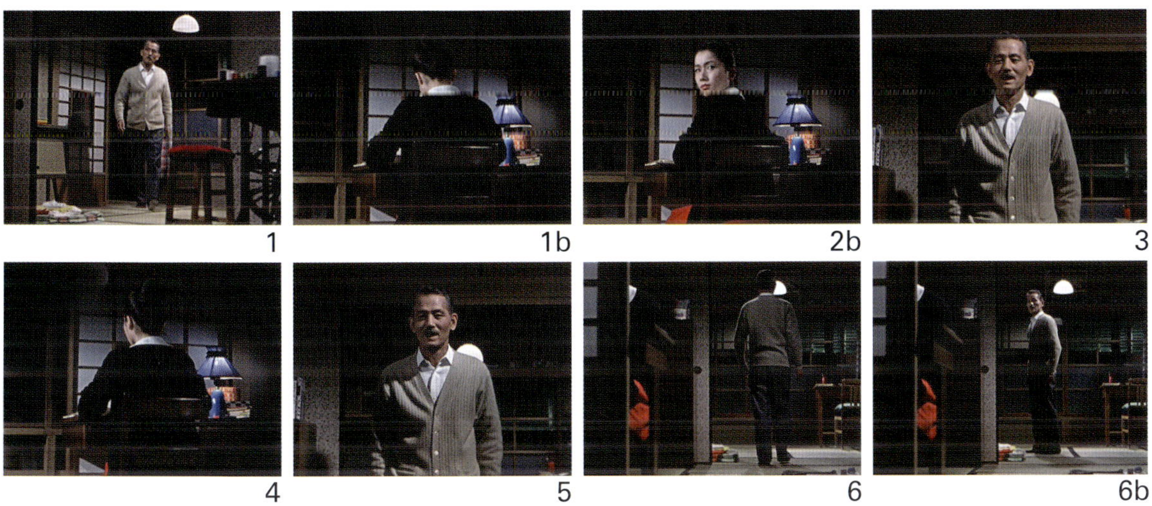

Figure 2.7 *An Autumn Afternoon* (1962). Director: Yasujirō Ozu. Cinematographer: Yûharu Atsuta.

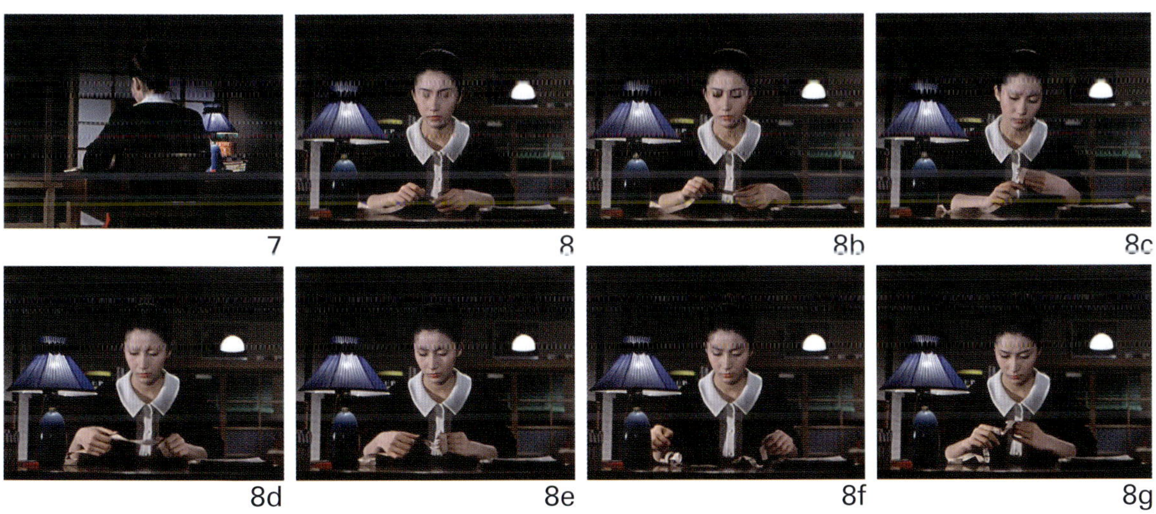

Figure 2.8 *An Autumn Afternoon* (1962). Director: Yasujirō Ozu. Cinematographer: Yûharu Atsuta.

allow effects that considerable motion and variety might disrupt. Michiko runs her hand along the back of her hair (not pictured here). The limited physical movement and emotional restraint, along with camera stasis, imbue the gesture with immense sadness. Afterward, Ozu repositions the camera to frame her face in medium close-up. (Shot 10) Once the scene transitions to Michiko facing the camera, her limited physical action plays out in a fifteen second static shot without interference from camera movement or shot change. But more importantly, the viewer is included now in Michiko's dismay, made more palpable by her one simple activity: she coils a tape measurer around her hand, uncoils it, and then coils it again. The stillness of the visual field gives the moment a stirring power.

In covering Michiko's reaction with a fifteen second, static, medium shot, Ozu allows the scene to play out without the interference of camera movement or shot change through a cut. The resistance to directing our attention more energetically with camera demonstrates a trust in performance (posture, facial expression, gesture) and conviction that camera stillness allows the viewer the time and emotional space to engage, uninterrupted, with the character.

The static shot in close-up

All of the film sequences exampled in this chapter thus far rely, primarily, on medium and medium wide shots. Consistently among them, the pace from shot-to-shot is deliberate, if not slow. This is not the only option. The well-known shower scene in *Psycho*, directed by Alfred Hitchcock, provides a striking contrast, pummeling the viewer with static close-ups of very short duration. Several sources report a total of seventy-eight camera set-ups for the shower scene and seven days of filming.[3] A set-up refers to the camera angle, shot size, and staging.

The scene portrays the murder of Marion Crane, a guest at the Bates Motel, while taking a shower. Written about at length and with great insight, extensive analysis here is not needed.[4] It is useful to know that a scene running slightly more than three minutes has fifty-five cuts and is constructed primarily with static shots. The shots of longer duration occur before and after the murder, at the beginning and end of the scene. The quickest cutting—shots of short duration (thirty-three static shots in twenty-one seconds)—occurs during the stabbing sequence at the center of the scene. Here are fourteen shots from the center of the sequence during which the stabbing occurs.

The frantic pace, made with shots that last less than one second, combine with shot repetition to intensify the action while also prolonging it. The viewer never sees the knife pierce flesh. The scene construction implies that visualizing the approach of the knife expends more drama than an image of contact or penetration. Anticipation is, after all, the root of suspense. As you can see from the fifteen shots, the image of the perpetrator with raised arm, knife in hand is repeated (Shots1, 5, 7, 14). Other shots are also repeated (Shots 2 and 6a; 3, 10, and 12). This staccato of shot repetition with intermittent variation aligns Hitchcock with other directors who make use of formal properties in designing a scene.

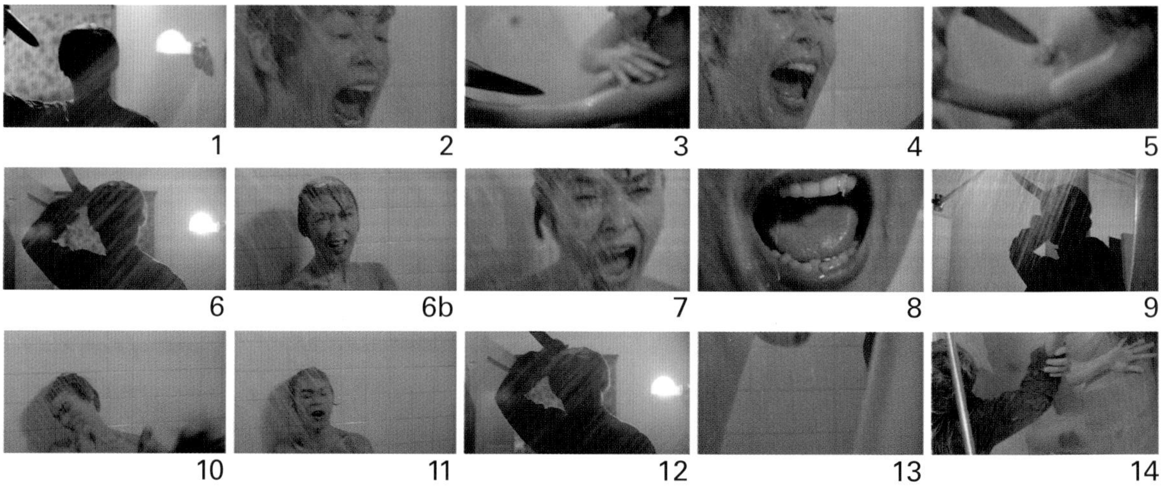

Figure 2.9 *Psycho* (1960). Director: Alfred Hitchcock. Cinematographer: John L. Russell.

Formal properties

Many directors who favor building action in the static frame make use of formal properties in a shot's composition, as well as in the sequencing of the static shots. As such, the arrangement of various elements in the frame works to *unify otherwise disparate elements with the result of rendering a design, structure, or pattern*. The word "form" has a Latin root, "forma," which means to shape or to mold. It implies not so much the shape or arrangement of elements, as the **method of arrangement**; not so much the integration of various components, but the **manner** of integrating them.

Pattern and variation

The mind will work to make patterns. In viewing even a landscape through your living room window, the mind accentuates repeated geometric shapes, colors, and figure movements. It follows that the application of formal properties in a film shot, sequence, or entire film will depend on **repetition**. The pattern made by repeating elements becomes an organizing or unifying principle. The pattern can then be varied or interrupted to create emphasis or dramatic tension. Pattern and variation as a formal strategy to organize and unify dramatic elements is a concept as old as Aristotle and can be applied to all things crafted: a painting, a sonata, a play, a scene from a window, and certainly a movie.[5]

Repetition of line, shape, and color

The images shown here from the Jim Jarmusch film, *Mystery Train*, are framed with a static camera. They register his ease with formal construction, using, in particular, elements borrowed from painting and photography. Light and shadow, line, texture, shape, composition, and color conspire to effect formal precision and coherence. In this shot from the film's credit sequence, Jarmusch also makes use of a window view. The camera is static, but the images passing in front of the window, of course, are not. The static shot in the opening scene of *Mystery Train* is animated by carefully chosen portraits of the American landscape seen through the window of a moving train.

Jarmusch combines a formal symmetry of line, angle of line, and shape with the junkyard heap of abandoned cars, which are framed through the window of the train like a painting or photograph. Without being stiff or stilted, the images read as a deliberate composition. The colors, while varied, are contained—each color inside the train appears in a paler version outside the window. The car heap, while seemingly random, repeats the basic shape of a smashed car and the given number of colors. The rectangle made by the window also repeats in smaller proportions several times in the frame.

The repetition of "shape" as an organizing principle occurs in another shot during this sequence. Jarmusch employs the same camera set up. The image is altered slightly by the figure movement of the young man and woman

There's a reason why you can watch older films—whether or not they're American films or foreign films—why you can watch a film by Akira Kurosawa or François Truffaut or Orson Welles. Filmmakers who had true command of the craft, even when they're working with big bulky equipment, and trying to find ways to creatively find choreography with the subjects, with the characters and the environment.

—John Singleton *6 Filmmaking Tips From John Singleton*, Film School Rejects. May 9, 2019.

Figure 2.10 *Mystery Train* (1989). Director: Jim Jarmusch. Cinematographer: Robby Müller.

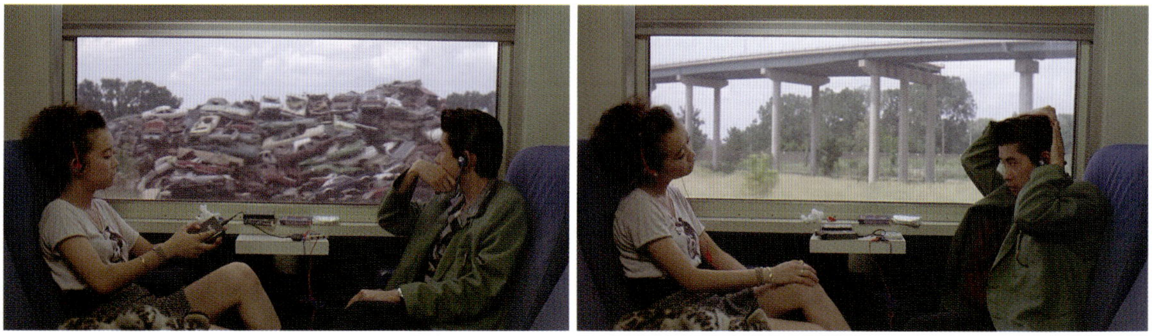

1 2

inside the train and drastically by the vista as it passes through the window: the concrete pilings supporting a highway ramp, blue in concert with their blue seats in the train. The Japanese couple is traveling to Memphis; they're tourists. These sightings through the window of the train become photographs of an American landscape. Seen through the eyes of the Japanese couple traveling in America for the first time, the "picture window" images are riddled with irony, made more ironic by the formal compositions. It is not uncommon for Jarmusch to apply formal strategies in his depiction of people at the margins of society—their in-between moments of life. And not only people, but physical structures and landscapes are represented formally. In so doing, he makes a claim to his viewer on behalf of their value. The discarded, worn, used up, and forgotten are reconceived as beautiful. Here, we find our Japanese tourists on Chaucer Street in Memphis. Throughout the film, the Japanese couple can be seen walking the streets of Memphis, like cutout characters pasted onto the landscape with their red luggage in tow.[6]

The camera tracks alongside as they pass in front of the yellow "twin-set" houses. One unit mirrors the other. Door and window, both in need of paint, with matching chairs (also yellow) fronting the porch, and on the left, the fabled white picket fence. The couple cannot be missed with their red suitcase like a blazing flag, marking them as outsiders. As they move up the sidewalk, it happens again—another "twin set" of houses, varied in color with the same shape, design, and placement of props. At the very least, the formal strategy in *Mystery Train* includes a commitment to visual symmetry, the repetition of shape and design, a preference for coupling, and a controlled color palette—all formal aspects that movies share with the visual arts.[7]

Because movies occur in time, as well as space, they can just as easily borrow "forms" from the temporal arts: music, drama, and dance. Gesture, movement, the way characters or props are grouped, tone or manner of speech, and pace are also means by which to affect a "method of arrangement." Jarmusch, to be sure, appropriates many of these formal tools, as well. Think of the Japanese couple moving through the streets of Memphis, carrying by way of a bamboo stick their red suitcase.

Figure 2.11 *Mystery Train* (1989). Director: Jim Jarmusch. Cinematographer: Robby Müller.

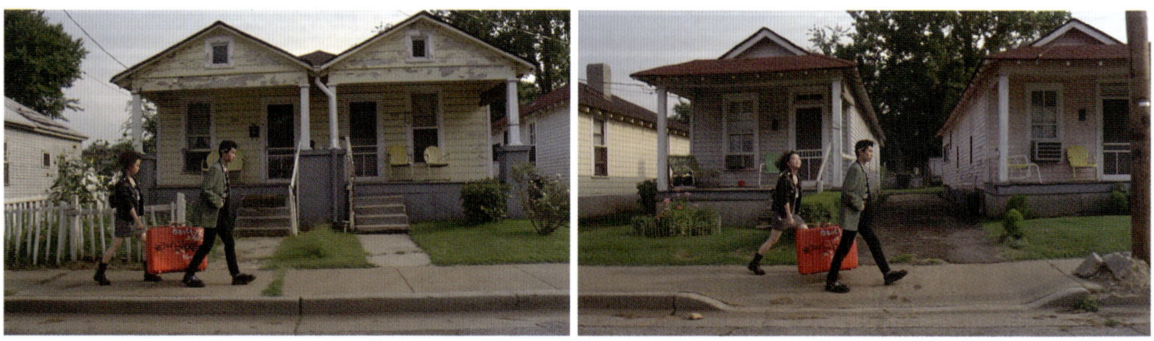

1 2

Narrative progression

As much as movie making owes its manner of formal construction to the visual and temporal arts, there are also aspects of generating form that emerge from the medium itself. One such aspect depends upon a movie's capacity to present images at different moments in film time.

The style of Andrew Haigh's 2011 film *Weekend* resembles the kitchen sink realism of British films from the 1950s and 60s.[8] Into that realism, Haigh infuses a repetition of certain visual elements that work as structural scaffolding. The film exemplifies the way in which formal properties can work in tandem with a realistic style and lend the film narrative authority. A touching romantic drama, the movie charts the relationship between two young men (Russell and Glen) over the course of a weekend after a one-night stand. Much of the film takes place in Russell's one bedroom flat in a high-rise apartment building in Nottingham. On three different occasions, after time together, Glen leaves the flat (Saturday morning, late day Saturday, and Sunday). A window view, again, works a central visual motif. Each time Glen leaves, the departure is pictured through the same window in Russell's apartment, each time the camera tilts slightly to follow Glen up the sidewalk. This consistency allows the filmmaker to chart story development by varying elements in the three departures. In each departure, for example, Glen wears a hoodie. The color of the hoodie changes from red to yellow to black. During the first two departures, Russell stands at the window watching Glen leave. During the last two, Glen stops in his path along the sidewalk, turns around, and looks up to Russell in the window. The third time, which marks a last goodbye, Russell doesn't go to the window. The pattern set by Russell's appearance in the first two departures (silhouetted in Shots 2a and 2b in Figure 2.12) gives his absence (a variation) a stronger effect. In this third departure, Glen stops, turns, looks up, and he will see no one standing in the window (Shot 3b).

Creating graphic parallels

The use of repetition is also an opportunity to build associations through color, shape, and framing across different sets of characters or locations. The correlation between the images accumulates as a value greater than each incident of occurrence. It can work to add dimension to story events, evoke a mood or

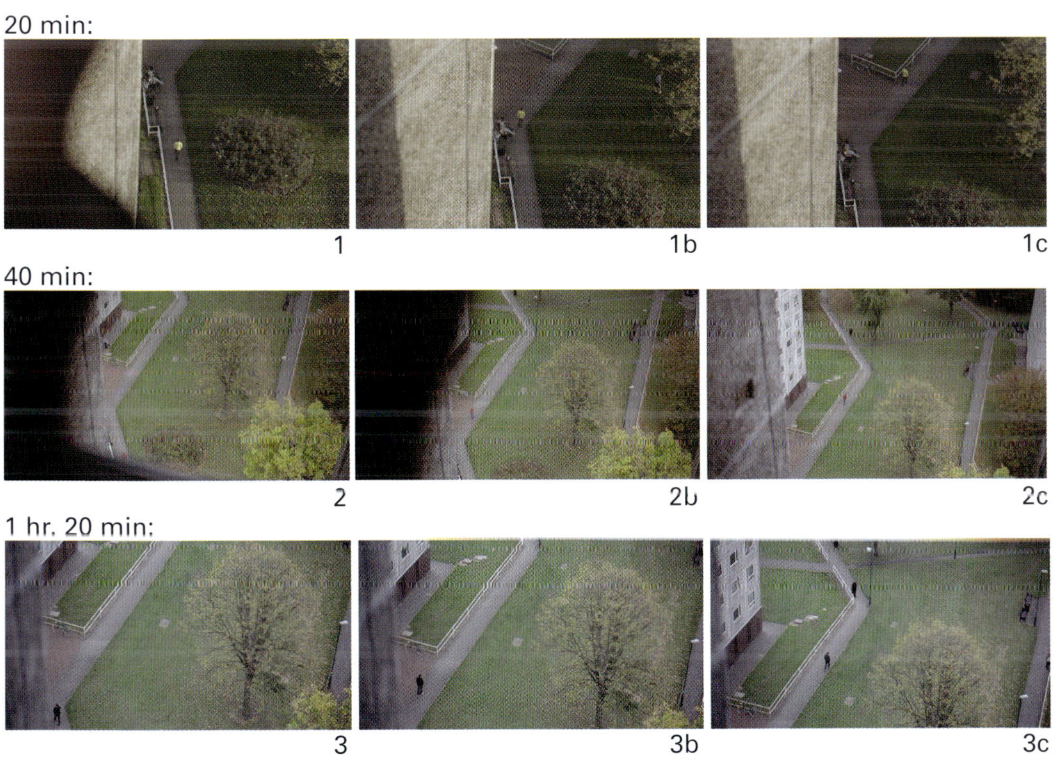

Figure 2.12 *Weekend* (2011) Director: Andrew Haigh. Cinematographer: Urszula Pontikos.

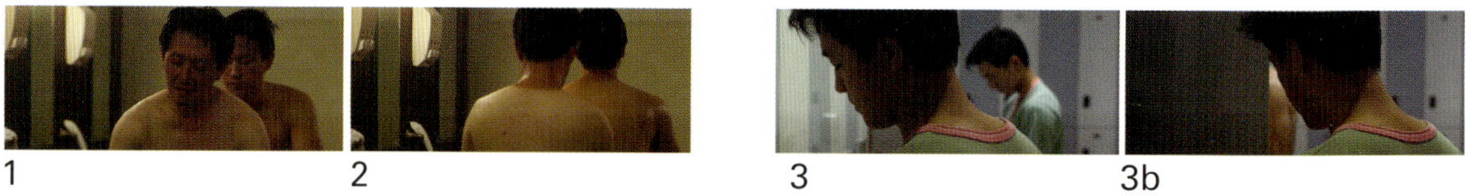

Figure 2.13 *Spa Night* (2016) Director: Andrew Ahn. Cinematographer: Ki Jin Kim.

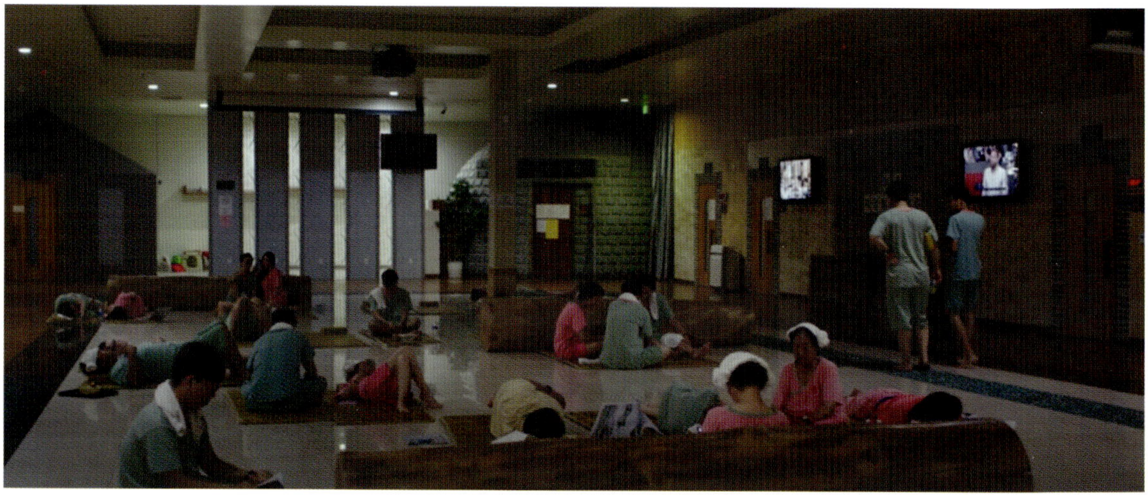

Figure 2.14 *Spa Night* (2016) Director: Andrew Ahn. Cinematographer: Ki Jin Kim.

theme, or further narrative development. At the very least the film's visual structure will be reinforced.

The opening scene of Andrew Ahn's 2016 film, *Spa Night*, provides a vivid example. David, the protagonist, visits a Los Angeles spa with his parents. The film opens with father and son, paired characters stacked in the frame, one occupying the foreground and the other, the middle ground (Figure 2.13). The closeness of father and son scrubbing one another in the sauna (Shots 1 and 2) becomes a kind of residue when we see David in the locker room with another young man (Shot 3-3b). The story told in *Spa Night* is one of emerging sexual identity. David, an eighteen-year-old Korean-American, is divided by loyalty to his parents and his own growing awareness of his attraction to men.

The two sets of shots are separated by a scene in which the parents and David share a picnic meal in the spa's lounge area (Figure 2.14).

The director's affection for formal composition is apparent with the use of repetition inside the frame (color, shapes, video screens, and columns). David's mother turns the conversation to marriage, encouraging David to settle on a Korean wife, so that they will all speak the same language. The marriage-talk ends with a cut to David entering the locker room. David, in the foreground, stands near a young man positioned deeper in the frame (Figure 2.13, Shot 3). Even without the development within the shot—the young man taking off his shirt, David turning his gaze on him (Shot 3b)—the graphic parallel in the compositions draws the closeness that occurred earlier between father and son into this moment.

Reinforcing character dynamics

Visual motifs dominate Wong Kar-Wai's lyrical film of longing, *In the Mood For Love*. Clocks, telephones, shoes, distressed walls, and even physical actions are repeated as when Mrs. Chan carries her sea-green thermos to the noodle shop, night after steamy night. The nine shots of Figure 2.15 occur in a single scene. They do not represent static shots, but one **tracking shot** in which the camera tracks left from Mrs. Chan to Mr. Chow and then right again, to Mrs. Chan—joining them and separating them in one shot.

The story centers around two neighbors in a cramped, Hong Kong high-rise drawn together by the illicit affair between their spouses. At

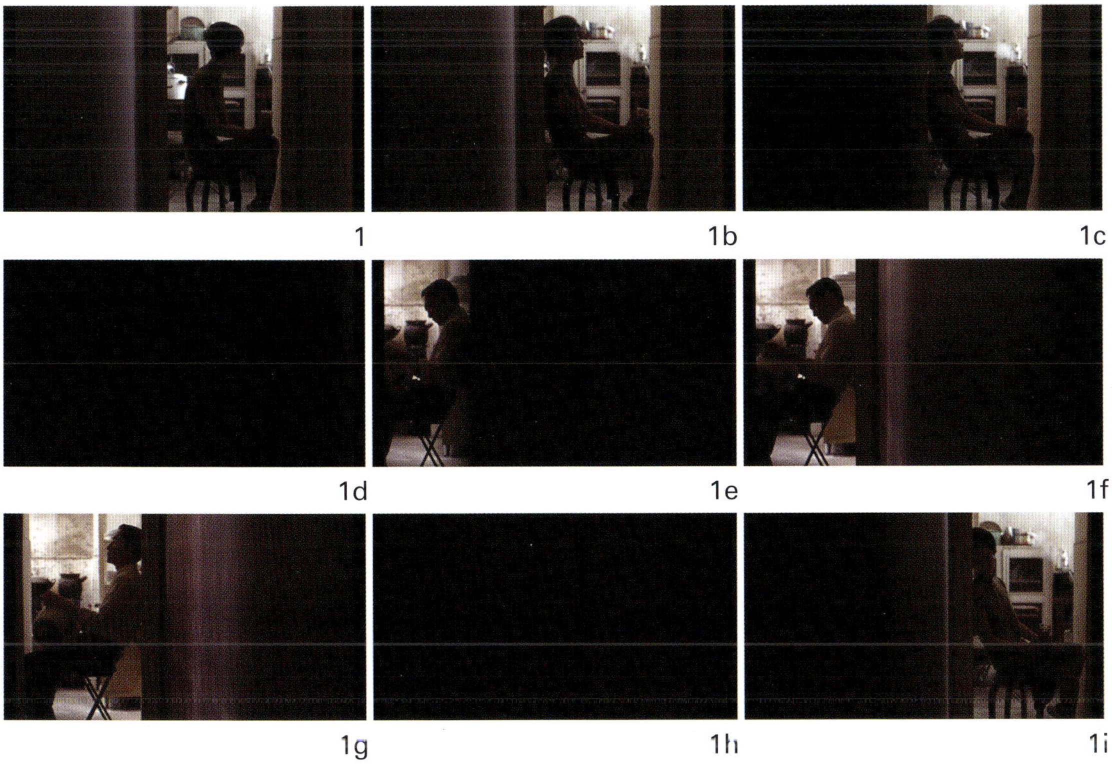

Figure 2.15 *In the Mood for Love* (2000). Director: Wong Kar-Wai. Cinematographers: Christopher Doyle, Pung-Leung Kwan, Ping Bin Lee.

first, they spend time together as a measure of solace. This leads to tenderness between them, and eventually they fall in love. For reasons of shame and pride, they refuse to acknowledge their mutual affection, leaving one another twice abandoned.

The scene is photographed through the eye of a camera that tracks laterally back and forth between the two characters, Mr. Chow and Mrs. Chan. The tracking camera stresses their connection, and at the same time, the impassable wall between them. Imagery emphasizing their togetherness alongside their separateness occurs many times in the film. In this segment, it is not only the framing that binds them, but a parallel in their body language. As the camera tracks in each direction, each character leans forward in profile. Then, as if giving into the longing, overcome by "mood," each leans back against the doorjamb, faces turn toward the camera. Here, formal construction makes use of camera movement, figure movement, composition, set design, costume, staging, and score (a vocalist sings from the radio). These elements combine to create added pressure on the story's central, unyielding conflict: Mr. Chow and Mrs. Chan are inescapably bound and inescapably separate.

> The process (of shooting a film) is based on two very basic elements—the people who are doing it together, and the space in which we work. The style comes from the space, the process, the limitations we have, the people with whom we work. It's not me imposing something on the film. It's the film emerging from those characteristics, those conditions, including weather. The film is not a style, it's a predicament.
>
> —Christopher Doyle. "Christopher Doyle (*In the Mood for Love*) Interview" *The Seventh Art*, July 19, 2016. Christopher Heron, Pavan Moondi and Brian Robertson.

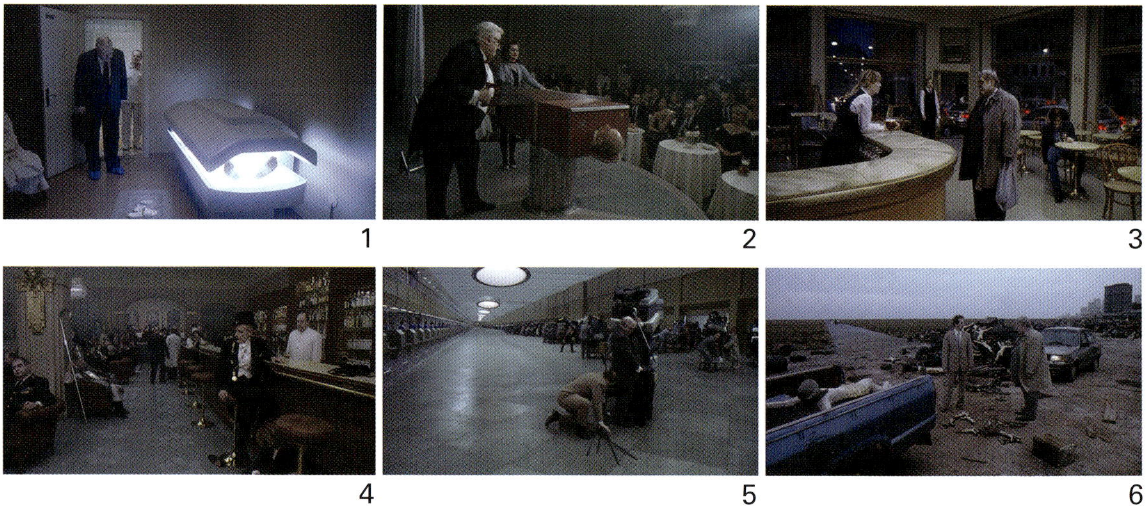

Figure 2.16 *Songs From the Second Floor* (2000). Director: Roy Andersson. Cinematographers: István Borbás, Jesper Klevenås.

Scaffolding for narrative complexities

Formal treatment dominates the recent work by Swedish director Roy Andersson. The signature style of his films depends on the marriage between visual storytelling and formal treatment, inspiring an ambitious use of mise en scene. His second film, *Songs From the Second Floor* is made up of forty-six scenes and forty-six cuts, an indication from the outset that a "method of arrangement" is in play. Each scene is confined to one shot: a meticulously constructed image framed through a static camera. Actually, in *Songs From the Second Floor* there is *one* camera move, a dolly, which occurs about midway through the film. The duration of each shot/scene varies, but many shots last for as long as two to three minutes. As we move further along in our discussion of camerawork I will take up the particular challenge a director faces when rendering a static shot of extended duration. In *Songs* this convergence creates the effect of endlessness suited to the film's meditation on lethargy, on the worn out and the humiliated, on the living dead. This effect is offset by situations pictured or enacted within a framing that bends the tone toward irony. Many are hilarious. Reviving this effect on the printed page is impossible. The six still frames demonstrate the precision of shot construction within each tableau. In addition to creating static shots with formal precision, Andersson gives each shot volume. Depth, for example, can be suggested by a door, or window, or diagonal, or vanishing point, or action staged in every field: foreground, middle ground, and background.

There is a startling variety among images that also share graphic parallels: the depth of composition in scenes 1, 2, and 3 that reaches toward a vanishing point in the center of the frame and in scenes 4, 5, and 6 a curved shape extending from the left toward the center of the frame. The parallels also work in concert with other formal tools to give the story, with its episodic structure, **narrative coherence**. Even as the individual vignettes deviate from the cause and effect chain of action in conventional narrative story telling, they are held together by familiar compositions and framing. The film's formal sensibility dictates choices of light, shadow, line, texture, shape, composition, and color.[9] Each shot has a painterly precision. In *Songs from the Second Floor*, the precision in each composition serves to balance a worldview that portrays a dreary unnamed city, populated by characters vacillating between impotence and despair. Formal treatment as a strategy for taming narrative complexities is not a new idea—not in the visual, dramatic or literary arts, certainly not in filmmaking. Here, the formal crafting of exquisite compositions also demonstrates the way a movie's treatment strategy can work as a *counterpoint to story events, creating a plurality*. This plurality (i.e., "the world is dreary and chaotic" *and yet* "the world is lovely and precise") allows a movie the ground, where stance is concerned, to quarrel with itself. The treacherous and sad world of *Songs* is also funny and beautiful. Surprisingly, like life.

Discussion questions

1. What additional similarities in the framing exist from one shot to the next in *An Autumn Afternoon*, Figure 2.5?
2. What, for example, is the role of geometric shapes?
3. As seen in *Mystery Train*, color works as a formal element. Is this also true for the shots in *Spa Night*, Figure 2.14?

Notes

1. Bruno Dumont states frankly during an interview featured on the Fox Lorber DVD release of *Humanité* that he is not interested in a "cinema of desire." This describes the movie-going experience in which a viewer seeks to identify with characters or merge with the dramatized world on the screen.
2. Yuharu Atsuta photographed many of Ozu's later films including *Good Morning (Ohayu)* and *Tokyo Story*.
3. *The Psycho File: A Comprehensive Guide to Hitchcock's Classic Shocker*, by Joseph W. Smith III, gives a thorough account of the shower scene during every phase of production. In so doing, it illuminates Hitchcock's working style and rigor as a director.
4. In June of 2015, Gary Susman, movie writer for *Rolling Stone*, authored a *moviefone* post entitled "*Psycho*: 25 Things You (Probably) Didn't Know About Hitchcock's Classic." "Number 12: The shower murder is one of the most studied montages of film ever made. It contains at least 70 edits in just 45 minutes."
5. The discussion of form in this chapter limits itself to the application of visual techniques toward cinematic storytelling, resulting in a particular treatment or style. It does not include modes or forms of narration.
6. Stylistic similarities can be seen in the works of Jarmusch and Kaurismaki. *A Man Without a Past*, for example, organizes space in front of the camera by taking full advantage of formal properties shared with the visual *and* dramatic arts. In addition to a static camera that takes great care with framing, character movements are often choreographed. Like figurines, they make ordinary human gestures in unison as if wound-up with the same turn-key. The effect is comical, but also touching, given the truthfulness coloring the comedy with substance and depth.
7. *Paterson*, Jim Jarmusch's 2016 film, exploits the director's interest in coupling as a formal device with all kinds of visual duplicates, including the repeated sighting of identical twins by Paterson, the bus driver who is the film's protagonist.
8. Kitchen sink realism (also known as kitchen sink drama), is a term used in Britain during the 1950s and 60s to describe a trend in the narrative arts for portraying gritty stories about an urban working class.
9. Andersson's production period on a film can run for as long as two years. The luxury of time is due, in part, to a warehouse purchased by him with funds from years of directing television commercials. (Samples of these TV commercials can be found online.) The movie sets are built in the warehouse and dressed by a team of collaborators who participate in each phase of the production process. Each set piece is subjected to a fanatical attention to detail. Andersson is also known for as many as twenty-five takes of each shot. *Tomorrow's Another Day* (directed by Johan Carlsson) documents the production of Andersson's 2009 film, *You the Living*. In it, the working style of Andersson and his team is thoroughly explored.

3

The close-up

Filmmakers discovered very early in the history of cinema that audiences grasped quickly the logic of changes in shot size. Viewers could easily observe the transition to a close-up in a scene of wide or medium shots without losing a story's thread. The close-up became an essential tool in filmmaking, enhancing the dramatic effects of a given scene. Achieved through altering camera proximity or manipulating the focal length, a close-up interjected into a scene works to provide emphasis, alter pace, portray a relevant prop, or visualize a character's response. Occasionally, the close-up functions as a **cutaway**—a break in the flow of action to give the viewer visual information pertinent to the plot.

In D.W. Griffith's 1919 film, *Broken Blossoms*, the close-up accomplishes a variety of narrative goals. In the scene pictured in Figure 3.1, its purpose is to clarify and emphasize aspects of the plot. This close-up is a cutaway. Lucy, the protagonist, framed in a wide shot prepares to go to town. Before leaving, she leans over to lift a brick in the floor. The cut to the close-up not only highlights her action, but also emphasizes what is buried underneath.

While cutaways have become an essential tool in visual storytelling, the most common use of the close-up, throughout film history, has been to picture the human face.

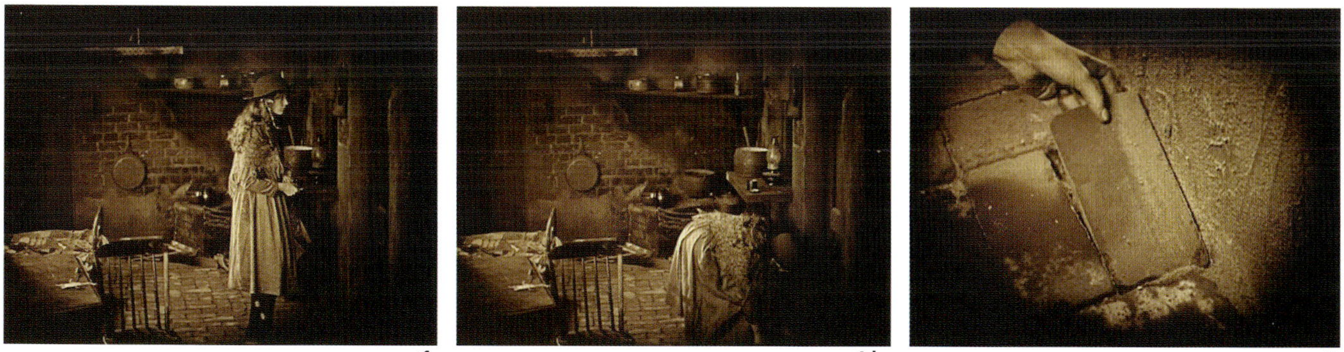

1 1b 2

Figure 3.1
Broken Blossoms (1919). Director: D.W. Griffith. Cinematographer: G. W. Bitzer.

This chapter focuses on the variety of dramatic effects that occur through the use of the close-up. The technique has been, from the outset, one of the fundamental tools in visual storytelling and yet, even in the twenty-first century, the dramatic effects occasioned by its use continue to be revised and expanded. Highlighted here are films that demonstrate inventive and purposeful application of the technique.

Among the effects discussed are the capacity of the close-up to interrupt time and space, to underscore character experience, upend technical convention, add punctuation or emphasis to a scene, and obscure background elements. We will also explore the atypical use of the close-up as the prevailing shot size against which wider shots are interspersed.

Interrupting space and time

If the conventional use of the close-up is to emphasize a subject or object present in a wider frame, the close-up can also interrupt space and time by implanting elements not present in the wide shot, elements that evoke memory, fantasy, or obsession. For example, Karoly Makk's 1971 film, *Love*, portrays an aging woman who clings to the past. This attachment to the past is conveyed through close-ups that intrude on the action occurring in the present tense. The close-ups are cut between shots of the character suggesting that the disparate images between belong to her, that is, they spring from her imagination, or in this case, her memory.

The "memory shots" (Figure 3.2, Shots 2, 4, 5, and 6) are interspersed among the shots of the aging woman (Shots 1, 3, and 7) so that the viewer understands that she is the source. Also, and this is crucial, the director orients the viewer by introducing this strategy for juxtaposing memory and the present very early in the film. The close-ups in the sequence include physical objects and people, though there is the added remove in her remembering people through replication—either as a painting or photograph.

As viewers, we're encouraged to assume that the close-up in shot 5 is the old woman as a young girl, given the graphic visual parallel to the close-up in shot 3. The sequence also argues on behalf of the power of framing the human face in close-up. Our attention is drawn immediately to these two shots. It is this pull that corrals our discussion through the remainder of this chapter, as we focus on the intimate access a close-up provides to a character's face.

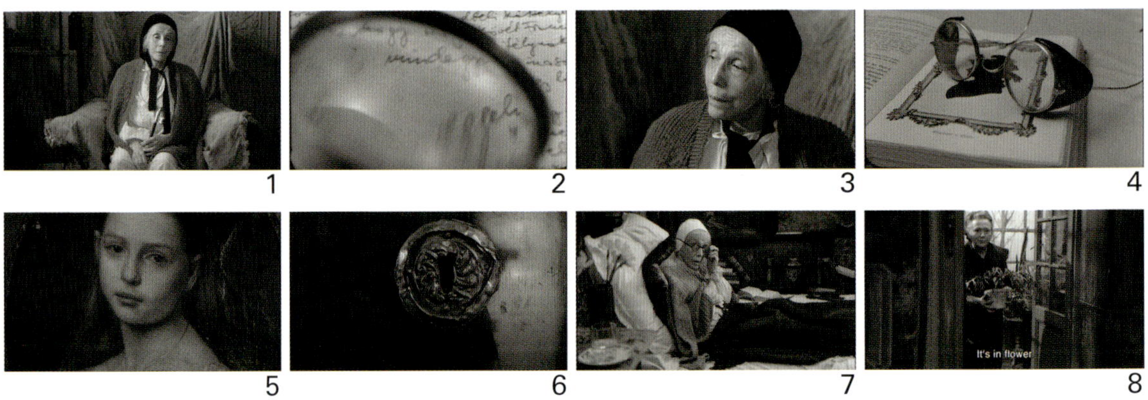

Figure 3.2
Love (1971).
Director:
Károly Makk.
Cinematographer:
János Tóth.

Narrative progression

An example of this occurs in Oscar Micheaux's 1925 feature film, *Body and Soul*. Like the sequence cited from *Love*, Micheaux's movie also makes use of a close-up to interrupt the flow of action with a memory sequence. But this is not its primary function in the scene.

Micheaux was the first major African-American film director. A published writer, his work as a novelist drove him toward complex story lines which posed narrative challenges in translating page to screen. These challenges were met with an imaginative and idiosyncratic use of film language as the grammar was taking shape. In *Body and Soul*, one can see Micheaux's mind working to convey visually the recognition between two characters that share a past not dramatized on screen (their shared past takes place before the film story begins). One of the two characters is an escaped convict posing as a pastor, Reverend Isaiah Jenkins, (Paul Robeson, in his debut performance). The second character, Yello-Curley Hinds (Lawrence Chenault), is his former jail mate. Yello-Curley, new to town, is invited to a Sunday service during which he discovers his former jail mate preaching from the pulpit.

The scene is comprised of twenty-seven shots, fifteen of which are devoted to a shot/reverse shot strategy of Yello-Curley Hinds in close-up (Shots 3, 5, 7) and Reverend Jenkins framed in a medium shot (Shots 4, 6, 8). The other twelve shots include a master shot in wide facing the congregation (Shot 1), a medium wide of the pulpit (Shot 2), two intertitles, and the three shot memory sequence showing Yello-Curley behind bars, framed on either side by the familiar image of Reverend Jenkins in medium shot. The scene closes with a wide shot of the pulpit from behind the congregation.

Narrative progression

The conventional strategy for integrating a close-up into a scene is to establish context (place, time, character(s)) in a wider shot before cutting to a close-up. Once the given moment in the story is contextualized, the close-up informs that context, adding emphasis or directing our focus.

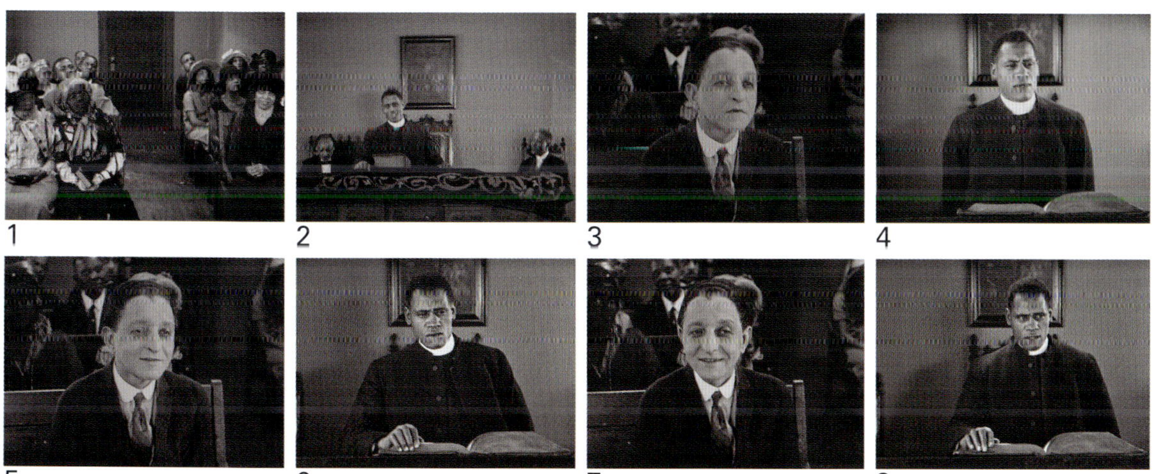

Figure 3.3
Body and Soul (1925). Director: Oscar Micheaux. Cinematographer: Uncredited.

The first third of the scene is pictured in Figure 3.3. One can see, even in eight shots, the way in which the close-ups of Yello-Curley Hinds are staged as a map of narrative progression through the scene. The viewer witnesses his recognition of Reverend Jenkins as his ex-jail mate. This leads to Yello-Curley's recognition by the reverend, and his pleasure in being recognized. The scene ends with Yello-Curley's delight over what the reverend's masquerade may mean for him. (Figure 3.4)

The narrative progression also charts Yello-Curley's transition from passive bystander to provocateur. In seven close-ups interspersed through the scene, Yello-Curley becomes an agent of action—without speaking, without any physical movement other than subtle changes in his facial expression. The relentless return to his face charges the scene, exacerbating panic and discomfort in Reverend Jenkins' over the possibility of having his masquerade exposed.

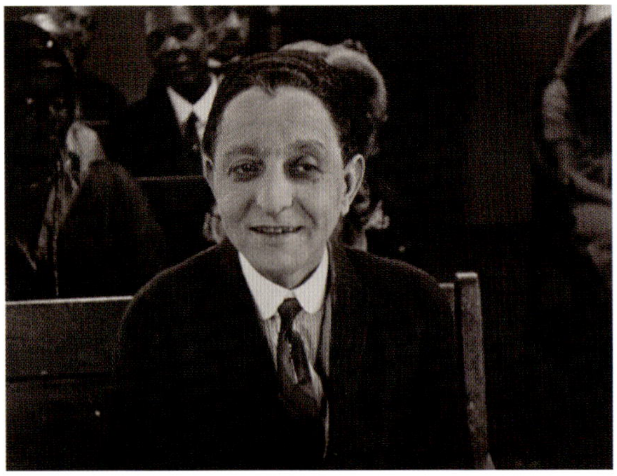

Figure 3.4
Body and Soul (1925). Director: Oscar Micheaux. Cinematographer: Uncredited.

Matt Zoller Seitz: You also do a lot of things where you've got close-ups of people where there's nothing in the frame except their face—it's almost like they're a painting. Why do you do that?

Ava DuVernay: Because the terrain of the face is the most dynamic thing you can point the camera at, to me. I love production design and bells and whistles and all of that. I love a techno-crane as much as the next gal, but a great actor's face? What else should we be looking at?

—The Vulture TV Podcast, Sept. 6, 2016

Shot/reverse shot

In the scene cited from Oscar Micheaux' *Body and Soul*, a shot/reverse shot strategy drives the editing, but only one of the characters is framed in close-up. Quentin Tarantino's World War II drama, *Inglourious Basterds*, makes use of close-ups for each of two characters. It is difficult in still frames to recreate the dynamic of two characters facing off against one another, but one can see in Figure 3.5 that the close-ups are matched, shot to shot. A Nazi colonel visits a local French farmer as part of a routine local inspection for sheltered, runaway Jews. The scene, to be sure, is a confrontation, though the colonel takes care in giving the farmer the impression that he is not suspected of harboring Jews. The friendly visit becomes both more suspenseful and more treacherous as the colonel begins to insinuate Jews might be living below the floorboards of the farmer's house. Until the final moment of revelation and admission (Shots 8 and 9), Tarantino uses the close-up to taunt the viewer in what is staged as a poker match with very high stakes. So desperate are we to unriddle the motivation, knowledge, and intention of the colonel, we study his face for the slightest hint of what he might know. Likewise, the viewer is privy to the fact that Jews are hiding there, in the basement, and watches the farmer with rapt attention in hopes that he does not give away what we know.

Throughout this volley of shot/reverse shot, the camera works to keep them evenly matched in shot size. When the camera moves in to a tighter close-up of the farmer, as it does from shot 2 to 2b, the cut to the colonel just after is also a tighter shot (Shot 3). Too, their faces fill more of the frame as the close-ups tighten toward the climax of the scene. The farmer begins to weep (Shot 8) and the Nazi colonel eyes him with smug conviction (Shot 9). In the confrontation between colonel and farmer, the portion of the frame filled by each character is matched and increases as tension rises in the scene.

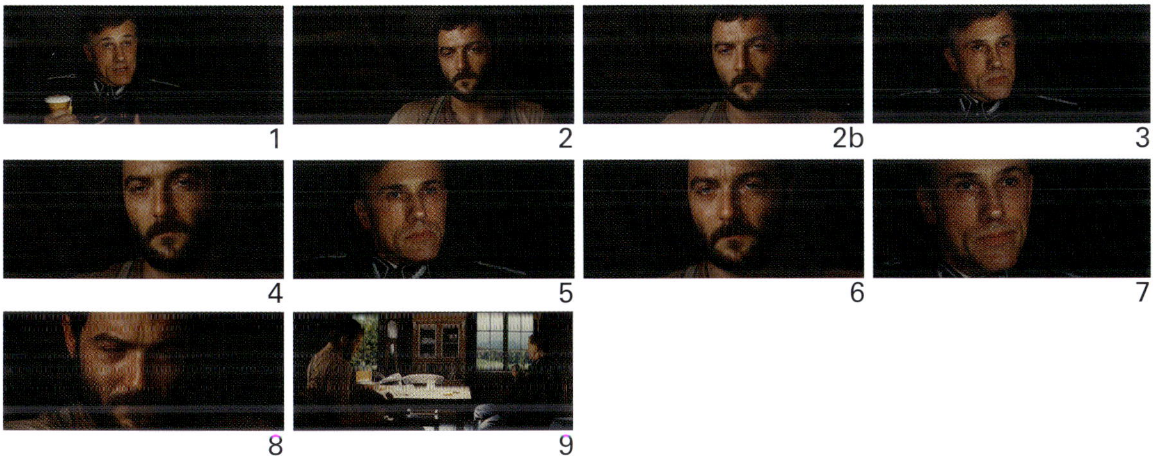

Figure 3.5
Inglourious Basterds (2009). Director: Quentin Tarantino. Cinematographer: Robert Richardson.

Revising convention

Body and Soul and *Inglourious Basterds* observe the basic convention: wider shots establish context followed by close-ups. Directors have been toying with the convention for some time. We've seen an example of this in the prologue of *KAOS*, which withholds the establishing wide shot to invest our attention in the interaction between characters and the nesting bird. *The Graduate*, directed by Mike Nichols, also dispenses with the convention of context. The movie begins with a tight close-up a young man (Dustin Hoffman in the role of Benjamin Braddock). The subjective experience of the main character gains focus from the beginning (and, as we soon learn, drives much of the action of the film). Unlike Yello-Curley Hinds whose facial expressions activate the drama in the scene from *Body and Soul*, Benjamin Braddock's face is noticeably expressionless—dazed, lifeless. After several seconds the shot widens to reveal the context. He's on an airplane (and we learn later, flying home from college).

By suspending the usual treatment, we are led to understand that the character's subjective (and in this case, psychological) experience precedes the action of the film, and will certainly inform it. The emphasis the film gives to Benjamin Braddock's interior life is more than sufficient reason to begin the film with a close-up.

In Steven Soderbergh's biopic, *Erin Brockovich*, a close-up also functions as the first shot. Here it works less to forge a bond with the character's interior life than a strategy for delivering defining character traits. For the first minute or so, the face we see on the screen is more Julia Roberts than Erin Brockovich. But with each line she speaks, character traits imbue the image and pull the story away from Roberts into the character of Brockovich. This break with convention doesn't cause the viewer disorientation: the context is easy to grasp—we discover readily where she is, what she wants, why she's there. The greatest advantage of the close-up in this scene is the way it privileges us with a close view of an abrupt mood change registered on Robert's face when the job interview goes sour. (This is an important narrative detail that will impact the plot on more than one occasion.) Throughout the film, Julia Roberts gives the character of Erin Brockovich a readable and expressive face. Soderbergh introduces this performance strategy in the movie's opening scene with the close-up.

Despite differences in emphasis, *The Graduate* and *Erin Brockovich* deliver close-ups in a way that provide enhanced experience of character without sacrificing for too long our understanding of context.

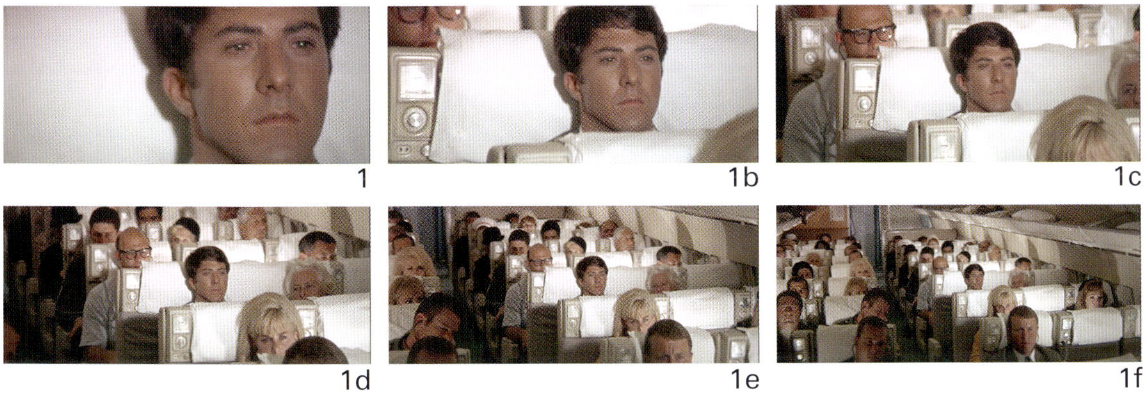

Figure 3.6
The Graduate (1967). Director: Mike Nichols. Cinematographer: Robert Surtees.

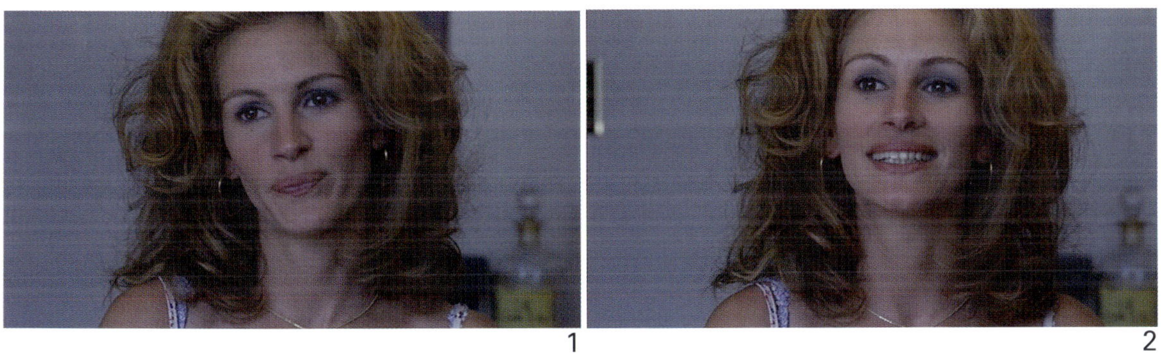

Figure 3.7
Erin Brockovich (2000). Director: Steven Soderbergh. Cinematographer: Edward Lachman.

Subjective experience

In the character close-ups we've sampled thus far, the close-up creates an emotional register by way of a character's reaction or non-reaction. This acts as a call to plant our attention inside a character's immediate experience. We've already seen one example of this in the film *Ordinary People*, where shots become tighter and tighter until Colin turns into close-up with his outburst. In Satyajit Ray's first feature, *Pather Panchali*, it is the bystanders of an outburst who earn the close-ups.

Nothing mitigates the challenge of making life on screen. That is the most beautiful challenge of all.

—Mira Nair, *Filmmaker Magazine*, March 7, 2016.

Figure 3.8 *Pather Panchali* (1955). Director: Satyajit Ray. Cinematographer: Subrata Mitra.

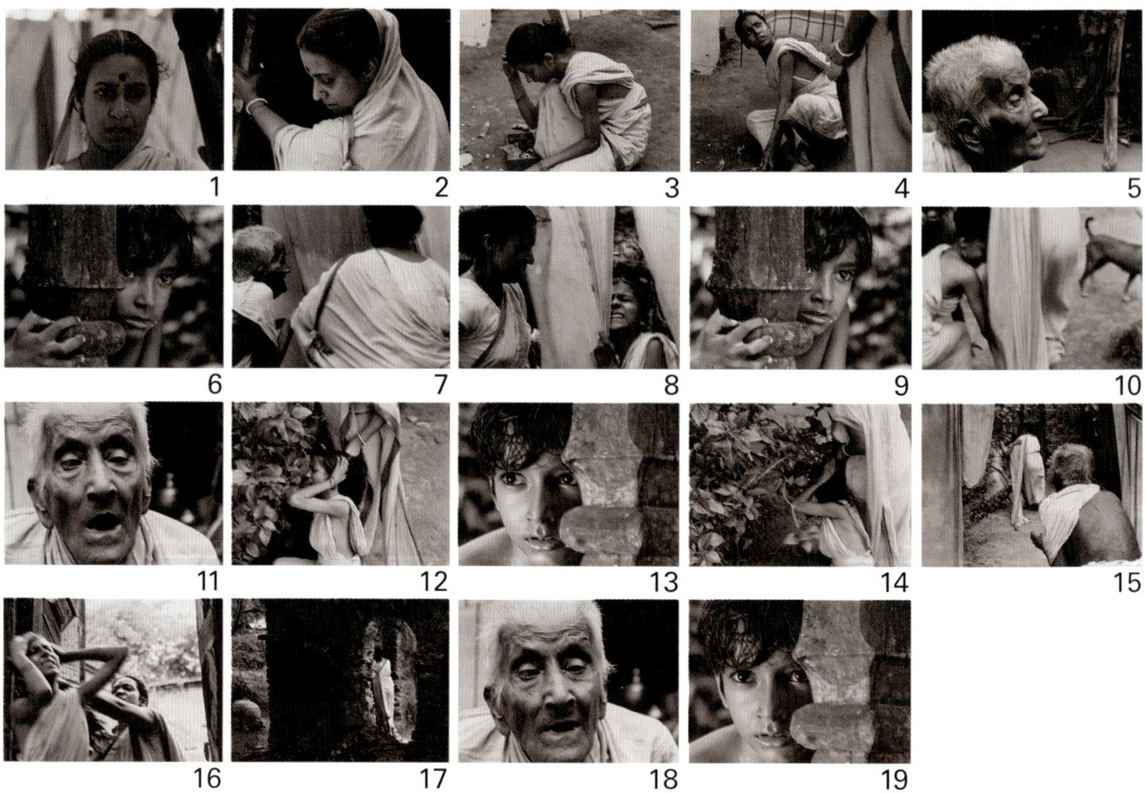

The movie tells the story of Apu's early life with his family in rural India. In the scene pictured (Figure 3.8) Apu's mother confronts his older sister, Durga, after neighbors accuse Durga of stealing. The quarrel escalates and the mother throws Durga from their home. The elderly Auntie tries to intercede, but to no avail. Apu ducks behind a post, dazed, looking on. Within the scene's coverage, nine of nineteen shots are single shot close-ups.

Even as the scene grows violent—with the mother dragging Durga by her hair across the ground—the shots are framed predominantly as medium shots. The scene reserves its widest shots for the moment just after Durga is thrown from the courtyard, when the split screen created by the stone wall dividing mother from daughter has its greatest visual power and meaning.

The close-ups of Auntie and Apu are reaction shots. In the first and last instance of their reactions, the shots are consecutive: a close-up of Auntie followed by Apu. In the middle of the scene, Auntie is seen in a close-up between shots of the mother and daughter fighting, on either side of which are additional close-ups of Apu. There is also a shift in Apu's close-up (pattern and variation intertwined) with his face on the left side of the post for the first two close-ups, and on the right side in the last two. The scene demonstrates a symmetrical shot structure without sacrificing at all the realistic treatment of everyday events in small but telling details.

Auntie's reaction in close-up, given her age, has a harrowing effect. Each time her close-up repeats, it punctuates the scene with the force of her wisdom and compassion. Young Apu, in contrast, lives at the cusp of new experience. Despite circumstances of rural poverty and his father's long absences, his innocence has deep roots. He takes pleasure freely in learning to read and write, in the sight and sound of trains, and in the company of his sister. When she is confronted by the neighbor and then, more aggressively, by their mother, Apu remains hidden, silent, and watchful. Apu is not merely a witness. He absorbs life lessons that chip away at his innocence. At one moment he winces. The close-ups give emphasis to Apu's shock and dismay, but also to his newfound awareness of a flawed and complicated world.

Subtracting context

Lucretia Martel's second feature film, *The Holy Girl*, not only draws us into character experience but also confines us there. The story focuses on the sexual and spiritual awakening of two adolescent girls, Amalia and Josefina. In Figure 3.9, the camera's commitment to restricting space around the characters can be readily noticed. The still frames depict the opening sequence in which a female soloist is heard singing over the credit sequence. The singing continues into the first shot: a static medium shot of six adolescent girls, with fixed attention. Two of the girls are crowded out of the frame. We discover the source of the singing (and their attention) in the second shot. Each subsequent shot, also static, continues to crowd and confine the characters and with no spatial orientation of an establishing shot. Repeated shots of the singer and our two protagonists, Amalia and Josefina, form the visual spine of the scene.

Noticeably missing is a wide shot establishing location, circumstance, or context. A woman sings liturgical music. A man accompanies her. A group of young teens listen. At one point, the singer begins to weep and turns to collect herself. She continues singing and it happens again. Two of the girls seem particularly struck by her reaction. This is all we know. Transmitting full and explicit story information is not Martel's priority. We are, through close-ups and crowded medium shots, pressed into character experience, even without context. The use of close-up and crowded medium shots act as a strategy for giving emphasis. The emphasis is weighted by what we are *not* shown, by what is subtracted. The context will emerge, in part, as the movie unfolds. But clarity is suspended in favor of conveying intensity. The intensity carries us forward. Introducing characters in close-up who will not be seen again gives a greater value to the experience portrayed than any individual.

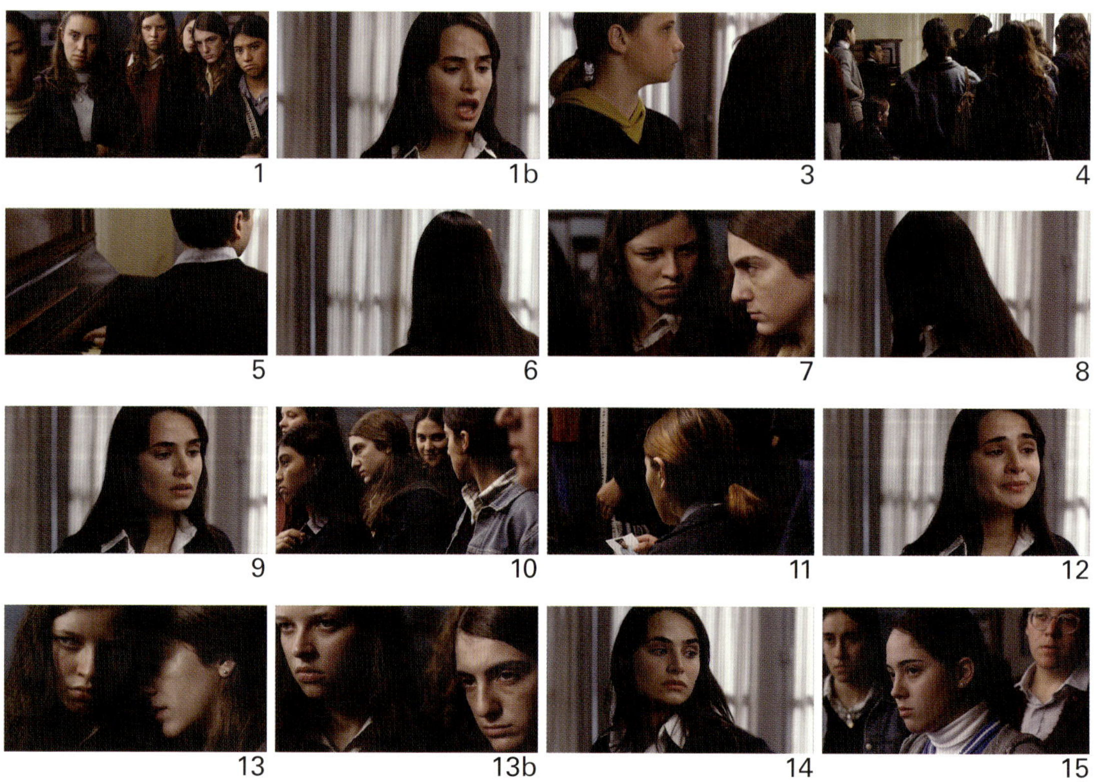

Figure 3.9
The Holy Girl (2004). Director: Lucretia Martel. Cinematographer: Félix Monti.

Predominant frame

The close-up used as the predominant framing device in a narrative feature film is, at the very least, unconventional. Anyone drafting a shot list or storyboard for even a short script understands the challenge of reducing the vocabulary of shots to close-ups. The wide, establishing shot locates the viewer, creates context, and provides essential narrative information. A wide landscape shot can also have pure, cinematic value, as seen in *Lawrence of Arabia* or John Ford's westerns. And, as we have already seen, juxtaposing shots of varying sizes can exert added dynamic tension on a given scene.

Nevertheless, two contemporary directors have taken on the challenge of creating feature films with a camera strategy that privileges the close-up. The two films, *Son of Saul* and *Blue Is the Warmest Color*, exploit the prevalence of close-ups in surprising and meaningful ways. Each does so with different intent and unique effect. Their remarkable ambition does not, however, supersede their predecessor, Carl Theodor Dreyer, who radicalized cinema in 1928 with the predominance of close-ups in his silent film classic, *The Passion of Joan of Arc*.

Much of the critical writing about Dreyer's film and its use of close-up is easily accessible so a lengthy discussion here is unnecessary. Suffice it to say that despite construction of expensive sets intended to replicate Rouen Castle, the exhaustive interrogation of Joan of Arc by the French clerical court unfolds almost exclusively in close-ups. There is much to learn from Dreyer's use of this camera strategy. A variety of camera angles add to the dramatic effect. Too, it is useful to note that the dynamic between Joan of Arc and her inquisitors is staged through matching eye lines of the characters. (Figure 3.10) The predominance of close-ups requires skillful casting and places a particular demand on the quality of performance. In *The Passion of Joan of Arc*, Renée Jeanne Falconetti, as Joan, also brings to the role a presence and depth that allows a viewer entry into the character's experience.

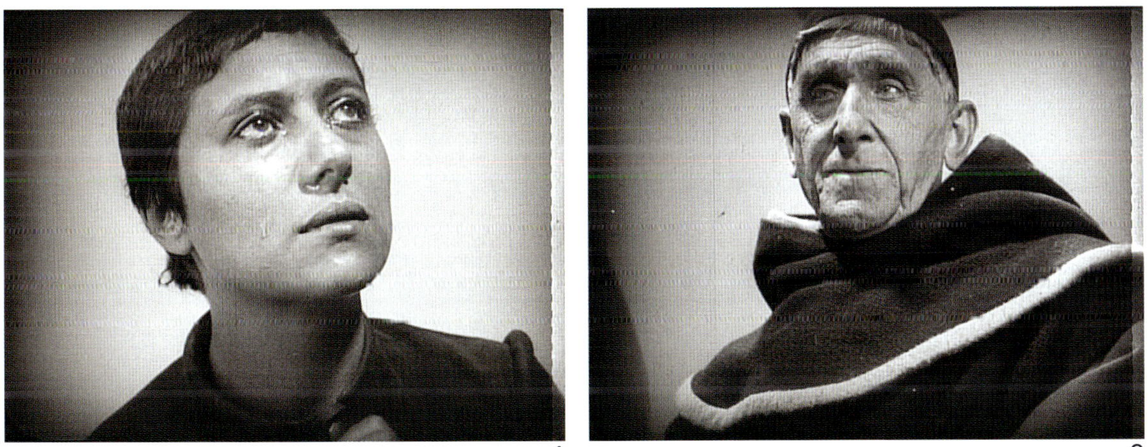

1 2

Figure 3.10 *The Passion of Joan of Arc* (1928). Director: Carl Dreyer. Cinematograper: Rudolph Maté.

Obscuring background

In the 2015 debut feature film, *Son of Saul*, by director Lázló Nemes, the camera boldly confines the coverage to the character of Saul Ausländer and restricts this coverage to a predominance of close-ups. Even when he is among a group of men, the frame is tight, with the men filling the borders of the frame, and often spilling out of it. Saul is a member of the Sonderkommando. These select groups of Jewish prisoners were forced to assist the Nazis with disposing of the corpses in the gas chambers. Set in Auschwitz, the camera's close watch of Saul strains to find any evidence of the kind of personal experience conveyed so palpably in *The Holy Girl* or *The Passion of Joan of Arc*. It delivers instead his stoic, numbed reaction to the daily tasks of ushering men and women into the gas chamber, scavenging valuables from the victims' clothes, dragging their dead bodies from the chamber, and scrubbing the floors. The claustrophobia created by the camera continues even after Saul discovers a young boy still breathing, after the gassing. The viewer witnesses Saul as he becomes more urgent in his actions, but in no way more expressive. Too, the strategy of combining a hand-held camera with long takes lends authenticity to the fictional portrait of a world rooted in historical fact.

Figure 3.11 reveals the way in which the tight frame of the close-up serves another indispensable purpose. It does not, as in the scene from *The Holy Girl*, obscure context. No, the context of *Son of Saul* is very clear. Rather, it limits the viewer's vision of horrors associated with that context. Concealed, for the most part, by Saul's head and shoulders, we see, in fragments, naked men and women in the background as they are readied for the gas chamber. The film takes immaculate care in creating an authentic physical environment, even if seen only at the edges of the frame or deep in the background. In this scene, which occurs at the beginning of the film, arriving prisoners are told to strip for showering, after which they will be given soup and assigned a work task. Saul oversees this activity and after ushering them into the gas chamber stands outside the door (Shot 1h), waiting for the wailing and urgent cries for help to end. Even as background fragments or mere sound effects, the horror prevails. Perhaps more so given our need to strain to decipher it. How much more vivid the image we, as viewers, are required to conjure.

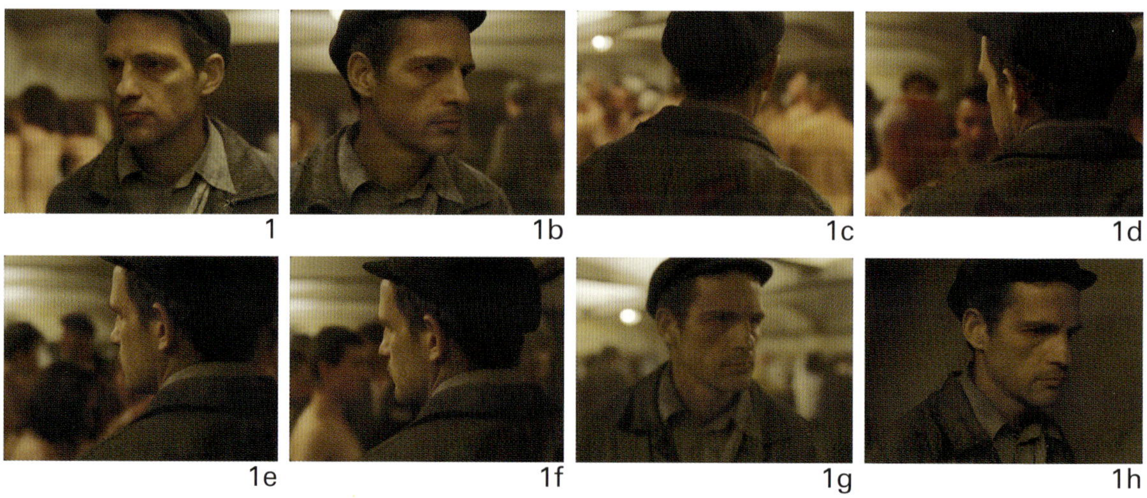

Figure 3.11
Son of Saul (2015). Director: Lázló Nemes. Cinematographer: Mátyás Erdély.

Erotic gaze

The 2013 coming-of-age romance, *Blue Is the Warmest Color*, obliges the viewer to endure the vicissitudes of first love by the force of camera on the character's fresh face. The character: Adèle, a fifteen-year-old high school student living in the northern French town of Lille. Her life is made up of the customary exchanges of adolescence until the blue-haired Emma, older, more sophisticated (an art student at École des Beaux-Arts) and more seasoned at love, enters her life.

A sighting of Emma on the street startles Adèle with a bolt of desire. Later, during her first foray into a lesbian club, also depicted in close-ups, she sees Emma again, at a table with friends. Eye contact is made and minutes later Emma joins Adèle at the bar where they have their first conversation. Their exchange is bookended with two wider shots, giving the viewer a brief glimpse at the crowded club. In between, a string of close-ups documents the tête-a-tête. This strategy breaks with the convention of punctuating a scene with close-ups. Here, wide shots work as punctuation. Before exploring the camera strategy for this documentation, it's worth looking briefly at the first wide shot, pictured in Figure 3.12.

Adèle is pictured in the center of the shot that precedes a long sequence of close-ups. The composition provides a sense of the crowded nature of the club while also, through lighting, drawing the viewer's attention to Adèle, seated at the bar. When the scene cuts to her close-up in the next shot, it does conform to convention—establishing a location before cutting to a tighter view of some aspect. In this instance, we've been prepared for this aspect by the glow of light around Adèle.

Emma arrives. Their dialogue consists primarily of the usual "get to know you" banter. It is, by turns, playful and informative. But the subtext, with its erotic charge incited by their mutual attraction, whips up the drama in the scene. It is this dynamic that the shots foreground. In fifteen minutes of screen time, the scene unspools more than sixty close-ups. These close-ups are created with two cameras, a variety of angles, singles and two shots. It includes shots from behind the bar, behind the actors, over their shoulders, at right angle, at left angle. Single shots dominate the beginning of the scene, and as the conversation relaxes into an easy back and forth, the close-ups convert to two-shots, and tight two-shots, at that. While only a few shots from the scene are replicated here, it is a useful exercise to analyze the scene in entirety, focusing on the motivation for shifts in camera position in stitching the scene together.

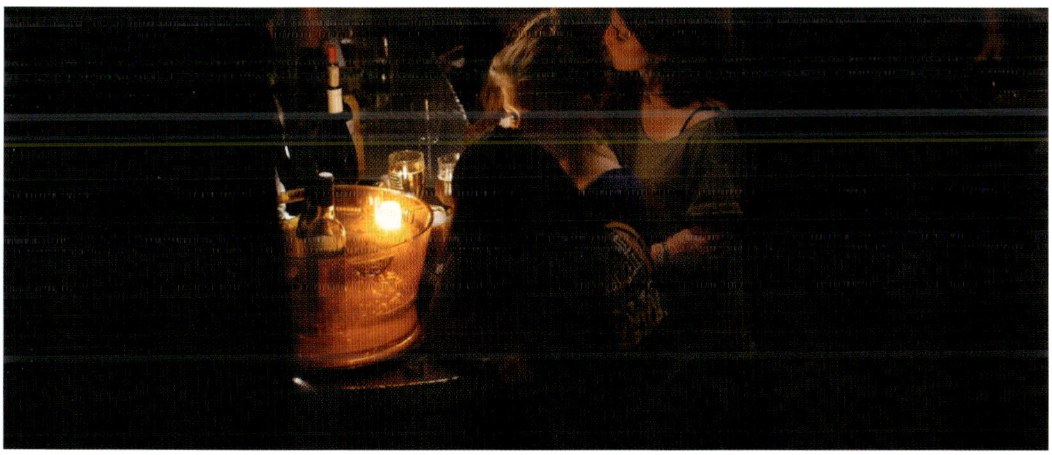

Figure 3.13 *Blue Is the Warmest Color* (2013). Director: Abdellatif Kechiche. Cinematographer: Sofian El Fani.

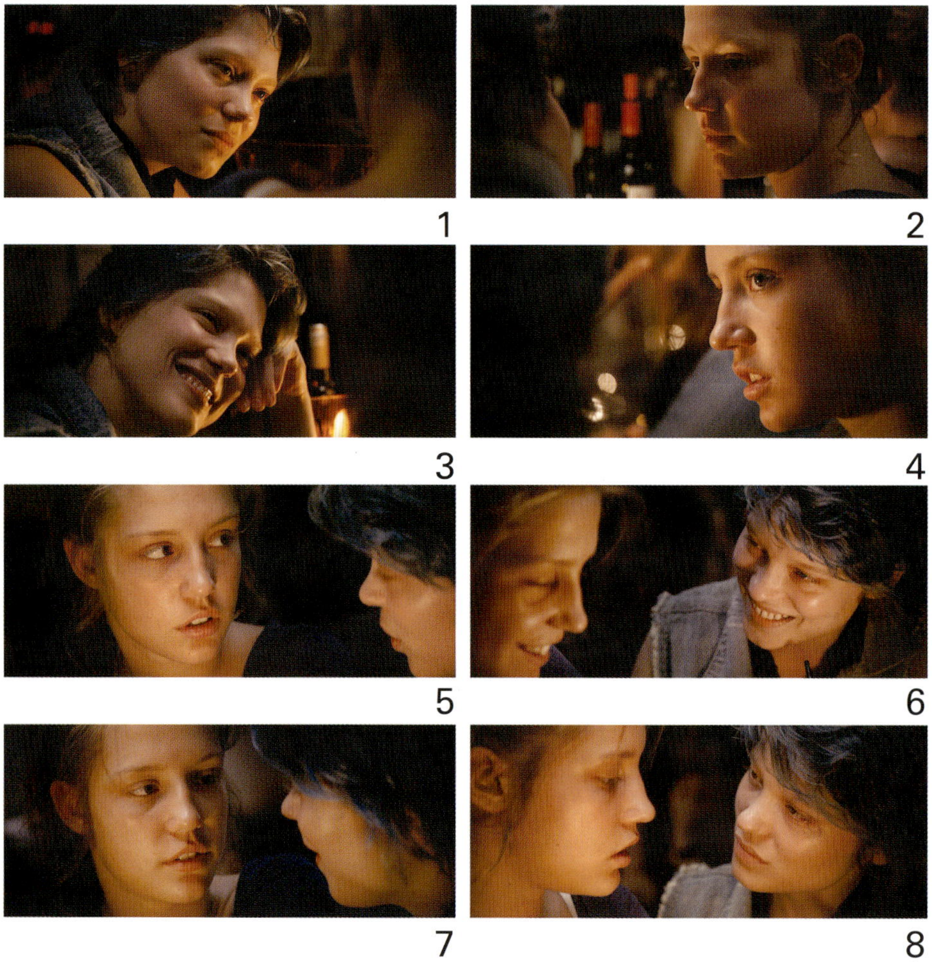

Figure 3.13 *Blue Is the Warmest Color* (2013). Director: Abdellatif Kechiche. Cinematographer: Sofian El Fani.

The close-ups make of their exchange, a dance, giving the viewer intimate access to the force of Emma's laser-like attention which unsettles and arouses, though Adèle never loses her footing. "Why do they call it a school of fine arts?" she asks Emma. "Are there ugly arts?" Adèle's self-possession, despite youth, fuels the attraction. And this is also visually conveyed. In the miscellaneous shots pictured in Figure 3.13, the magnetism between them is palpable. The camera keeps them close. Single shots prevail at the beginning of the scene (Shots 1–4). As their flirtation deepens into open exchange, Adèle and Emma are framed predominantly in two-shots (Shots 5–8).

Beauty shot: glamour personified

It seems appropriate to follow the discussion of *Blue Is the Warmest Color* with a nod to the close-up as a frame for portraiture reveling in beauty. In fact, no discussion of the close-up would be complete without highlighting its relevance to what has come to be known in film vernacular as "the beauty shot." Much as it sounds, the beauty shot emphasizes the attractive qualities of an actress or actor. It rose to prevalence during the decades of the star system in Hollywood, when major film studios invested in any stylistic treatment that might add to the star value of a given talent.

As early as the 1930s, the **beauty shot** became a significant part of narrative filmmaking and continues to this day. More often than not, the beauty shot is synonymous with a close-up. Figure 3.14 includes close-ups from six movies that span motion picture history. One can see the critical role of lighting that works to surround a character with a golden glow. And while female talent has been privileged by the occasion, frequency, and quality of the beauty shot, it has not been limited to female protagonists. The fame quotient of Leonardo DiCaprio skyrocketed after the release of *Titanic*, resulting in a Leo-mania worldwide that included the sale of memorabilia (T-shirts, coffee mugs, etc.) made from his "beauty shot," close-ups in the film.

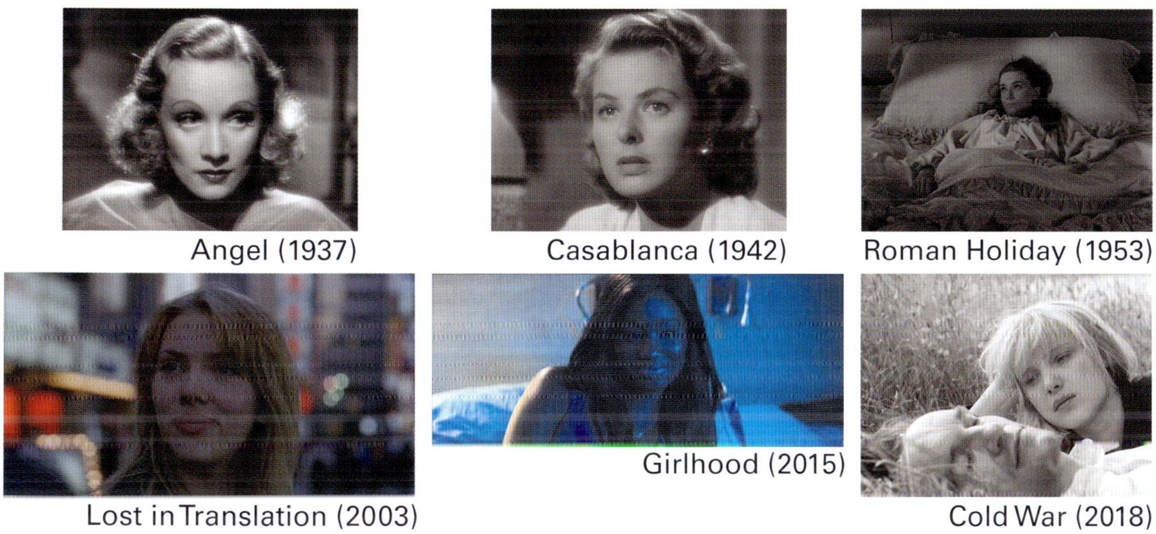

Figure 3.14
The beauty shot.
During the Golden Age of Hollywood (1930–1960) audiences and film studios alike expected to see movie stars portrayed as beautiful. More recently, the beauty shot as close-up has been used as counterpoint, beautifying talent who may not conventionally be seen as such.[1]

In the mirror: self-discovery

Agnes Varda's 1962 contribution to the French New Wave, *Cleo From 5 to 7*, continues to enchant audiences over fifty years after its release. The story follows Cleo in and around Paris during a two-hour wait for results of a medical test she fears will shortchange her future. With a hand-held camera, in black-and-white photography, Varda portrays Cleo's transformation from a fearful, self-absorbed, and doll-like pop singer to a woman capable of friendship, empathy, and human connection—despite Cleo's providence about her own fate.

As much as the film is a story about a young woman's awakening, it can also be seen as Agnes Varda's essay on beauty.[2] It exploits the beauty shot self-consciously, as a technique used to objectify character and to glorify appearance over substance. Many of Cleo's close-ups occur as a reflection in a mirror—that is, Cleo looking at herself, celebrating her own beauty, or as a point of view shot from a man's perspective (Shots 1 and 2). In Varda's film, the close-up is used thematically, as both representation of the character and commentary *about* the character. As Cleo develops the capacity *to look*, rather than simply to be *looked at*, the close-ups, as single shots, end. She is seen thereafter in close-up, but always with another character in the frame. The sampling of Cleo's close-ups pictured in Figure 3.15 represents their order in the film. In shot 5, Cleo's eyes are covered. She wears shades to avoid being recognized after playing one of her

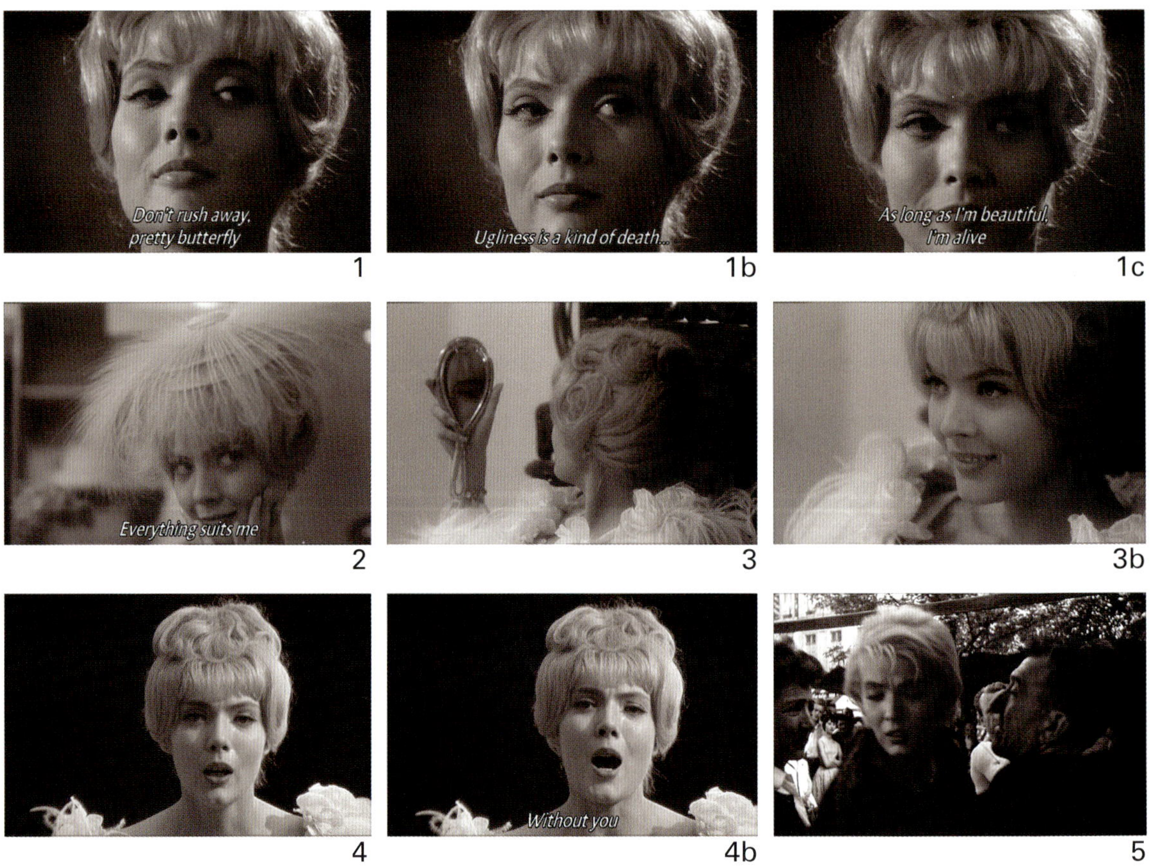

Figure 3.15 *Cleo From 5 to 7* (1962). Director: Agnes Varda. Cinematographers: Paul Bonis, Alain Levent, Jean Rabier.

songs on the café jukebox to gauge the patrons' interest (Shot 5). To this she overhears a woman complain about the café's "noise." This second café scene marks the last time we see single shots of Cleo in close-up. Her next close-up (Figure 3.16) and all of her close-ups thereafter, are two-shots. In Figure 3.16, Cleo moves through a crowded sidewalk. A street performer bids his audience, "Open your eyes." And so, thereafter, Cleo does.

Dramatizing a character's awakening is also the project of Jonathan Glazer in his contemporary science fiction film, *Under the Skin*. Like Cleo, a female protagonist discovers what it is to be human, though in Glazer's film, literally human, as in Homo sapiens. Arriving to earth as an extraterrestrial, she inhabits the body of a young woman and, driving around in a van, picks up men. With each seduction, she takes them into a warehouse where she lures them naked into a pool. Once submerged in the liquid void, she leaves them and resumes her solicitations.

The mirror, again, functions as an essential prop. The close-ups seen in Figure 3.17 render and fragment the character's face in the van's mirror while she cruises the streets of Glasgow. If the mirror in *Cleo From 5 to 7* demonstrates Cleo's preoccupation with her image, here, in *Under the Skin*, the reflections portray the arc of character development, from disassociation to confrontation with human essence.

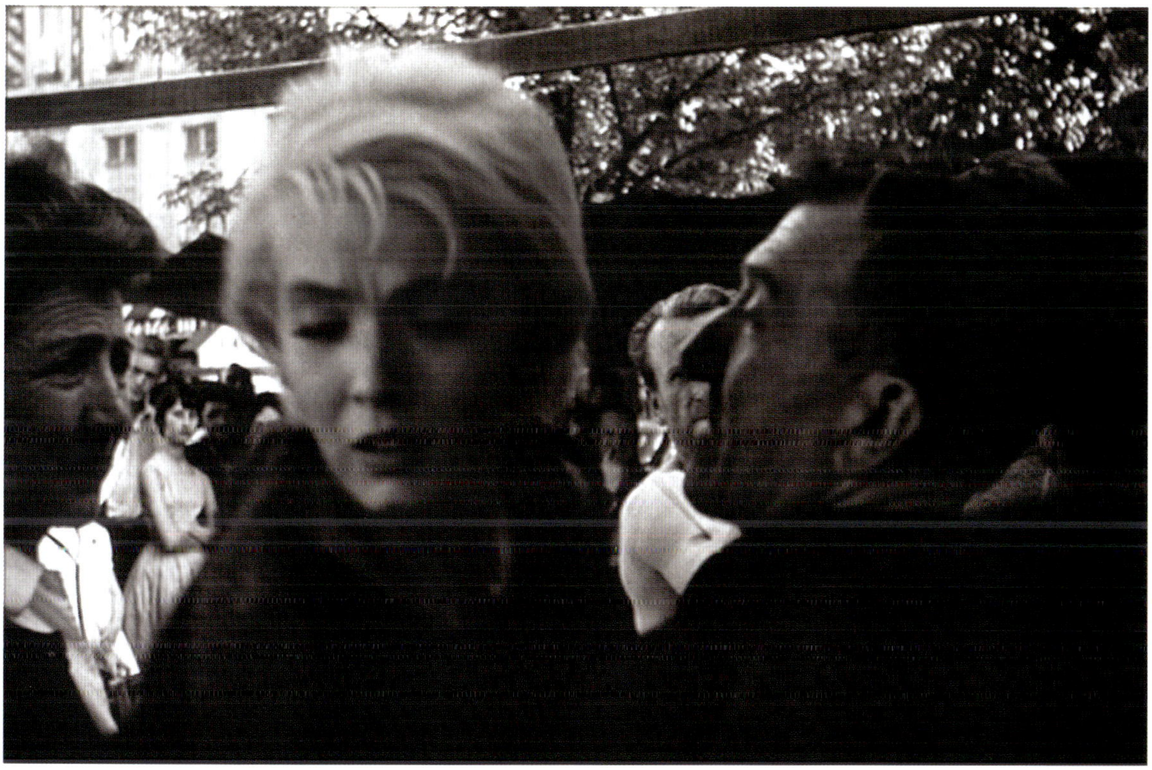

Figure 3.16
Cleo From 5 to 7 (1962), Director: Agnes Varda. Cinematographers: Paul Bonis, Alain Levent, Jean Rabier.

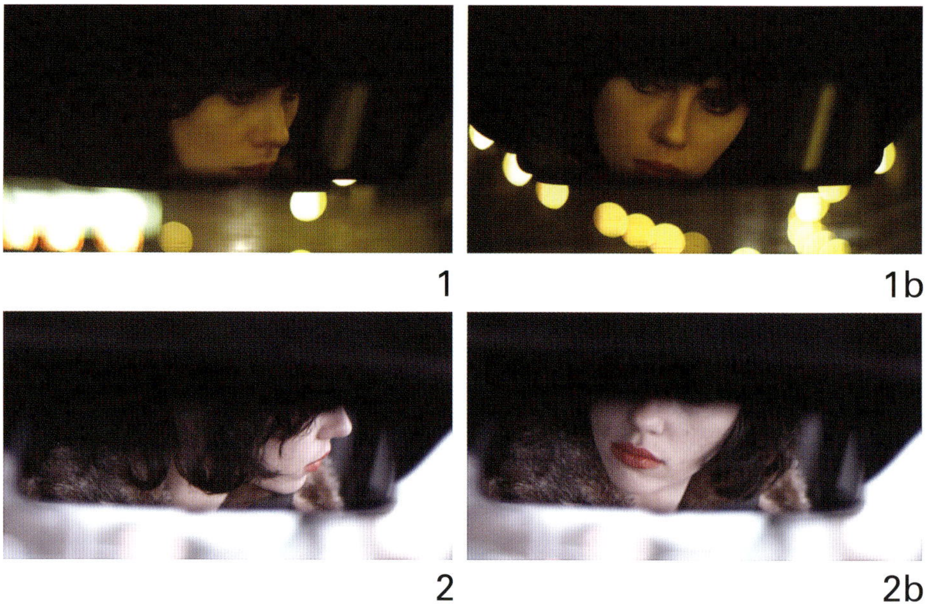

Figure 3.17 *Under the Skin* (2013). Director: Jonathan Glazer. Cinematographer: Daniel Landin.

Later in the film, at a critical moment of narrative development, the unnamed character finally looks *at* herself. Darting down the stairs of a warehouse after a successful abduction, she passes a mirror on the wall in a dimly lit hallway. She stops, double-taking her image (Shot 3). For two long minutes of screen time, she studies her face in the mirror. This self-study is given to the viewer as a close-up. A gradual shift in lighting marks the only technical change in the image as her face brightens, while her eyes, distant and detached up until this moment, register her human presence. *Anagnorisis* is a term of Greek origin that refers to the moment in a drama in which a character makes a critical discovery. The character's two-minute study of herself in the mirror qualifies as such a moment.

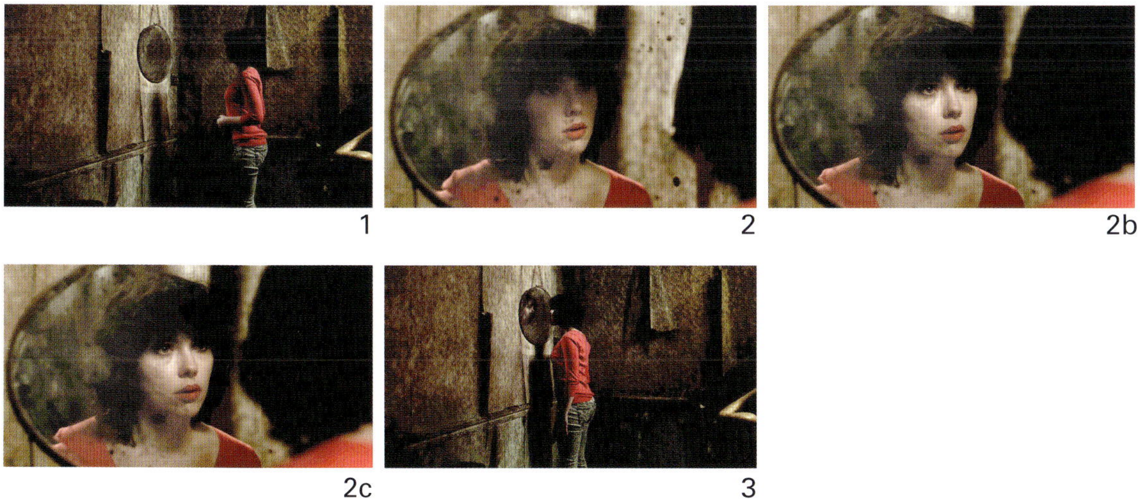

Figure 3.18
Under the Skin (2013). Director: Jonathan Glazer. Cinematographer: Daniel Landin.

The sequence ends (Shot 5) by returning to the frame of the first wide shot (Shot 3), though her proximity to the mirror changes. Startled, her head turns as motivation for two point-of-view shots (not pictured here): a fly buzzing around the glass panel of a door, and a wider shot of the door, next, the extreme close-up of the alien's human eye. (Figure 3.19) The character's awakening to the prospect of being human is given to the viewer as this tight close-up of her eye, reflected in a mirror.

A handful of additional close-ups follow this moment in the film, as when she tastes her first bite of chocolate cake or later receives her first romantic kiss (not unparalleled events). But it is the mirror that does its work on her, after which reflected close-ups no longer appear.

Figure 3.19
Under the Skin (2013). Director: Jonathan Glazer. Cinematographer: Daniel Landin.

Discussion questions

1. Consider the viewer's close proximity to a character in a shot within a given scene. How critical is the shot duration with regard to the close-up?
2. Examine the beauty shots in Figure 3.14. How are the focal planes and lighting managed and to what effect?
3. Analyze the shots in Figure 3.13 from *Blue Is the Warmest Color*. What might be the motivation for changes in camera position?

Notes

1. The dynamic between female beauty and narrative film has been the subject of much writing. John Berger, Molly Haskell, Laura Mulvey, Mari Ruti, and Hilary Neroni are among the writers who have explored, in print, the representation of the female in film.
2. Hilary Neroni's book-length study, *Feminist Film Theory and Cleo From 5 to 7*, takes on the representation of women in film through a close reading of Varda's film. (Bloomsbury Press, 2016)

4

The moving camera

While the first films were recorded with a stationary camera, even the Lumiere brothers intuited the value of camera movement and began placing the camera on moving vehicles. This created the seamless visual treatment of space and time. As such, the moving camera enters film language as a tool for building correspondences, connecting subjects to a given environment and to each other.[1] The moving camera also emerged as an essential narrative device, used for revealing vital story information. These revelations occurred through a lexicon of basic camera movements: the **dolly**, **pan**, **tilt**, **crane shot**, and **tracking shot**. Eventually, the capacity to change the focal length of the camera lens allowed for the **zoom**, a shot which simulates movement, even as the camera remains stationary. The technological advance of the Steadicam afforded the filmmaker any movement that could be achieved by a person walking. Today, the **drone** increases the movement possibilities of aerial cinematography.

With the moving camera, pace and direction of movement are critical considerations. Added to this, the interaction between camera movement and figure movement expand the possibilities for visual dynamics. Among the many dramatic effects, the moving camera can be used to establish tone or stance, to replicate character dynamics, to confound viewer expectations, to evoke theme, or to exaggerate a character's state of mind.

Freedom of camera movement must have exhilarated the first generation of directors. Action was no longer confined to space in front of a stationary camera but could extend to any space capable of being captured. The effect was profound. Alterations in distance and perspective could be staged in continuous time and space. This gave filmmakers more latitude in managing the flow of story information through pace and direction of the camera's movement.[2]

The moving camera was quickly absorbed into the language of visual storytelling. A robust narrative depends on stirring anticipation of what will happen next. The moving camera also evokes anticipation—sparking the viewer's interest in what will be seen next.

The moving camera also gives the visual storyteller a tool for building correspondences. The seamless treatment of space and time connects subjects/objects to the environment and to each other. A camera movement can also be choreographed to establish a relationship between the first and last frame within the shot. For example, if you look ahead to Figure 4.14, a scene from Antonioni's *L'Avventura*, the camera movement in combination with figure movement revises the power dynamic of the two characters from first frame to last (Shots 1 and 1j). In the first frame the man looms over her. In the last frame of a continuous movement, the female dominates. This shift within the framing of the shot corresponds to shifts in the power struggle between the characters. The continuous shot binds them even as the staging and camera position reveal their discord.

The dolly

In the previous chapter, we explored dramatic effects achieved through a cut to the close-up. Here we begin the discussion with the effect created by camera movement that alters the shot size from a wide to close-up. *Notorious*, Hitchcock's 1946 spy thriller is a well-known example. Physical props are essential to the movie's plot, and given to the viewer with cinematic flourish—a combination of image and musical score. Figure 4.1 depicts one such scene. Alicia, pictured in the first shot, has been recruited by a US government agency to infiltrate a Nazi organization. She insinuates herself into the world of Alex Sebastian, a leader of the group. He falls in love with her and proposes marriage—a proposal Alicia accepts to accomplish her goals. At a dinner gathering, Alicia notices agitation among his group around certain wine bottles and is eager to inspect the cellar. For this, she needs the cellar key kept in her husband's possession.

Just before a lavish party, Alicia enters the outer chamber of her husband's room while he dresses (off-screen). In the first of the still frames of Figure 4.1, Alicia eyes her husband's key chain on his dressing table. This is followed by a point-of-view shot, a medium wide shot of the room in deep focus—every element in the foreground, middle ground, and background is clearly depicted. The camera dollies in toward the object of Alicia's interest, ending in a close-up of the keychain on her husband's table. The keychain's position on the dressing table and the relative positions of Alicia to the table, and table to the door (behind which her husband, Alex, can be heard) are critical factors in creating tension within the scene. Continuous coverage through the dolly reinforces these critical distances, keeping them relative to one another, even as the dolly brings the keychain into detailed focus.

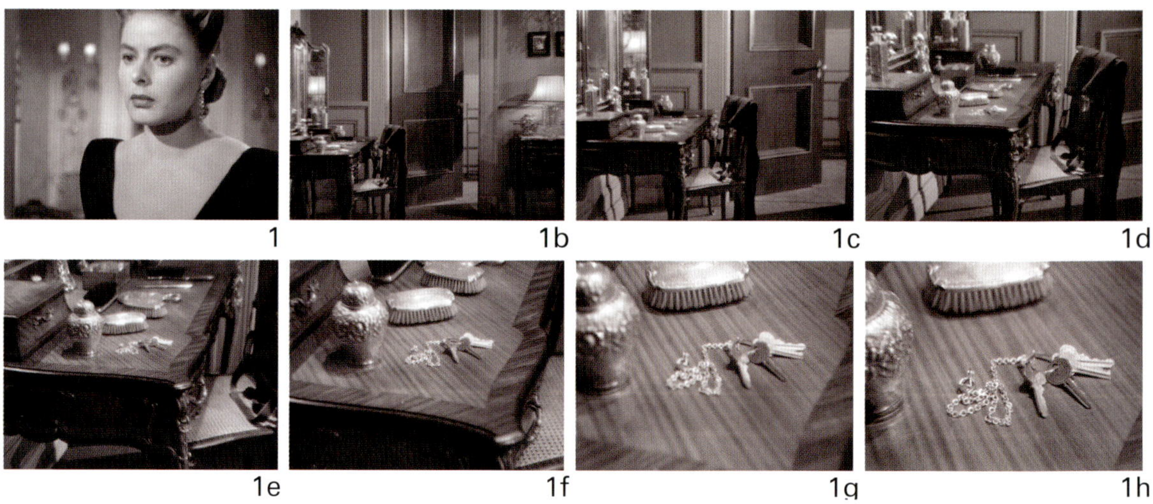

Figure 4.1 *Notorious* (1946). Director: Alfred Hitchcock. Cinematographer: Ted Tetzlaff.

There is no correlation between the way in which the human eye works when seeing an object of interest and the push of a camera dolly toward a close-up of that object. In this scene from *Notorious*, the dolly movement isn't intended to mimic human vision. It represents, instead, the mind aroused by the object, which has been seized by its focus.

In less than one minute of screen time, the cellar key will be the object of another camera move to close-up. In the celebrated crane shot, the camera descends from an extreme wide shot at the top of the staircase to an extreme close-up of Alicia's hand holding the key. This has been written about at length and does not need further discussion here.[3] The first and last frames can be seen in Figure 4.2. Unlike the earlier shot, this camera move is objective, that is, not from a character's point of view. At our last sighting of the key, Alicia tosses it onto the carpet of the dressing room to avoid being caught with it in her possession. Now, in the midst of a room crowded with party guests, we discover the key in her hand.

Hitchcock demonstrates immense technical skill in his shot design—in this film and others. But the camera strategy is always tied to story and the desired dramatic effects. The crane shot triggers a discovery, one that both relieves and intensifies viewer anxiety.

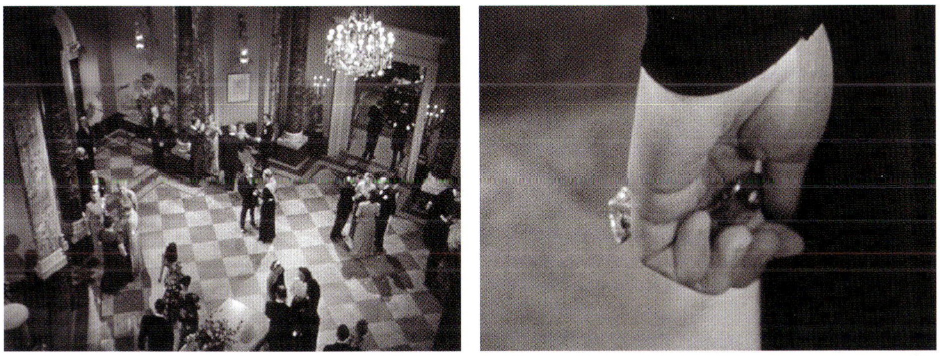

1 1b

Figure 4.2
Notorious (1946). Director: Alfred Hitchcock. Cinematographer: Ted Tetzlaff.

The pan

If the forward dolly drives the viewer's attention to a particular subject or object in the frame, the pan, a lateral camera movement, left to right, or right to left, works to connect characters and/or objects, building associations among the various elements. Sciamma, collaborating with her cinematographer, Crystel Fournier, makes elegant and repeated use of the pan in the 2014 French film, *Girlhood*.[4] Living in the poor suburbs on the outskirts of Paris, the African-French, 16-year-old Marieme is at the hub of these connections, even as the film charts her journey to connect, first and foremost, to herself. Marieme's coming-of-age includes the part-time care of her younger sister while the mother keeps the household afloat as an overtime, night-shift worker cleaning offices. In the scene pictured in Figure 4.3, Marieme's younger sister aggravates the pull between desire for autonomy and a sense of responsibility. Lying in bed, arm outstretched, the camera floats (panning right) toward Marieme's face (Shots 1–1d). Her arm jostles, Marieme turns. Following her gaze, the camera floats back (panning left) to find the source: the younger sister, where it lingers on their clasped hands (Shot 1g) before cutting to a wide shot of the shared bedroom (Shot 2). The continuous movement of camera substantiates the connection between the sisters by keeping them in uninterrupted space. It also inflects the moment with a discovery that occurs in real time. The viewer is included in both the camera's exploration and the moment of intimacy found. The slow, lyrical pace of the camera panning left to right, and then right to left suits this small, quiet moment between the sisters, and enlarges it.

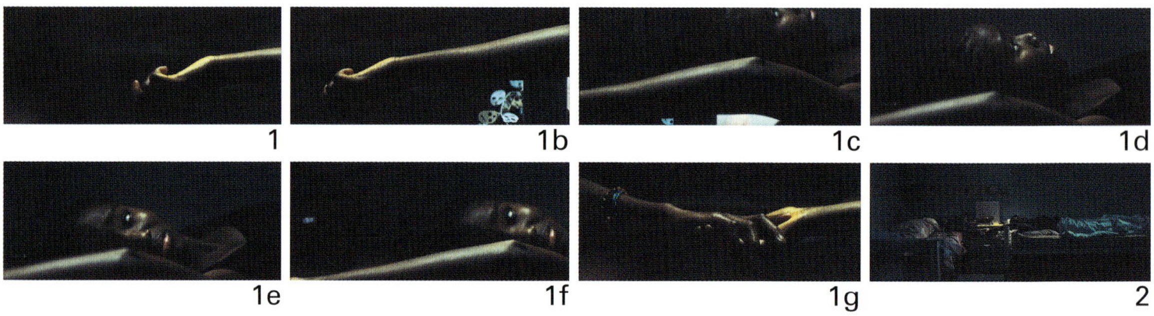

Figure 4.3
Girlhood (2014), Director: Céline Sciamma. Cinematographer: Crystel Fournier.

The color palette we used, between blue and green, can produce a gloomy effect and never enhances the actors. But our actresses, since their skin is warm, can handle these types of colors. We could push colors to a point, impossible with white skins.

—Crystel Fournier, ARRI Interview: Crystel Fournier about "Girlhood" June 6, 2014.

The pan with moving subject

A moving camera has the capacity to excite anticipation. While the cut is a call to alertness, camera motion asks the viewer to follow action in real time and in so doing, becomes a structure for discovery.

The film, *Timbuktu*, directed by Abderrahmane Sissako, is as much a story of place as character. Islamic extremists have taken over the city, governing with a strict adherence to Sharia law, enforced by armed jihadists. Kidane, a cattle farmer, is living at some remove with his wife and daughter in the dunes outside the city. When a fisherman kills his prized cow for damaging a fishing net, Kidane goes to confront him. He takes off across the shallow waters of the Niger River. This crossing is portrayed in a long pan of a wide shot that keeps Kidane in the left third of the frame (Shots 1–1e). While the convention includes panning along with a moving subject to maintain the composition, here, despite the fury that drives Kidane forward, the camera seems to hold him back, even as he moves. The filmmaker has created a chase scene in which a character, while moving forward, never makes any headway in the frame. Too, the camera keeps the object of Kidane's pursuit, the fisherman, Amadou, out of view. This holding back and withholding exaggerates Kidane's desperation and offers relief when we discover, finally, the subject of his pursuit, Amadou (Shot 1e). Their confrontation brings the characters to the center of the frame with Kidane's shove of Amadou (Shot 1f). When Amadou pushes back, the camera follows him, panning left, repositioning Kidane in the first third of the wide shot. The men skirmish until a gunshot is heard: Kidane's gun accidentally fired.

When Kidane rises out of the water, gasping, he lurches forward (Figure 4.5, Shot 1j), leaving Amadou dead in his wake. The scene then cuts to an extreme wide shot during which the viewer sees Kidane's long trek through the Niger River back to shore, where the ruling jihadists will determine his fate. His loss of agency is reinforced by the tiny speck of a man he has become moving across the frame.

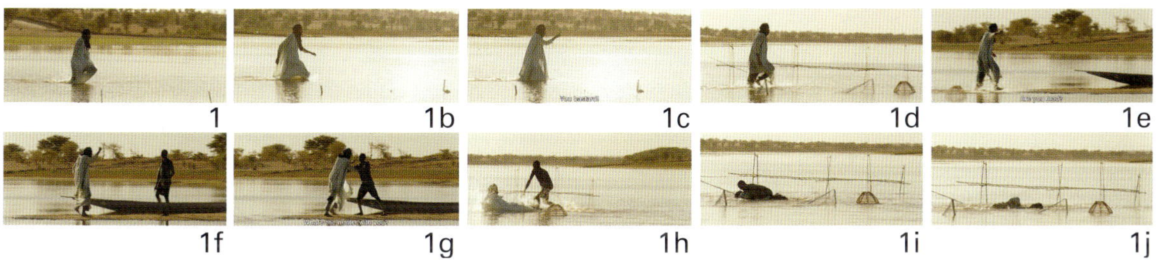

Figure 4.4 *Timbuktu* (2014). Director: Abderrahmane Sissako. Cinematographer: Sofian El Fani.

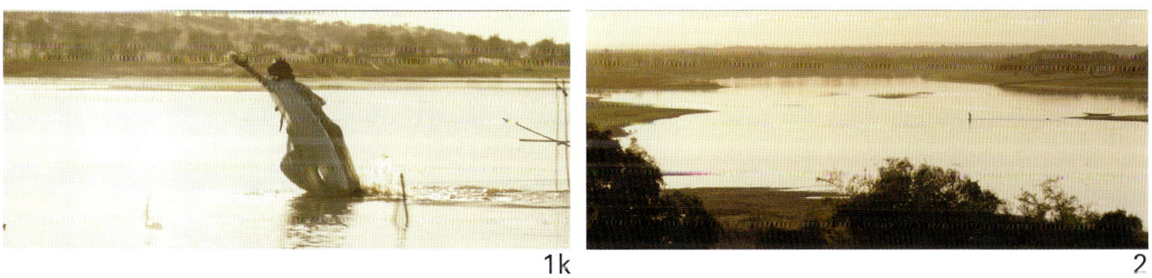

Figure 4.5 *Timbuktu* (2014). Director: Abderrahmane Sissako. Cinematographer: Sofian El Fani.

Pan and tilt: in search of the subject

Staging discoveries, yes, but also an attention to formal beauty, become the basis for the camera strategy in *Beau Travail*, Claire Denis' feature film collaboration with cinematographer Agnès Godard. The film is a loose retelling of Melville's *Billy Budd*. The early scenes introduce the camera's preoccupation with formal elements as it explores the environment, which may or may not include characters. The primary characters are soldiers in the French Foreign Legion, newly arrived in Djibouti to begin training. The scene depicted in Figure 4.6 depicts the men undergoing an endurance exercise. Of little interest plot-wise, the camera with its lateral motion (a pan) and upward motion (a tilt) treats their activity as ritual, giving the scene mythic proportion. The slow, deliberate camera pans across shadows in the sand before tilting up to reveal first one man (Shot 1e), and then, in turn, the others (Shots 1h–1o)—arms raised and eyes closed.

Revealed last is Gilles (Shot 1o), the legionnaire who will emerge as the main character, fulfilling the camera movement's promise of discovery. The continuous motion also connects Gilles to the other men and this reflects his fate. The section chief, envious of the respect Gilles earns from his fellow soldiers, takes action against him.[5]

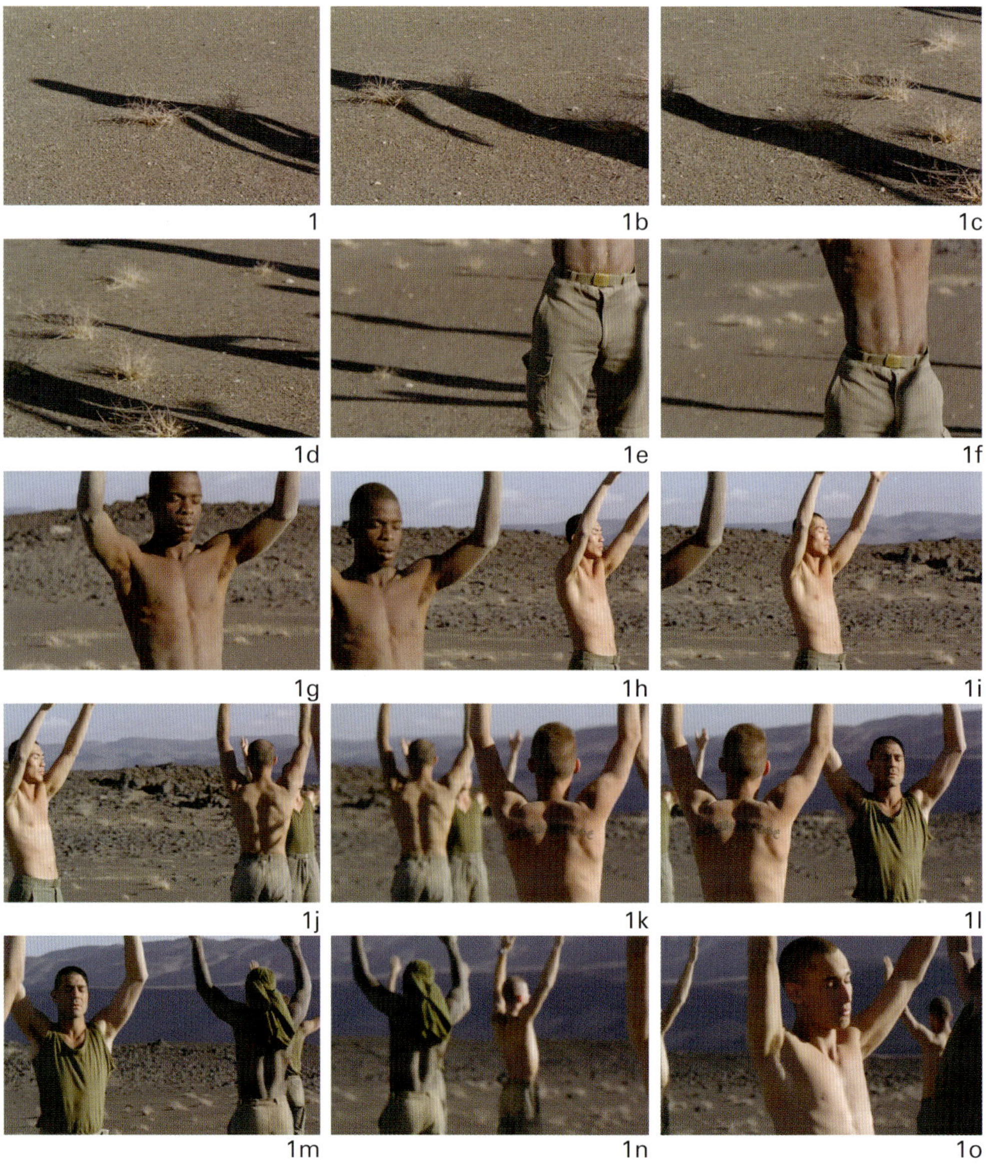

Figure 4.6 *Beau Travail* (1999). Director: Claire Denis. Cinematographer: Agnès Godard.

Camera movement and figure movement

Staging discoveries with camera movement or dynamic moments of revelation is synonymous with the energetic camera work found in Martin Scorsese's films. There is an immense variety of shot size, camera angle, and position, as well as duration and pace of the camera's movement, along with shifting camera directions.

Revealing narrative information

The shots pictured below are from the 1990 film, *Goodfellas*, a collaboration between Scorsese and cinematographer Michael Ballhaus. Scorsese's enthusiasm for keeping the camera in motion is facilitated in this film by the **Steadicam**.[6] The Steadicam, an apparatus attached to the camera and worn by the camera operator, frees camera motion from the horizontal grid required for dolly shots and tracking. Because the field within the frame is more accessible (any place reachable by walking, any space wide enough for the camera operator and camera), the image will often appear to have greater volume.

During an early montage, the protagonist, Henry Hill, tells his audience in voice-over narration about his induction into the Italian mob.

The camera, at first, seems to illustrate narration, beginning its move with a low-angle, close-up: the front of the car, from the level of the grillwork. As Henry says, "wise guys would pull up," the camera tilts up and moves forward to reveal Henry behind the steering wheel as the car ignition turns over. The camera sweeps around to the driver's side, almost caressing the car, as Henry says, "and here I am this little kid, I can't even see over the steering wheel." The camera continues its move, the car drives out of frame, as Henry finishes his narration, "and I'm parking Cadillacs." The camera slows and stalls. Up until this point, image and narration are in sync, though dynamically, given the camera's tilt and the variation between speed of car and speed of camera motion. The car vanishes from frame. Peering from behind barbwire fencing are four schoolgirls, books in hand, and a boy, just Henry's age (Shot 1e). Their envy is palpable. More dramatic than any voice-over testimony, the sight of Henry's classmates gaping from behind the fence reveals his clout in the eyes of his peers. The camera, which seems at first to illustrate the narrative leads to revelation: a visual cue for young Henry's rising status in his world.

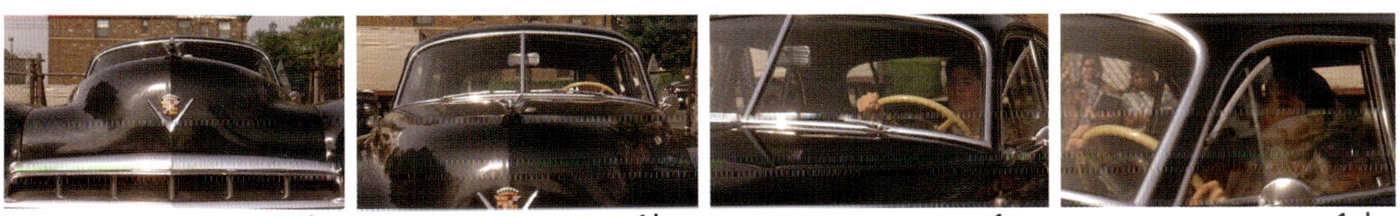

1 1b 1c 1d

Figure 4.7 *Goodfellas* (1990). Director: Martin Scorsese. Cinematographer: Michael Ballhaus.

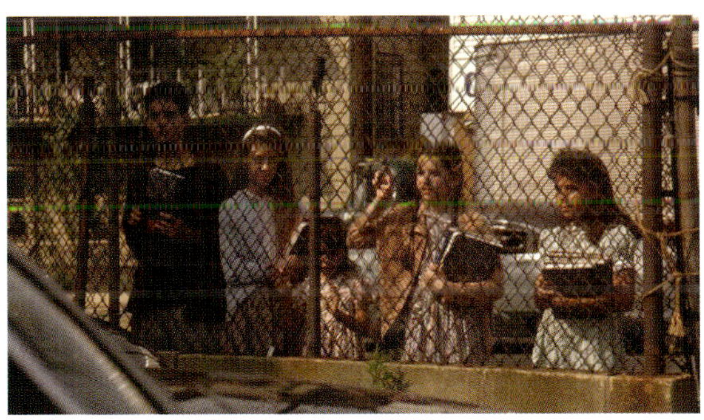

Figure 4.8 *Goodfellas* (1990). Director: Martin Scorsese. Cinematographer: Michael Ballhaus.

The dolly shot and the zoom

The dolly shot and the zoom can alter the perceived distance from viewer to subject. The **dolly shot** is a movement of the camera forward, backward, laterally, or even curved (depending on the tracks the camera dolly runs along or the path the camera operator wearing the Steadicam takes). This motion differs from the zoom, which also moves the viewer closer to the subject through changes in shot size achieved through changing the focal length of the lens. The zoom lens, refined in the mid-1960s to accommodate this purpose, made it possible to track optically without moving the camera. But, unlike the dolly, the zoom does not create the effect of moving through space—it creates the effect of space wearing away as the camera zooms in, or space building up around the camera as it zooms out. To a large extent, the zoom undermines a sense of perspective by confounding the spatial reality of any given scene. The dolly, on the other hand, leaves space intact.

In the scene represented by Figure 4.9 the camera tilts (up and down) or glides (laterally). It also moves forward—into a subject or object. Once again, the scene is underscored by Henry's narration. It begins with a long tracking shot that starts on a brightly lit counter of sandwiches on a tray. The camera moves right to Henry, tilting up to frame him in a medium shot as he, part narrator and guide, leads the camera into the darkened room. There we see the first poker table where one of the players scoops up cash in the middle of the table (Shot 1d), and then the camera travels on in continuous movement to the next table, also brightly lit (Shot 1e), where another poker game is played, poker chips piled in the table's center, the frame, again, featuring the men's hands. The camera continues gliding across the room through a throng of men milling about, passing Paulie, seated on a stool, facing the camera (Shot 1f). The camera movement stops on a frame divided between a floor-length green curtain and a pool of darkness (Shot 1g). "It was when I met the world," Henry says. "It was when I first met Jimmy Conway." The door opens and Jimmy, lit with radiance, steps into the darkness (Shot 1h).

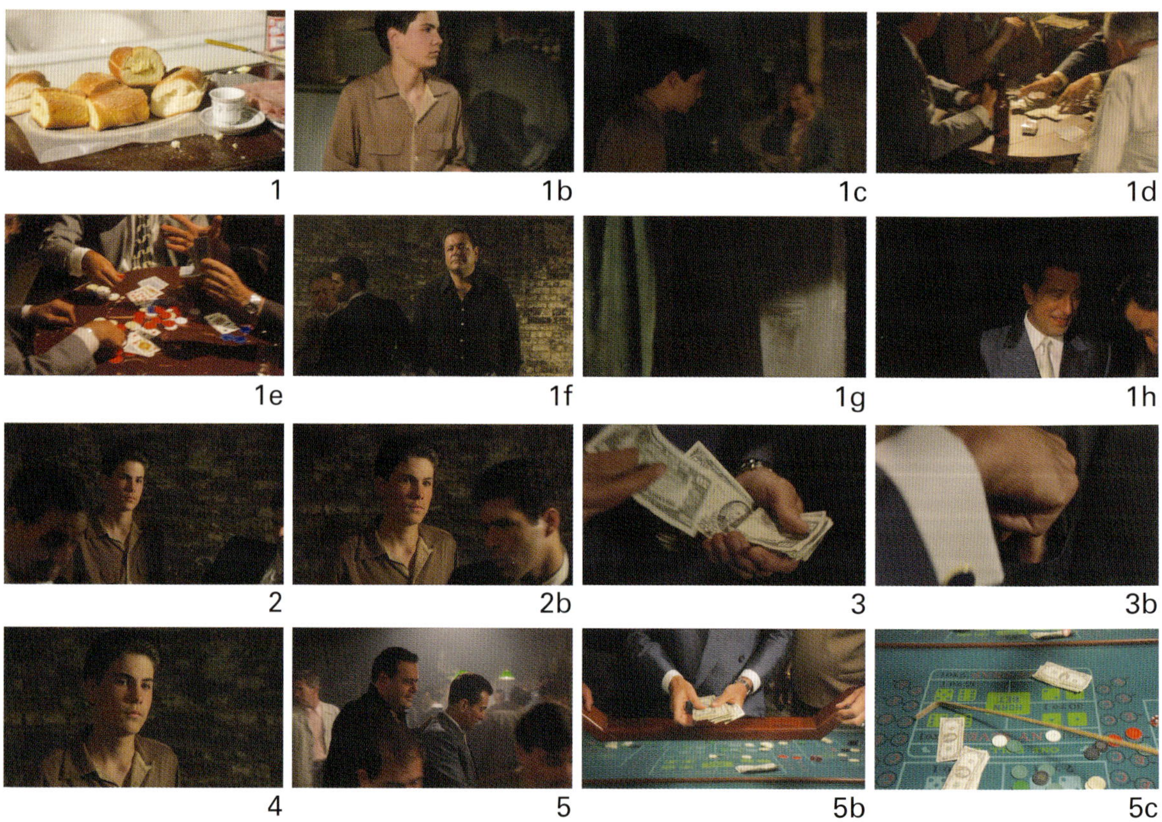

Figure 4.9 *Goodfellas* (1990). Director: Martin Scorsese. Cinematographer: Michael Ballhaus.

The choreography of the camera tugs our attention from place to place and asserts control over our growing awareness. The fluidity conveys the sense that any part of the room can be penetrated. There is the pretense of a tour, with Henry as guide, but as continuous movement in time and space, it does the deeper narrative work of connecting objects to one another and to the surroundings: a coterie of characters bound by drinks, cards, poker, and money in this world of underhanded activity. The activity of any one character (or prop) is firmly established as a part of the larger collective, amplifying the atmosphere of solidarity among them—the sense of family.

Revelations through camera movement don't end here. This sequence begins on a brightly lit counter of lunch foods resembling a church picnic, at the end of which is Henry. Henry, carrying his "picnic" sandwich, walks into the interior of the clubroom and disappears. The camera movement not only connects Henry to this interior world, but, for the remainder of the shot, loses him in it. From brightly lit ham sandwiches to the curtained door of darkness, the moving camera parallels the arc of Henry's fate as a character. In fact, the interaction between camera movement and lighting in the scene emphasizes certain elements in the frame that contribute to our deeper understanding of character.

The long tracking shot that begins the scene is punctuated by a cut to the medium shot of Henry, a point-of-view shot (Shot 2), cuing the audience to the object of Henry's interest: Jimmy and his stack of bills. Henry watches as he tucks money into the front pocket of the doorman's jacket (Shots 3 and 3b) reinforcing one of the scene's visual motifs: hands seen in close-up. The camera cuts back to Henry as the move toward him continues, framing him in close-up (Shot 4), reinforcing Henry's interest in what he sees.

When the camera leaves Henry, it resumes its coverage of Jimmy at the door, greeted now by Paulie. The camera follows the two men in profile (Shot 5) until they arrive directly in front of the camera at the casino table. Without a pause, the camera tilts down, stalling only to reveal Jimmy's hands, shuffling through his money, and then tilts down further as he slaps several bills on the table (Shot 5b). The rake pulls the money across the table, left to right, a motion that in an elegant graphic cut brings Henry to the table, left screen to right (Shots 5c and 6). The rest of the scene converges the important elements in the scene as the pace picks up, shot to shot.

In surveying the twenty-four still frames that define the scene, one can discern quite a bit about the way in which the scene is shaped through camera movement and shot duration. The first moving shot lasts for one third of the scene (Shots 1–1h). The pace picks up in the middle third (comprised of four shots), but it is in the last third (a total of seven shots) that character interaction combined with shot variety and brief duration charge the scene with an excitement akin to Henry's thrill at being a part of this world and what it might mean for him. The second time Jimmy Conway tucks money into a front pocket it is Henry's (Shots 3b and 9).

Henry's close-ups are achieved through a forward motion of camera and coincide with moments of epiphany—jolts of awareness that show his wide-eyed induction into the world of mobsters. Shifts in proximity, from medium shot (or medium close-up) to close-up also occur in the context of lateral camera motion: a combination of pan (the environment) and forward motion (toward Henry). The camera movement converges Henry's moments of discovery with accumulating impressions of the environment. The shot design mimics, if not foreshadows, his soon-to-be-complete immersion in this world.

In each of these scenes from *Goodfellas* the camera movement, shot size, and staging produces a dramatic revelation—the school children clinging covetously to the fence, the darkened world of the casino, Jimmy Conway with his fat wad of cash, stuffing a twenty dollar bill into Henry's pocket. Even as voice-over narration describes Henry's world, *how* it is pictured adds thematic dimension, specific and cumulative: goods changing hands, money changing hands, money equated with power, and power as a force—sexy and irresistible, certainly to young Henry. The vitality of the camera work gives the world to us as Henry experiences it: dynamic and seductive, with endless possibility.[7]

Expectation and discovery

Camera movement can control expectation and awareness toward moments of discovery that include elements of surprise. For example, location, production design, blocking, staging,

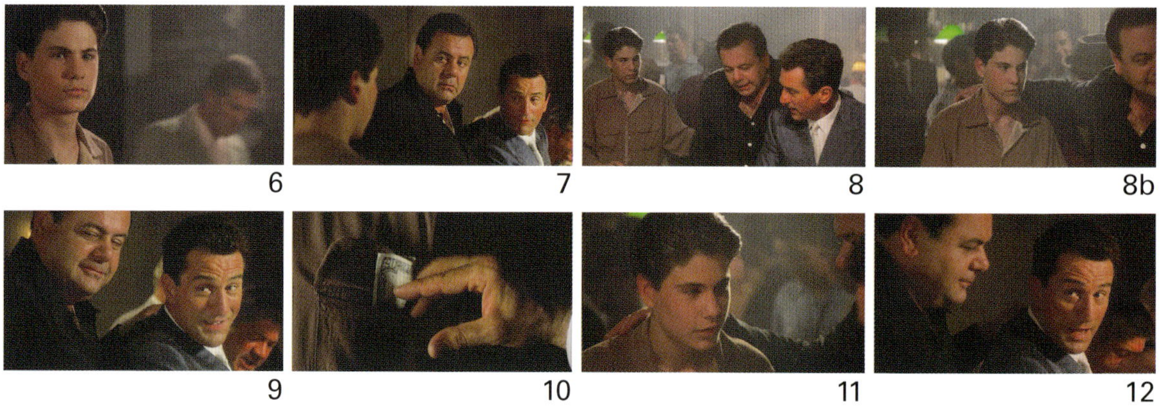

Figure 4.10
Goodfellas (1990). Director: Martin Scorsese. Cinematographer: Michael Ballhaus.

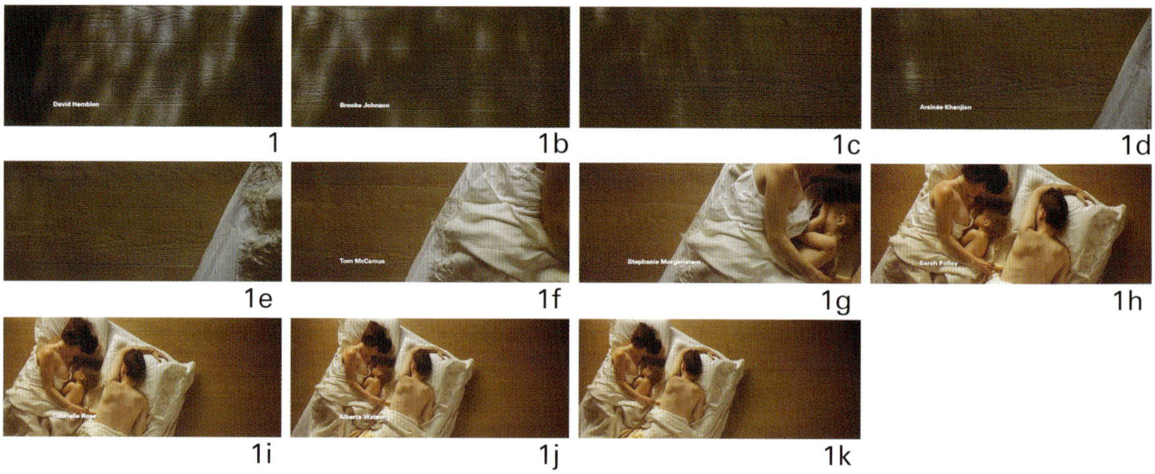

Figure 4.11
The Sweet Hereafter (1997). Director: Atom Egoyan. Cinematographer: Paul Sarossy.

I saw *8½* just two weeks before shooting my first short film at NYU, *What's a Nice Girl Like You Doing in a Place Like This?*, and the impact was overwhelming because of the fluidity of the camerawork and the beauty of the black and white. I fell in love with the moving camera so much in that film that I also fell for everything about Italy—the cafés and the fashion.

—Martin Scorsese, *Scorsese on Scorsese*, Faber and Faber, 1989.

and lighting—all elements of mise en scene—will interact with camera movement to encourage assumptions that are then, through continued movement, upended or overturned.

In the opening sequence of Atom Egoyan's film, *The Sweet Hereafter*, the camera tracks across a paneled surface assumed to be the paneled surface of a wall. As the camera continues tracking, an overhead view of a bed emerges correcting the assumption with new knowledge of the surface as floor. Egoyan enjoys exploiting camera movement to overturn assumptions supported previously by composition and staging. The viewer assumes the camera faces a wall, rather than looming overhead above a bed positioned like an island in the middle of a room where a family sleeps. These visual riddles often require the manipulation of elements within the frame. They depend on camera movement as a means for obscuring and then slowly sharing a startling revelation.

Counterpoint

Under the direction of Jean Renoir, the moving camera is one element interacting with other elements as point or counterpoint, not unlike the polyphonic composition of a fugue. He conceives of camera movement as if the Steadicam had already been invented, moving in multiple directions in any one shot. In his classic film, *The Grand Illusion*, photographed by Christian Matras, the movement exerts itself as a stylistic trope very early on—the pattern: to stage pockets of activity in different parts of a given space and to track or dolly, pan or tilt, from one center of activity to another. The camera's direction is often led by figure movement, conversation, sound, or, in some instances, by the will of the camera to make its own claims. The effect in *The Grand Illusion* is a visual connection among a group of French officers bound together by fate in a German prisoner of war camp during World War I. The camera movement not only reinforces the character camaraderie, it also emphasizes dramatic beats within the scene. Added to this, the choreography of the camera enacts a dramatic arc, with a beginning, middle, and end. The pace of movement, order of images revealed, duration, and action covered, accumulate and build to a climax, like a crescendo in a musical score.

The prisoners have staged an evening of cabaret. During the event, French prisoner, Lieutenant Maréchal, receives news of a French victory (Shot 1). "Stop! Stop!", he shouts, claiming center stage. "We've retaken Douaumont," he goes on to tell the audience. The sequence begins with two static shots: the first, Maréchal's entrance onto the stage. In the second shot, the camera leaps to the back of the theater, behind the audience, where Maréchal becomes a vanishing point of light. The wide shot gives the viewer a feel for the density of the audience, increasing, by sheer numbers, the effect of the news. This multiplies in one strategic stage direction: the men in uniform rise, their backs filling the frame (Shot 3).

At this point the tracking shot begins that makes up the remainder of the sequence (Shots 4–4m). The soldier/female impersonator rises into frame, tearing off his wig, commanding the musicians, "Marseillaise, please!" In a medium shot he leads the audience in a rousing chorus of the French National Anthem (Shots 4b and 4c). The camera pulls back, panning right, then tilting up to Maréchal, who leads the camera in the direction of two German officers, as he sings with gusto toward them. The camera tilts down to frame them (Shot 4e). As the officers turn to leave the theater, their movement leads the camera, altering its direction with a pan left. Rather than trailing their exit, the camera stops at the row of French officers, where it pushes forward, glides across the men, before panning right toward the small chamber orchestra, where it tilts up, returning to the female impersonator. It repeats the framing that began the tracking shot, gracefully bookending the clockwise motion of the camera.

The shot could have easily and effectively ended here. Instead, it acts as a pause or punctuation before reversing motion again, panning left back to the proud soldiers, several layers deep, standing in song. The camera stalls for twelve seconds as the last words of the Marseillaise are triumphantly sung (Shot 4m).

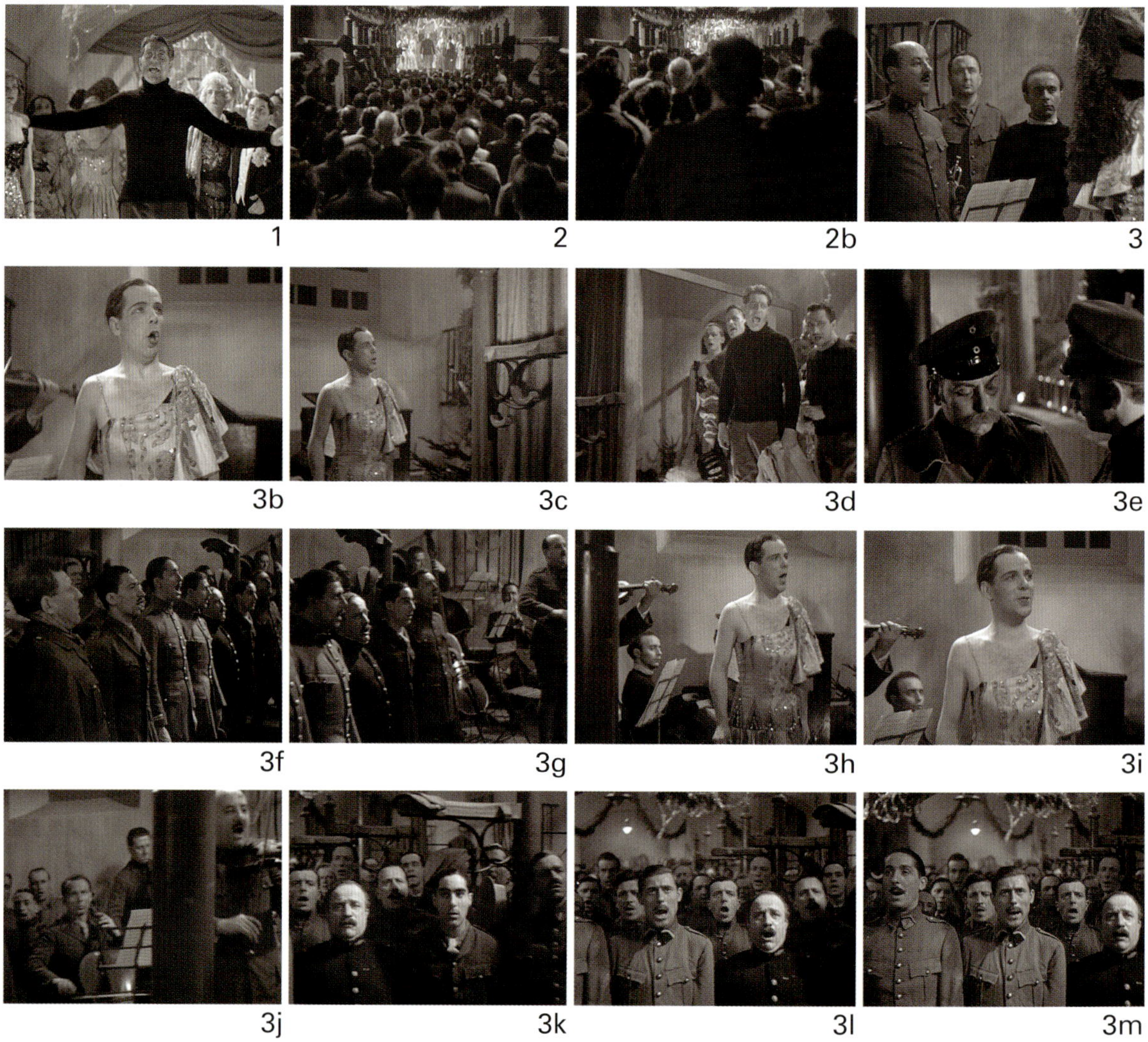

Figure 4.12 *The Grand Illusion* (1937). Director: Jean Renoir. Cinematographer: Christian Matras.

A tracking shot such as this required ingenuity, dexterity, and a skilled camera operator. Working with cinematographer Christian Matras, Claude Renoir, the director's nephew, operated the camera for this sequence. Renoir says of him, "He was supple as an eel and shrank from no acrobatics."[8]

It is a small but not insignificant aspect of this particular clockwise then counterclockwise motion that the two occasions of reversal reveal officers—first German, then French. That these officers are not personalized in the story of *The Grand Illusion* (that they are "extras") enlarges the capacity of the men pictured to represent any officer in any war. To finish the camera's extended tracking shot with the image of anonymous soldiers presses the impact beyond the lives of main characters or the movie stars who portray them, to the unknown swept into the grand tide of history made by all wars.

Tone, theme, and social commentary

The choreography of camera in *The Grand Illusion* epitomizes the use of camera movement to endow the portrayal of story events with an additional layer of dramatic inference. This inference colors the action with point of view. In Stanley Kubrick's 1957 anti-war film, *Paths of Glory*, shot in black and white by cinematographer George Krause, the stance is suggested by the camera's interaction with figure movement. Additionally, the moving camera serves to reinforce **subtext** and **tone** through control of **shape, speed**, and **direction.**

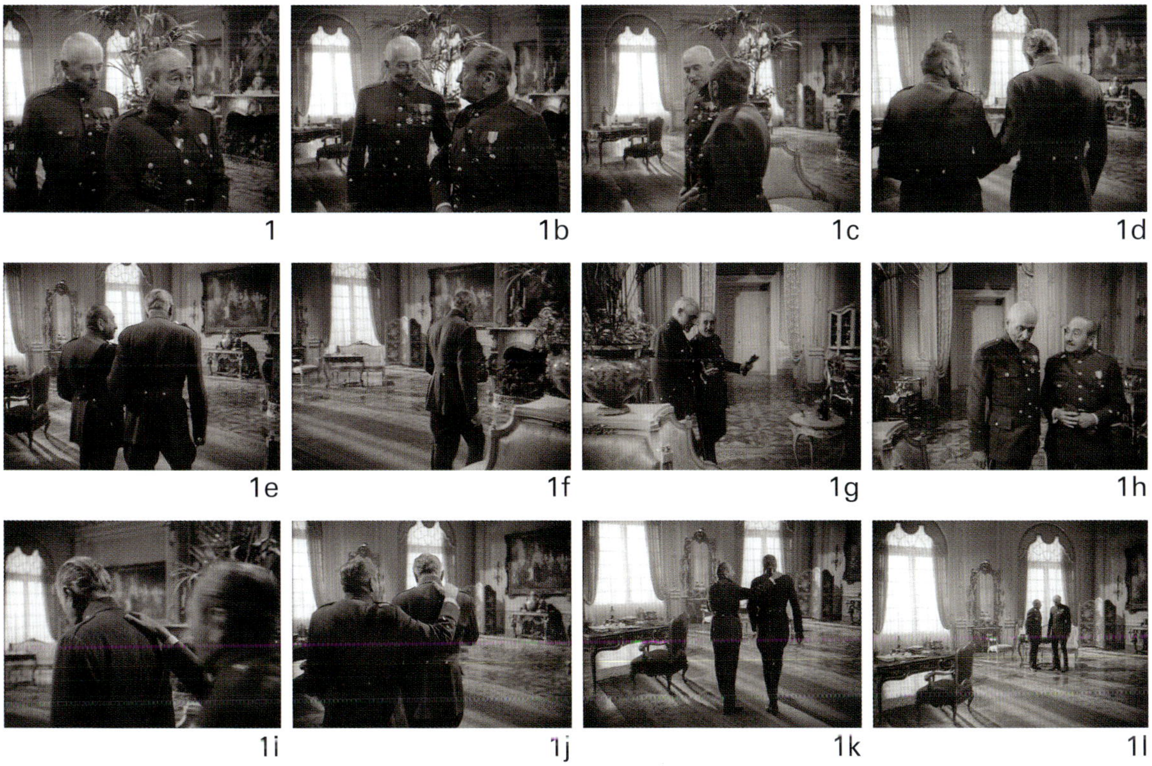

Figure 4.13
Paths of Glory (1957). Director: Stanley Kubrick. Cinematographer: Georg Krause.

The film also takes as its subject the First World War and is set in France. The movie begins with an exchange between two generals: a commander and a divisional officer. The commander challenges the officer to organize his troops to "take the ant hill," a strategic offensive that could bring about a turning point in the war. The officer refuses, respecting the weariness and morale of his troops. The commander offers bribes, promises of commendation, and advancement. "Not for all the stars, decorations or honors in France," the officer declares—though he soon capitulates, agreeing to the command. By the scene's conclusion, the commander's "I don't want to push you into it if you think it's ill advised," is met by the division leader's self-deluding reply, "Don't worry, George, you couldn't do that if you tried." During this prolonged negotiation, the two men stand, sit, walk around in unison, walk around individually as the other sits, and walk around in unison again. "Walking around" is not merely a figure of speech—the staging of the scene has the two men moving in circles, even as the dialogue seems to run in circles. The pace, direction, and duration of camera movement exaggerate the befuddling effect, particularly as it follows so closely, and without interruption, every pivot and turn of the two men.

Combining circular dialogue and figure movement with a camera moving in circular and semi-circular paths duplicates strategies across separate techniques. The effect is satire. Stating and restating the same theme with figure movement, camera movement, performance style, and casting lends the scene its comedic edge and ironic tone. Rather than a tension through techniques applied as point and counterpoint, the opening scene uses the effect of parody to comment on the role of military officers in wartime. Throughout the film, camera treatment of military officers cultivates this tenor while treatment of soldiers in the trenches delivers imagery with graphic sincerity and pathos, adding another phrase to the film's point of view.

Visualizing character dynamics

Camera movement designed in concert with character movement conspires in *Paths of Glory* to create a commentary on the action within the scene. Camera movement can also work with figure movement to create effects concerned less with social commentary than psychological

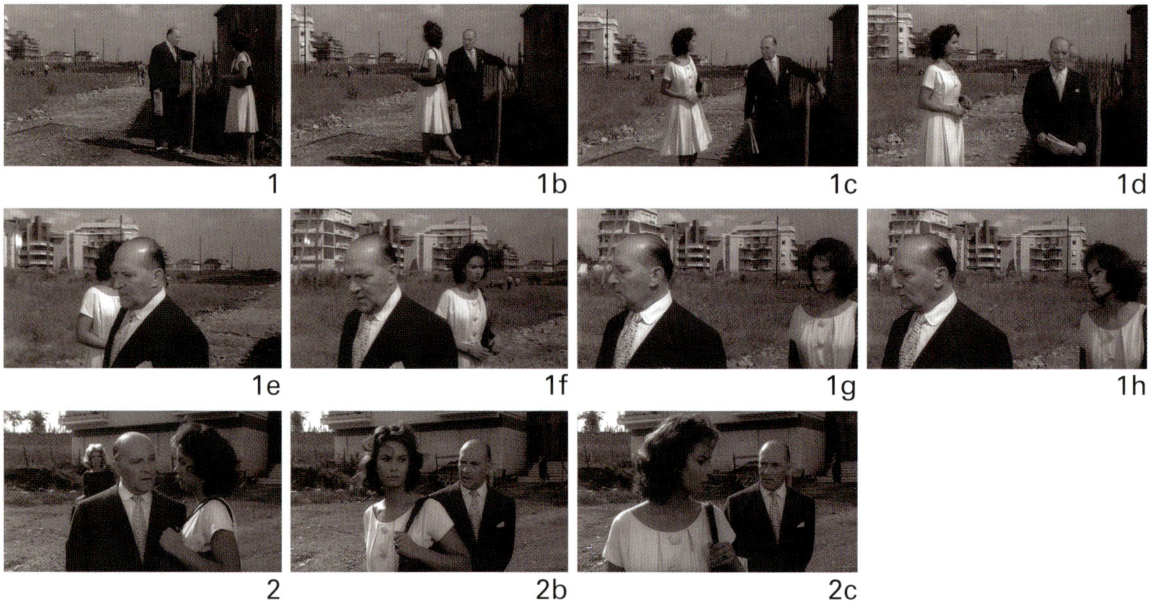

Figure 4.14 *L'Avventura* (1960). Director: Michaelangelo Antonioni. Cinematographer: Aldo Scavarda.

insight. In the films of Michaelangelo Antonioni, insight emerges from camera movement that frames characters to represent or illuminate the dynamic of their interaction. This **metonymic** use of camera is one of Antonioni's most inventive contributions to the language of film.[9]

Here is an example: in the opening scene of *L'Avventura*, Anna and her father exchange words before she leaves to meet her fiancé for a yachting trip. The father expresses discontent over what he sees as her unrealistic attachment to her fiancé. During the dialogue, respective movements in relation to the camera's position alter their height within the frame; one minute the father is taller, in the next, the daughter—replicating the struggle between them. The industrial background adds to what might be inferred about the father's work and stature. But more emphatic than this background is the blocking. Anna asserts her influence in the do-si-do of figure movement, gliding by her father twice to upstage him. The two never see eye to eye. The scene ends with Anna framed not merely taller, but in greater physical dimension despite the father's prophetic claim that the fiancé will never marry her. Notice the way in which their dynamic is exposed through a staging of camera and character movement. This works to establish a rumbling *below* the surface, deeper than subtext and perhaps not even within the reach of character, depicting visually the dissonance between them.

Dissonance and social malaise become catalysts for personal power in several Antonioni films and power struggles between characters drive the narratives. He gives the content a formal, abstract treatment, adding to film language a variety of techniques. In *Red Desert*, photographed by Carlo di Palma, the dynamic of disconnectedness between characters is compounded by their relationship to the environment. This "red desert" is an industrial no man's land with gushing towers of steam and smoke, and deafening eruptions of noise. It is against the constructs of this world that the following exchange occurs.

Ugo is a factory engineer in an industrial plant and husband to beautiful Giuliana. Corrado (in the trench coat), develops an attraction to Giuliana, having come to the factory town to recruit workers for a South American project. The scene depicted charts the earliest exchange between the two men as Ugo gives Corrado a tour of the plant. The dramatic arc of the scene begins with polite banter that becomes competitive until the scene's end when the two men are overwhelmed visually and aurally by the factory's expanse of machinery and industrial exhaust.

Shifts in the comparative height of the two characters reflect their attempts at one-upmanship. The dynamic occurs in a series of seamless maneuvers. At times, the camera repositions in a direction at odds with character

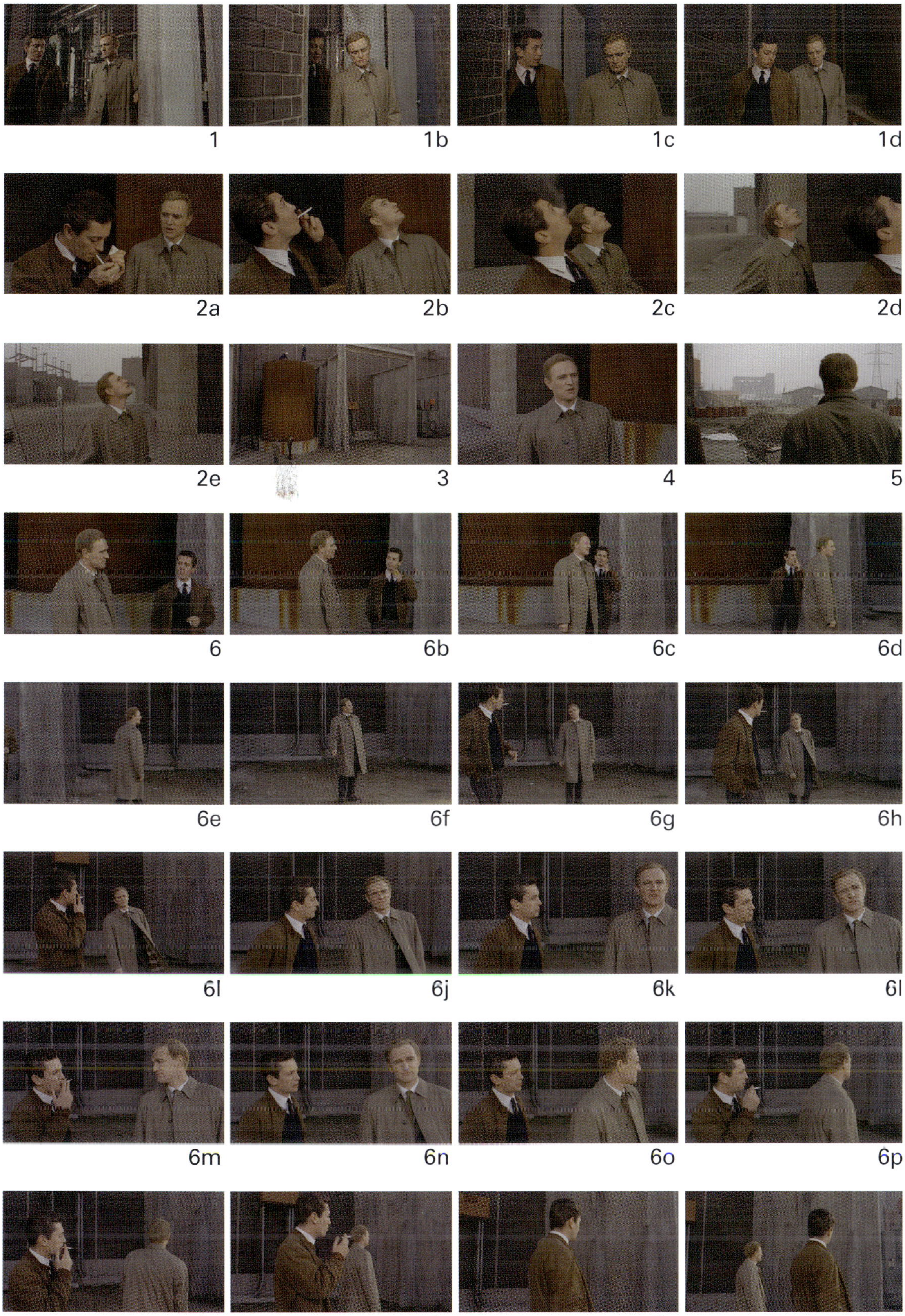

Figure 4.15 *Red Desert* (1964). Director: Michaelangelo Antonioni. Cinematographer: Carlo Di Palma.

Figure 4.15 (continued)

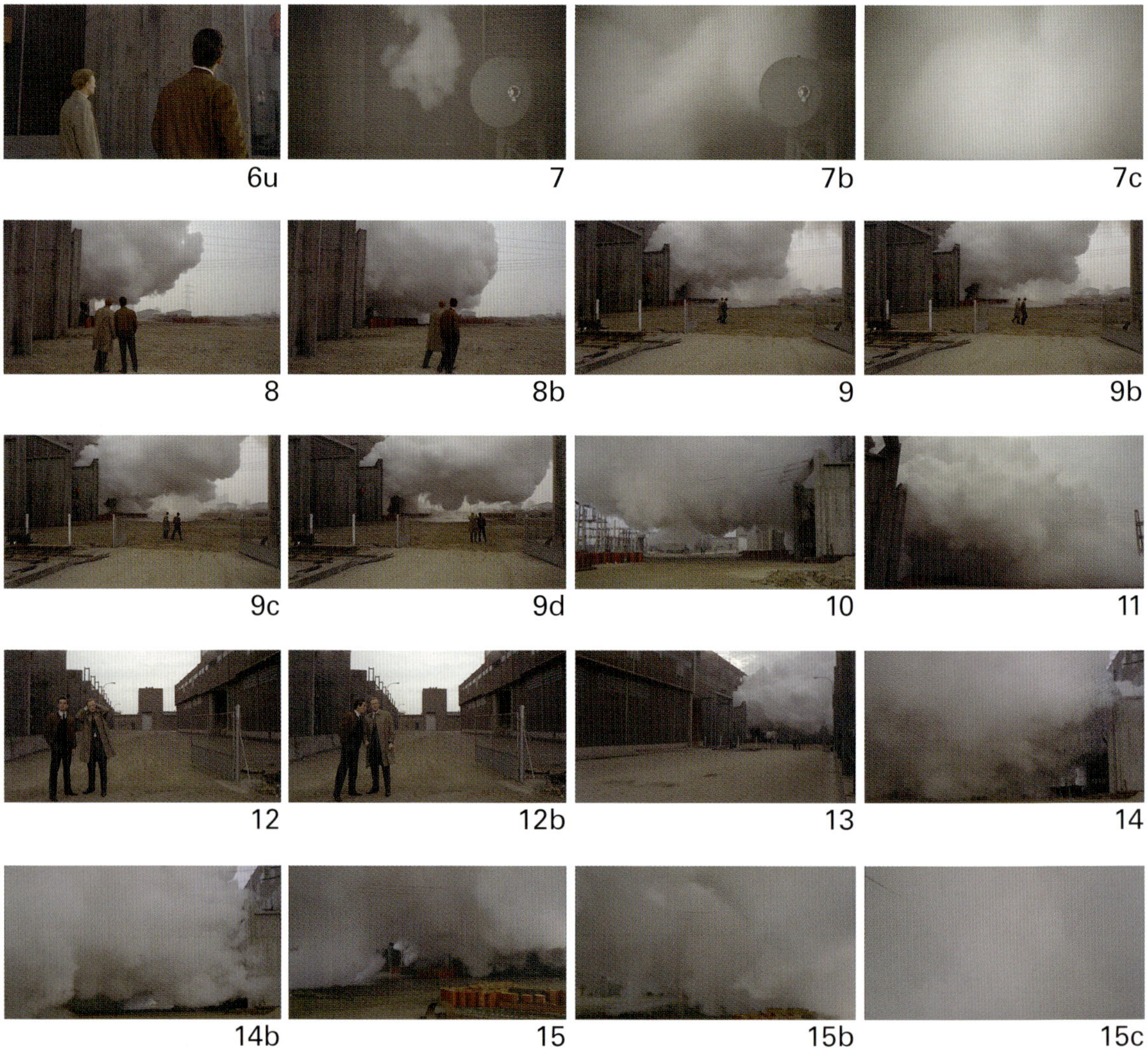

movement to achieve the visual inequality. At other times, it remains static as a character steps forward in the frame, diminishing the relative size of the other (Shot 6k). This dynamic is punctuated by occasional equality—including one shot when the men are diminished equally by a massive industrial silo in an extreme wide shot. So little occurs through dialogue compared to the impact created by visual imagery as the two men vying for power become overwhelmed finally by exhaust from the local factory.

The contest between them, made more visible by their shifting screen size, ends with a blast from the plant (foreshadowed by the third shot). An empty frame fills with steam and exhaust (Shots 7a–7c). The scene ends with a series of static frames that picture the men at equal height but in varying proportion to the billowing cloud. The film is not shy in giving the industrial complex the last word: size, scale, and racket of environment render the men unheard and inconsequential.

Tone, theme, personality

We've seen examples in which movement of camera has been designed to reveal new information, suggest subtext, connect objects in three-dimensional space, upturn narrative assumptions, establish tone, suggest social commentary, convey power dynamics, and/or insinuate character psychology. Compare these strategies to the camera technique in Paul Thomas Anderson's 2002 love comedy, *Punch-Drunk Love*. Collaborating with cinematographer Robert Elswit, using a Steadicam, Anderson reconceives and expands the conventional motivations for camera movement by giving the camera personality—expressive, coercive, even petulant—a demonstration propelled by *Punch-Drunk Love's* thematic engine.

A war of the sexes is the subject of the film, but the protagonist, Lena, makes sure that both sides of the affair win. The object of her affection is Barry, who sells wholesale bathroom supplies out of a warehouse in Southern California. The obstacles to their love include Barry's seven sisters (who tease, nag, and cajole), a phone sex extortionist, and Barry himself, with his tendency to punch through plaster walls (a habit he can't seem to break). This fiercely contemporary "song of love" is told with classic visual references to movie romance and a score ridden with trills and percussion by John Brion.

A total of five shots represent the first portion of a sequence in which Elizabeth brings Lena to her brother's workplace to make an introduction (not knowing the two have already met). The first of these shots—a pan toward the warehouse entrance, punctuated by the brief stasis of Barry standing in the white wash of morning light—reverses as Barry, in response to something startling, darts back across the warehouse where he trips, falls, and, recovering himself, catches up to a camera pan that turns seamlessly to follow him diagonally toward his office, then into his office, stalling only when he stops to "take his pose" next to a harmonium (Shots 1a–1g).

In this short opening sequence, the sudden stops and shifts of the camera's relentless tracking of Barry's movement signal not only its independent agency but also a degree of attunement that conveys both subjectivity and purpose. The felt sense of the camera as a presence in the scene continues as the girls arrive. The second shot sweeps past the vertical handles of bathroom plungers and toward the warehouse entrance, where it collides with Elizabeth and Lena, who are making their way into and through the warehouse at a clip apace with the camera (Shots 2–2c). The camera and the girls converge at what appears to be a right angle (Shot 2d). When the girls make a hurried turn in the direction of the camera (Shot 2e) and toward Barry's office, the camera suddenly reverses, as if their force of presence and intention pushes the camera away and over in a blinding swish pan (Shot 2f), which stops

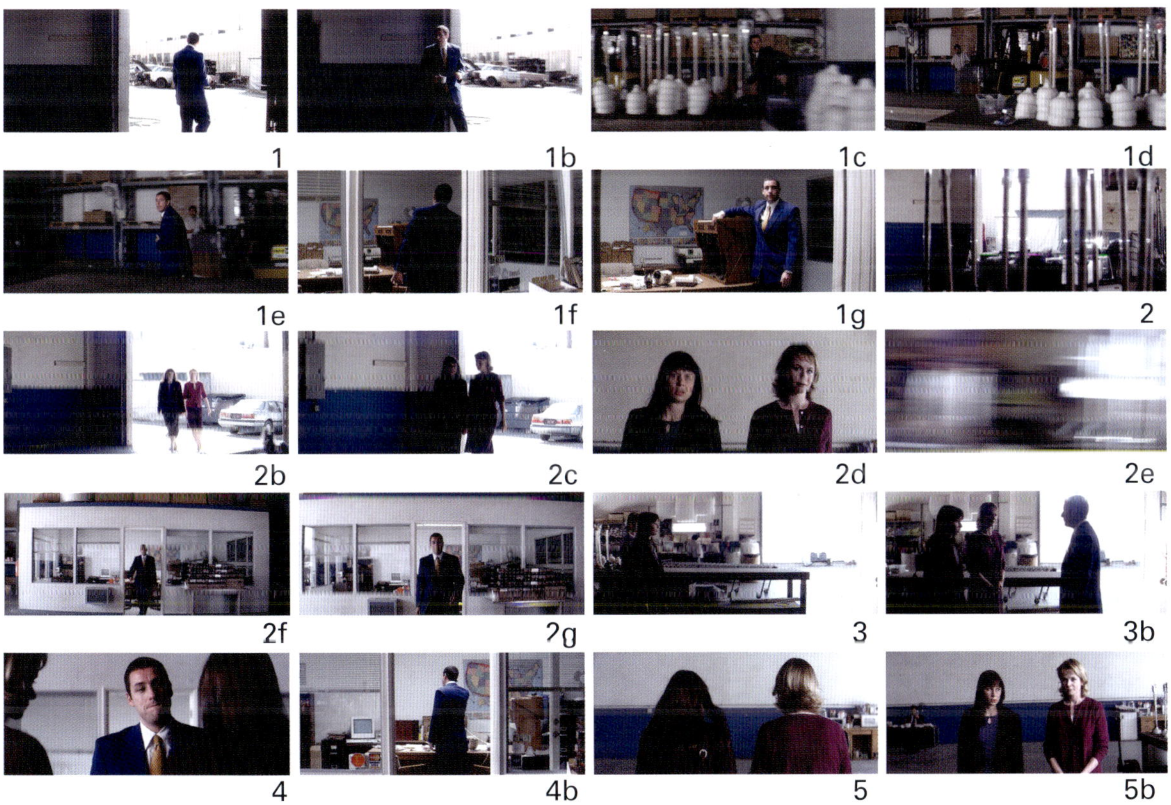

Figure 4.16 *Punch Drunk Love* (2002). Director: Paul Thomas Anderson. Cinematographer: Robert Elswit.

at Barry's office. Here, the camera steadies for merely a second as Barry steps into the doorframe, before inching toward him again, ending the second shot (Shots 2g–2h).

The third shot reveals their meeting, tracking alongside the girls as they make their approach (Shot 3). When Barry enters the frame, the camera movement stops (or so it seems) (Shot 3b), but as Elizabeth natters on with her endless stream of commentary and questions, the camera inches toward them, slowly closing in (Shot 3c). "We're going to eat, do you wanna come with us?" Elizabeth asks without any pause of punctuation. "Yea, I can't," Barry replies, mixing his message. The camera continues its crawl. "You don't wanna come eat with us?"

A fourth shot frames Barry in the center of a medium close-up, the two girls on either side seen from the back, his sister's questions now interrupted by the intercom, "Telephone, Barry, line 2." Barry turns and runs to take the call as the camera edges up behind and between the shoulders of the girls, again inching slowly toward Barry (thirty seconds worth), until he's framed in medium close-up (Shot 4), trapped in the mechanics of his infatuation.

Throughout the film, as in this scene, the camera is manic, pesky, and adolescent—like Cupid himself, darting toward the action or tagging along at varying paces, agitating the orderliness of Barry's life, trapping him in the spin and whirr of first-time love. The clever movement of camera that continues—for example, even when Barry tumbles and disappears from frame—lets us know that something bigger is in motion than Barry's dumb life, and he had better stay apace with it. And this is what he does: he springs to his feet and darts into his office, leaving the broken mug scattered in shards across the warehouse floor. Alternately giddy and hesitant, the camera replicates, enacts, and sets to motion, as it is set to music by the Brion score, the spirit of intoxication decreed by the film's title, *Punch-Drunk Love*.

The subjective camera/state of mind

The optical vantage point, or sight line, is the most common application of a subjective camera. The subjective experience of a character can be conveyed, as well, through fantasies, memories, or dreams. The challenge for any filmmaker is to establishing transitions to and from these subjective "states" through choices related to editing and camera style. It is also possible to represent a character's state of mind through camera movement, position, or lens. Extreme close-ups, shots skewed or tilted, movement fast or slow, can serve to enhance the viewer's impression of the world as experienced by the character.

Collaborating with cinematographer Gianni de Venanzo, Fellini employs all three of these strategies in *8½*, in which entire sequences of objective storytelling are overthrown in favor of depicting the protagonist's state of mind. In fact, Guido's state of mind is the story's central thread. He is a famous Italian film director suffering a mid-life crisis. He travels from Rome to a nearby spa in an effort to recover from a state of immense anxiety and psychic paralysis. The sources of his anxiety follow him there: producer, critic, mistress, wife, foreign press, production team—all with expectations and demands, and all hovering near. Adding to his confusion, the Cardinal of the Roman Catholic Church checks into the spa at the same time he does, a nice narrative nudge to Guido's vulnerability to Catholic guilt.

The movie's third scene takes place in the courtyard of the spa where the guests come to take their daily portion of the healing mineral water. We have seen Guido leave his hotel room. Afterward, there is a series of traveling shots that deliver the impression of a point of view: characters nod in close-up or wave in acknowledgement. The camera seems to mimic a traveling gaze. The convention of establishing point of view through eye-line is upturned—we do not even see Guido, much less his eye-line—in favor of who and what is being seen. (It also gives Fellini the opportunity to merge Guido's point of view with his own—the film having been inspired by circumstances in Fellini's life.) The identity is never made explicitly clear, though we assume it to be Guido, or Fellini himself, or Guido as Fellini. Consider, finally, the terrific variety of techniques that work to give the traveling shots visual complexity: camera movement, varying shot size, characters positioned within various fields of the frame, costuming, casting, and performance. And scored under it: Wagner's *Ride of the Valkyries*.

In a later scene, the camera and figure movement conspire with framing to convey Guido's intensifying anxiety and feeling of entrapment. Again, state of mind is the camera's objective.

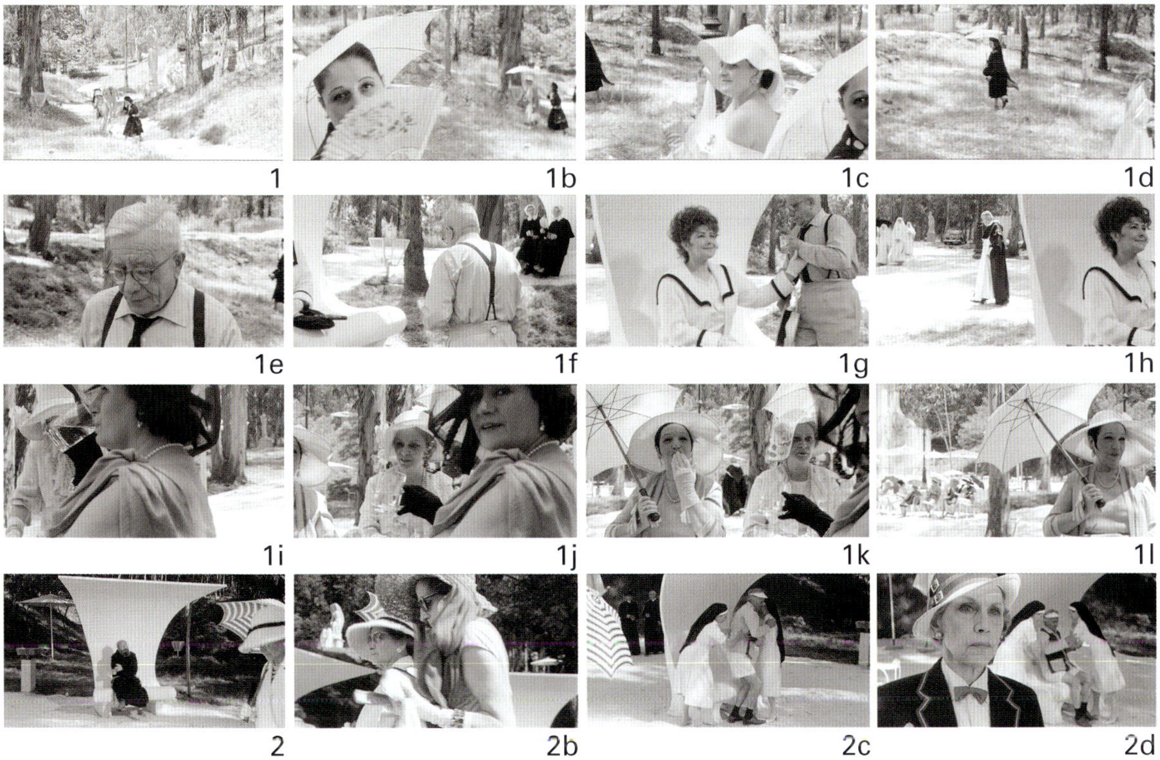

Figure 4.17 *8½* (1963). Director: Federico Fellini. Cinematographer: Gianni Di Venanzo.

Guido enters the hotel lobby. He is approached, called, clutched, encircled, and intruded upon—each intrusion another demand. In some instances, Guido escapes by seeking out one character to avoid another. But everywhere he moves, the camera, like each character, gives the impression of hovering close. "Don't take me by the arm. It bothers me," he tells his oldest, dearest colleague, Conocchia (Shot 1l). Guido's only recourse is to stay in motion, but the camera persists, framing him in close-up, characters crowding into shots or framed in reverse shots, also close-ups. Repeatedly, a third character will intrude upon the framing of a two shot (Shots 1j, 2c, 4d, 5, 5e, and 7). As the scene builds toward its end, the two shots are backgrounded by increasingly large clusters of onlookers, culminating in a last wide shot of Guido, flanked by his entire entourage (Shots 14a–14b). With punctuation not unlike the use of the wide shot in *KAOS*, the frame holding Guido in close-up and medium close-up opens wide intermittently. This is motivated by Guido's more forceful effort to free himself, charging across the lobby, taking distance from those crowding in on him as well as the hovering camera (Shots 1d–f, 1s, and 8a–b).

A high-angle camera looks down across the floor of the hotel lobby. Guido manages for a moment to escape the picks and probes of the human swarm by moving toward his producer and kneeling before him as he descends the stairs (Shot 8b). In this shot, Guido is finally alone and given room to breathe by camera framing and the circle of space around him. The camera, however, reverts quickly to its

First-person camera

Positioning the camera to reveal character point of view is often referred to as a **subjective camera**. It occurs most often by juxtaposing the sight line of the character in the frame (eyes cast in a specific direction) with a shot of the object or subject of their gaze: a technique referred to as the **first person camera**. The sequence of shots implies connection, as in the opening of *KAOS*: three single close-ups of characters look down, followed by one shot of a male bird perched on a nest of eggs.

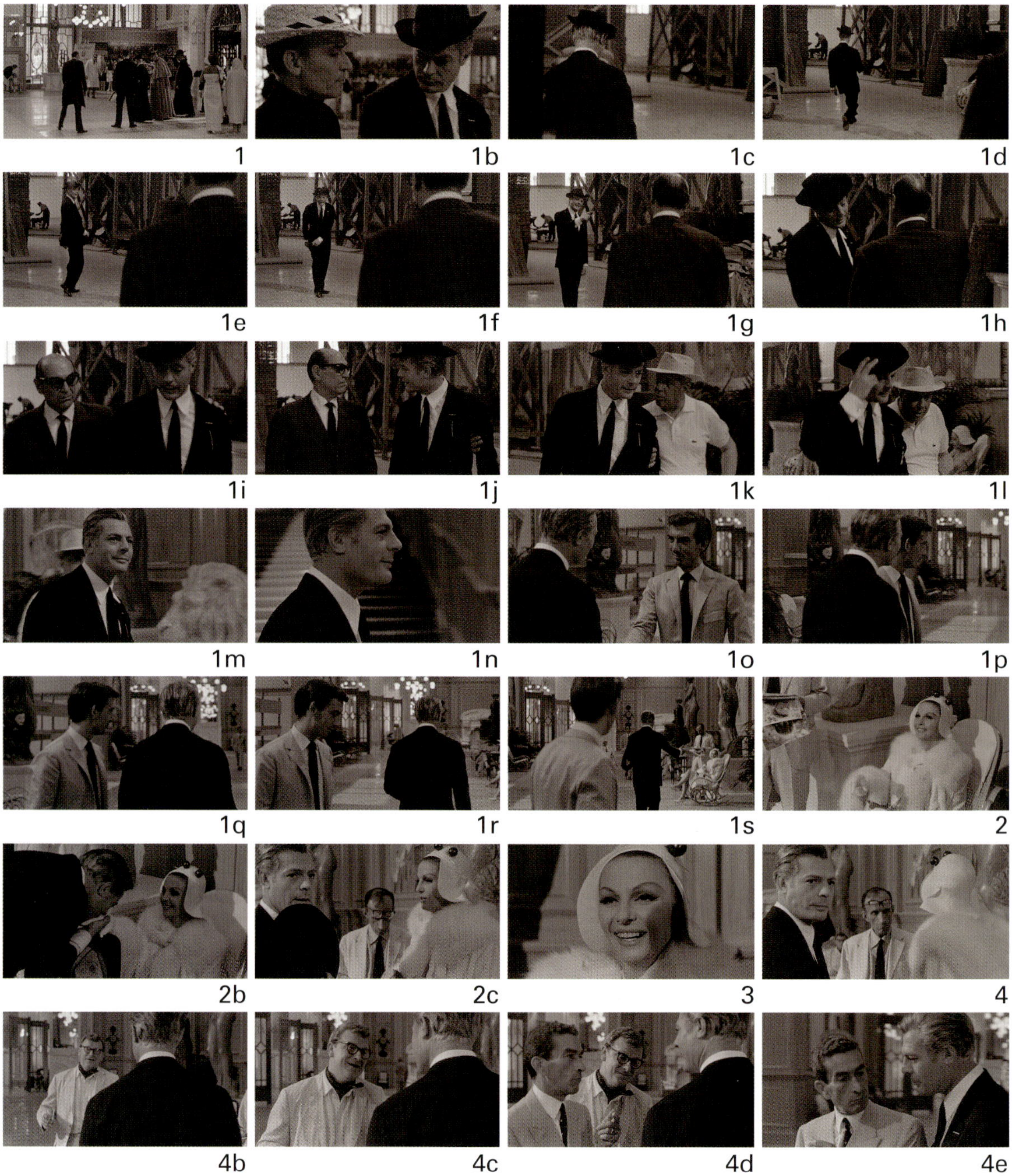

Figure 4.18
8½ (1963).
Director:
Federico Fellini.
Cinematographer:
Gianni Di
Venanzo.

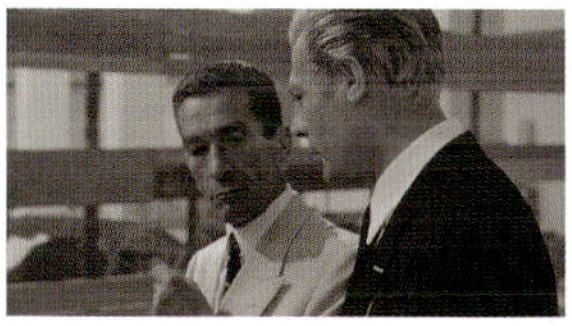
4f

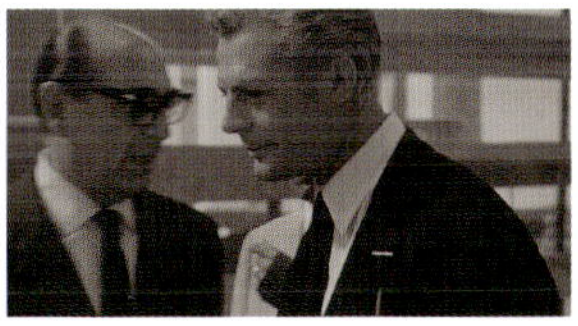
4g

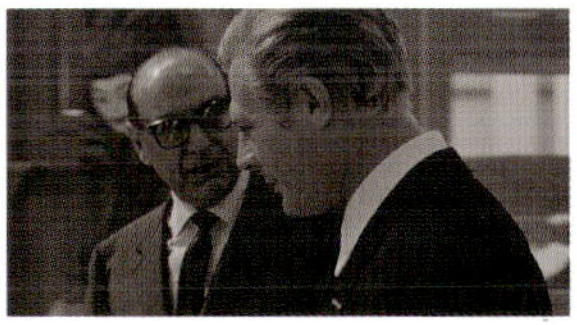
4h

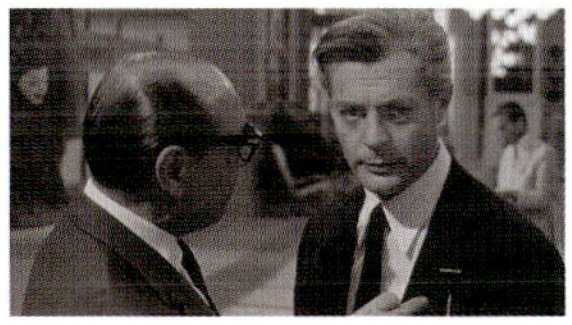
5

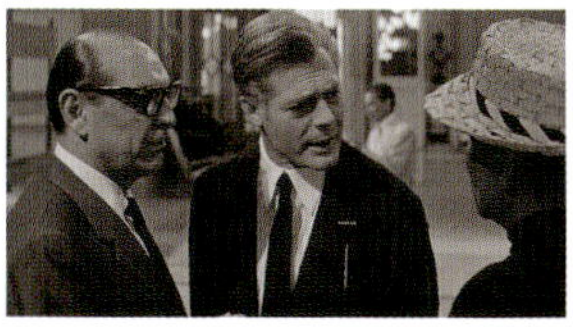
5b

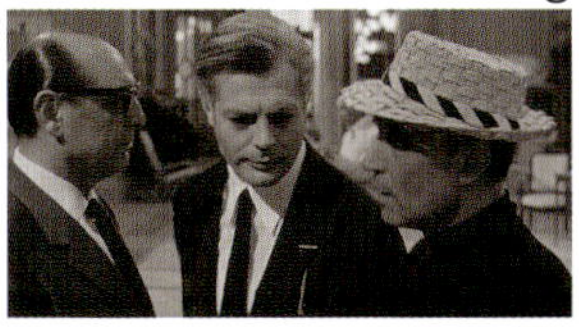
5c

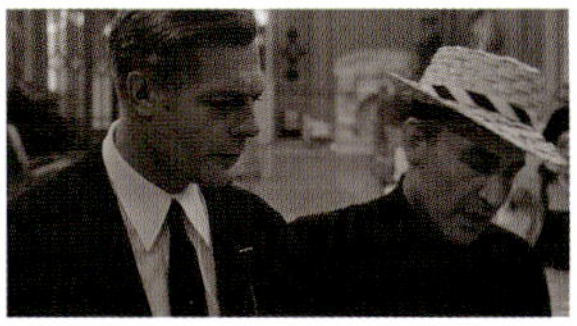
5d

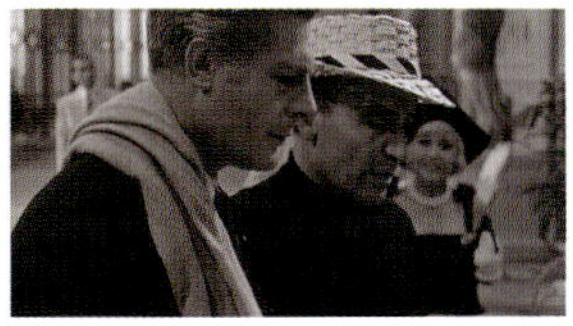
5e

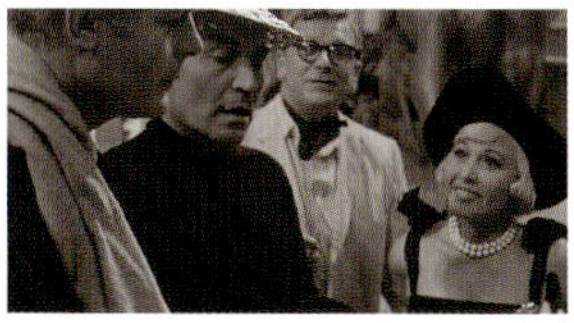
5f

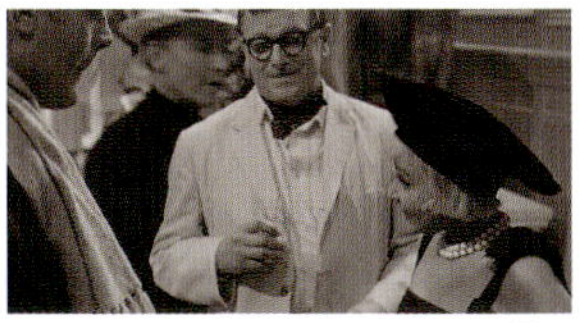
5g

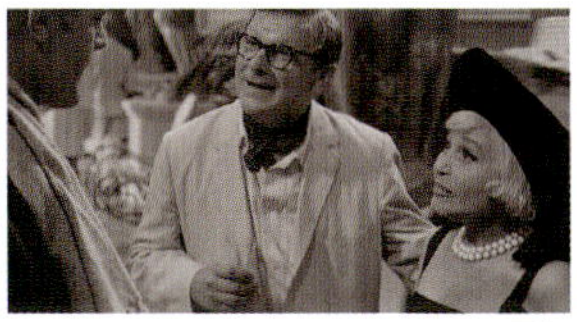
5h

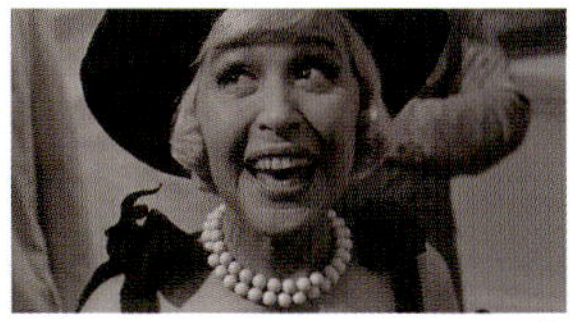
6

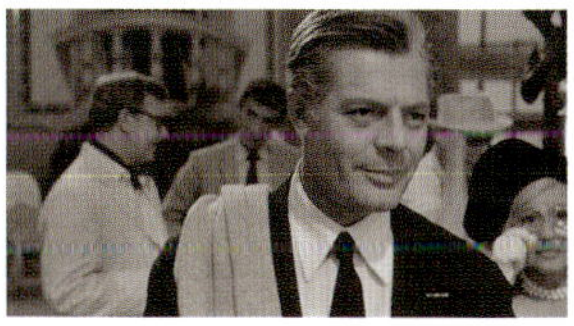
7

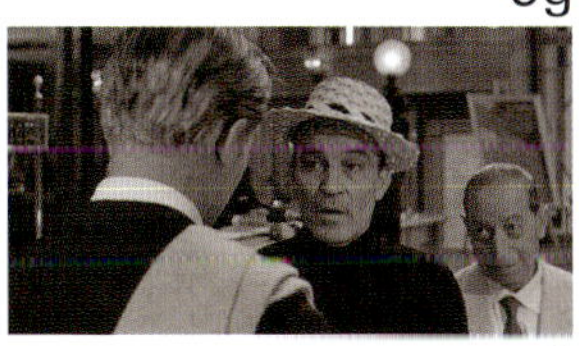
8

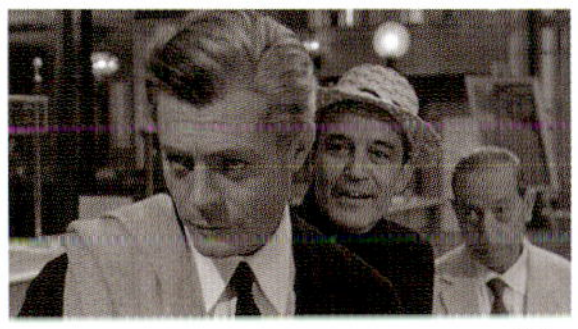
8b

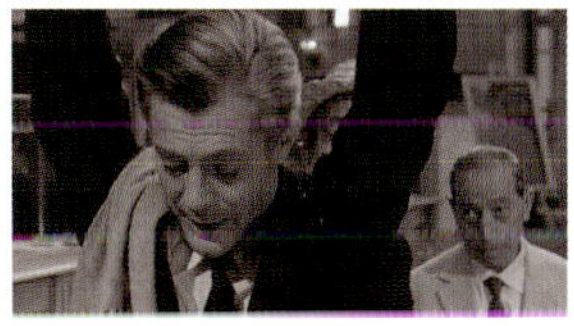
8c

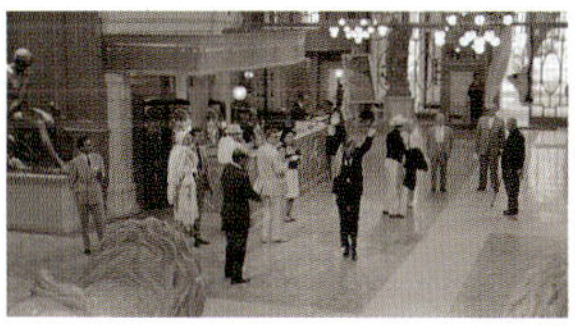
9

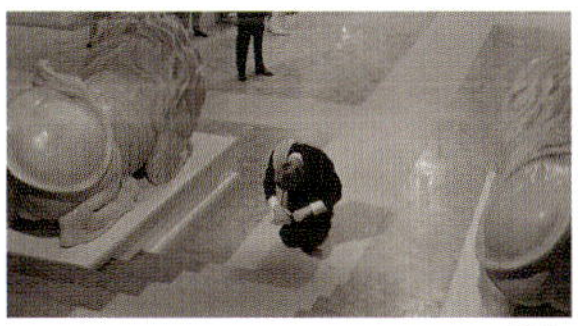
9b

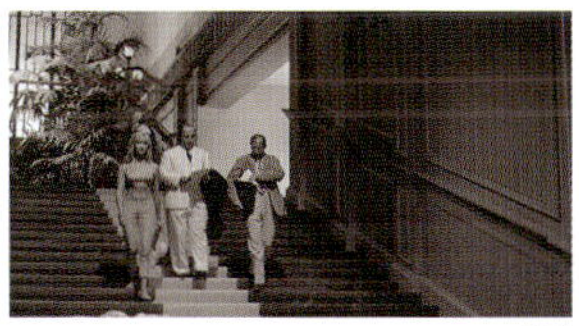
10

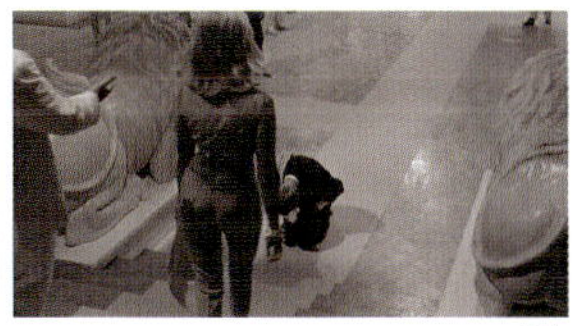
11

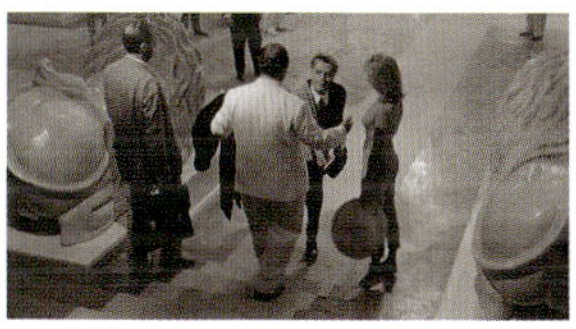
11b

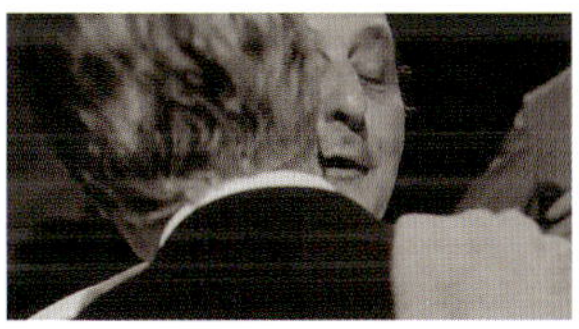
12

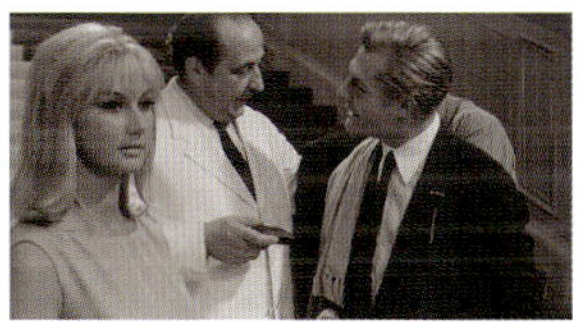
13

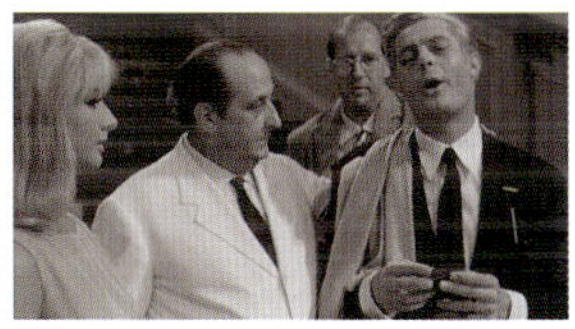
13b

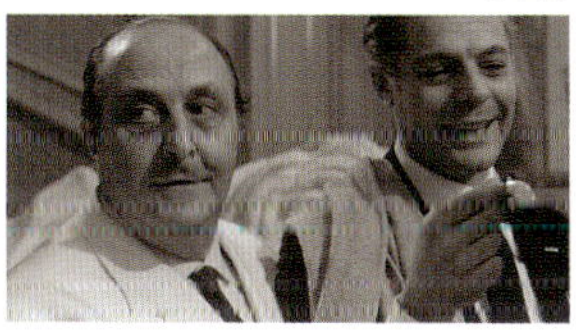
14

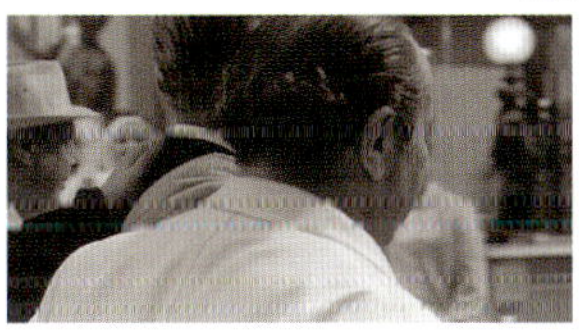
14b

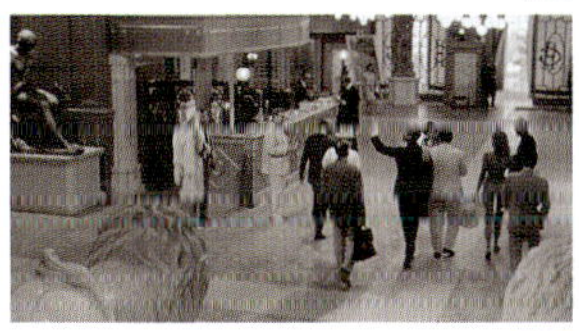
15

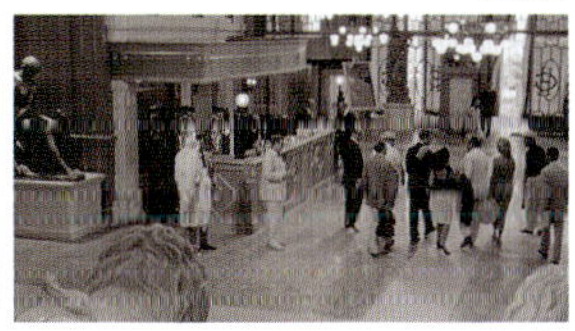
15b

close-ups: the producer, his girlfriend, and Guido crowded into the frame as the producer confers on Guido the gift of a wristwatch (time ticking away) (Shots 11 and 13). In the last shot, the producer and his retinue cluster around Guido and are joined by Guido's entourage—half on one side, half on the other. Guido leaves the lobby in an extreme wide shot, accompanied now by the entire cast of characters, more people than ever. Camera movement, figure movement, and framing conspire to remind the viewer that despite Guido's flailing efforts to escape, he is trapped in a world of his own making—*even* in the wide shot (Shots 14–14b). At the conclusion of an interview with film critic, Charles Thomas Samuels, the interviewer says to Fellini: "in *8½* Guido is constantly asking to be freed." Federico Fellini responds: "I am Guido."[10]

By now the interrelatedness of camera style to story must be obvious. This includes not just narrative events but also the conceptual understanding of those events as conveyed in themes and/or recurring motifs. The bluntness inherent in the camera style of *Humanité* is as appropriate for Dumont's haunting drama as the lively play of camera is suited to the romantic project of Lena and Barry in *Punch-Drunk Love*. Likewise, it seems somehow more affecting that Apu's induction into the social boundaries of Indian culture in *Pather Panchali* is given to us in static close-ups. And just as fitting that Henry Hill's wide-eyed initiation into the world of the mob is captured by the camera's deliberate forward motion or that Guido's sense of entrapment is exaggerated, visually, by a camera crowding characters into his tightly framed close-ups. In each case, the suitability of camera style to story demonstrates the kind of "right" choices in rendering the "logic" of narrative events: a camera strategy in sync with how a particular story can best be told.

Discussion questions

1. What role does environment play with regard to the moving camera?
2. How do framing and composition further activate the moving camera?
3. Carefully compare shot 6 in Figure 4.15 from *Red Desert* with the shot from *L'Avventura* represented in Figure 4.14. Do you notice any similarities in each of these two moving shots?

Notes

1. Hutchinson, Pamela. *A window on infinity: rediscovering the short films of the Lumière brothers*. Theguardian.com, May 23, 2016.
2. The "zoom" also functions as a technique for effecting movement through a change in shot size. A zoom occurs by changing the focal length of the camera lens. It does not require movement of the camera body.
3. Photographs of the crane shot in action (taken by Ingrid Bergman's love interest, the photojournalist Robert Capa) can be found online at the website: cinearchive.org—On the set of *Notorious*.
4. *Girlhood* is the third collaboration between Céline Sciamma and director of photography, Crystel Fournier. In *Girlhood*, the camera strategy makes repeated use of the pan. Look, for example, at the early scene in the subway car. Blocking isolates Marieme on one side of the car, against the three girls of the gang she is eager to join. A dance effort to iPhone music is captured by a camera, which pans back and forth, loosening the stiffness between them. The most impressive pan occurs right to left, as it glides across a row of African-French high school girls, twenty or more, standing in the plaza of a shopping complex. This portraiture with musical score has no plot value. Its work is thematic and stylistic, celebrating the faces of these young women.
5. Claire Denis recruited Bernardo Montet to choreograph the training exercises enacted by the soldiers in the film. The choreography was based on the actual exercises performed by the French Foreign Legionnaires.
6. The Steadicam was introduced in 1975 by its inventor, cameraman Garett Brown. It was first used in 1976 by cinematographer Haskell Wexler, working with Brown as his camera operator in the film *Bound for Glory*. The film went on to win the Oscar for Best Cinematography that year.
7. The muscularity of camera work in *Goodfellas* includes a zoom out in combination with a dolly in. The image occurs during the lunch counter scene and coincides with Henry's stunned awareness that his long-time friend and mobster, Jimmy Conway, has set him up to be killed.

8. Jean Renoir, writing about camera work in *The Grand Illusion: My Life and My Films*, Da Capo Press, 1974.
9. For a more thorough discussion of metonymy see *How to Read a Film: The World of Movies, Media, and Multimedia*, by James Monaco (Oxford University Press), in particular the chapter entitled, "The Language of Film: Signs and Syntax."
10. This exchange concludes the remarkable interview between Fellini and Samuels published in *Encountering Directors*, a book-length collection of interviews with formidable Western European film directors of the 1960s. All men, all Caucasian, but articulate and forthcoming in response to Samuels' probing questions.

5

The wide shot and mise en scene

The wide shot in cinema refers to a category of framing and has a precedent in landscape painting and photography. In addition to establishing place, the wide shot also works to locate characters in place. The position of characters—their size in the frame and their proximity to camera and to one another contributes to the composition's mise en scene. This interaction between the wide frame and mise en scene (elements staged within the frame) allows for a variety of dramatic effects. Characters can be seen as connected or isolated, free or entrapped, depending on the shot construction. A wide shot and its given mise en scene might also work as a pause in the forward progression of the story—a form of punctuation before the next sequence of action begins. The relative vastness of the wide shot makes it possible to organize mise en scene so that the frame is divided into different areas of activity, which go on to serve intended dramatic effects.

The wide shot, occasionally referred to as a long shot, has a deep history of use in the visual arts before being employed as a category of framing in film. In particular, landscapes have been the subject of an entire genre of painting. Think of *The Gleaners* by Jean-Francois Millet with its backdrop of land and sky against which characters are set. Like the framing in Millet's painting (Figure 5.1), a wide shot in cinema typically shows characters in full view in a given environment. This gives emphasis to the interaction between characters and place. Millet privileges the status of the laborers by centering them in the foreground of the painting.

Through its generous framing, the wide shot emphasizes a story's environment. This empowers the filmmaker to manipulate the dynamic between character and environment to create dramatic effects. Compare the effect, for example, of the images in Figure 5.1 and Figure 5.2. Much has been written about the influence of painting on filmmakers. Subject matter, set, costume design, color palette, and, of course, composition are aspects of filmmaking that have benefitted from the influence of painting Figure 5.2 is a still frame from *The Harvesters* (2018), a feature film set in South Africa. Its evocation of Millet's painting is obvious. Their subject is the same: gleaners in a farm field. Both are wide shots. Each image positions the characters in the center of the frame. The horizon line cuts across the upper third of each image. And yet, in the film still (Figure 5.2), the characters seem more merged with environment, engulfed by it, as if they, too, not unlike the wheat, grow out of it. What accounts for this?

In this chapter we will explore the use of the wide shot to invoke a character's sense of entrapment, isolation, fear, helplessness, and general psychological state. Also exampled here are compositions that construe character in relation to environment to convey the struggle for autonomy or need for intimacy. These examples provide tools for managing the proportions between character(s) and the space inhabited. Each of the films chosen demonstrates a confidence and/or ingenuity in managing composition and shot size toward bold effect.

As director of photography, I am in charge of whatever goes in to the making of the image so I am head of the camera, grip, and electric departments. I'm number two to the director so one of the most exciting parts of my job is conceptualizing the visual language that goes into the image. During prep, I sit down with the director and talk about what their visual and narrative influences are. I try to get into the director's mind's eye in order to be able to enhance and execute that vision. It becomes, for me, a collaborative vision.

—Ellen Kuras. *Indiewire* interview, November 25, 2002.

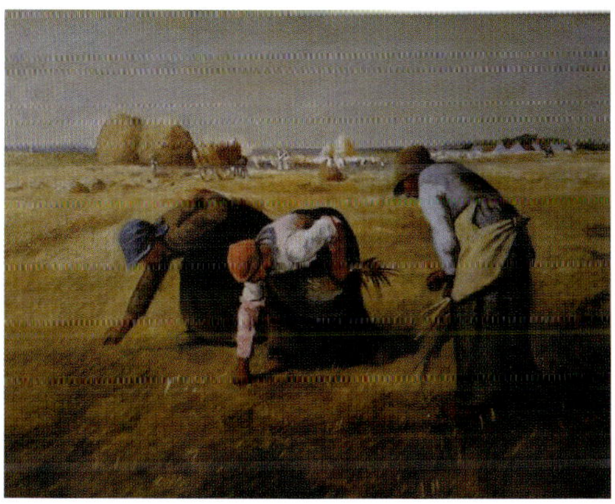

Figure 5.1
The Gleaners (1857). Painted by Jean-François Millet.

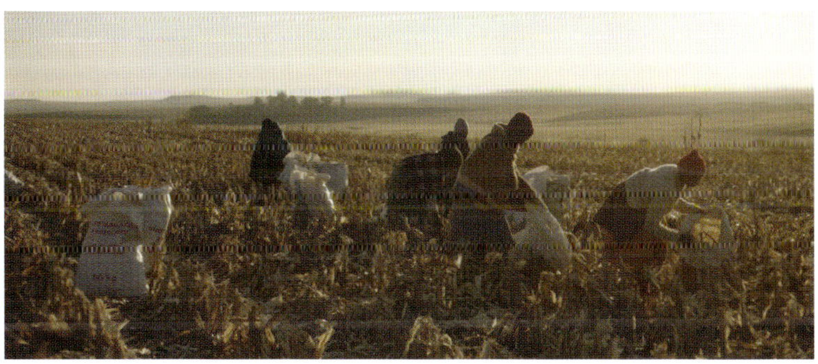

Figure 5.2
The Harvesters (2018). Director: Etienne Kallos. Cinematographer: Michal Englert.

Mise en scene

Any discussion of dramatic effects achieved through the wide shot leads to the interaction of framing with another technique: **mise en scene**. This will include choices related to the width, height, depth, and volume in each frame, moving or static. The camera's role in suggesting dimension is obvious, but effective mise en scene also depends on elements placed within the frame that work to focus the viewer's attention. This will include particular elements of a given location, set design, color, costumes, lighting, even weather, added to by the staging of action in front of the camera. Given mise en scene's province of organizing elements within the frame, one can see its value in any wide shot.

In the first image of Figure 5.3 elements of mise en scene interact with the wide shot to depict Johan as blending into the landscape. Contributing to this effect are the mist, the lighting, color unity, his right-to-left movement, alongside the right-to-left movement of the cattle. In the second image (Figure 5.3, Shot 2) Johan is pictured in the center of the frame, facing his father. For sure the strong color contrast with vivid red and green farm equipment, as well as tractor's framing of him, go a long way against having him disappear in the frame. In the second image, however, Johan is trapped. The strong foregrounding of farm equipment—color, shape, and size—diminish and enclose him. These two images sum up the possibilities available to Johan in the story told by the film, at least insofar as he is capable of imagining: he can disappear or endure an environment that stifles and entraps him, without regard for his value or identity.

Mise en scene

The concept of mise en scene finds its way into moviemaking from the world of theater, originally French theater. In theatrical terms, mise en scene refers to props, characters, stage sets, and backdrop—elements manipulated to transform a proscenium into a world of three dimensions. It is this three-dimensional space that mise en scene references in filmmaking. Whereas theater works within the boundaries of a stage, a movie, as we have seen, is made within the boundaries of the camera's frame.

Camera, space, dimension

The three examples cited here occur in films that rely extensively on the interaction between character and place. In the first of these, wide shots combine with a chilling use of mise en scene to create a film of modern horror. The other two examples occur within stories of migration. In visually compelling but vastly different terms, the characters face a "new world."

At the center of Todd Hayne's 1995 film, *Safe*, is Carol White, a housewife living with her husband and stepson in the San Fernando Valley. Her escalating sensitivity to a near-perfect environment—interiors, exteriors, even what she eats and drinks—leads her, finally, to a toxin-free incubation cell at a New Age "wellness center" in the desert. The management of space, and of character in relation to space, reveals a careful, almost obsessive preoccupation for working with a frame's dimension.

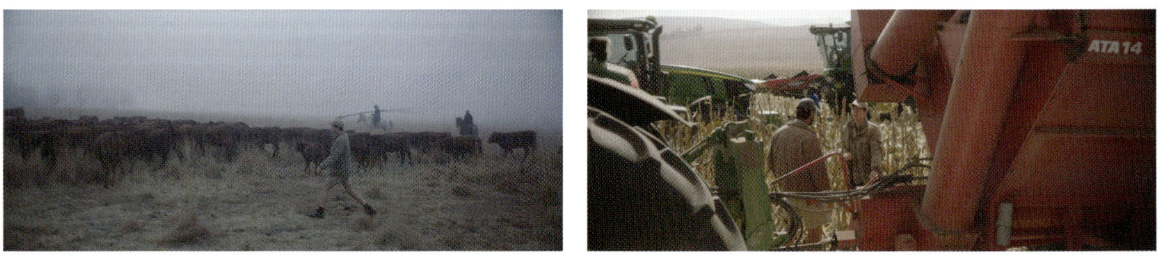

1 2

Figure 5.3 *The Harvesters* (2018). Director: Etienne Kallos. Cinematographer: Michal Englert.

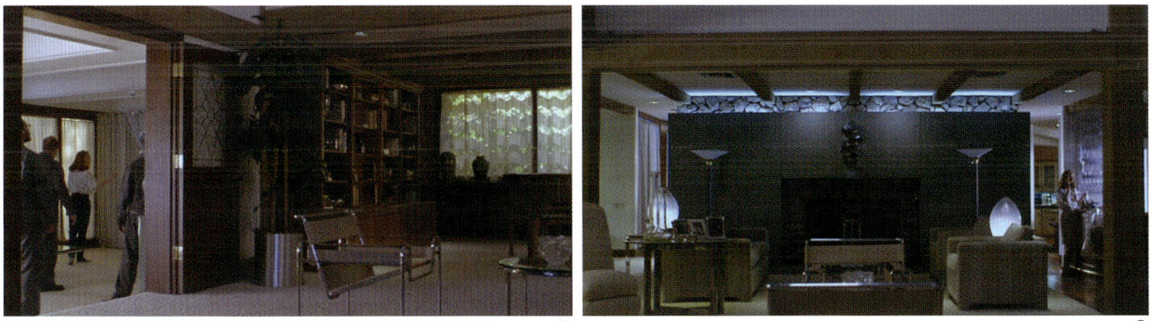

1 2

Figure 5.4
Safe (1995).
Director:
Todd Haynes.
Cinematographer:
Alex
Nepomniaschy.

A simple tool for analyzing the mise en scene in a given wide shot is to assess the way in which the frame's dimensions are reinforced by elements within the frame. Notice the way window light in Figure 5.4 (Shot 1), defines the width at each end of the frame. Height is emphasized by the potted plant rising through the center of the frame, and reinforced by the vertical graphics of the bookshelf, the interior doorway, and the sky-lit ceiling in the left third of the frame. Despite the repeated use of verticals in the frame, the room is enclosed, floor and ceiling included. This strategy is repeated in interiors throughout the film, reinforcing Carol's entrapment. Depth is also created by window light and, too, by Carol's position. Here, the film really makes use of the wide shot by rendering Carol in miniature, given all else in the frame, including the men foregrounded in the shot. Visually, as well as narratively, the environment overwhelms her.

In the second image of Figure 5.4, light, again, serves to mark the width of the frame; height organized, again, through repeated use of verticals. The vertical beams serve to create a frame within a frame. Once again, the frame confines the room by including floor and ceiling Unable to resist the use of deep space, the film repeats the strategy of positioning Carol at distance from the camera. Here, she's seen again as a small figure within the right sliver of the frame. Salmon-colored walls and warm rose light, in combination with her pale pink skirt (a color which dominates Carol's wardrobe), contrast with the green wall and blue light emanating from the stemware. Again, the camera diminishes Carol in her environment.

The strategy for emphasizing deep space in Figure 5.5 is clear. The sliver of depth works to divide the frame and also provides a space for the protagonist to step into (Shot 1b). Carol's size in the composition is diminished by her relative size compared to the housekeepers in the foreground. Repeatedly in the film, Carol's size and position in the wide shot is as important as her action or activity in the shot. Here, the rosy colors mark the middle ground. Width is emphasized with color: the housekeeper's blue uniform, rag, and the blue seen through the open space above the left counter. The blues form a zigzag of unified color leading from foreground (her uniform) through middle ground (the blue reflection on the left) to background (with the blue painting on the wall). Verticals reinforce the frame's height and yet

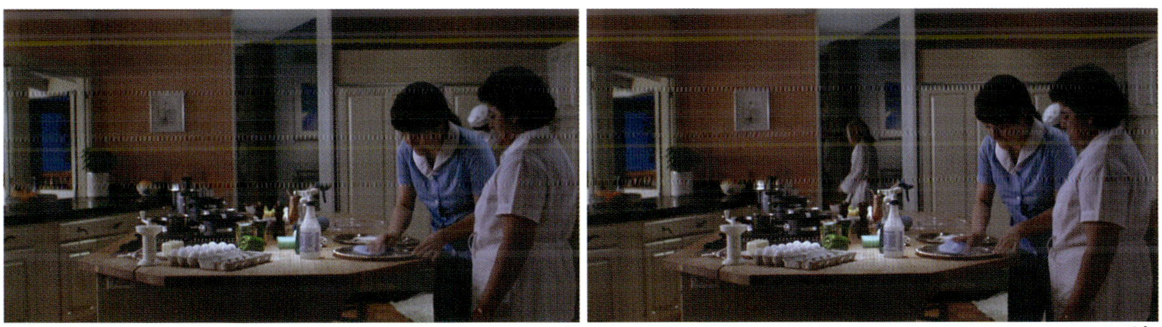

1 1b

Figure 5.5
Safe (1995).
Director:
Todd Haynes.
Cinematographer:
Alex
Nepomniaschy.

again, the ceiling is visible, confining the space—in addition to depth, width, and height.

The shot also demonstrates an effort with density, giving weight to the foreground with the workers, the table, and various props sitting on it. In Figure 5.5, chemical products are placed in the foreground as the housekeeper, Fulvia, shows her assistant how to polish the silver and clean glassware while workmen in white apply varnish or sealant to the new kitchen cabinets. Through camera placement and the other elements of mise en scene, the seemingly benign daily tasks of suburban life occur as "bigness" compared to Carol: small, powerless, and overcome.

These screen shots from *Safe* could just as easily be found in a 1990 edition of *House Beautiful* or *Architectural Digest*. But as images that accumulate to tell a story, they possess a persuasive intensity. The protagonist is minimized in every shot. While spacious and luxurious, the interiors are restricted by definite borders of walls and ceiling. This strategy of mise en scene, with sealed-tight frame and character placement in the background, reinforces the "portrait" of Carol as trapped in a world of toxic hazards—with its sprays, waxes, varnish fumes, chemically treated carpets, furniture, and fabrics. This all results in our increasing discomfort.

Safe demonstrates the value gained when a filmmaker analyzes the script for the purpose of visualizing the relationship between character(s) and environment. What role does location play in the story, and in what proportion, relative to a given character? Does this relationship alter over the course of the film? How will the camera interpret this?

Characters in space

Made over thirty years earlier, the French-Senegalese film, *Black Girl*, demonstrates striking use of techniques that visualize the dynamic between character and place. An attractive, young Senegalese woman, Douanna, moves from Dakar to the South of France as the domestic servant employed by a wealthy French couple. Her hopes of enjoying cosmopolitan life are dashed when she discovers the tight rein the couple maintains. The film traffics between her current situation in Antibes and flashbacks of her former life in Senegal. Place serves as a fundamental story element. As such, the camera's coverage of each location provides an opportunity to imbue each image with added dimension.

Interior spaces dominate the portion of the story set in the resort town of Antibes, on the Côte d'Azur. They include the main living area, the kitchen, bathroom, and Douanna's sleeping quarters. Favored among them are scenes that take place in the main living area (Figure 5.6), as much for the amount of time Douanna spends there, performing her daily tasks, as for the characteristics of the room. It has two portals. One door leads outside, the other is an open entrance to the kitchen, trafficked more frequently by Douanna. More than once she can be seen through the doorway, backgrounded in the kitchen. (Figure 5.6, Shot 3).

There is consistency in the use of static wide shots to depict the living area, but the compositions vary. For sure, the mise en scene in each composition insures our view of the mask on the wall, a gift brought from Senegal by Douanna for her new employers. Design elements—set design and costume—also do their work in these wide shots with the vivid contrast of black and white that begins with the striped floor. Douanna dresses elegantly considering her daily housework—a source of irritation to her female employer, who insists that she wear an apron.

One of the more striking contrasts occurs when a shot of Douanna in her bedroom, ever

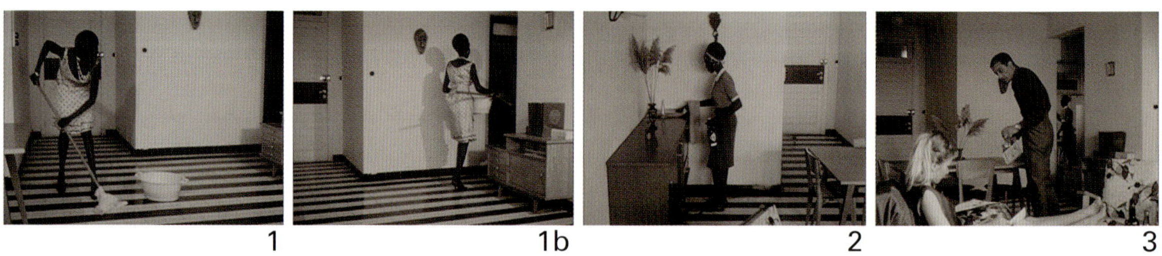

Figure 5.6 *Black Girl* (1966). Director: Ousmane Sembène. Cinematographer: Christian Lacoste.

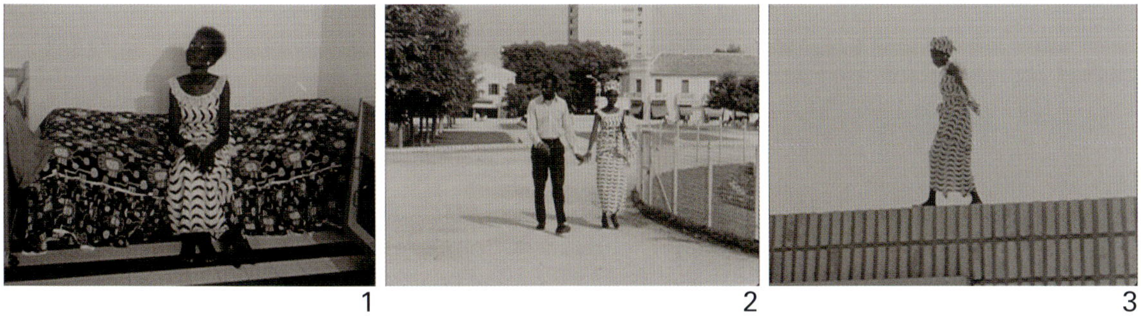

Figure 5.7 *Black Girl* (1966). Director: Ousmane Sembène. Cinematographer: Christian Lacoste.

beautiful in Senegalese garb, cuts to a flashback (Figure 5.7, Shot 2). In the same dress, Douanna saunters along the streets of Dakar with her boyfriend and then, later, hops playfully on the rim of a local monument. In the first of these three shots, she is centered on her bed, against the wall, head tilted toward a ceiling we cannot see. Entrapment is suggested by the shallow space behind her and the gesture of looking up. The sky serves as a consistent feature in the wide shots of Dakar and the compositions, expansive. The walls in the apartment work as a compositional element in counterpointing the open spaces that define Douanna's hometown in Senegal.

The world Doanna is so desperate to leave gives her more room to live.

Image as caesura

One could make an entire study of the use of wide shots in Carpignano's debut feature, *Mediterranea*, so consistent is the application and with such purposefulness. The film tells the story of two young men from Burkina Faso, Ayiva and Abas, whose great hope is a better life in Italy. The journey from Africa is harrowing, the arrival fraught with challenges. As a story of migration, place is central to the story's telling.

Caesura

This term is a late-Latin word meaning to cut, break, interrupt or pause.

The film's primary locations include the African desert of their crossing, the Mediterranean Sea, and the Southern Italian town of Rosarno, where they land. The camera strategy is hand-held, a shooting style discussed at greater length in chapter seven. Much of the film depends on medium shots and close-ups, which maintain proximity to the two men, while also confining the viewer to the limits of their experience. Close-ups of Ayiva, in particular, are common. They document his increasing dismay as the daily grind of life in Italy upends his hoped-for vision. The wide shot functions as release.

In many sequences dominated by medium shots and close-ups, the wider frame pictures the back of Ayiva's head foregrounded as he takes in the view. In the section of the film devoted to life in Rosarno, this strategy is particularly affecting, charting Aviya's reckoning with reality as compared to the "new world" he had imagined,

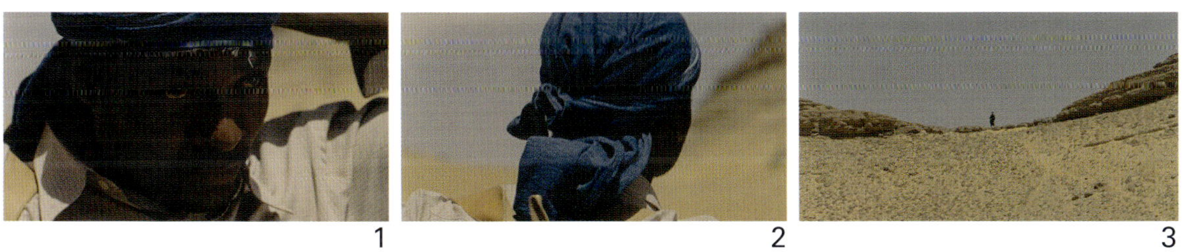

Figure 5.8 *Mediterranea* (2015). Director: Jonas Carpignano. Cinematographer: Wyatt Garfield.

and for which he risked his life. If Ayiva is not in the frame, the wide shot will be preceded by his close-up, as in Figure 5.8, securing his point of view. We see him in a frontal close-up (Shot 1), then from behind (Shot 2), followed by a wide shot of the view he faces (Shot 3).

The scene represented by Figure 5.9 pictures a portion of the treacherous desert crossing the two men make with a group of others seeking asylum in Italy. Look at this sequence of shots! Once the viewer has been oriented to the specific action, the camera frees itself to portray snatches of a yellow scarf (Shot 3), shadows in the sand (Shot 2c), then the top of Aviya's head against the dunes (Shot 5b). The pace of cutting generates an energy that enhances the strain in making their way over the dune. And then comes the release (Shots 6–6e). In shot 6, the pace slows with the camera following a man over the crest of the sand dune. It tilts up away from him to reveal the vast expanse of what remains to be accomplished. In this instance, it is not so much a subjective point of view shot as an objective and majestic glimpse of the trials ahead. Point-of-view shots are central to film's storytelling strategy, capturing Aviya's increasing awareness of the life he has chosen, for which he risked and forsaken so much.

The dynamic between these extremes does not require much explication. As the travelers make their way over the sand hill, we're on top

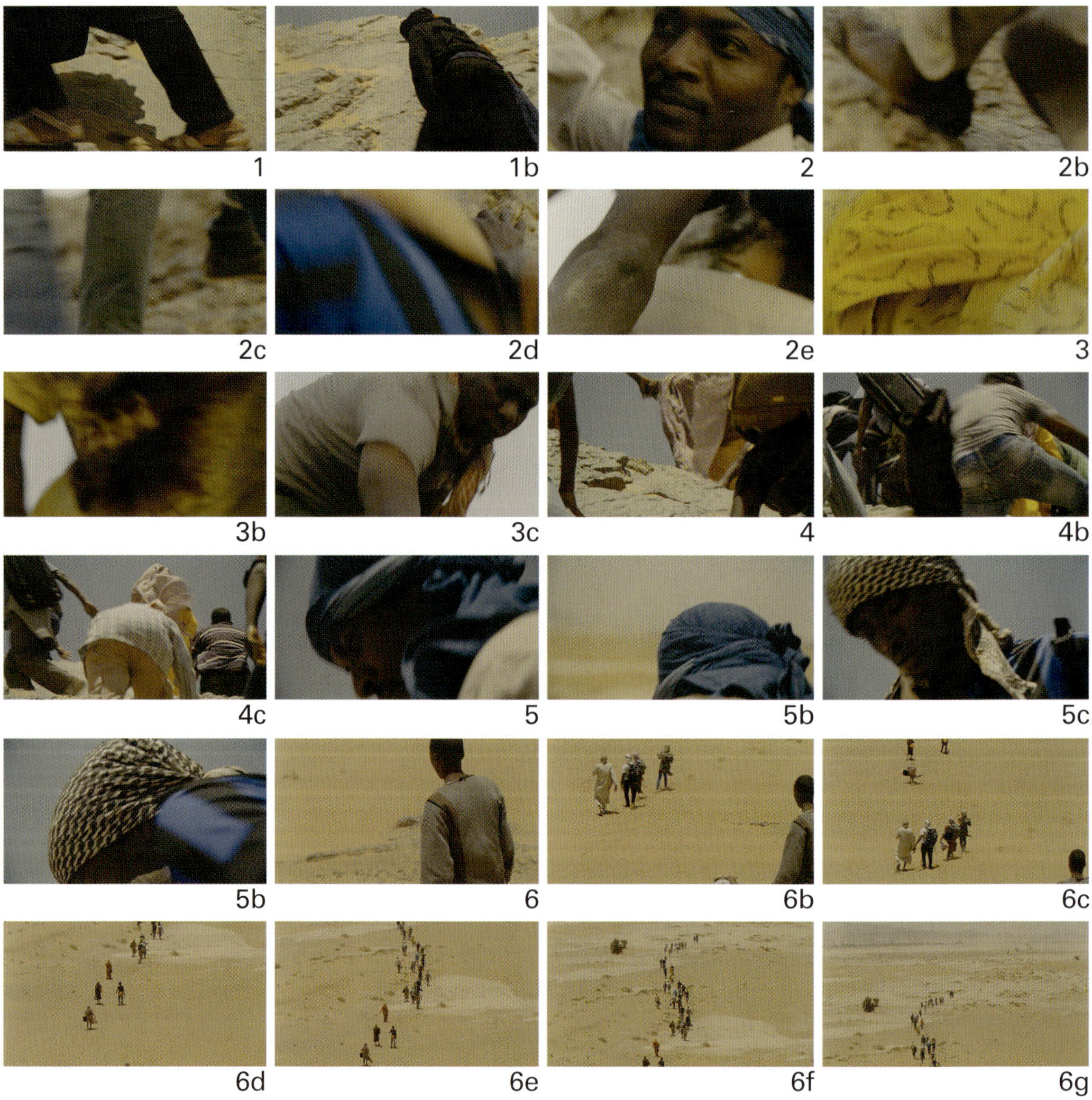

Figure 5.9 *Mediterranea* (2015). Director: Jonas Carpignano. Cinematographer: Wyatt Garfield.

of them, in hand-held fragments, merged with the challenge of climbing the steep hill. The urgency of the action is sustained by the pace of cutting. Images are abstracted with the tight hand-held close-ups. Then, the pace quiets in a continuous take of an ever-widening shot that gives the viewer context as well as time to absorb it. We see the travelers as tiny creatures dwarfed by an immense and unforgiving landscape. The very shot that effects a visual release conveys a sobering, if not constrictive, narrative reality. Combining opposite effects in the interaction between technique and story—i.e., a wide shot that relaxes tempo while it also induces greater dramatic tension—is a common strategy in *Mediterranea*. It enhances the dramatic power of a given moment, a potential the film exploits vigorously.

When you're filming a journey across vast landscapes, there's a temptation to show the scale of the locations and the insignificance of the characters in relationship to them. But when you're climbing over rocks in the desert, it's much more about the physical struggle and what's right in front of you. Throughout the film, we tried to avoid the temptation of classical beauty and focus on the human experience.

—Wyatt Garfield, "Wyatt Garfield Takes Film to Its Extremes on 'Mediterranea.'" *Kodak.com*, August 20, 2015.

Connecting characters in space

In the spring of 2001, the Taiwanese director, Edward Yang, met with a group of graduate film students in New York City. He expressed his commitment to the wide shot as a storytelling technique. Yang's 1999 film, *Yi Yi*, demonstrates not just interest in but great acuity in managing elements of mise en scene within a wide shot to give a story moment more substance and dimension.

Set in Taipei, *Yi Yi* makes a close study of the trials of the extended Jian family, drawing us through their conflicts and desires to the movie's theme: the loosening hold of tradition on urban dwellers at the end of the twentieth century. Figures 5.10 and 5.11 picture wide shots that stretch over the first ten minutes of the film. The images act as shorthand for the way a natural symmetry and serenity are overtaken by the architecture and motion of city life. The first shots open on a tree-lined park on the occasion of the wedding of the oldest brother. In the first of these, the family stretches across the frame under a canopy of trees that mark the width and height of the frame (Shot 1). The family members, at some distance from the camera, establish depth. Pulling attention deeper, an archway of light marks the center of the frame, creating a vanishing point.

This bucolic paradise continues into the second shot, in which fifteen-year-old Ting Ting and her seven-year-old brother, Yang, come together under the spreading branches of a shady tree (Shot 2). The breadth of the tree widens the frame while also giving it height. Ting Ting and her brother are positioned just off center to the right, under the arch of the tree's branches, balancing the density of the tree to create orderliness in the frame's composition. The characters are placed in the middle ground, at considerable distance from the viewer's

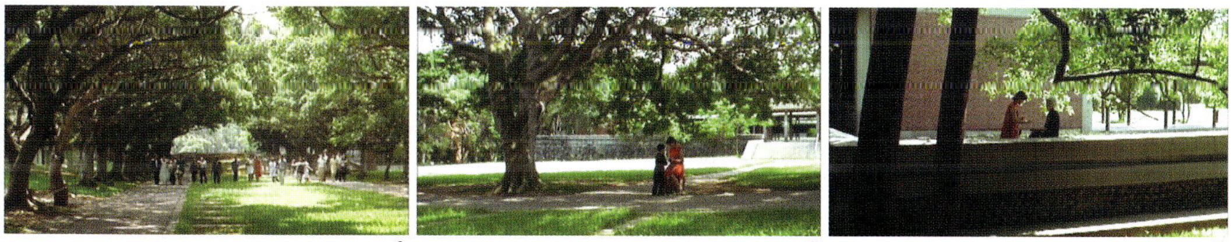

1 2 3

Figure 5.10
Yi Yi (2000).
Director:
Edward Yang.
Cinematographer:
Wei-Han Yang.

gaze—a placement similar to the treatment of the protagonist in *Safe* but with an altogether different effect. Whereas in *Safe*, such positioning "belittled" the character in relation to her environment, here it works to create a palpable sense of intimacy. Why is that? To begin, the wide spreading tree umbrellas them in sunlight softened by shade. The earth green and lake blue set off the warm and vibrant red of Ting Ting's dress. But even more persuasive in establishing the tone of endearment is the physical posture of the characters. Their heads are bowed toward each other. He is showing her something, which they look at together. This fixed attention on a third thing, something not her, not him, but outside of them, draws them to one another, endowing their interaction with closeness. The camera distance adds privacy to what is already personal.

This effect is repeated in the second shot when Ting Ting brings something to show her grandmother (Shot 3). As in the earlier shot, the setting builds a quiet around them. Ting Ting bends slightly toward her grandmother, signaling a tone of deference and respect. The grandmother, the family's matriarch, remains upright as she extends her hand to receive Ting Ting's finding. In contrast to *Safe*, in which camera distance serves to exaggerate subjective experience, here it lends the scene objectivity, adding to viewer perception the understanding that the exchange being observed is familial and private. And yet, throughout the film, Yang upturns convention by using the wide shot as the ground for emotional connection among characters. He also risks the counterpoint: character despondency or loneliness conveyed in medium shots or close-ups.

Shot 4 of Figure 5.11 portrays urban life intruding upon the personal and private as Ting Ting ushers her grandmother from a cab into their apartment. Leafy branches of trees are still visible as background, obstructed somewhat by the unloading of moving trucks that occupies the middle ground of the frame. The grid in the foreground sections off the frame, giving it width and height; Ting Ting and her grandmother occupy a small portion in the left. Ting Ting, in her red dress, captures the viewer's eye, accentuating depth.

The remaining elements of the natural world in shot 4 give way to an entirely architected world of grids, verticals, flat planes of color, and shiny surfaces in shot 5 as Ting Ting and her grandmother enter the family's apartment building. Here, the director converges a close-up of the security monitor with a wide shot—the image featured in the frame of the monitor. In the last of the shots (Shot 6) Ting Ting and her grandmother exit the elevator and introduce themselves to Lili, who, with her mother, is moving into the apartment next door. Here, we can really see the director's interest in organizing a wide shot with respect for formal properties: the vertical red stripe in the foreground repeated in Ting Ting's dress and the gold light and coloring of background, which draw our eye to their interaction. The strip of bright daylight silhouetting the grandmother, a vanishing point positioned precisely in the center of the frame, is reminiscent of the opening shot of the park; but the canopy of trees is here replaced by the structure of the hallway. For the moment, any trace of the natural world, and the traditional values associated with it, have disappeared.

This elegance in the work of integrating mise en scene with wide shots is characteristic of the films made by Edward Yang. Although it has not been a point of discussion here, it is very much worth exploring the visual parallels in construction among the shots. What similarities of composition, for example, exist in the shots represented in Figure 5.10, or likewise, in Figure 5.11?

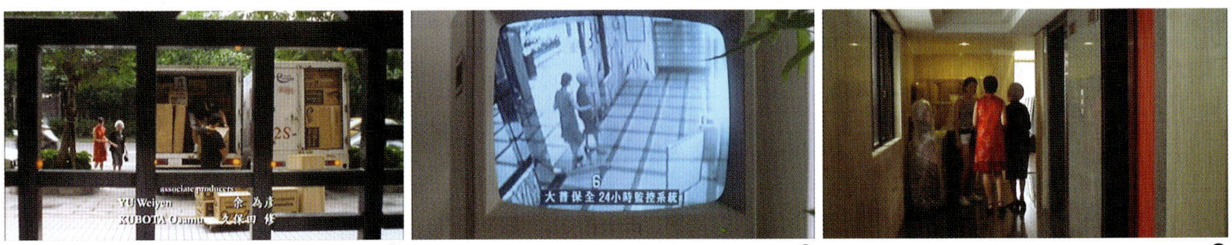

1 2 3

Figure 5.11
Yi Yi (2000).
Director:
Edward Yang.
Cinematographer:
Wei-Han Yang.

Isolating characters in space

In Nuri Bilge Ceylan's quiet story, *Distant*, Yusuf comes to Istanbul to stay with his cousin, Mahmut, after a factory closing in his small hometown leaves him unemployed. Mahmut, a successful photographer, turns out to be a willing, but not particularly welcoming, host. At the beginning of the film, Yusuf arrives at his cousin's apartment. As the scene unfolds, Mahmut doesn't seem to be at home and Yusuf, waiting idly for his return, sets his eye on an attractive girl in the street.

Of the five (mostly static) shots that make up the scene pictured in 5.12, the first, third, and fifth shots have the same composition: a wide shot of a street lined with apartments. In this composition, the street makes a diagonal through the frame and vanishes in the distance. This long road reaching into the distance brings to mind the earliest work of the Lumiere Brothers referenced in the Introduction—with the camera positioned to create a diagonal, increasing depth.

The accentuated depth, along with Yusuf's slow walk up the empty street in real time

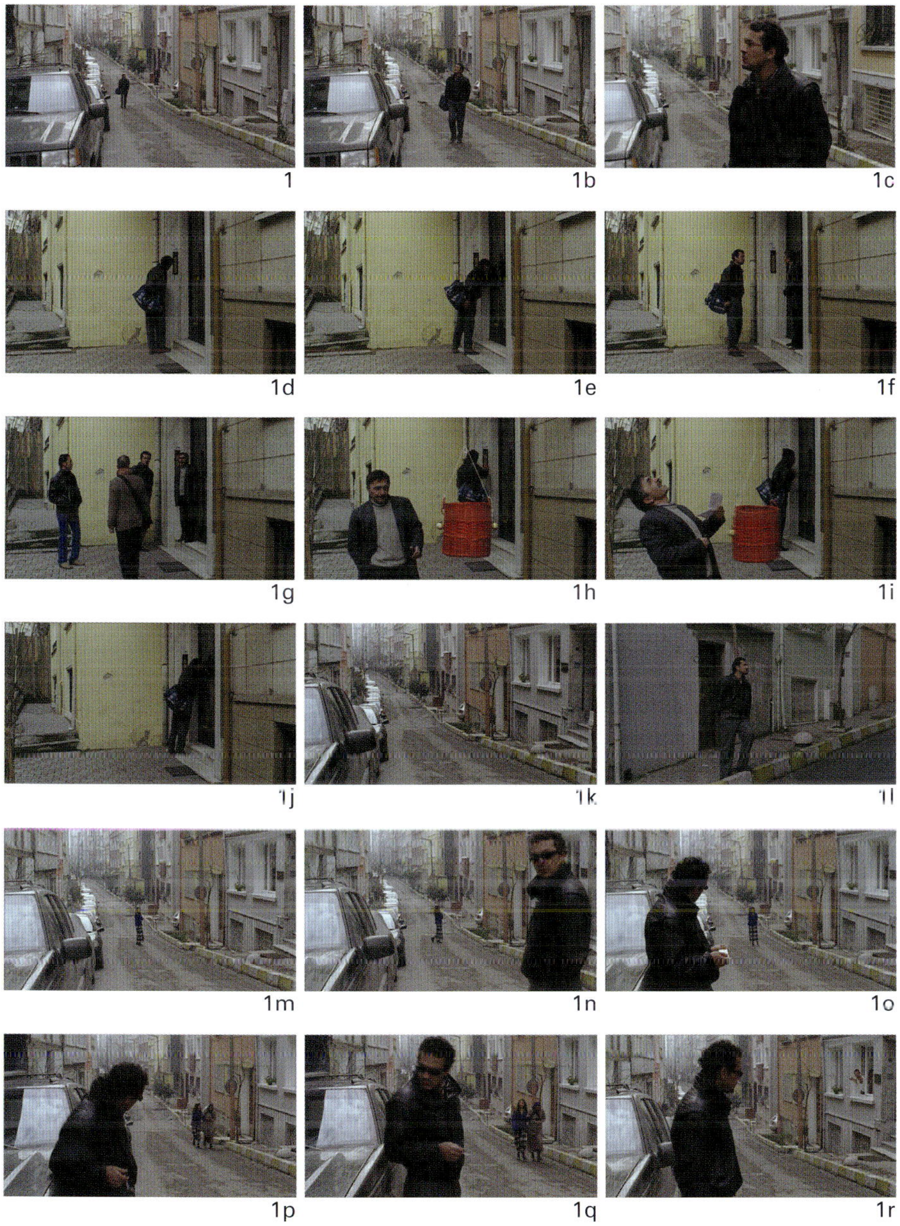

Figure 5.12
Distant (2002). Director: Nuri Bilge Ceylan. Cinematographer: Nuri Bilge Ceylan.

(Shots 1–1c), works to give the basic narrative action (arriving in a new town) added layers of loneliness and isolation.

The second shot reinforces Yusuf's loneliness and status as an outsider with the addition of characters and activity. Again, the frame is a wide shot (Shots 2–2g). Again, the shot is mostly static and events occur in real time. The main action—Yusuf ringing the doorbell repeatedly with no answer—complicates as residents of the building enter and exit with little or no concern for Yusuf's situation. In fact, the blocking and staging add significant dimension by keeping Yusuf isolated in the background (nearly unseen) at precisely those moments when he is accompanied most. A man, who seems to be the superintendent of the building, knows his cousin, but does not allow Yusuf entrance. Yusuf is rendered inconsequential throughout and no more effectively than when the surprise of a red basket lowers from an upper window into the foreground of the frame (Shots 2e–f). The shot ends as it begins, with Yusuf left alone at the door, pressing the bell.

The third shot repeats the first. Deep in the frame a cat scoots across the empty street beside a man who stands at the curb. The fourth shot has Yusuf leaning against a tree, waiting (also a wide shot). He looks back in the direction of the street leading to the fifth and final shot, repeating the composition of the first and third. This time, our eye, like Yusuf's, is drawn to an attractive young woman who seems to be waiting. Her power at holding our gaze is delivered by her costume, her position in the frame (center), and movement (blocking)—all elements of mise en scene.

Life heats up on this quiet street in Istanbul. Yusuf steps into the frame, collar turned up and shades on, hoping to attract her attention. Again, blocking and staging are pivotal, as is costume. Despite the use of wide shot, Yusuf dominates the composition as a dark figure positioned in the foreground. He leans against the car, lights a cigarette, eyes fixed in the direction of the attractive young woman. A second woman emerges. Arm in arm they walk up the street toward him. Making their approach, Yusuf repositions himself against the car and as he does, the car alarm sounds. The women smile, (politely avoiding laughter) as Yusuf jumps away from the parked vehicle. An exasperated car owner leans out a window to stop the alarm with his remote as the women walk out of frame. Yusuf waves an apology, also leaving the frame, his departure not just a failed connection but humiliation. As an echo of his loneliness, the shot is "empty" now but for the man at the window gesturing in annoyance, the frame's background held intact by a woman in the distance walking up the street, the foreground anchored by a woman walking toward her.

Deep space

Victor Erice's 1973 feature debut, *The Spirit of the Beehive*, uses an odd set of narrative elements for staging a story that nods in the direction of a horror film. Two children, a bee farmer, and his wife live in a remote Castilian village in Spain. The year is 1940 as the Spanish Civil War comes to an end. Ana, the younger daughter, becomes haunted by images she sees in *Frankenstein* during a traveling movie show that comes to the village. Particularly affecting for her is the scene in which the monster accidentally kills a girl child. This haunting drives her actions, and through them the plot, which unfolds as a series of laconic episodes, many of which portray Ana's attempts to quell her trepidation.

The wide shot becomes an essential technique in *The Spirit of the Beehive* toward elevating the viewer's anxiety about Ana's safety. We scan the dimensions of each frame in every direction for harmful intrusions. The mise en scene expands the geography of possibility.

In the scene pictured in Figure 5.13, a static wide shot lasts for the duration of the scene. Ana and Isabel decide to visit an abandoned barn, looking for traces of Frankenstein. Isabel taunts her sister, fanning Ana's apprehension. "See the house with the well?" Isabel says to her. "Does he live there?" Ana asks. "Yes," Isabel tells her, "You want to go there?" Off they go into the deep space until they appear swallowed up by the landscape. The director will often have the characters walk or run away from camera into the frame's depth, staging a disappearance in front of the viewer's eyes. Of course, we presume there will be no monster sighting. (Nothing in the film's tone portends the supernatural.) But what else might be found there? Or rather, whom else might they encounter?

In the scene that follows (not pictured) the two girls arrive at the barn. Ana's sister is the

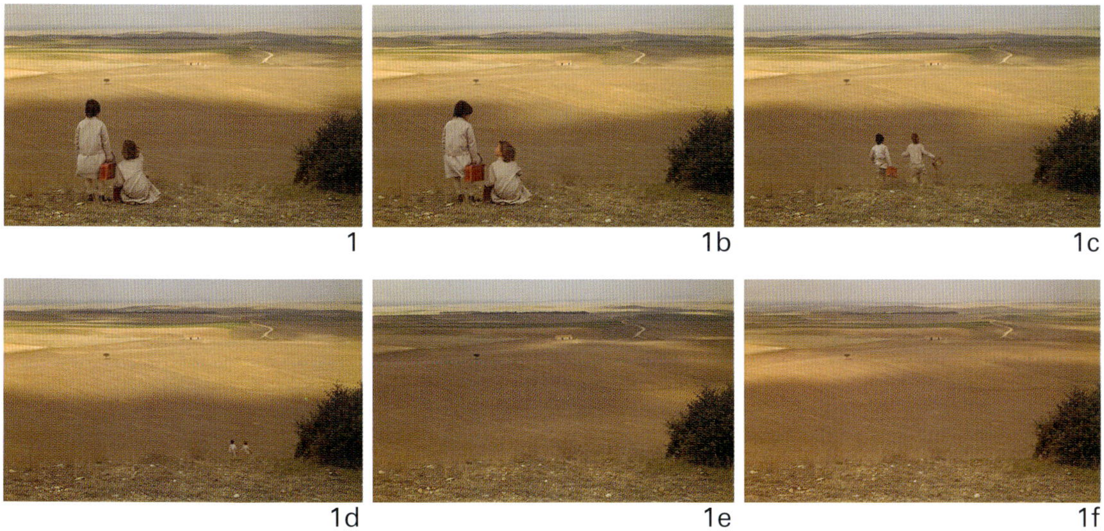

Figure 5.13 *The Spirit of the Beehive* (1973). Director: Victor Erice. Cinematographer: Luis Cuadrado.

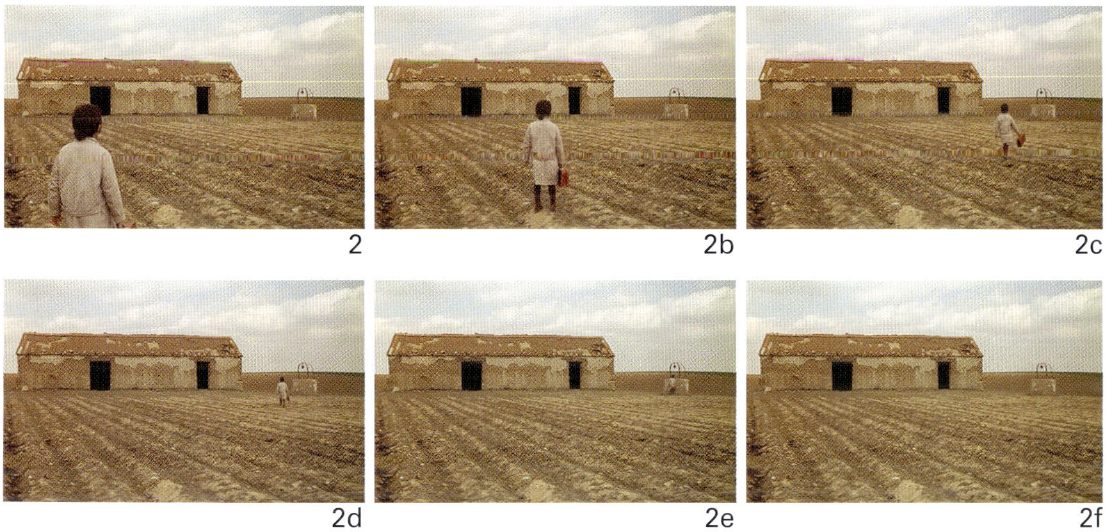

Figure 5.14 *The Spirit of the Beehive* (1973). Director: Victor Erice. Cinematographer: Luis Cuadrado.

one who dares to enter. She finds nothing and they dart off. Minutes later, Ana returns alone (Figure 5.14). In the terrain of her psycho she imagines that Frankenstein might only appear to her. Again, the scene makes use of a static wide shot. We see Ana cross the rows of farmland toward the well, all but disappearing in the frame. The camera's stubborn refusal to follow her leaves her unprotected, exciting the viewer's fear. We do not often associate a static wide shot with intimations of shock or horror. But once the filmmaker converges the possibility of an intruder with the innocence of a child, the static wide shot magnifies the effect.

I never tried to achieve the beauty of the image. I tried to achieve the beauty of truth. I always took as my motto what Robert Bresson said: You don't have to make images that are beautiful. You have to make images that are necessary. And Bresson is a filmmaker who was, first of all, a painter.

—Victor Erice, Andrew, Geoff "An Interview with Victor Erice," *A-BitterSweet-Life*, Edwin Adrian Nieves, July 29, 2011.

Character psychology

It is one of the marvels of film language that a camera technique can achieve entirely different effect depending on its purpose, placement, and application. The static wide shot, for instance, in Figure 5.15 from Ava DuVernay's *Middle of Nowhere* also minimizes character against a vast, empty landscape and yet, unlike *The Spirit of the Beehive*, it does nothing to suggest an intruder. What is the effect? That depends, in large part, on the story and the visual storytelling strategy that precedes it.

At the center of DuVernay's debut feature-length, narrative film is a young woman faithfully waiting out her husband's eight-year prison sentence. A dedicated, registered nurse, Ruby takes her marriage vows to heart, making weekly visits to see Derek, encouraging him with good cheer and faith in the future. Her devotion to marriage, "for better, for worse," begins to weary, taxed by Derek's indiscretions in prison, as well as sweet and playful overtures from Brian, the bus driver who works Ruby's route to and from the hospital.

The characters and dynamics between them are captured exclusively in medium shots and close-ups. In particular, the camera charts the loosening of Ruby's resolve in close-ups and medium close-ups, letting the viewer witness the subtle changes in her expressive face. Ruby begins to lose her bearings; the gleam disappears from her eyes.

The first assault on her resolve occurs when the daily calls from Derek mysteriously end. During her visit to the prison she learns that he's been confined to solitary for three weeks due to his complicity in a prison brawl. When we next see Ruby, she's waiting for a bus at the roadside. The vastness surrounding her in the wide shot is not staged to excite the viewer's anxiety as in *The Spirit of the Beehive*. It is, in this instance, a reflection of Ruby's experience.

During the interior sequence in which Ruby meets with a prison administrator, the coverage is limited to a series of shot/reverse shot medium close-ups, tinted with a palette of gray and blue that dominates the film. The cut from muted interior to bright sunlit exterior is already startling. More startling, the transition from a subjective read of Ruby's reaction in close-up to an objective view of her state of mind. This occurs through the wide shot, centering her against an almost featureless landscape. She's in the "middle of nowhere"—internally and externally. Ruby has lost her compass, the environment telegraphing her psychology. More poignant still are Ruby's size in the shot (small) and her action: she faces the camera and then she turns away, her back to us, facing "nowhere."

Shallow space

A film in which a troop of French Legionnaires relocate to West Africa will, by the very nature of its story parameters, give value to character interaction with location. In chapter four, Figure 4.7 depicts the men during a training exercise as camera movement controls the viewer's field of vision toward a discovery or revelation. Here, we revisit the film for the striking way Claire Denis' *Beau Travail* exalts the visual conditions of spare shot construction in locations that are vast. Both are achieved without sacrificing the use of wide shots. The shots are stark and graphic with flat planes of color, backdrops of sea or sky, and the human form treated more as figure than character. Atmosphere becomes a critical narrative element, often more impactful than a plot turn.

In the sequence represented by shots 1 and 2 of Figure 5.16, the sky becomes a wall

Figure 5.15 *Middle of Nowhere* (2012). Director: Ava DuVernay. Cinematographer: Bradford Young.

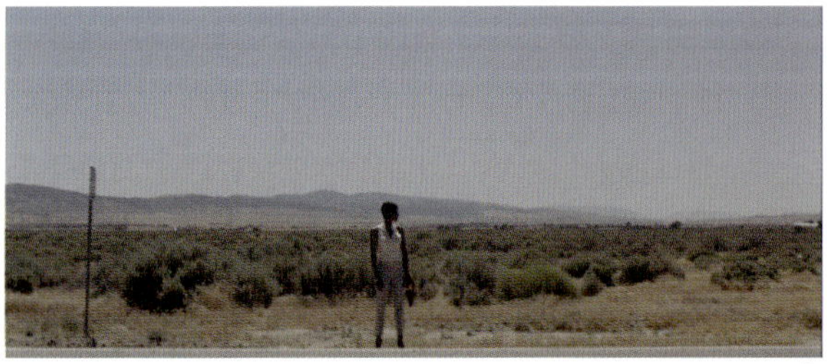

1

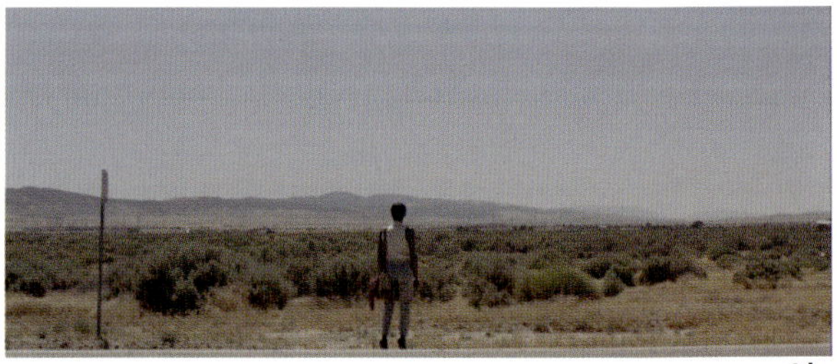

1b

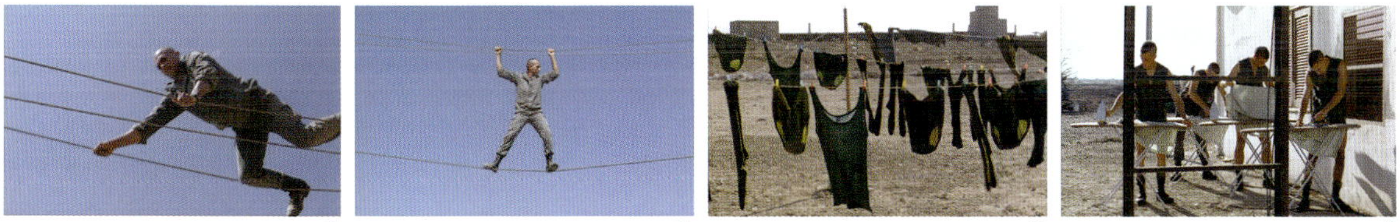

1 2 3 4

Figure 5.16
Beau Travail (1999). Director: Claire Denis. Cinematographer: Agnès Godard.

surface. Dimension is suggested through the three parallel cables, establishing width, along with the position of the Legionnaire who gives the frame volume (Shot 1). In the second shot, depth and volume disappear with the Legionnaire suspended in space against a field of blue sky.

The three horizontal lines of high wire (Shot 1) are repeated in the three lines of clothes flapping the desert air (Shot 3), creating graphic parallels among the compositions. Too, even as a wide shot, it works to contain, or inhibit, the endlessness of desert. This occurs again in shot 4, which pictures the Legionnaires ironing behind three horizontal metal bars, repeating form and color. The director, in collaboration with her cinematographer, Agnès Godard, applies a discipline to each shot that includes the application of line, texture, and color. This visual precision reinforces the rigor and confinement that define the daily lives of the Legionnaires.

In a later sequence the image surface sacrifices dimension for color when an offshore explosion fills the frame in orange and red—a shot that lasts for nearly ten seconds (Figure 5.17, Shot 1). It dissolves into a surface of green, then a green-blue of sea that reveals the protagonist rescuing an injured Legionnaire. Look at the pockets of fire floating on the surface of the water (Shot 2c). You can see that the fascination with sea, sky, gravel, salt, fire, sand, and the musculature of the physical body drives the aesthetic and dictates mise en scene in the wide shots of *Beau Travail*.

Order in chaos

A river city landscape overcome by stench and swamp is the setting for Lynne Ramsey's first film, *Ratcatcher*. The story takes place in Glasgow during the infamous 1973 garbage strike. Given the choice of subject matter, we could reasonably expect the stylistic treatment to deliver a gritty feel with a handheld camera and found locations. But no, Ramsay uses her camera to deliver formal, static compositions (evidence of her background as a still photographer) and a mise en scene that favors lyrical sensibility. The story centers around the lives of children who live in the rundown tenements. In one sequence, the protagonist, James, visits a friend, Margaret Ann, who has just moved into a newly built apartment across town with the added feature of an indoor bathroom and bathtub. This is James' great hope for his family: to leave the tenement housing for a decent dwelling. This will be postponed by the ongoing strike, as his father is a garbage collector. Having just combed lice from his sister's hair, James visits Margaret Ann, where he watches (or tries not to watch) as she takes her bath (Figure 5.18, a selection of 6 shots in sequence from a scene comprised

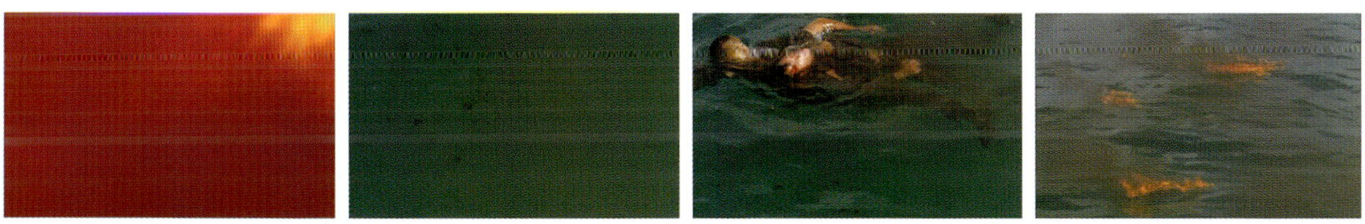

1 2 2b 2c

Figure 5.17
Beau Travail (1999). Director: Claire Denis. Cinematographer: Agnès Godard.

of many more). At one point, unable to resist the luxury, James climbs into the tub with her. Despite piles of clothes and the mismatch of fabrics and textures, the children—nubile, bony, slippery with wetness, and pink against the blue cast of tile and wallpaper—are beautiful. The pink is repeated in the plastic tray sitting in the adjacent sink and in the bright pink soap. The medium shots and close ups, even if rendering only portions of their bodies, never sacrifice the tenderness between them.

The sequence culminates in a wide shot (Figure 5.19). The children sit, wrapped in towels on a "sofa boat" eating sandwiches. They are watching the TV, which we hear as it reports the ongoing garbage strike. In a room that reads a monochrome of off-whites and beige, James and Margaret Ann are the pink of youth and promise: their towels, their drinking glasses, their flesh. The physical closeness of the two characters on the sofa, their fixed attention on the TV, along with synchronized gestures (taking a bite of sandwich or raising a glass at the same time) give the scene levity and charm. They are the lovely order, the lyrical beauty in a world ridden with detritus, lice, toxicity, and rats. This is what Lynn Ramsey accomplishes through the wide shot and mise en scene.

The proscenium: setting the stage

One of the obvious challenges of staging a scene in a wide shot is that the filmmaker, in collaboration with the cinematographer and production designer, must determine the dimensions of the frame, as well as the placement of each object set within it. For certain kinds of **location shooting** the choices may be limited to camera placement and lens, as with

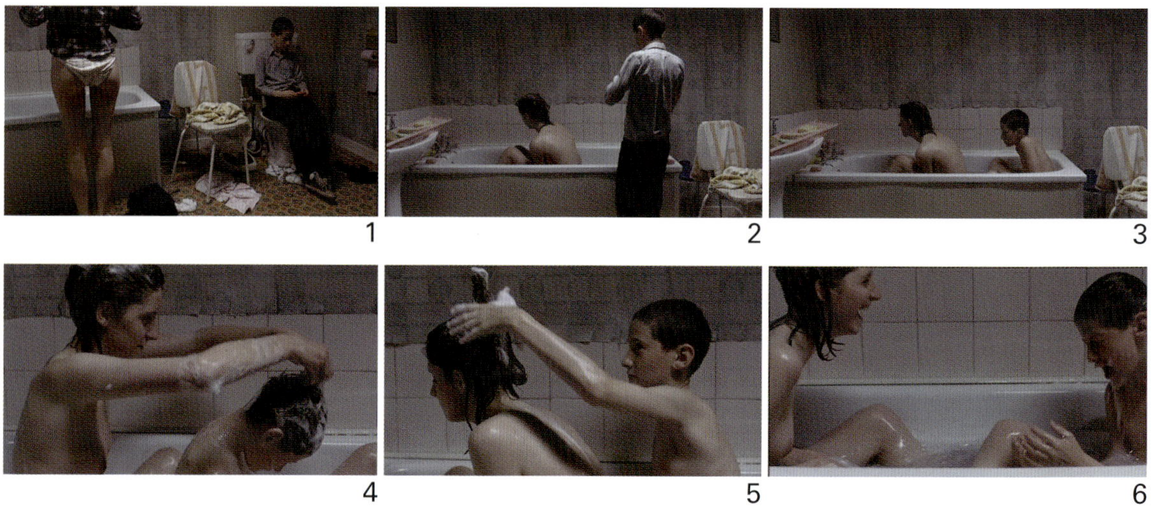

Figure 5.18 *Ratcatcher* (1999). Director: Lynne Ramsey. Cinematographer: Alwin H. Küchler.

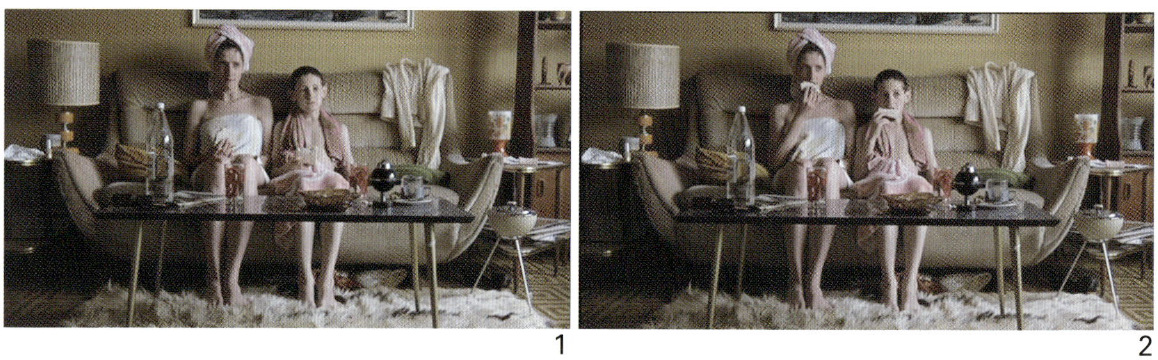

Figure 5.19 *Ratcatcher* (1999). Director: Lynne Ramsey. Cinematographer: Alwin H. Küchler.

the wide shot of the desert in *Mediterranea* or of the countryside in *Spirit of the Beehive*. Locations that require more elaborate set dressing depend on close attention to every detail.

We can see this challenge met in a scene from Claudia Llosa's haunting film, *The Milk of Sorrow*. The movie centers around Fausta, a young woman scarred after years of hearing horror stories that occurred during years of conflict between the Peruvian government and a ruthless guerilla group. We learn of these events as Fausta's mother, a victim of these horrors, lay dying beside her. The stories of rape and violence plague Fausta, compromising her capacity to enjoy even the happiest occasions.

One such occasion is the upcoming wedding of her cousin, whom we meet in the scene pictured in Figure 5.20. It begins with a wide shot of a courtyard, outside a family home at the foot of low-lying Andean mountains. The position of the stationary camera creates inside the frame a theater-like composition, reinforced by the table situated in the center of the frame's middle ground. The shot makes strategic use of mise en scene with the rich layering of colorful design elements in every plane of action and vivid use of set pieces along with physical props (Figure 5.20, Shots 1–1k).

Additionally, the static shot is animated by activity staged to fill the frame with motion that runs in all directions: a boy on a bicycle, soccer balls retrieved, one dog leaping, and another lusting after a kitten. Added to this, the cousin enters from an arched doorway in the background, wearing her wedding gown, seeking approval from her father who sits at the table. The long train of the dress becomes a curtain in the frame, floating across it to the right, and then in the foreground, even obscuring her father, before she turns to Fausta who arrives off screen. When we cut to Fausta in the medium shot, the visual and kinetic vitality of the previous frame disappears instantly, replaced by her somber presence, backgrounded by a dull brick wall (Shot 2). The one brightness in the frame is a hot pink bird cage at the periphery, echoed by her soft pink sweater, the print of which repeats the flowering branch growing alongside the cage. We have seen earlier in this chapter the use of wide shot as punctuation after a series of close-ups or medium shots. Here the wide shot is what expands; it is the long rambling sentence, punctuated by the medium shot of Fausta wearing her pointed grief.

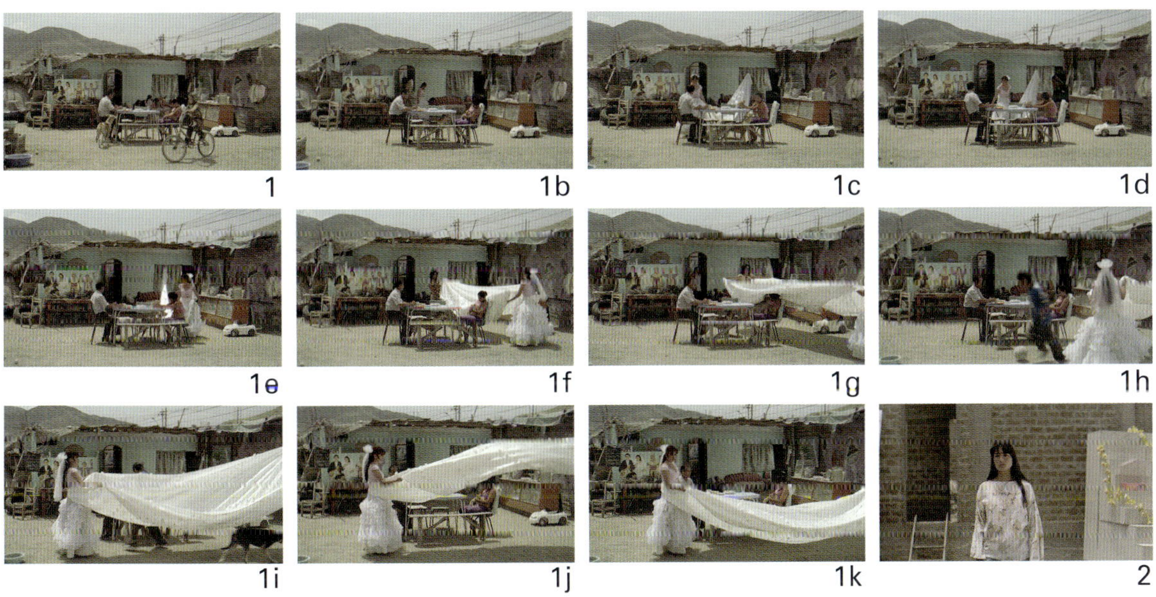

Figure 5.20 *The Milk of Sorrow* (2009). Director: Claudia Llosa. Cinematographer: Natasha Braier.

Figure 5.21 *What Time Is It There?* (2001). Director: Tsai Ming-Liang. Cinematographer: Benoît Delhomme.

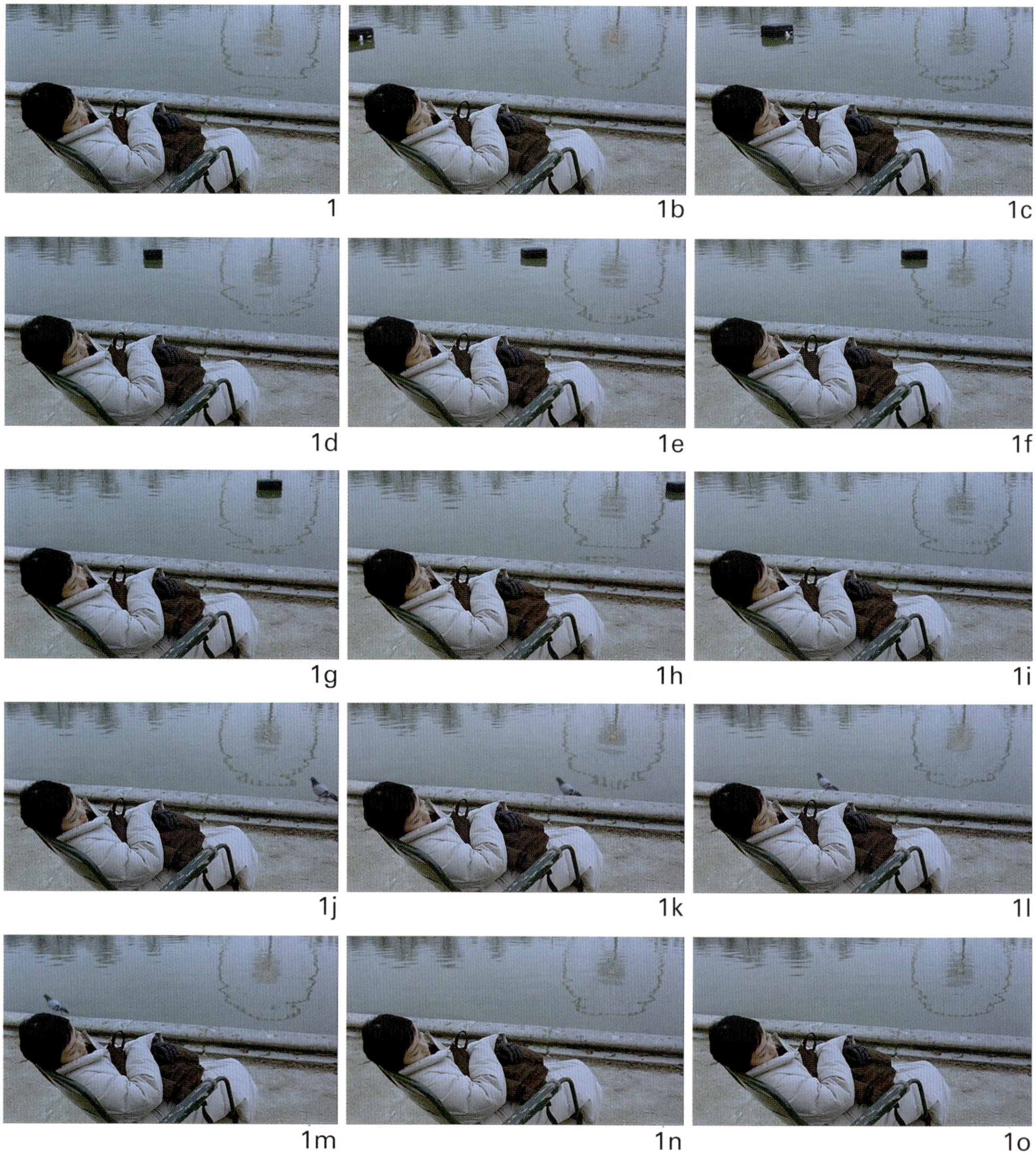

Dividing the space

A slightly slanted horizontal line divides the screen in the penultimate scene of Tsai Ming-Liang's *What Time Is It There?* The lovely Shiang-chyi, after persuading Hsaio Kang—a street vendor of watches—to sell the watch he's wearing (with two dials for two time zones), travels from Taipei to Paris. While Hsiao Kang treats their brief encounter as an oasis of relief, Shiang-chyi navigates the life of a foreigner in Paris. Exhausted by loneliness, she collapses in a chair next to the reflecting pool at the Place de la Concorde. Floating across the pool is her luggage, having been stolen and rifled through by a group of boys as she dozes.

The duration of the entire scene, the last in the film, is just over six minutes. This shot, the second in the scene, is an uninterrupted "long take" of one minute and twenty-one seconds. Its framing emphasizes the two dimensions of height and width: the horizontal line of the pool's edge marks the width of the frame, and the reflection of trees, a darkened blur along the upper rim of the frame, reinforces its height. Set against the wide patch of gray-blue, the luggage and Shiang-chyi's hair, each a vivid black, accentuate perspective and a modicum of depth. But there is no vanishing point. The camera's downward tilt eliminates this. And there is no horizon line, unless the raised border of the pool is seen as horizon, and the water seen as sky. There is only piece of luggage floating by and the squiggly ring around a circle of light reflecting the nearby Ferris wheel. The shape, size, and position of the wheel's reflection resembles a clock and formally balances the character, Shiang-chyi. Slowly, through this framed flatness of real time, the luggage drifts from screen left to screen right. And then after it has disappeared from view, as if reincarnated in another form, a pigeon walks the pool's rim right to left. And so it goes.

Discussion questions

1. In what particular ways do wide shots privilege mise en scene?
2. What are the considerations for mise en scene in a film with color photography? What specific considerations for mise en scene are required for black and white photography?
3. What is the difference between an establishing shot and a wide shot?

6

The long take

Every moviegoer riveted through the opening scene of Orson Welles' *Touch of Evil* knows the power of the **long take**. This, of course, refers to a shot's duration. Any shot that continues coverage for an extended period of time before transitioning with a cut, dissolve, or fade is considered a long take. The long take has been employed as a technique with great skill and invention since the beginning of cinema. As technical changes allowed for greater length in stock, filmmakers took advantage of duration as a means of sustaining continuous space and time.[1] Currently, digital technology has extended this length and revolutionized this limitation.[2]

In the most basic way, a cut acts as a call to renew the viewer's attention by way of a change in visual imagery. It is the most common means of transitioning from one shot to the next. It is also an efficient means for advancing the story with new information or re-orienting the viewer. Postponing the cut with a long take burdens the filmmaker with finding other means to captivate the viewer and advance the story.

Techniques

In early cinema, the prevailing strategy for advancing story and maintaining viewer attention during a long take involved **camera movement** across different **centers of action**. In chapter four, we discovered the way in which camera movement, regardless of shot duration, arouses anticipation, exciting the viewer's interest in what might be revealed as the image unspools. The long take exploits this effect with a camera tracking from one area of dramatic action to the next in continuous space and time. This strategy, established as convention, drives the opening 3:20 minute shot of *Touch of Evil*, which, through its athletic choreography, demonstrates the "gold standard" of the convention. Tracking forward, backward, diagonally, craning up, circling back, the camera's motion is constant as it covers the various story elements, each of which serves as a center of action: the bomb ticking, the bomb placed in a car, a couple riding in the car, a second couple walking alongside the car, the crossing at the border. Welles further animates the long take with variation in shot size: close-up, wide shot, extreme wide shot, and medium shot. Deployed as an arm of the narrative, the camera introduces the viewer to the particulars that become critical dramatic elements of the scene. All this occurs while arousing, minute-by-minute, suspense. When the cut comes, finally, at the end of the shot, we see what has just been heard: an explosion, providing horror and a strained relief to the uncertainty built up by the meandering long take.[3]

The camera movement in the opening shot also allows for changes in perspective. This approximates the effect of editing. The viewer's focus throughout the take is changing, shot to shot. But, unlike shots separated by a cut, the dramatic effect depends on keeping the viewer located in continuous proximity *with* the bomb. Once the bomb is planted in the convertible, the action occurs in real time, keeping the viewer inside the shot, increasing our investment in the outcome. The suspense intensifies when the second couple is introduced, portrayed in the film by movie stars Charlton Heston and Janet Leigh, signaling their value in the plot. They appear walking alongside the convertible toward the US/Mexico border. They stroll away from the car, and then appear next to it as they arrive at the checkpoint. This escalation gives the cut an even greater impact when it finally occurs, coinciding, as it does, with the explosion.[4]

Actualités

Even the one-minute movies by the Lumiere brothers might be considered long takes, given the continuous time and space of each shot. They exhausted the length of film stock available in the late 1800s when they were made.

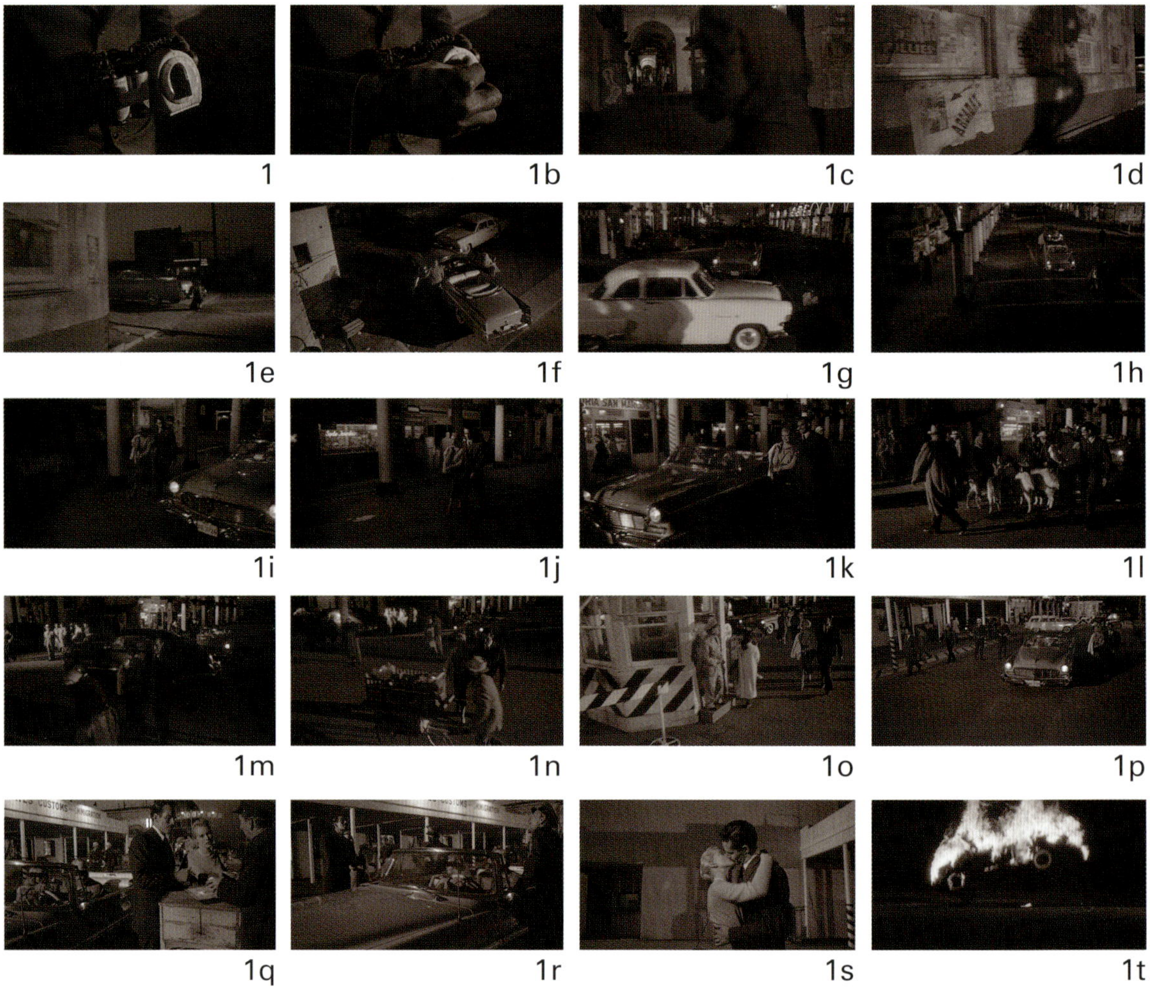

Figure 6.1
Touch of Evil (1958). Director: Orson Welles. Cinematographer: Russell Metty.

Staging action with an ensemble

For sure, staging different centers of action animates a long take to hold a viewer's interest. But a more substantial effect is in play. The smaller segments of dramatic action are unified through geography, adding influence to their relationship. Imagine, for example, a shot portraying a child on a swing. The camera pans to a nearby tree, behind which a man sharpens a knife. The living distance between these actions—swinging, sharpening—binds them in space *and* time, elevating their association and relevance to one another.

The films of Jean Renoir reveal his interest in the long take to unify various actions and/or characters. Working within the convention, nearly defining it, Renoir crafts different centers of action that he yokes through camera movement toward an added dimension of story. We've seen an example of this in the scene from *The Grand Illusion* analyzed in chapter four. Citing it here again, for fresh purpose, reveals the way in which the fourth shot in the sequence enacts a long take. This shot exploits time and space to create visual connection among a group of French officers bound together by fate in a German prisoner of war camp during World War I.

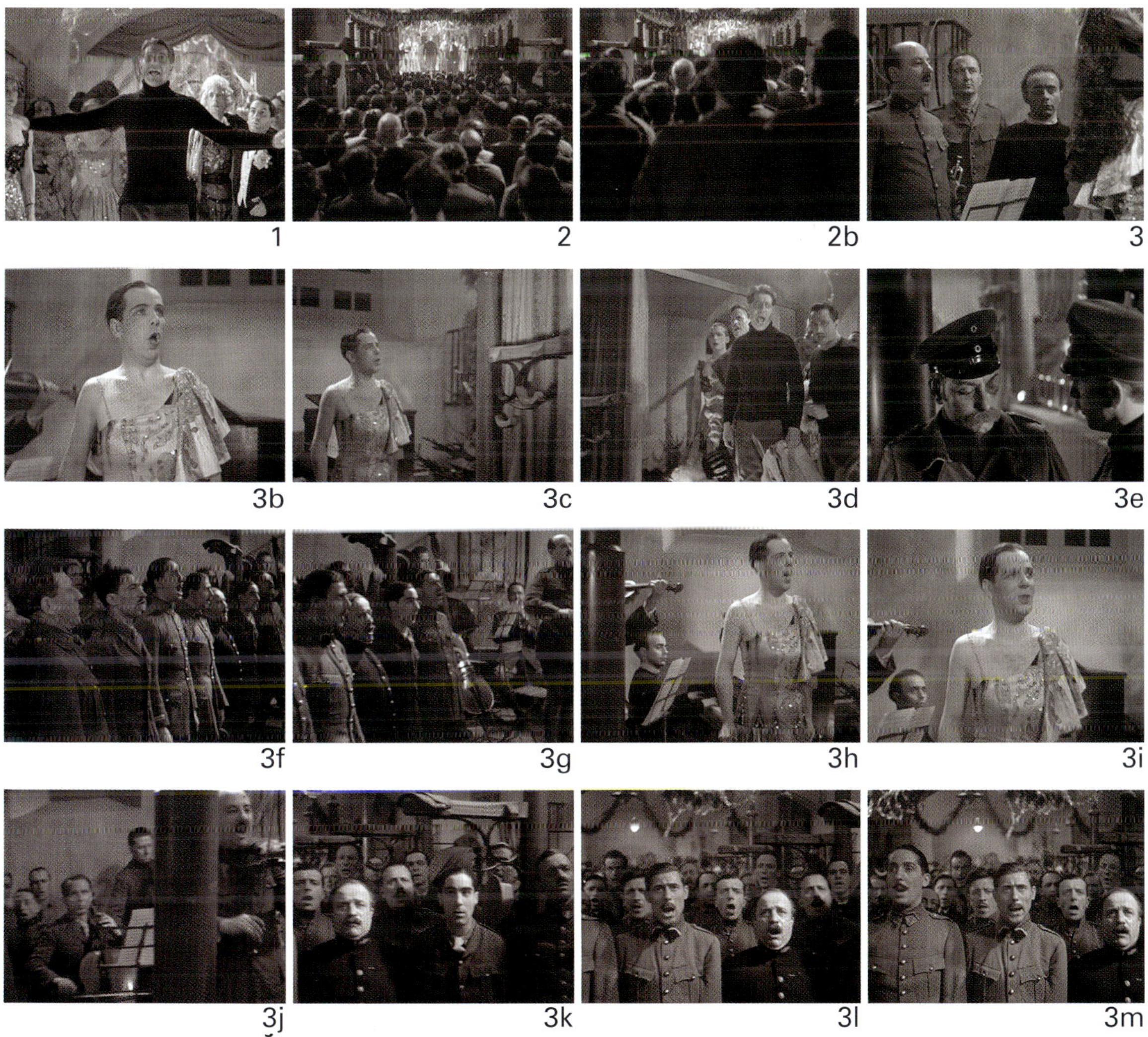

Figure 6.2
The Grand Illusion (1937).
Director:
Jean Renoir.
Cinematographer:
Christian Matras.

The prisoners have staged an evening of cabaret. If you remember, this is interrupted when the French prisoner, Lieutenant Maréchal, receives news of a French victory (Shot 1). A rousing version of the national anthem begins with one voice (Shot 4b), and swells to include all of the officers, onstage and in the audience. The camera movement in the single long take (Shots 4–4m) includes tilts, pans, counterclockwise and clockwise tracking, and stasis. The tracking across different "actions" reinforces character camaraderie, building association among them, while also excluding the German officers (Shot 4e). The camera pivots at just the moment it frames the German officers (Shot 4e), and turns away from them, giving emphasis to their exclusion before it rests on the group of "unnamed" soldiers singing "La Marseillaise." As mentioned in chapter four, a tracking shot such as this requires immense dexterity and a skilled camera operator. Claude Renoir, the director's nephew, operated the camera for this sequence.[5]

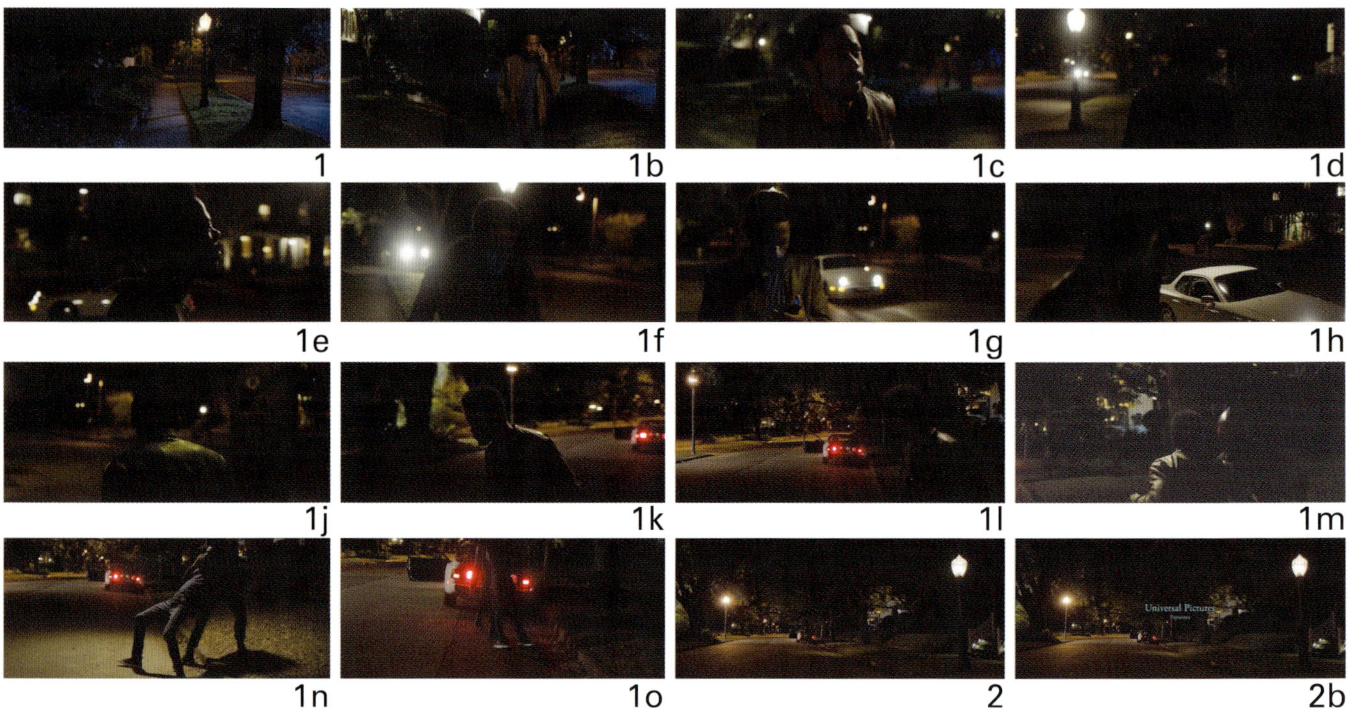

Figure 6.3
Get Out (2017). Director: Jordan Peele. Cinematographer: Toby Oliver.

Staging action with an individual

Action staged with camera movement in a long take for the purpose of unifying and/or separating elements within the frame continues to be a widely practiced technique. Eighty years after the release of *The Grand Illusion*, Jordan Peele in his debut feature film, *Get Out*, applies the technique to startling effect in the movie's opening. Working with cinematographer Toby Oliver—known for inventive treatments within the horror genre—the two apply this technique to a scene staged in upscale suburban America.

The one-take sequence acts as a prelude, a short film within the film. It does not include any of the main characters or locations that appear in the main body of the film. Nevertheless, it establishes atmosphere, providing a ready window into the film's tone.

The story is simple. A young black man has lost his way in a suburban neighborhood one night. He's on the phone with an intimate friend, complaining about the situation: "I feel like a sore thumb out here," he says, in what he calls a "creepy, confusing suburb." The only sounds are the random barking of a dog and the low hum of cicadas. After the call ends, he talks himself through the directions to his destination when a car passes by. The car turns around, and turns again, to follow him, sealing his fate.

As with the scene in *The Grand Illusion*, the long take in *Get Out* includes camera movement that varies in pace, direction, shot size, and angle. Managing this with a Steadicam has obvious advantages, but the choreography is equally impressive and thoughtful in its design toward specific effect. The desired effect is not a spirited camaraderie but suspense, dread, and horror, with a comedic tone.

The long take begins with a wide shot of an empty suburban sidewalk. We hear our character's voice, and then he enters, frame right. We learn quickly that he has lost his way and is uneasy in his surroundings. This is reinforced by the space around him that the wide shot affords, as the camera tracks backward keeping his pace. When the call ends, the camera stops, pivots, and then follows him from behind. This allows for a view of an approaching car.

As the car passes him, the camera pivots again, (Figure 6.3, Shot 1c) into a wide shot (Figure 6.3, Shot 1d), following our character, frame left in close-up as the car's action fills the right side of the frame. Through this strategic movement and reframing, the viewer knows *before* our pedestrian that the car has turned around and travels back toward him.[6] When our character eventually notices the car inching along the road beside him, he makes an about face and walks briskly in the opposite direction. "Not today, not me," he mutters to himself.

The camera tracks the character's movement, while also affording the viewer the benefit of a wide shot, which reveals the car pulled over by the curb, door open. When the camera pans again with our character, it opens the frame to the right, where the attacker enters, lunging toward him. The worst happens. The score plays "Run, Rabbit, Run" as his body is dragged to the trunk of the car. The shot ends with a cut to an extreme wide shot of the perpetrator loading him into the trunk. The credit sequence begins.

Running the scene in continuous time eliminates the possibility of any action occurring during gaps in the visual record. This is both reassuring and, under the particular narrative circumstance, harrowing. But the real suspense and horror are ratcheted up through continuous space. In frames devoted to our character, we, as viewers, see only what surrounds him. When a threat enters the space (a hovering car), we are lulled into omniscience, which makes the ferocious attack from the sidelines more sensational. We, unlike him, did not see it coming.

> (In *Get Out*,) the warmth in the imagery at the estate was intended as a bit of a visual false security in a way, but of course there is something very strange under the surface. I also played with color in the night scenes both inside and outside the house, using special lighting gels and camera settings to bring a range of cyan, greenish and aqua tones into the 'moonlight' and ambiance rather than a straight up 'blue' vs 'warm' feel.
>
> —Toby Oliver, *American Cinematographer*, May 5, 2017.

Continuous space

Working in continuous space and time becomes an essential storytelling asset for the Hungarian director, Miklós Jancsó. He deploys long takes throughout his 1967 film, *The Red and The White* and does so with athleticism. Set in 1919 Russia during the outbreak of civil war after the Revolution, *The Red and The White* charts skirmishes between Red soldiers and the counter-revolutionary Whites that culminate in a massacre. Photographed by Tamas Somlo, the cinemascope frame widens the location—a hillside landscape along the Volga River that runs through Central Russia.

From the beginning of the film, Jancsó establishes a pattern of organizing long, fluid camera movement episodically. If we look closely at the occasions for the use of long takes, certain patterns emerge. First, the takes grow longer as the film progresses, with the longest (nearly six minutes) occurring toward the movie's end. Second, each of the long takes covers an exterior sequence of confrontation that builds to a chase or killing. Third, each sequence will reveal a character in close-up (often at the beginning or end of the take), widening to a long shot featuring groups of characters against a vast, unyielding landscape. The **variation of shot size** is not surprising given the need to hold our attention for the duration of the take. But what is startling is the elegance of the compositions: as the camera continues it's motion, each pause in framing offers pictorial loveliness, a strategy for demonstrating authority without the emphasis of a cut.

The most chilling effect occurs by staging wartime confrontations in the uninterrupted time and continuous space allowed by the long take. The White Shirts are ordered on foot to the Volga River, then away from the river, and then back into the river where they are executed. Here is an example.

The still frames in Figure 6.4 include the first four shots of the film. The first three shots are of short duration. I include them to show the careful crafting of the opening sequence, particularly in terms of graphic compositions. The first shot, static and frontal, depicts men on horseback in the distance riding over a hill toward the camera. The second follows action (men on horseback) from right to left. The third pans left to right (also men on horseback). Then the long take begins (Shot 4a): a close-up of a man holding a rifle. He darts into the center of the frame where he stops and fires his rifle. The camera follows him, (tracking alongside a fence) toward the river, then into the river and crossing the river until in the distance, men on horseback are seen galloping in his direction. He turns back, traipsing through knee-high water to the riverbank and ducks behind the brush (Shots 4g and 4h). The camera tilts up to focus on another man in the hills across the river, running from the horsemen toward the river. "Get in the river," one of the armed horsemen shouts. He is ushered at gunpoint through the river and then along the fence (the camera tracking beside them). At the end of the fence, they stop. One dismounts and asks, "What are you? Georgian? Armenian?" he camera dollies toward them. "Hungarian," the man tells him. Back to the river they go (Shots 4t and 4u), the camera tracking again alongside them. The man is shot (Shot 4v). The soldier returns, mounts his horse, rides toward the river, then away from the river, galloping out of frame, the camera following his direction (Shot 4y). At this point, the camera returns focus to the man hiding in the river brush. He stands, emerging from the brush and moves into the river, again, walking upstream, obscured somewhat by the overgrowth, as the shot ends.[7]

It's difficult to replicate the to-ing and fro-ing in still frames. But we can at least see a blueprint of the blocking and staging. Looking closely, you can sense the effect of rendering the action in real time and continuous space rather than through a series of cuts. At the very least, we're aware from the shot's beginning of the soldier hiding in the bushes, still in our field of view, as other men are killed. The choreography of men ushered to and fro in what seems like a kinetic version of military folly sets a tone that will be unwavering throughout the film.

The pattern of camera and figure movement continues as the story unfolds, as we invest in the fate of certain members of the White Brigade. The pattern repeats right up until the final scene when, at a moment of climax, the staging varies. The action no longer occurs in alternating screen directions, to and fro. Instead the White Shirts march away from a camera that is, like the first shot, static and frontal. The men in Red, off-screen, fire their rifles. In the distance, the White Shirts collapse, disappearing into the tall grasses that grow beyond the river's edge.

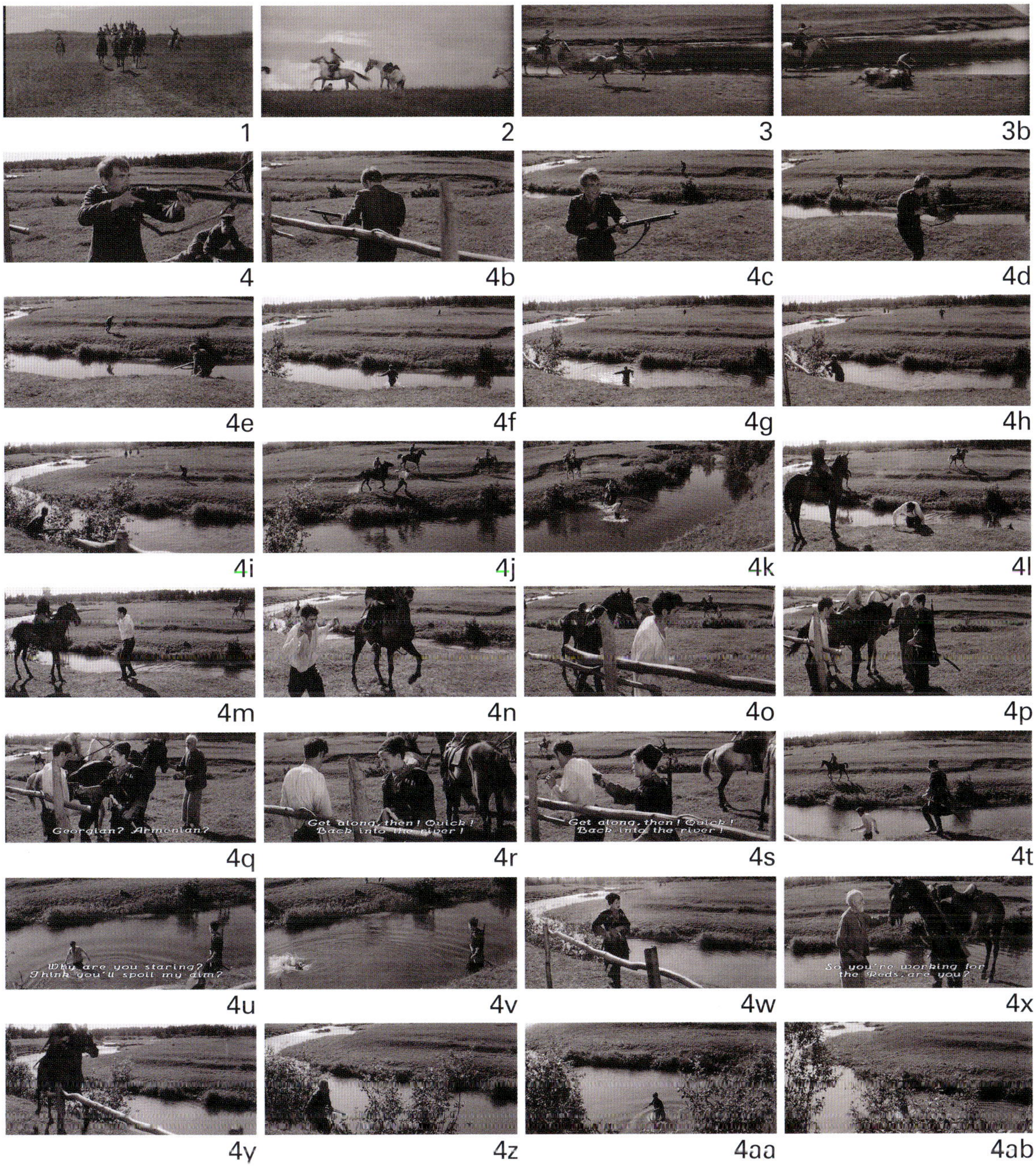

Figure 6.4 *The Red and The White* (1967). Director: Miklós Jancsó. Cinematographer: Tamás Somló.

Continuous time

The conventional application of the long take—breaking action into smaller segments, shots of varied size and focal length—is strategically revised in the film of Bela Tarr, a contemporary Hungarian director, in *Werckmeister Harmonies*. Filmed in black and white, the movie uses the long take to relay sequences in real time. But these are not so much centers of action as recorded activity, the daily tasks of living, uninterrupted by the cut. The effect is to keep the viewer weighted in moment-to-moment life. The life most often viewed is that of Janos, witness and caretaker, in a small town on the Hungarian plains. The town awaits the arrival of a circus, including a large trailer that parks in the town center holding the stuffed carcass of a whale. The anticipation of the event stirs tensions among the townspeople leading to acts of chaos and political upheaval. Steady in this storm is Janos, whose innocence becomes a measure for the strife that emerges.

Included here are the frames from two consecutive scenes shot in one take. In the first, Janos makes his way on foot from a local tavern to the home of the aging Gyorgy Eszter, a musicologist for whom he provides care and assistance. It is night. The street is lit in patches. Janos, in silhouette, walks through the alternating fields of dark and light toward the camera. At the outset he is positioned slightly above the frame's center. The camera slowly, imperceptibly at first, moves farther and farther away from him as he continues to walk toward it, the pace of camera more rapid than the pace of Janos' stride. As a consequence, Janos diminishes in size as the horizon line rises to the upper portion of the frame. By the end of the long take, the frame is filled with darkness but for a tiny figure in silhouette, staged against a thinning field of light. The take endures for one minute and fifteen seconds of time. There is also score, melodic and haunting. We can see that the shot is as much a visual ode to figure, darkness, and light as it is a record of a man walking on a street.

The second scene, also a long take, will last for six minutes and twenty-two seconds. Here, Janos arrives at his uncle's home to go through the ritual of helping him to bed and closing his house for the night. Any impatience on our part to hurry toward dramatic charge is met with fastidiousness in the visual account of nightly tasks carried out by Janos. The shot begins and ends with window light (Figure 6.6, Shots 1 and 1ad). Variation in shot size occurs during the long take, enlivening it, but the camera's fundamental attitude is one of watchfulness. Its movement, while inspired by figure movement, is not slave to it. Look, for example, at Shots 1s–1t. Janos goes into the bathroom to complete another mundane task and the camera follows him but then moves in on him, as if to more closely inspect his activity. In *Werckmeister Harmonies* the long take serves as an effective technique for exalting the simplest of human activities: walking, lighting a water heater, drawing the curtains, turning off lights. He accomplishes these tasks without complaint. Any weariness on our part in witnessing the ritual in real time only casts his spirit of kindness in greater relief.

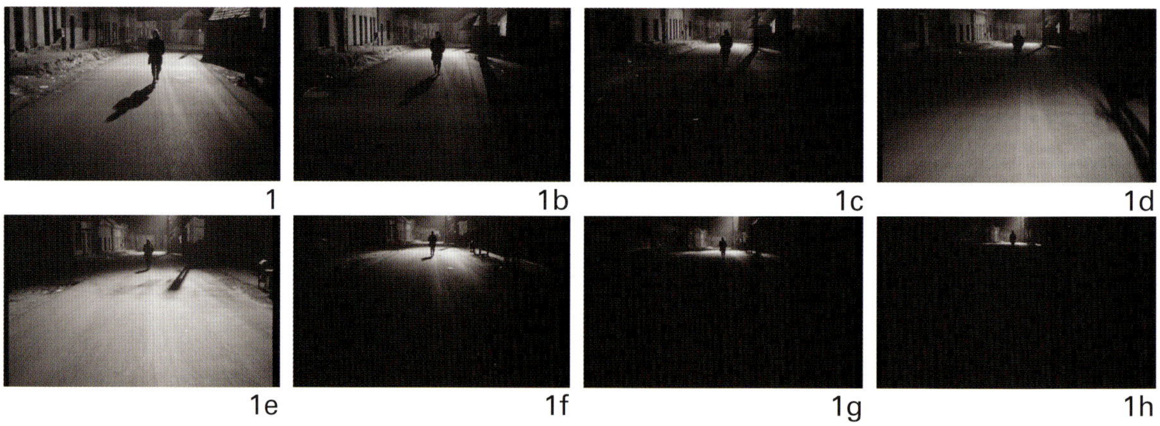

Figure 6.5 *Werckmeister Harmonies* (2000). Director Bela Tarr. Cinematographers: Gábor Medvigy, Rob Tregenza, Patrick de Ranter, Miklós Gurbán, Emil Novák, Erwin Lanzensberger.

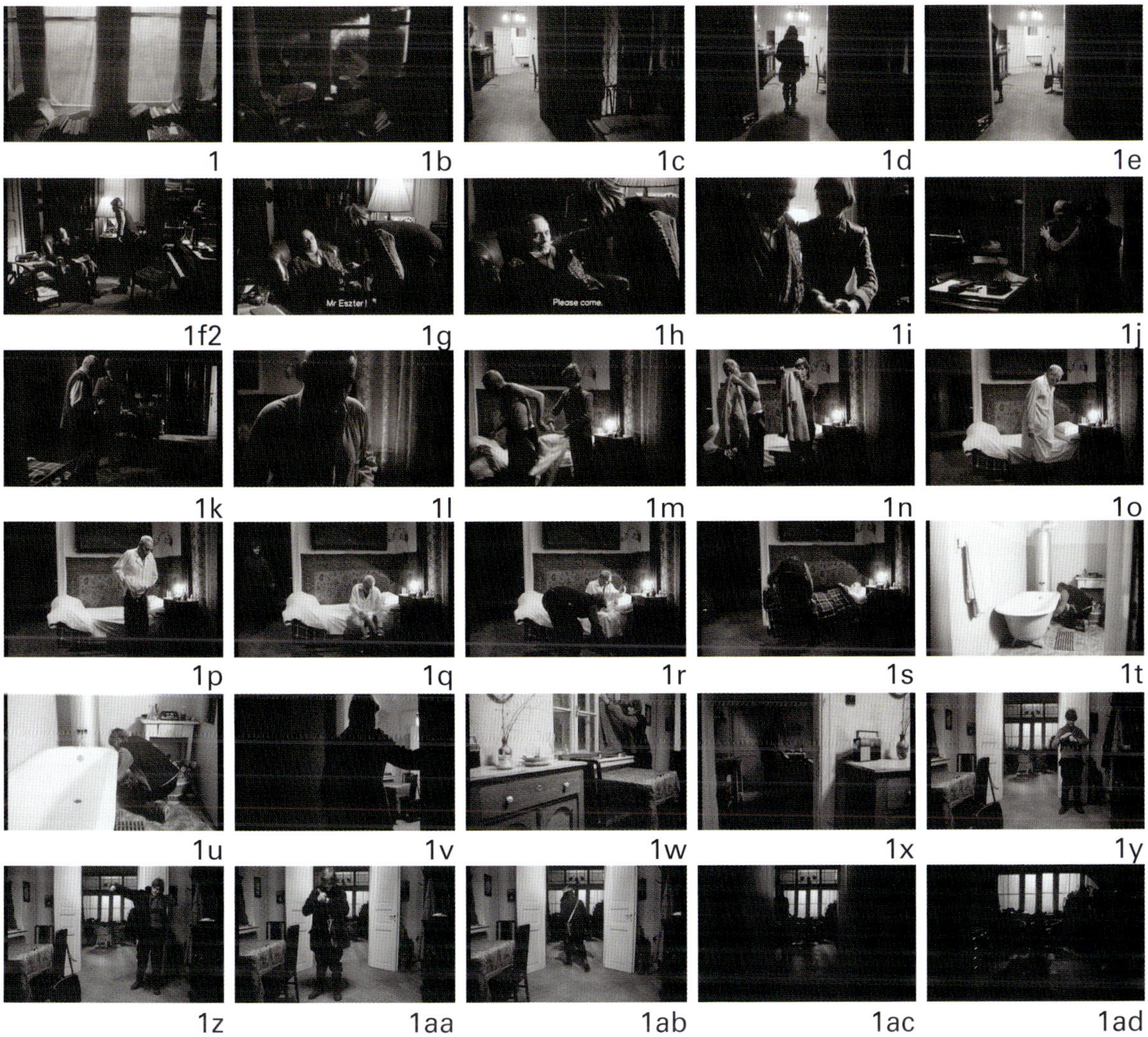

Figure 6.6 *Werckmeister Harmonies* (2000). Director: Bela Tarr. Cinematographers: Gábor Medvigy, Rob Tregenza, Patrick de Ranter, Miklós Gurbán, Emil Novák, Erwin Lanzensberger.

Continuous space and time

Gus Van Sant's regard for the films of Bela Tarr is part of written record.[8] This record is no more convincing than the movies made by Van Sant since 2002. Whereas *The Red and the White* by Jancsó depends on the long take to yoke various actions in time and space, Tarr and Van Sant use the long take as an extension of time and an expansion of space for purposes of ritual and inclusion. In *Elephant*, Van Sant uses the technique to enhance the monotony of incidental moments, which a narrative interest in conflict or dramatic intensity might overlook. Set against impending violence, these quiet, more casual moments arouse our sense of anticipation and dread.

Elephant takes place on an ordinary day in an American high school with students going about their customary habits: class work, lunch break, sports practice, hallway exchanges, extracurricular activities. Everywhere they are taking their time, oblivious to the imminent threat cooked up for them by two of their classmates. The long take reinforces their naiveté and conspires in accumulating succession—long take after long take—to give value to these casual occurrences as the stuff of life, or certainly the stuff of young lives on the cusp of a future with promise and possibility.

If you know the movie, you've seen the overall strategy: the camera follows a particular character for a given stretch of time. Occasionally, the camera will begin with one character and then, as two characters meet, continue with the second one. The film does not progress chronologically but doubles back on itself. This kind of structure asserts an interest in our observing the whereabouts and activities of each member of a select cast of students during the few hours leading up to the snipers' attack. In some instances, this will mean that we view the same exchange or incident more than once from a different point of view.

In the scene depicted, Eli makes his way down a long hall, the camera in front of him, keeping pace. Michelle, the figure in red, walks at the same pace but much further back in the frame. This gives the image depth already suggested by the four windows of light at the end of the hall. Eli's procession is interrupted by an off-screen voice, "Hey, Eli." The camera continues gliding back further to frame Eli as he stops to greet John. The camera remains static as the class bell rings. In the distance, Michelle runs past as Eli snaps a photograph of John. The two shake hands again, and Eli continues, stepping out of frame as the camera resumes its movement, now with John, following him from behind at a distance, which diminishes in increments for the remaining one minute seventeen seconds of the shot.

John will walk down the long hall, make a right turn, walk down another hall, make another right turn, and exit the building, the camera trailing. Once outside, he will have his moment with the dog, and greet the two boys toting their munitions, the camera still trailing. "Hey what are you guys doing?" he asks. "Get out of here and don't come back," they tell him as they head toward the building's entrance. The camera stops as John turns, "What are you doing?" he asks again, facing the camera, now, in close-up. In this rendering, the close-up becomes a form of dramatic action. It punctuates a long traveling shot in which the deliberate distance between camera and character erodes imperceptibly until John turns into his close-up at the exterior of the building. The viewer's sensory pleasure, accommodated by choices of casting (John's hair, eyes, cheeks, lips) and costuming (bright yellow T-shirt to match his hair), counters the disturbance registered by John's reaction, cued and reinforced by the camera's tight frame. Withholding conflict or rising action until the last five seconds of the shot electrifies the meeting—two student snipers walk past John as the camera frames him in close-up.

Elephant challenges the conventional application of the long take. Technically, the two-minute shot is broken into segments: Eli walking, Eli and John together, John walking, John greeting the dog, John outdoors, and John addressing the snipers—his classmates. With the

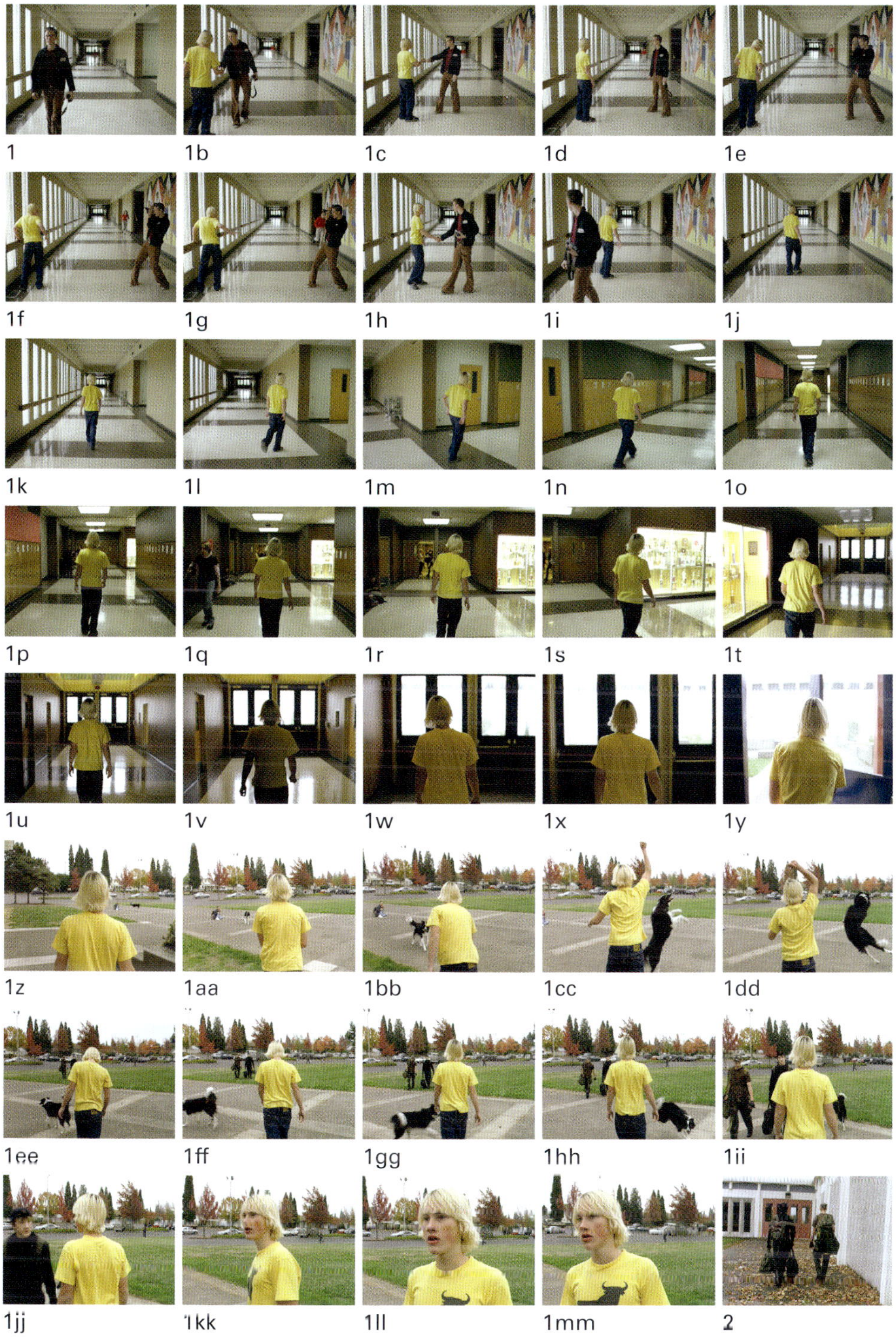

Figure 6.7
Elephant (2003). Director: Gus Van Sant. Cinematographer: Harris Savides.

exception of the command by one of the snipers," and possibly the exchange between John and Eli that begins the take, the segments are less divisions of action than activities. The long take is also constructed with varied shot size, beginning, as it does, with a wide shot and ending with a close-up. The variation in framing, a gradual adjustment, is potentially unnoticed until the final seconds of the shot when John turns into his close-up. The shot develops, no question. But the languorous coverage emphasizes the shot's seamlessness and gives value to the simple acts of greetings (bookending the shot) and walking, luxuries in light of the imminent alternative.

Field and ground

Our preoccupation in this book has been the narrative feature film. One exception seems worthy of our attention, particularly as it pertains to the long take. A music video directed by Michel Gondry demonstrates ingenious application of the long-take conventions: a moving camera over various centers of action. Gondry, an award-winning narrative feature filmmaker, secured his training as a director in the world of music videos, and a playful preoccupation with fantasy and deeply saturated primary colors mark even his earliest work. His technical skills include a capacity to stitch together fantasy and reality, and to do so in ways that endow the concocted world with absolute authenticity. Much of his work demonstrates a perseverance and exactitude in using the camera as a tool in service of a stylized vision, often invoking the lively dreamscape of a child. *Protection* is an accomplished music video (produced for Massive Attack) that consists of one long six and a half minute take, a sizeable cast, and complex set design. It also required construction and coordination of elements to achieve a number of staged optical effects.

The narrative material unfolds simply: a man comes to an apartment building on a rainy night with his daughter (presumably) to leave her with a woman who lives in the building. While this "drop off" occurs, the camera, like a benign voyeur, surveys and occasionally enters the rooms of various tenants including the apartment occupied by Tracy Thorn, who sings to the camera in her kitchen (and later from her TV room) (Shots 1m–1o). Toward the end of the six and a half minutes, the child is seen in one of the window tableaus standing on a chair as a woman beckons her to sit at the kitchen table for dinner (Shots 1ss–1uu). The video ends with the father in the elevator, descending, walking out into the rainy night, the child's car seat empty as he drives away.

The twelve window tableaus, each a thoroughly constructed set piece, represent twelve different "stories" and work to meet the demand of the long take for shifting perspective through camera movement and enlivening action episodically. Added to this is the pleasure of minute-to-minute surprise. The "real" time alluded to by the continuous take, for example, includes an ellipses. As the camera pictures the father and daughter (in the elevator), it moves to the right "through" a corrugated opening in the wall to reveal the father and daughter walking down the hall. (At one moment the frame depicts the father's feet rising in the elevator even as we see him walking down the hall (Shot 1h).) Other than this "jump," the fluid camera reads as continuous time.

The treatment of space is also arresting and provocative. The camera, seemingly aimless or offhanded, moves up and down, in and out, left and right, even diagonally—skating across the façade of the building, surveying the inhabitants through the twelve window tableaus, returning intermittently to Tracy Thorn singing. The long continuous take serves to unite these characters and their individual "stories" as part of one world. The specificity of props and activities renders each character unique, and the world they form collectively gains authority.

But the world goes awry: a man floats in his apartment, a baby crawls upside down in a kitchen cubicle. From the outset we experience dissonance. Something is off, but it is difficult to pinpoint exactly what it might be. The set, in fact, is actually six stories, but long rather than tall, resting flat against ground—the construction, with its compartments built on a sound stage, the camera hovering above it. The characters in most instances *are* lying against a wall (gravity) in positions and amidst props and set pieces that give the illusion of uprightness. (Tracy Thorn, for example, sings lying down). Mirrors also serve the construction (i.e., the exterior shot of "nearby" buildings, the upside down, crawling baby—never mind the camera's capacity to travel through walls from room to room or the color of the façade changing from lavender to grey to green, or the airplane flying at such close proximity outdoors). Such is the visual playing field of Michel Gondry, who, while adhering to the long-take conventions, uses the camera to rewrite the physical laws of the known world.

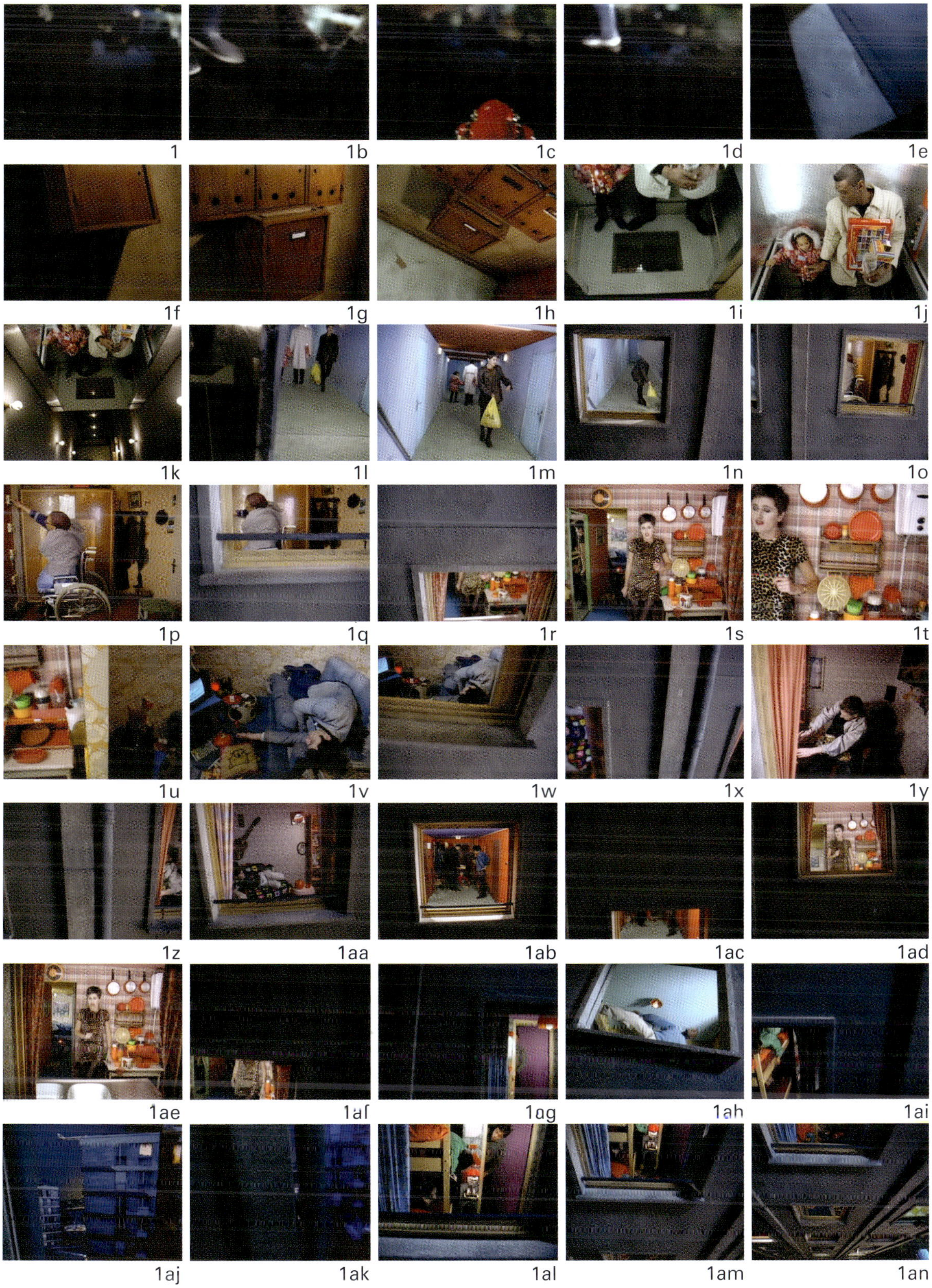

Figure 6.8 *Massive Attack: Protection* (1995). Director: Michel Gondry. Cinematographer: Tim Maurice-Jones.

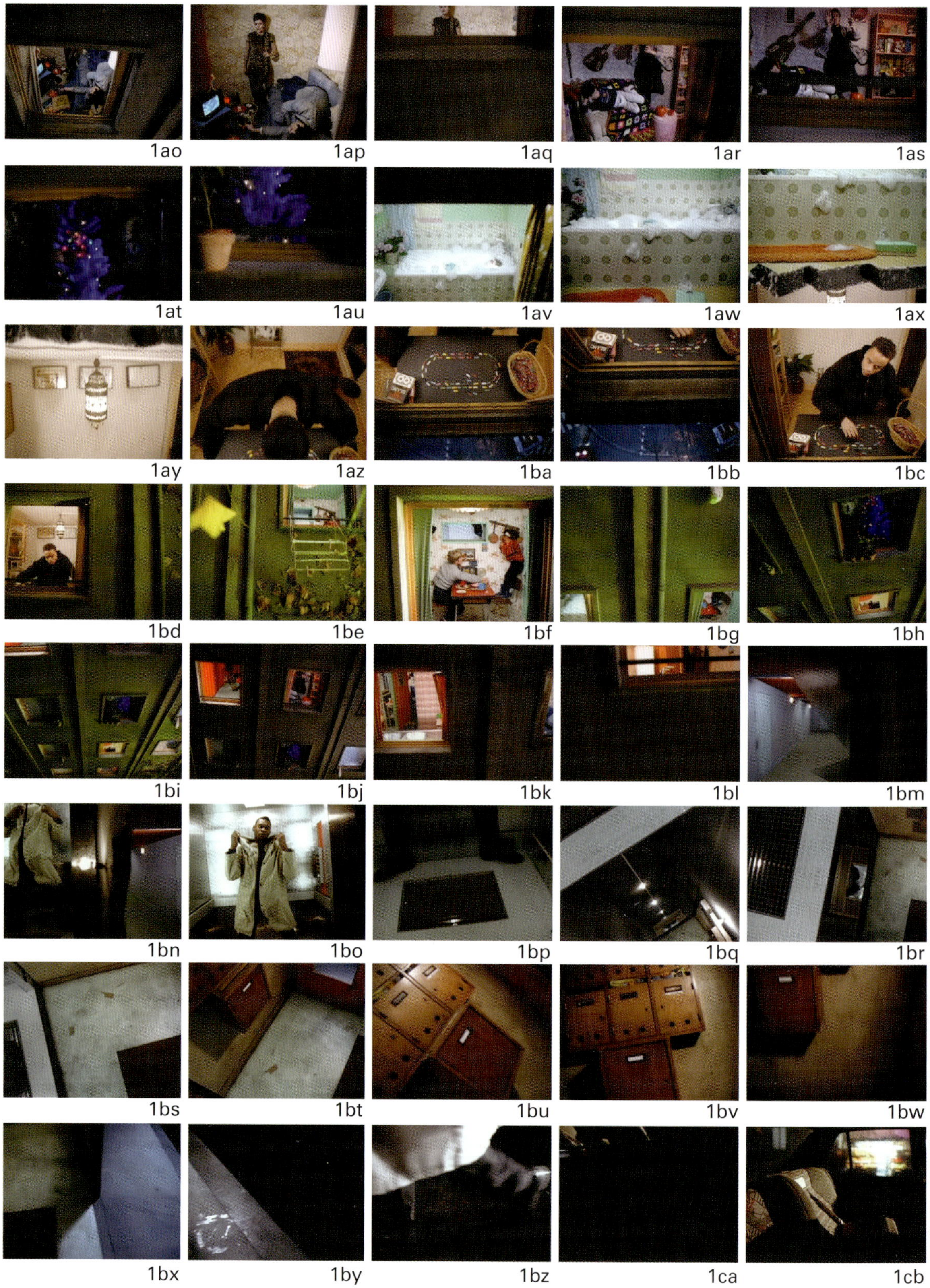

Figure 6.9 *Massive Attack: Protection* (1995). Director: Michel Gondry. Cinematographer: Tim Maurice-Jones.

Stasis

We've already seen, in the last two examples, effective use of the long take with character activity replacing centers of action. In *Werckmeister Harmonies* and *Elephant* the camera tracks the movement of characters from place to place, slowing the pace toward a close observation of the present and an unknown "future" to come.

A number of recent films push the limits of the long take even further by using a static camera. Entrapping the viewer in one place for a long stretch of time places a particular burden on the shot and/or scene, as well as the pace of dramatic progression. Directors Roy Andersson and Tsai Ming-Liang manage this burden with carefully crafted mise en scene, playful interactions, and the narrative principle of surprise. Included here, for our discussion, are several examples of long takes with a static camera, staged in varying shot sizes (medium, wide, and close-up), each crafted to yield a very different effect. If camera movement by its very nature excites anticipation of what is to come, the combination of a long take with a static camera makes a claim for the present.

The present is complicated for Otilia, a university student in Cristian Mungiu's film, *4 Months, 3 Weeks, 2 Days*, set in 1987 Romania. Otilia has been asked to help her naïve and self-involved roommate, Gabita, arrange an abortion, illegal in Romania at the time under an abortion law, Decree 770 enacted by Communist dictator President Ceausescu to reverse the country's low birth rate.

Otilia organizes a meeting in a hotel with the hired abortionist, who is stunned to discover the advanced stage of Gabita's pregnancy. Short of the exact amount of cash, other transactions are demanded to compensate, which compromises Otilia. In the midst of this trying experience, Otilia is obliged to leave Gabita to fulfill a promise to Adi, her boyfriend, who requests her presence at his mother's birthday dinner in the family home. Adi knows nothing about Gabita's abortion, and further burdens Otilia with his own self-interests. The single long take pictured in Figure 6.10 serves as the center of the sequence in which Otilia visits Adi's home.

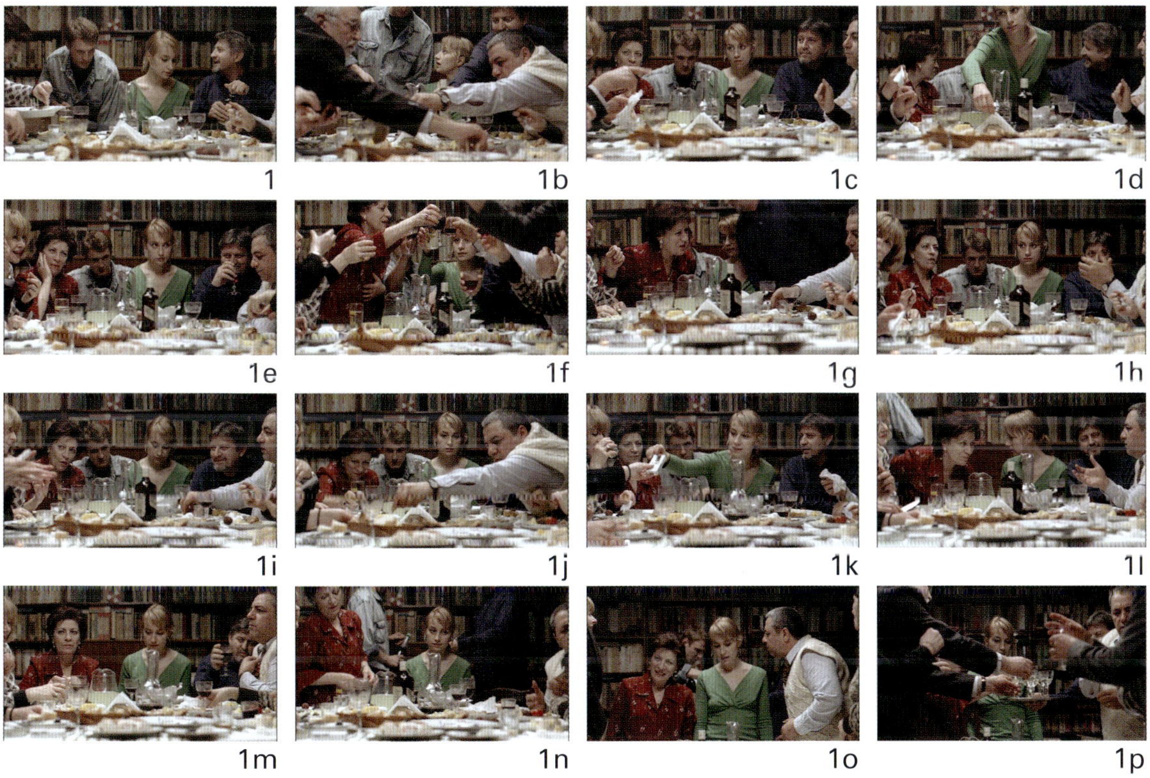

Figure 6.10 *4 Months, 3 Weeks, 2 Days* (2007). Director: Cristian Mungi. Cinematographer: Oleg Mutu.

The dramatic effect depends, in part, on Otilia's state of mind when she arrives. After securing cash for the abortion and providing additional compensation demanded by the abortionist, she's in no mood for a birthday party. Never mind what has been all day Gabita's laissez-faire attitude, and now, Adi's sense of entitlement.

Otilia sits sandwiched between her boyfriend, Adi, and his father, positioned in the center of the frame. This does not protect her from being upstaged several times during the take when the arms of guests reach across the table in front of her, obscuring our view. Class differences between Otilia and Adi come to light through dialogue, unsettling Otilia further. "Simple folk often have a better sense than the educated," one of the guests will say after Otilia reports her father is a soldier. Other slights take place, as when a guest chastises her for smoking in front of Adi's parents as she reaches to light a cigarette. Otilia persists in suffering the accumulated slights with restraint, while we, the viewer, are locked by the static camera in her experience, desperate for release. Her discomfort and the obliviousness of the others becomes our burden. Like her, we cannot forget Gabita, who Otilia has been unable to reach by telephone, or any of the other sufferings brought on by the day.

Stasis and distance

In the previous chapter we explored advantages of the wide shot in emphasizing environment and encouraging dynamics between character and environment. What happens to the dynamic when a static camera of a wide shot is sustained on screen in a long take? What is required of the film to compensate for the combination of distance and duration in a medium that depends on motion? The following four films give insight into the effects of this combination of techniques and demonstrate the close tether to story and tone achieved by their application. The psychological thriller *Cachë* uses the long take of a wide shot to hide fateful story information and in *A Ghost Story*, the techniques serve the movie's thematic intent as a meditation on loss. Mise en scene adds dimension to an extreme wide shot covered in a long take that conveys the resolution of a love story in *Through the Olive Trees*, and *Certain Women*, a trilogy set in the American Northwest, takes advantage of this same strategy to sear into the viewer's mind the particulars of place.

Stasis and wide shot

Static wide shots of significant duration begin and end *Caché*, a movie set in France where the film's title "caché" translates as "hidden." The two long takes function as a pair, interacting with one another. The first pictures a residential street of apartments, viewed from a cross street (Figure 6.11), assumed to be an establishing shot, locating the film in the present tense. As a wide shot it invites the viewer to scan the frame for meaningful action or activity. And yet, in the first minutes, none seems to occur. Frustrating viewer expectation through manipulations of technique is one means that *Caché* employs to unsettle the audience, keeping viewers on alert. At some point, minutes into the shot, we hear voices. Through dialogue we discover that the image is a recording. We learn soon after that a videotape has been sent to the protagonist, showing this: his apartment exterior on the street where he, and his wife and son, live. The unspoken message: someone's watching you. So begins the thriller.

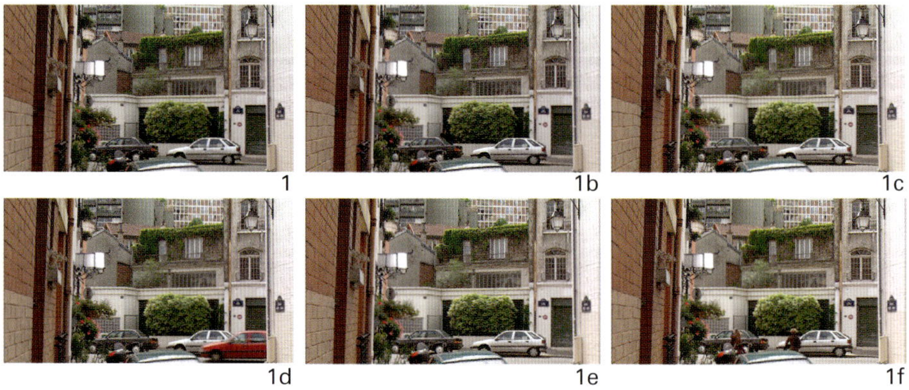

Figure 6.11
Caché (2005).
Director:
Michael Haneke.
Cinematographer:
Christian Berger.

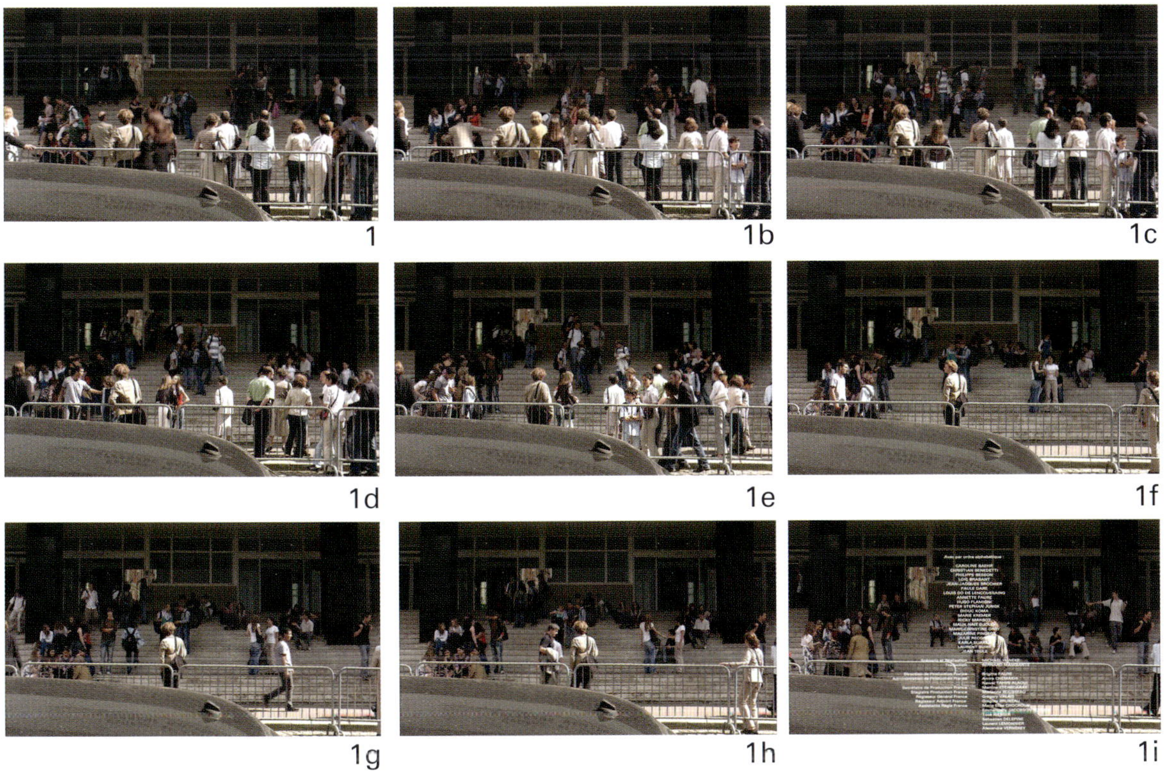

Figure 6.12 *Caché* (2005). Director: Michael Haneke. Cinematographer: Christian Berger.

When at the end of the film, the camera stalls again in a wide static shot; we are in front of the school attended by our protagonist's eight-year-old son. The scene outside the school is livelier, the frame more crowded with people and activity. Here, at the movie's end, we know to survey warily the six-minute shot, looking for a sign of reassurance or foreboding. It appears, eventually, hidden in the shot, for even the most fastidious observer to miss.

David Lowry's low-budget feature, *A Ghost Story*, makes repeated use of long takes to create atmosphere, and to lure the viewer into a world in which pathos is elevated above action or activity.[9] For the most part, the long takes occur as wide shots, staging character(s) against environment in dramatic and evocative ways. This is certainly true in the scene depicted in Figure 6.13. It occurs at a critical point in the story, thirteen minutes into the film.

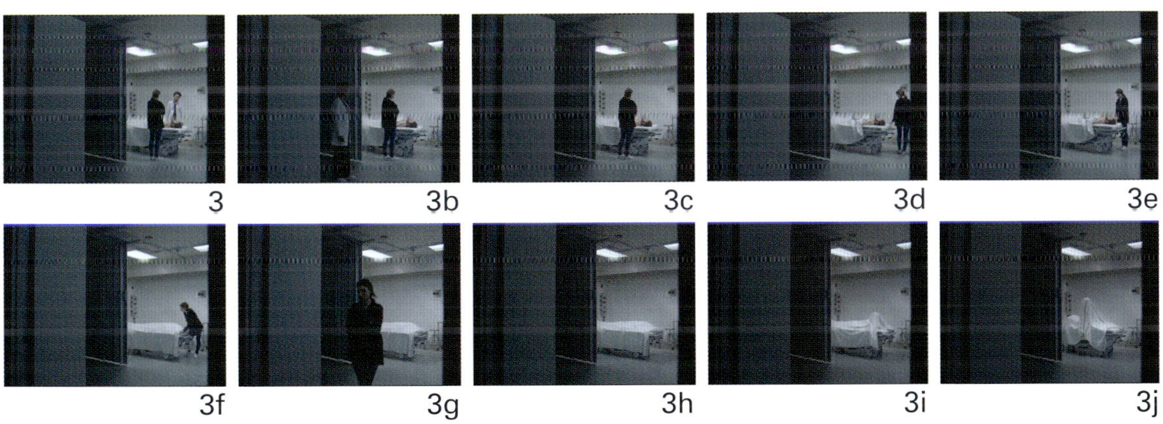

Figure 6.13 *A Ghost Story* (2017). Director: David Lowery. Cinematographer: Andrew Droz Palermo.

The scene is covered in a wide shot, a single long take of three and a half minutes. *A Ghost Story* explores the relationship between a married couple, M. and C., before and after C. is tragically killed in an automobile accident. In the scene, M. is shown her husband's body by a hospital nurse who then leaves M. alone with his corpse. Intimacy between the couple has been established in the film's earlier scenes, inspiring the viewer to watch closely as M. studies her husband's face. Her physical actions are spare: she walks to the other side of the gurney, pulls the sheet up over her husband's body, covering his face, and exits the room. This is accomplished in one and a half minutes, leaving the viewer to gape for another full minute at a static wide shot of a covered corpse in a room in which nothing happens. The prevailing stillness in the frame witnessed in real time escalates the effect when suddenly an action occurs. The corpse rises, taking on his new persona as a ghost, while the wide shot preserves the viewer's status as an unobtrusive voyeur.

Stasis and extreme wide shot

The natural world is the backdrop for Abbas Kiarostami's 1994 film, *Through the Olive Trees*, though it is a landscape devastated by earthquake in Northern Iran. The village is Koker, and a film crew has come to make a fiction movie, casting locals for several of the film's main roles. It is through this casting that Hossein, a local stone mason, meets Tahareh, who plays his wife in the film within the film. Hossein becomes infatuated with Tahareh, who lives with her grandmother, having been orphaned by the quake. Tahareh is schooled and literate. Hossein is not and this disadvantages him when he implores the grandmother repeatedly to allow him to marry Tahareh—her response, emphatically, "NO." Much of the film is devoted to Hossein's pursuit of Tahareh as he takes advantage of their time together on set to recite to her his worthwhile qualities. She will not speak to him, other than lines she must deliver in the role of his wife. When the production ends, Hossein is frantic to restate his case as to why she should marry him despite their differences in background. He follows her from the set through the countryside for some distance making his claims. Tahareh, in front of him, goes over a rise, disappearing from view. Hossein stands at the top of the rise, which drops into a grove of olive trees, weighing his options (Figure 6.12, Shot 1). And then the long take begins.

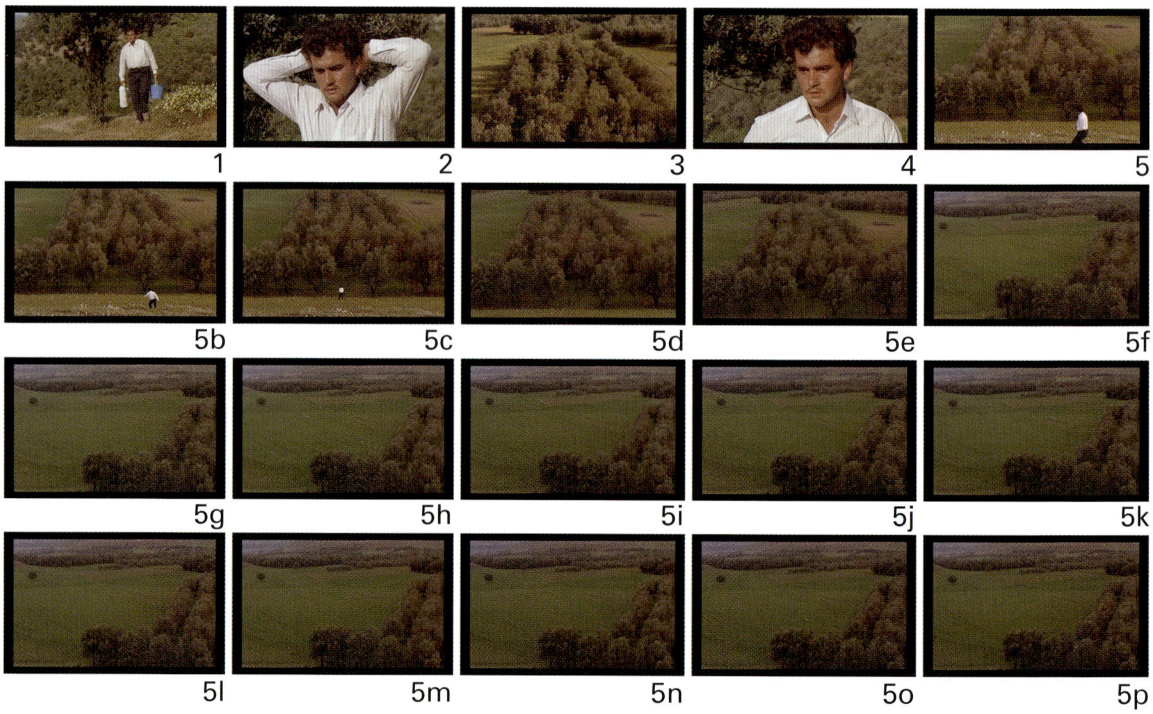

Figure 6.14 *Through the Olive Trees* (1994). Director: Abbas Kiarostami. Cinematographers: Hossein Jafarian and Farhad Saba.

The film offers a considerable number of long takes, making use of the technique to lace the film with comedy but also to quiet the need for more energetic forward movement of plot so that the subtle exchanges between and among characters might resound more deeply. The tedium and struggle of the locals in this aftermath becomes felt and lived-in through the patient camera. In the instance of this last shot of the film, Kiarostami manages to use the long take expressly for dramatic purpose—meaning without which he would have no ending.

Hossein makes the decision to continue to follow Tahareh over the rise and down a hill toward a grove of olive trees that open into large field. The camera, which has tracked their movements with handheld coverage since they left the film set, stops now, at the top of the rise, leaving Hossein to chase Tahareh on his own. The camera remains static in the extreme wide shot as the chase scene continues to unfold. Very soon, Hossein and Tahareh become white specks on a vast landscape of green. She is going home. He is zigzagging a path behind her. The last audible words we hear from him are in the close-up before he takes off down a hill after her and the camera washes them in green, and once more he pleas with her to marry him, "say yes," he begs. Then his descent. The shot lasts for over three minutes. For the first two minutes he follows after her, left then right, then left. As the two white specks crawl up the screen the distance between them shrinks, and one overtakes the other as their motion stalls. For several seconds the two white specks merge. One of them continues into a cluster of olive trees while the other, we presume to be Hossein, begins a lively trek back in the direction from which he came, running, leaping through the tall grass, and at one point swallowed up by it as he tumbles and falls. Hossein makes his way back under the umbrage of olive trees and the frame goes black, the story ends. We are left to suppose from the manner in which he spirits himself across the grass in our direction that Tahareh has finally agreed to marry him. Or put another way, we are asked to write the ending with cues from the extreme wide shot of a long take, informed by color and figure movement in the shot's mise en scene, and influenced, as well, by Dominico Cimarosa's lively "Allegro Giusto."

Each movie has an ID or birth certificate of its own. A movie is about human beings, about humanity. All the different nations in the world, despite their differences of appearance and religion and language and way of life, still have one thing in common, and this is what's inside of all of us.

—Abbas Kiarostami, *Film Comment*, July–August 2000 Issue.

Stasis and place

Location can occasionally be of such narrative consequence that value is gained by picturing it on screen for an extended period of time. This is particularly true when a given place or geography impacts story development, or when, for example, it serves as an obstacle or as a comfort to characters. Place has been at the heart of every film directed by Kelly Reichardt. This certainly applies to her 2016 feature film, *Certain Women*, a trilogy of stories set in and around Livingston, Montana. Locating the viewer in place becomes an essential strategy for conveying the movie's context, a context that weighs on characters as they go about their daily lives and informs the movie's tone.

Figure 6.15 *Certain Women* (2016). Director: Kelly Reichardt. Cinematographer: Chris Blauvelt.

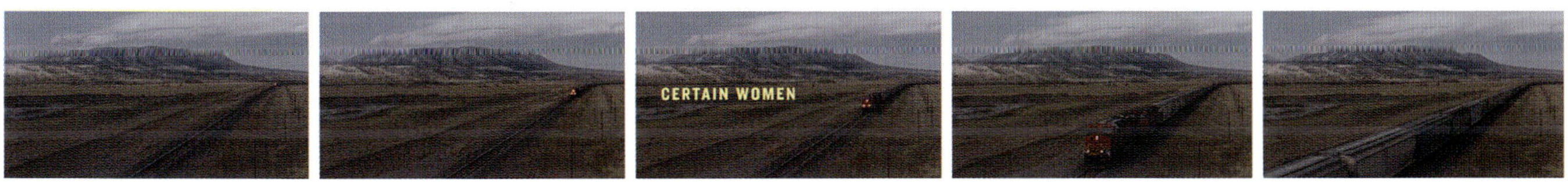

1 1b 1c 1d 1e

The movie begins with an extreme wide shot of prairie land that rises up to low-lying mountains, and cutting through this prairie, a railroad track. The camera is positioned above the valley, with the track running diagonally from screen right to the middle foreground of the frame. A whistle blows and a cargo train slogs up the track for the duration of the shot. No character is visible in the frame, and no character action, other than the work of the unseen train conductor presumed to be driving the train. On this extreme, unpopulated, wide shot the camera holds, initiating the viewer into the film's pace while also imprinting into the viewer's mind the Montana landscape of brown and grey, the snow clouds hanging over the mountain, and the train. All these elements converge to convey an image of isolation. This isolation will become a factor in each of the three stories. The rumbling of the train with its whistle and clang is heard as a repeating sound effect throughout the film, yoking the stories, and also serving as a reminder of just how remote Livingston, Montana, seems to be. It is cargo, after all, not passengers, being trafficked in and out of town.

Stasis and family matters

Like Roy Andersson and Yasujirō Ozu, the British director Joanna Hogg privileges the stationary camera. For Hogg, each film offers an opportunity to create sequences of elegantly constructed tableaus in which character dynamics brew, simmer, and boil. As in the films of Michelangelo Antonioni, locations seem chosen for the correlations that can be made between exterior landscapes and the characters' interior plight.

The windswept island of Tresco among the English Isles of Scilly is one such location in the 2010 feature film, *Archipelago* (Figure 6.16). A cottage on this island hosts a holiday for Edward, his sister, Cynthia, and their mother, Patricia. The arrival of Patricia's husband, William, looms as possibility throughout the film, though he never shows up. We feel his presence due to overheard telephone calls with Patricia, who seems driven by the conversation to anger and anguish in varying degrees. In William's place, a local artist, Christopher, has been recruited by Edward's mother to teach her to paint the surrounding landscapes; Rose, a professional cook, has also been hired to provide their meals. The mother and sister have prohibited Edward from bringing his girlfriend, Chloé, insisting the holiday is for family only (never mind the local artist). Chloé's absence becomes a nagging presence as tension grows among them. Edward is plagued foremost by what seems to be a crisis of direction—he has quit his city job for a chance at volunteer work in Africa but is altogether ambivalent about going. The film's drama is charged by tensions between and among these five characters and the two absent, who serve to pressure the conflict.

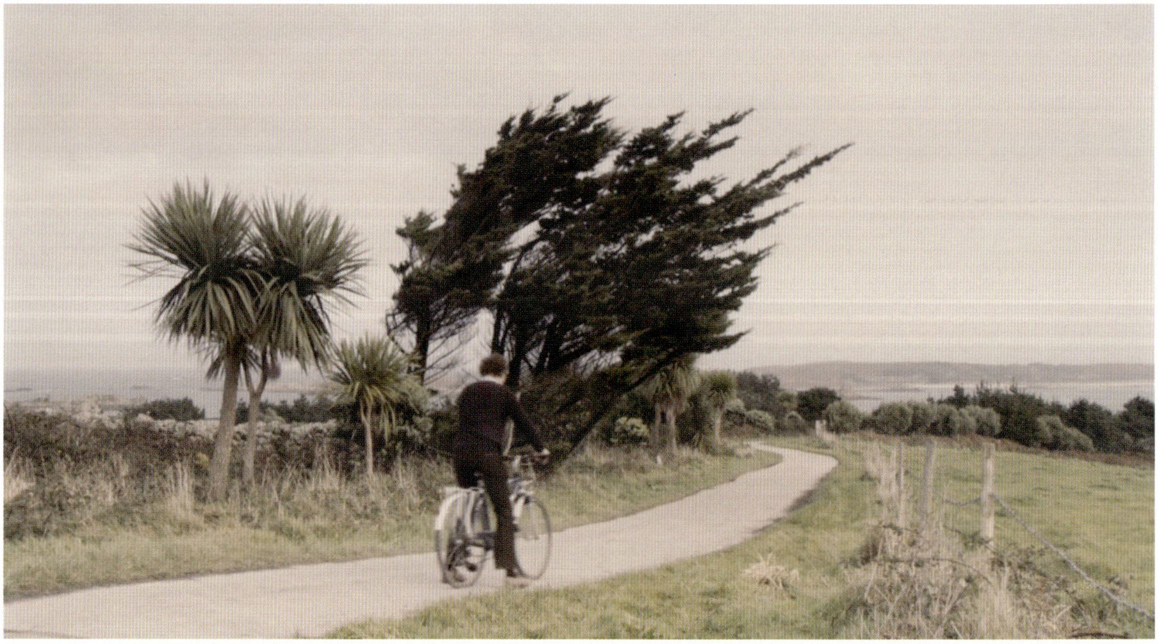

Figure 6.16 *Archipelago* (2010). Director: Joanna Hogg. Cinematographer: Ed Rutherford.

Over dinner one evening, small slights accumulate as Cynthia challenges every idea or position expressed by her brother, Edward, who holds forth at length with news about his job in Africa and his girlfriend, Chloé. The conflict escalates until Cynthia storms away from the table and out of the house. The mother sends Edward to comfort her, taking us into the night with its wild sound of wind and sea, overwhelming Edward's calls to his sister. This is followed by the scene pictured in Figure 6.17. Edward sits on a stool, silent, in the dimly lit living area, across from his mother. They say nothing to one another as they wait for Cynthia's return. Finally, we hear someone entering the house, slamming the door, stomping upstairs. The mother leaves the room to attend to her. Left alone with Edward, we hear, as he does, the mother's voice, "Cynthia, you don't have to be so angry." This spins Cynthia into a vocal rage, as Edward remains in the living area alone, listening, then standing to listen as Cynthia's rant continues.

The choice to keep our attention fixed with a stationary camera in a long take on Edward, alone in the living area, suffering the effect of his sister's behavior (rather than on his sister and her behavior) asserts the authority of family relations with their inextricable triggers and ties. It establishes, as well, the loneliness exacerbated by proximity to family, exposing the empty pockets of self that can't be filled by even those who have known us longest. Both are true. This is the terrain mapped by *Archipelago*, defined in the geographic sense as a group of islands—connected but apart.

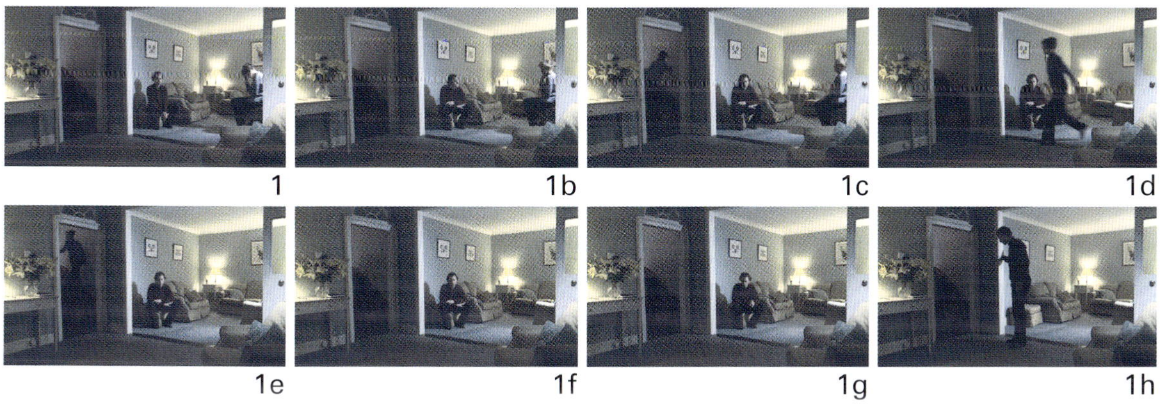

Figure 6.17 *Archipelago* (2010). Director: Joanna Hogg. Cinematographer: Ed Rutherford.

I'm interested in the dance of people and the way people interact with each other. I think if you cut things always to a close up or a medium shot you don't see what the rest of the body is doing. So, I think a lot of the story is told in how the characters are moving and how they move with each other within the frame. I think if you cut too quickly you don't get time to see those things.

—Joanna Hogg. Carnevale, Rob, "Archipelago—Joanna Hogg interview." IndieLondon.co.uk.

Stasis and friends

It is useful to ask, in each instance of a long take, which elements combine to sustain our interest in the drama captured in the take. This is particularly useful in a long take with a stationary camera. In the next example from Hong Sang-soo's 2004 film, *Woman Is the Future of Man*, the turns in well-crafted dialogue between two old friends charge the scene with dramatic beats. Capturing this in a long take with a stationary camera leaves no room for escaping the subtle jabs of one character to another and maintains the momentum of mounting insults in real time.

Technically, the long take exampled here includes camera movement. But the camera travels (three pans) to and from and back to a table where the two young men sit, a table that serves as an anchor to the scene, on which the camera remains static for over three minutes. Just after reconnecting, Lee and Kim agree to meet for dinner. Lee (screen right) has married and is a university art teacher. Kim (screen left) has just returned to the country after graduating from an American film school. From the outset, Lee's life choices are thrown into question by Kim's single status and ambitions to be an artist, a filmmaker, rather than to teach. This further undermines Lee's confidence as he works to sustain a position of authority over Kim, making judgements about his life choices, none of which matter to Kim. Their body language replicates the dynamic, as Lee leans forward, then back, then forward, crafted carefully to elevate tensions as the subtext bleeds into dialogue. Kim remains indifferent to Lee's insinuations and so Lee digs for a concrete offense to throw in Kim's direction. Lee accuses Kim of giving his wife an "American" hug when he last greeted her, a gesture that has fiercely offended Lee. When Kim is both baffled and remorseless over this accusation, Lee raises his voice, stands, and storms off. Kim remains unfazed, more interested in the attractive waitress who he solicits for a film role, and the lovely young woman waiting at a bus stop across the street, aware of Kim's gaze through the window.

The vantage point of the camera positions the two friends as equals (Figure 6.18). It also eclipses from view a clear sighting of their faces. We cannot see the expressions that accompany their reactions to one another. Only their body language with shifts in posture lets us witness the subtext that percolates to the surface in their exchange. In this way the camera is an onlooker, advocating neither of the two young men, letting each reveal himself. Such is the gift of real time and continuous space in the café.

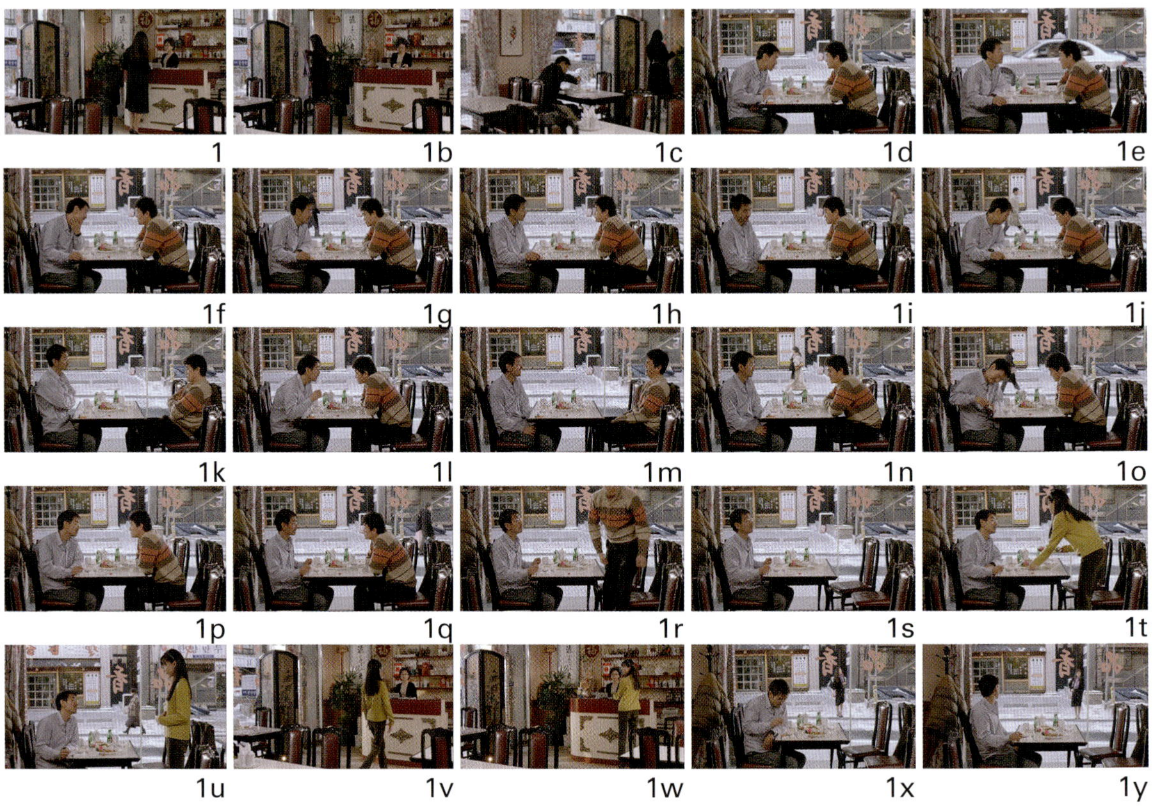

Figure 6.18 *Woman Is the Future of Man* (2004). Director: Hong Sang-soo. Cinematographer: Kim Hyeon-gu.

Stasis and the close-up

A static wide shot as the basis for a long take has the advantage of creating visual interest and dramatic tension through the interaction of character behavior and dialogue with elements of mise en scene. Mise en scene, as you remember from chapter five, includes set design or location, as well as the blocking and staging of actors—their proximity to one another and/or the camera. This advantage serves each of the last two examples, where distance from character to character correlates to power struggles in play. Imagine then the challenges in the choice to stage a static long take as a close-up of one character.

The static long take that ends the first scene in *Climates* privileges the stubborn record of a young woman's shift in mood. By stubborn I refer to the camera's insistence that here, the viewer is pressed into her emotional state. Not only is it a single shot, with a static camera lasting two minutes in duration, but a close-up, limiting the action within the frame to her face.

Isa is a young woman struggling to sustain a relationship with her somewhat older male companion, Bahar. The film charts the dynamic between the two characters like changes in weather—hence, the title, *Climates*.

The scene begins and ends with studies of Isa's face in close-up. In the middle, a series of five shots reveal space, time, and the strained dynamic between Isa and Bahar. The first of Isa's close-ups is followed by a medium wide shot of Bahar, establishing the location and also delivering the subject of Isa's gaze. The close-up repeats (Figure 6.19, Shots 3 and 4), and then Isa and Bahar are brought into the same frame. Rather than reinforcing their togetherness, dissonance is highlighted. Notice the way Bahar disappears behind one of the columns as Isa steps into the medium wide shot (Shot 5b). Again in shot 5, after their brief exchange and embrace ("Are you bored?" he asks. "No," she says), Isa sets off toward the crest of land rising above the ruins (Shot 5d). Now, Bahar steps forward, eclipsing her movement behind him. Shot 6 reverses perspective, framing the scene from the top of the hill. Now the shots focus on her, medium wide (Shots 7 and 7b) and then, her point of view (Shots 9 and 9b) when Bahar stumbles and falls, and then the close-up (Shots 10–10c): the long take.

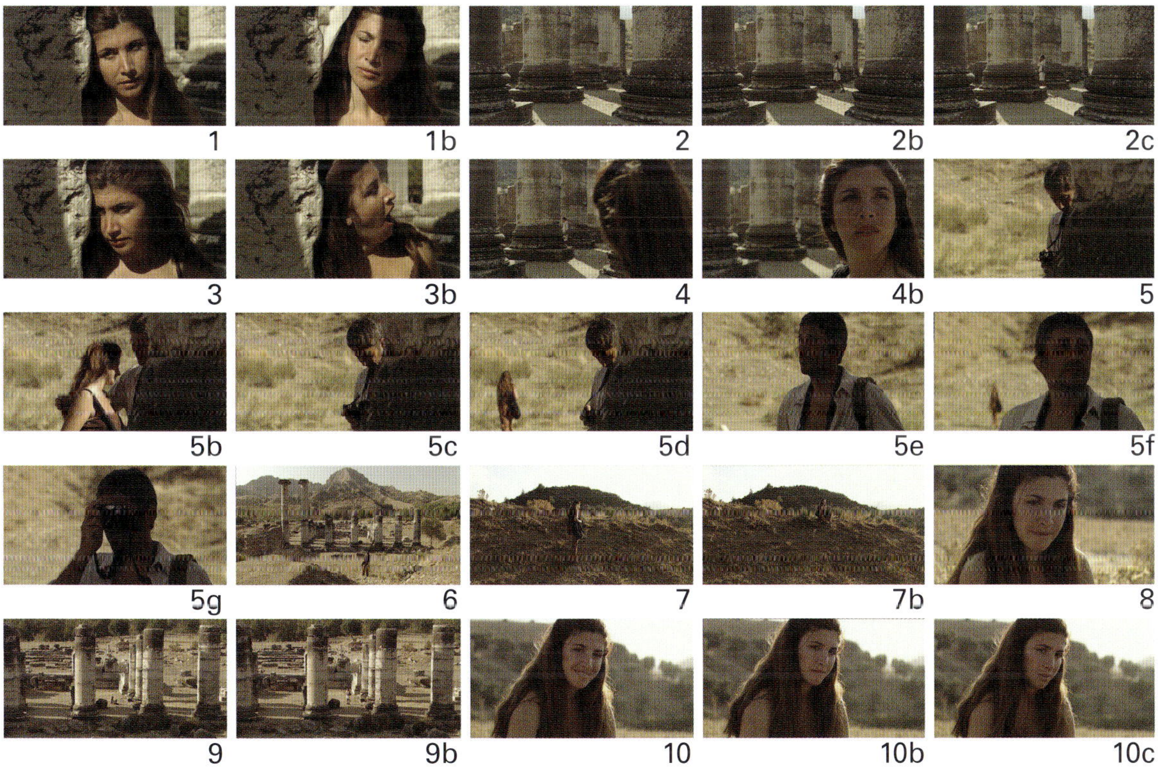

Figure 6.19
Climates (2006).
Director: Nuri Bilge Ceylan.
Cinematographer: Gökhan Tiryaki.

The still frames do not begin to replicate shot duration though you may grasp a sense, even if somewhat abstract, of the scene's rhythm. There are two relatively long takes. The longer of these occurs as the final close-up. The shots preceding it are the two of shortest duration in the scene. A variety of shot length, as well as shot size, animates a scene that is otherwise quiet in activity. Not only shot variety, but the rhythm varies as well, with the pace accelerating in the quick shot (a close-up, Figure 6.14, Shot 8) and the point of view shot (an extreme wide, Figure 6.19, Shots 9 and 9b) right before the long take. The long take lasts for over two minutes. This is a considerable span of screen time for a close-up. Here, the convention of close-up combined with shorter duration is overruled by narrative necessity. Isa's face maps the dramatic action that fulfills narrative expectations. This is no small credit to the quality of her performance. We see only her face and her mood shifting across it: amusement retreats into reflection that stirs disturbance, which prompts what seems to be an unrelenting sorrow. Then, the cut.

Meditative

Any discussion of the long take brings to mind the work of film director Andrei Tarkovsky. Tarkovsky's preoccupation with film time is documented in his book-length artistic testament entitled *Sculpting in Time*, in which he discusses the art of capturing the flow of real time in visually compelling ways.[10] Given Tarkovsky's inventive treatment of time, it's worth examining scenes from two feature films to demonstrate the variation within Tarkovsky's style rooted in story necessity or the nature of the project and its purpose. The scene selected from *The Mirror* affords the opportunity to study the long take within a scene, situated between shots of shorter duration.

This film, *The Mirror*, has the most unconventional narrative structure of any of Tarkovsky's films, based as it is on the memories, thoughts, and reflections of the protagonist, Alexei.[11] The scene depicted in Figure 6.20 represents a childhood memory. Alexei appears only in a cutaway, resting in a hammock with his sister (Shot 5). The camera doesn't trouble itself with locating the action explicitly from Alexei's point of view. Rather the camera evokes the quality of memory, with its languorous movement and preoccupations, resting as it does, for example, on the back of the mother's hair, braided into a loose knot above her bare neck.

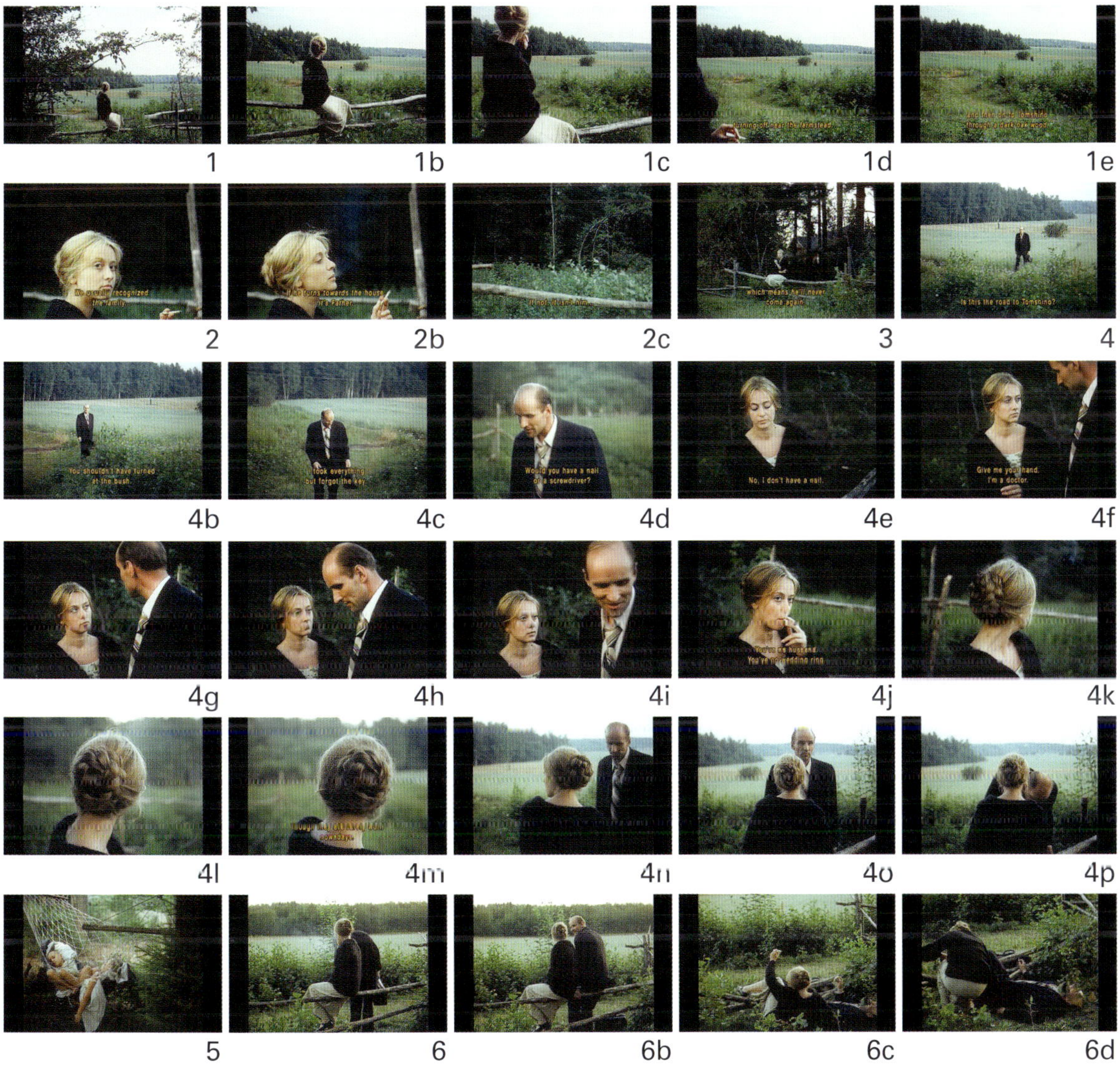

Figure 6.20 *The Mirror* (1975). Director: Andrei Tarkovsky. Cinematographer: Georgy Rerberg.

There is narrative progression, even if slight: Alexei's mother sits on a fence outside their country home, smoking a cigarette, waiting for Alexei's father, or so we discover deep into the scene through Alexei's voiceover narration, as a grown man. A stranger comes seeking directions for nearby Toshino. An exchange occurs between the mother and stranger, and then, remembering his destination, the stranger leaves. This is basically the sum of what happens and yet much more occurs in the subtle shifts of mood in Alexei's mother, and also in the stranger.

When the stranger arrives, he is eager to make connection. The mother, on the other hand, annoyed by the intrusion, resists his flirtations. When he departs, abruptly, she seems startled, as if his coming and now going has set her longing in motion again. The camera is also charged with rendering this experience.

The six-minute scene consists of eight shots of varying lengths. If you look at Figure 6.21 you can see that the fourth and sixth shot represent longer takes with shot 6 dominating the last half of the scene. The camera is patient even with shots of shorter duration (Shots 3 and 5), and notable for the way camera movement disguises shot duration with a lively choreography designed to interact with character movement. At times the camera is motivated by character movement, and at other times, decidedly not. This variation seems always to serve mise en scene, and the work that mise en scene can do in elevating atmosphere, as if the mother's mood, which infuses the scene, becomes what the child most remembers about this afternoon.

Certain observations about the scene can easily be made. There are only two static shots (Shots 3 and 5). Every other still frame in Figure 6.21 belongs to a moving shot, even if the camera temporarily hovers in one place. Even in shots 6e–6g, the camera moves in, ever so slightly, getting closer to the stranger before it tilts up as he stands. We can also see that Alexei's mother dominates the first portion of the scene, coinciding with her resistance to, and impatience with, the forward nature of the stranger: taking her pulse ("Are you nervous?" he asks her), bumming a cigarette, and sitting next to her on the fence. After the fence breaks, spilling the two of them onto the ground together, the camera's eye shifts to him as he waxes poetic about the schism between the natural world and human striving.

The long take of shot 6 transports the viewer through this shift, like changes in landscape viewed from a train. Any convention of covering character interaction with shot/reverse shot is abandoned entirely. Look, for example, at shots

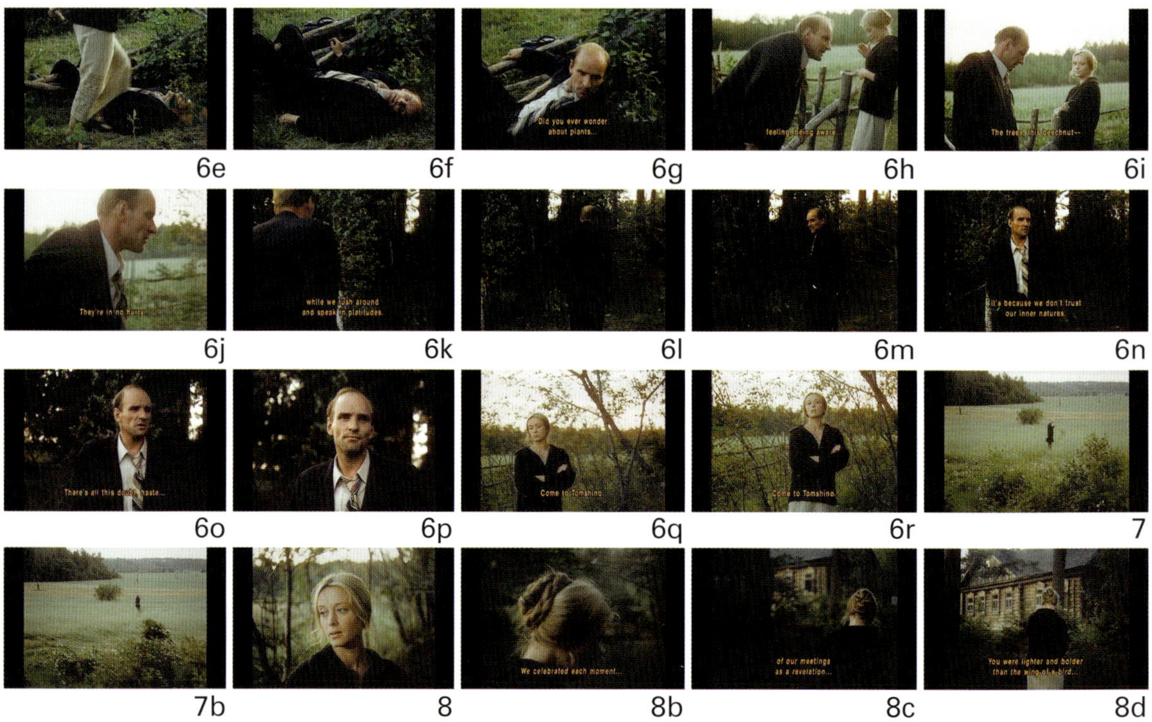

Figure 6.21 *The Mirror* (1975). Director: Andrei Tarkovsky. Cinematographer: Georgy Rerberg.

6n–6s. The stranger addresses Alexei's mother and she responds to him, unseen—we only hear her voice. The camera withholds her until the stranger leaves, giving her appearance, when we see her finally, more amplitude. Between shot 6s and 6t the stranger ducks out of the frame to retrieve his case and then he's off, back across the field of buckwheat toward Toshino, leaving her standing, arms crossed, alone (Shot 6t). "You're bleeding," she tells him, pointing to his ear where the ground must have scratched it. He's unfazed. The camera returns to her, in close-up, before she turns away from him, away from us, and walks back toward the house.

Inspired by a science fiction novel, Tarkvosky's fifth feature, *Stalker*, employs a camera that moves like an apparition, distancing its object, holding it at bay, drawing closer gradually while the object is fixed, careful not to disturb even the surrounding air. Occasionally, this takes the form of a long tracking shot, as in one scene in which the camera hovers above the surface of a stream investigating objects in the shallows. The water stream runs through the Zone, a place with obstacles and traps, quarantined and forbidden, into which Stalker has brought a writer and a scientist in search of "The Room." The Room is a place inside the Zone where one's deepest heartfelt wish may come true. The movie charts their day-long trek and arrival in the outer chamber, where conflicts sparked by inhibitions of entering The Room escalate and then, abate, though none has courage, finally, to go in.

At the end of their excursion, near the film's conclusion, 4:50 minute scene unfolds in which almost nothing happens. It begins as a medium wide shot of the scientist, following him with a pan toward the Stalker and writer who squat in a water pool facing the entrance of The Room (Figure 6.22, Shots 1–1b). The scientist sits beside them, the three men huddled together in a wide shot (Shot 1c). A formal composition centers the men. Behind them, a slab of concrete on the back wall etched with a vertical line marks the third point in a perfectly centered isosceles triangle. Camera movement is confined to a dolly that eases out slowly, almost imperceptibly, altering the frame from wide shot to extreme wide shot, distancing the travelers farther and farther from the viewer, and creating a frame within the frame. Figure movement is limited to the scientist's intermittent tossing of pebbles into the water puddled in The Room. The only words spoken, "it's so quiet," precede the primary action in the scene: a rain shower which comes on suddenly, the duration of which occurs in real time (Shots 1f–1g). The most spellbinding

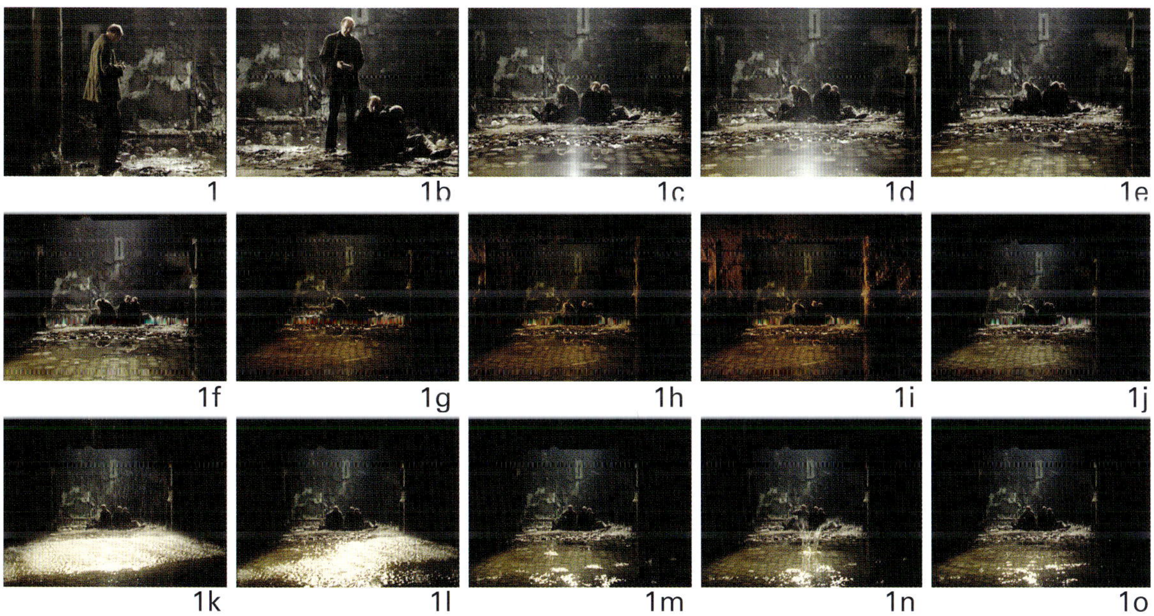

Figure 6.22
Stalker (1979). Director: Andrei Tarkovsky. Cinematographer: Alexander Knyazhinsky.

aspect of the scene is changing light, from silver blue to gold, to deeper gold (as clouds cover), to white gold (as it rains), and then finally (as clouds pass) to a glistening gold and blue: a beauty that comments upon the humbled defeat of writer and scientist incapable of entering The Room. The duration of shot, the near imperceptible camera motion and staging, along with an utter absence of action save for the rain, fosters a creeping awareness, almost as an afterthought, that we, the viewers, have been positioned by camera placement (heartfelt wishes in tow) in the center of The Room.

It was from a weekly visit to the cinema that you learned (or tried to learn) how to strut, to smoke, to kiss, to fight, to grieve. But whatever you took home from the movies was only part of the larger experience of losing yourself in faces, in lives that were not yours—which is the more inclusive form of desire embodied in the movie experience. The strongest experience was simply to surrender to, to be transported by, what was on the screen.

—Susan Sontag. *Against Interpretation, And Other Essays,* 1966.

Epiphany

For Tarkovsky, the long take asks a viewer to sink into lived experience, moment to moment. It gives weight to small actions and choices made within a stretch of time, even the choice to do nothing. It seems fitting to follow the discussion of the scene from *Stalker* with the climactic long take in Alfonso Cuarón's feature film, *Roma*. Cuarón admits to rereading Tarkovsky's *Sculpting in Time* as preparation for the making of the film.[12] For sure, the camera strategy privileges the unfolding of events in real time, and includes several long takes, one or two of which equal the athleticism in staging that occurs in *The Red and the White*. In the climactic scene, the camera movement is simple (Figure 6.23). Slowly, it tracks left, then right, then left, then right, then left, pausing at intervals for character interaction. The characters interacting include the mother and her four children, along with their live-in maid, Cleo, the film's protagonist. While the camera movement is straightforward, the staging is majestic: characters backlit by a late-day sun at the beach, the long take uniting a family as they stride to and from the edge of the surf, to and from one another.

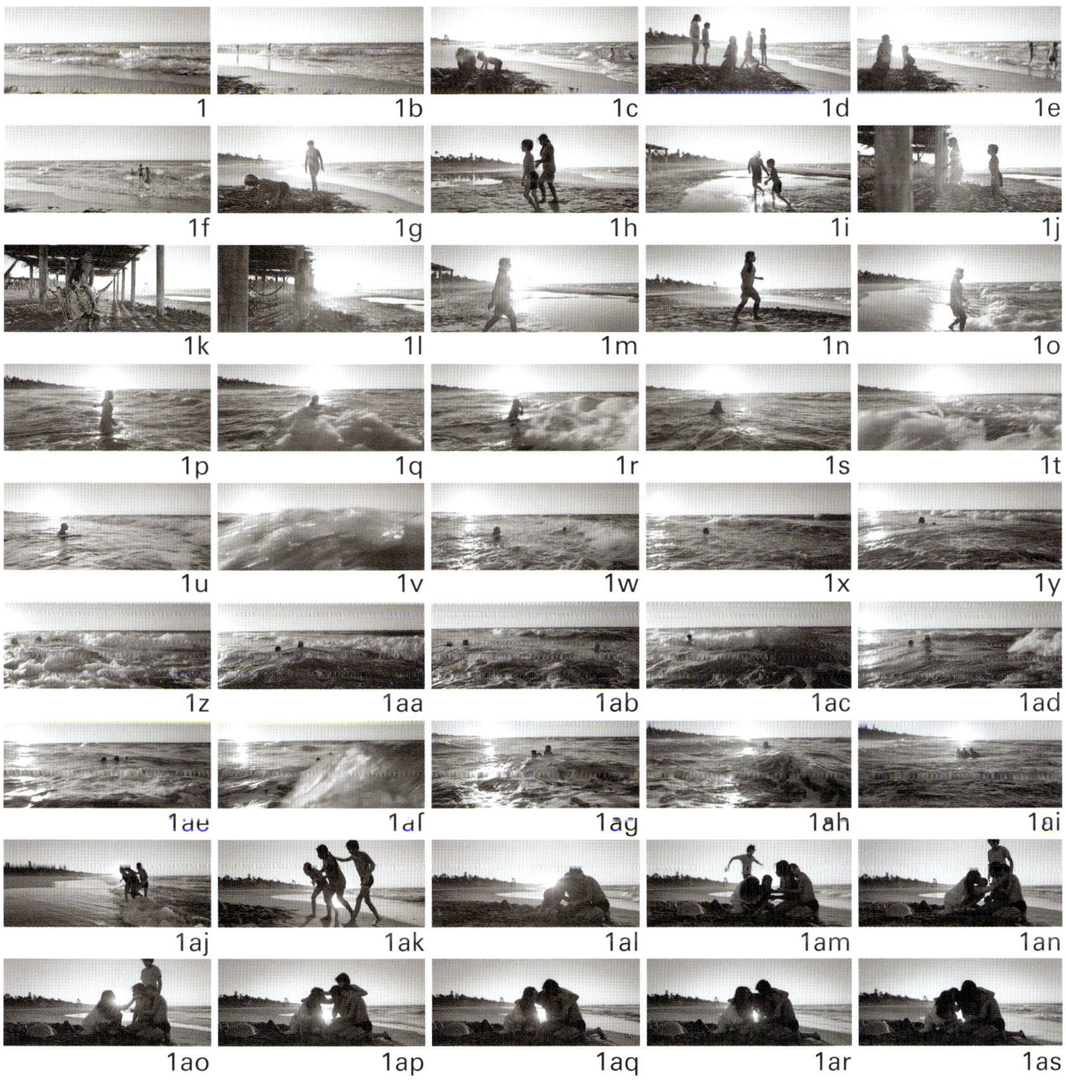

Figure 6.23
Roma (2018).
Director:
Alfonso Cuarón.
Cinematographer:
Alfonso Cuarón.

The shot culminates with Cleo's fearsome rescue in real time of two children caught in the tide pull of the sea, more alarming still given that Cleo doesn't know how to swim. When she carries the children back to shore, the mother and two other children run to meet them. The shot ends, as in *Stalker*, with the characters huddled together in a wide shot. Here, in *Roma*, this fatherless family—mother, her four children, and Cleo—nestle together on the sand in a communal embrace (Figure 6.24). This embrace is the story's stroke at a resolution, giving the film its epiphany.

Figure 6.24
Roma (2018).
Director:
Alfonso Cuarón.
Cinematographer:
Alfonso Cuarón.

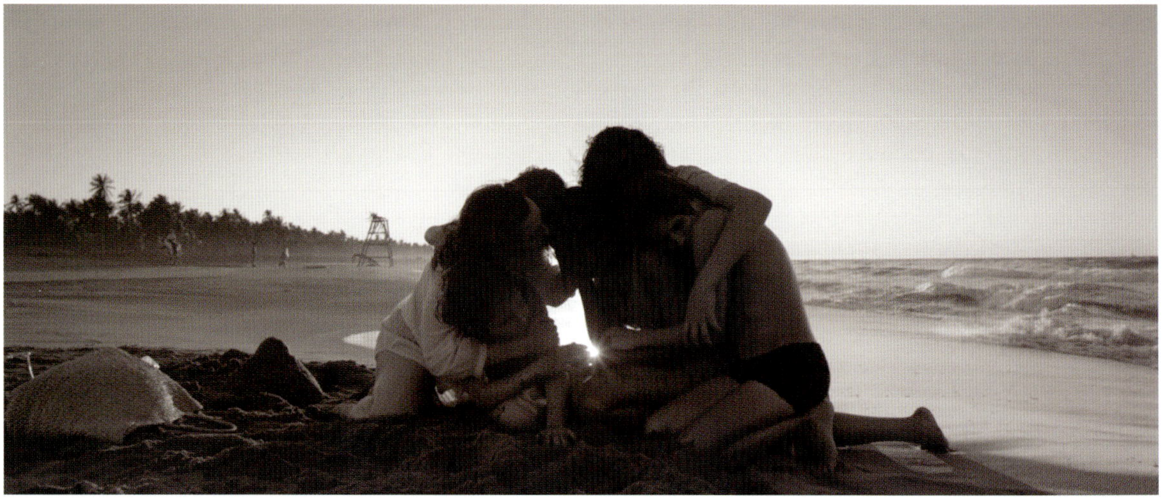

For the beach scene, we had to build a jetty, and put a techno-crane to keep the same height. And the day before we shot, tropical storms weakened the jetty. Every time we tried to shoot the scene the cameras would derail. I wanted to have six takes before the sweet spot of the light. We couldn't get anything, it was derailing 45 seconds after saying action; we would get the beginning. Luck. When the sweet spot came the camera didn't derail and we have the only good complete shot. I didn't want to keep on going. I was afraid of safety and also because the light was not worth it.

—Alfonso Cuarón. Thompson, Anne. "Alfonso Cuarón tells Lubezki How He Filmed 'Roma'—Even One Quiet Shot Needed 45 Camera Positions." *IndieWire* December 14, 2018.

Long takes in sequence

A **continuous shot feature film**, also known as a one-shot feature, is a movie filmed in one long take with a single camera, or constructed to convey that impression. The advent of digital technology made this more readily doable and in 2004, director Alexander Sokurov offered an example with his film, *Russian Ark*. In 2014, Alejandro González Iñárritu set out to make a movie in which action appeared to unspool transition-free, optimizing the advantage of digital filmmaking. The result became the celebrated, manic-paced story, *Birdman*. And there is *Rope,* Hitchcock's notable effort shot on film, with transitions hidden inside the edit to give the effect of a one-take movie.[13]

The directors of the 2019 film *The Body Remembers When the World Broke Open* had hopes of shooting the entire movie as one long take.[14] The film is the joint effort of Kathleen Hepburn and Elle-Máijá Tailfeathers, who share credits for writing and directing. Tailfeathers also performs in the film in the role of Aila, alongside Violet Nelson as Rosie. The two characters drive the story. Their lives converge when Aila rescues Rosie, an expectant mother, after domestic violence leaves her stranded in the street. Both women are indigenous to the First Peoples of Canada, but the bond of heritage doesn't overcome the tension incited by their differences in lifestyle and need.

Interest in telling this story in one take grew out of the desire to portray the interaction between Aila and Rosie as authentic, giving breath to their moments of awkwardness and silence. Test shoots with cinematographer Norm Li persuaded them to capture the movie on 16mm film. This required conceiving a way of crafting the transitions, given the eleven-minute limit of a film mag. The one hour and forty-five minutes of screen time in *The Body Remembers When the World Broke Open* is stitched together with twelve cuts.[15]

The film is particularly ambitious in all aspects of its camera strategy. In addition to shooting the entire story as a series of long takes, much of the action is covered in close-ups, creating a visual landscape dominated by faces. A handheld camera in combination with the film's long takes gives the story a fidelity of character and place.

Satisfying the convention of the long take, there is plenty of camera movement in the film, because there is figure movement, and the camera faithfully follows each character. The characters serve as the centers of action. The differences between Aila and Rosie are apparent as early as their introductions. We meet Rosie first, traveling on a bus, then walking, and then arriving at an apartment, before settling in (Figure 6.25, Shots 1–1n). The first of the twelve transitions (a cut) introduces Aila, replacing Rosie in the frame (Shot 2). Now Aila walks down a hall, arriving at what appears to be a doctor's office, where she readies for an exam. Despite the prevalence of close-ups, the viewer is able to glean a significant amount of narrative information from what lies in the periphery, surrounding each character. The directors are careful to situate Aila and Rosie in environments that set them apart and stage the action so that pertinent elements of the background can be seen. This includes, for example, graffiti covering the wall as Rosie walks from the bus through her neighborhood, or the poster of a baby in the examining room where Aila readies for her medical appointment (Figure 6.25, Shots 1c and 2g).

It is apparent from the images in Figure 6.25 that the use of the long take gives value to incidental moments, embedding any dramatic intensity within them. But the most striking effect of filming the two women in continuous space and time, and at such close range, is not just the authenticity conveyed, but the intimacy forged between the audience and the characters. The camera, patient and relentless, insists that we take the lives of Aila and Rosie to heart.

A personal technique of mine while operating the camera is to imagine what a character is going through and to instinctually reflect that feeling through operating. It was important to tell the story from the perspective of the characters.

—Norm Li csc. *Canadian Cinematographer Magazine*. October 2019.

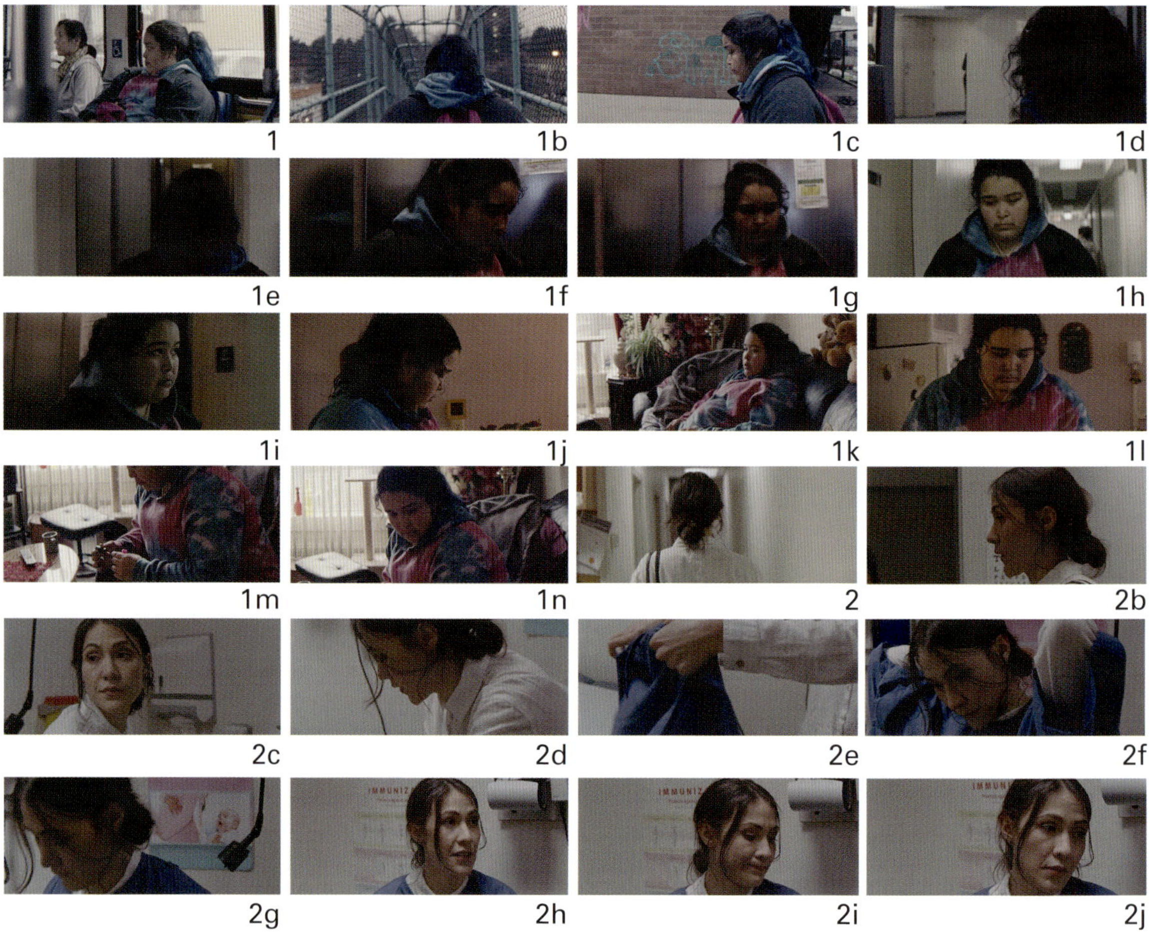

Figure 6.25 *The Body Remembers When the World Broke Open* (2019). Directors: Kathleen Hepburn, Elle-Máijá Tailfeathers. Cinematographer: Norm Li.

Discussion questions

1. With the long take we can glide from one center of action to another, what is the effect on plot when there are no breaks as with traditional editing?
2. Can you think of a scenario between two characters which would be served by the continuous time and space associated with the long take?
3. In *Birdman* (Figure 6.25) consider the images during the long take, what do you imagine was the motivation for framing the character(s)?

Notes

1. Early practitioners of the long take include Orson Welles, Kenji Mizoguchi, Carl Dreyer, Andrei Tarkovsky, Jean Renoir, Miklos Jancsó, Theo Angelopolis, and Alfred Hitchcock, who made an entire feature film of eleven-minute long takes to enhance the sense of entrapment in his suspense thriller set in a single apartment: *Rope*.
2. Alexander Sokurov exploited the new technology in his single-take, feature length movie of one hour and thirty-nine minutes. *Russian Ark*, set in the Russian Hermitage

Museum of St. Petersburg, provides the viewer the opportunity to experience the effect of a cut by enduring its absence. This was made possible, of course, by digital video. The new technology has launched an ongoing conversation among filmmakers. "Film lasts longer than digital. That's one of the problems that we're confronting at the ASC (American Society of Cinematographers). We have meetings on this stuff all the time." This, from an interview with cinematographer Ernest Dickerson in the online publication *Shadow Act*.

3. Robert Altman stages his own version of the shot at the opening of *The Player*, a film about a powerful producer working for a big studio whose life is threatened. In this instance the meandering camera covering the various "centers of action" provides the exposition, connecting characters in place.
4. Orson Welles stages a second and third long take in *A Touch of Evil*, occurring fifty-nine minutes into the film, in the apartment of Sangez, a suspect for the bombing. Centers of action are limited to the variety in blocking and staging, which create compositions that reflect power dynamics among the characters.
5. Jean Renoir, writing about camera work in *The Grand Illusion*. *My Life and My Films*, Da Capo Press, 1974.
6. Narrative film requires the manipulation of story knowledge, that is, who knows what, when. This includes the characters within the story and also the viewer. The story may progress so that character(s) and viewer are both surprised by a dramatic event. On the other hand, a story can be staged so that the viewer knows what is coming while the character does not. This is often the narrative strategy used by Hitchcock, in which suspense is excited by the viewer's anticipation of an event about to happen. This is the strategy in *Get Out*.
7. Jancsó is well known for his tracking shots, which required immense skill in laying the dolly track and creating action on either side of it to effect greater movement. Today's Steadicam would have relieved him and his camera team of many hours of conceiving, building, and executing these carefully choreographed shots.
8. In 2018, *Filmmaker Magazine* published an article by Scott Macaulay prompted by a Gus Van Sant retrospective in New York City. The article, entitled "Three Interviews with Gus Van Sant About his Long-Take, Béla Tar-Influence 'Death Trilogy'" explores this influence.
9. David Lowery reputedly made *Ghost Story* for $150,000 with limited crew over a spare number of days. This can be read about in articles from *The Guardian*, *Indiewire*, *Vulture*, *Filmmaker Magazine* and other film journals and online publications.
10. Andrei Tarkovsky, *Sculpting in Time*, (New York, Knopf, 1987).
11. *NY Times*, April 13, 1975. By James F. Clarity. *NEW FILM STIRS SOVIET AUDIENCE: "Mirror" by Tarkvosky Is Unorthodox and Popular*.
12. Gayané Kaligan interviews Alfonso Cuarón for www.mugglenet.com. During the interview, Cuarón discusses his preparation for *Roma*, which included rereading Bresson's *Notes on Cinematography* and Tarkovsky's *Sculpting in Time*.
13. A discussion of camera technique in *Birdman* can be found at https://www.rollingstone.com/movies/movie-news/flying-high-again-alejandro-gonzalez-inarritu-on-the-making-of-birdman. Techniques used in *Rope*, Hitchcock's film, are explored in V. Renée's article, "Understanding the Hidden Editing in Hitchcock's 'Rope,'" https://nofilmschool.com/2013/10/understanding-hidden-editing-in-hitchcocks-rope.
14. A discussion of the directors' original ambitions can be found in an interview with the cinematographer, "Long Take Norm Li, csc," *Canadian Cinematographer Magazine*. October 2019.
15. A thorough and generous discussion of the camera strategy is on record in the interview with Norm Li, the cinematographer. The interview details the method devised for transitioning from one long take to the next. "Long Take Norm Li, csc," *Canadian Cinematographer Magazine*. October 2019.

7

Handheld camera and the legacy of documentary film

It goes without saying that smart phones with video camera capability have had an enormous impact on the way in which we record experience. They have also insured that a vast population has had experience in recording and viewing visual imagery captured by a handheld camera. Of course, this was not always the case. Handheld camera technique emerged as a common means of image capturing during the late1950s when portable film equipment made it possible to execute camera movement without a tripod, dolly track, or crane. Exploited by documentary filmmakers, handheld film cameras liberated directors from transporting heavy equipment, encouraging greater mobility in recording events. One particular style came to be associated with handheld technique known as cinéma vérité, also referred to as observational cinema or direct cinema.[1] Advanced by documentary filmmaker Jean Rouch, it exploited the improvisational capacity of the handheld camera, treating it as a tool that could reveal or discover what is true in any situation.[2]

As a result of the widespread use of cinéma vérité in shooting documentaries, the handheld camera technique became synonymous, even in narrative films, with immediacy, authenticity, and real-life events. This association continues today. Consider any handful of movies employing this technique: *127 Hours*, *The Revenant*, *Gummo*, *Thirteen*, or *Winter's Bone*. In fact, many of the stories told by these films have a basis in actual circumstance or, at the very least, gain dramatic value from the implication of truthfulness. While the choice of handheld camera is not limited to life-like narratives, any decision to use it will take into account the effect of a camera technique historically linked with authentic experience.

Because of this link, filmmakers choosing handheld technique need to consider ways of balancing the improvisational nature of coverage with an organizing principle. Or put somewhat differently, what element(s) might be privileged in the shooting that will allow for visual coherence? Each film discussed in this chapter demonstrates the use of handheld camera toward a different emphasis. And for each example explored, we will be examining the ways in which the applied handheld technique solves the problem of unifying the immense variation in images that gives the handheld coverage its dynamism and veracity.

In the year 2000, it was a change of century, and I changed my life in a way. I discovered little [handheld] cameras, and I started to understand that I could film alone. That's how I made *The Gleaners and I*.

—Agnès Varda, *The Guardian*, interview, September 2018.

Character psychology

The coincidence of cinéma vérité technique with the vision of filmmaker John Cassavetes could not have been more fateful. Handheld technique became one of the hallmarks of his fiction films, so suited it was to the kind of stories he translated into film. These are stories filled with characters whose eruptions of personality undermine their need to be close and connect, and in some instances threaten their own wellbeing. While his films were meticulously scripted, performance allowed for latitude in line delivery and also in blocking and staging.[3] The handheld camera proved a perfect tool to get close to the raw emotions evoked by human interaction, while also capturing these spontaneous aspects.

A Woman Under the Influence, made in 1974, tells the story of Mabel, a wife and mother whose volatile behavior frightens her husband so much that he feels obliged to commit her to an institution. The film follows Mabel and Nick, and the three children, before, during, and after Mabel's return home from her time in the institution.

The scene represented by Figure 7.1 depicts Mabel (before she is institutionalized) going to a bus stop to wait for her children's return from school. We see her underdressed for winter climate, pacing erratically, barking at women passing by who will not give her the time, mocking them with gestures, walking into the middle of traffic looking for the bus, and when the bus arrives, jumping up and down gleefully to greet her children.

The handheld coverage works to keep Mabel in the center of the frame while also allowing for significant space around her. This requires continuous tracking, given her pacing and charging to and fro. As viewers, we feel the camera lurching after her, which in turn makes the effect of her erratic physical motion more vivid and more disturbing.

Notice the difference in coverage between Figure 7.1 and the scene represented by Figure 7.2. The later scene occurs after Mabel has returned from six months of treatment, when Nick still holds out hope for a domestic life of calm and balance. He invites extended family to come for dinner to celebrate her return, at the end of which Mabel's efforts at self-control go awry. When Mabel takes to standing on the sofa, singing, Nick asks the family members to leave. A chase scene occurs within the house. Mabel sequesters herself in the bathroom, making use

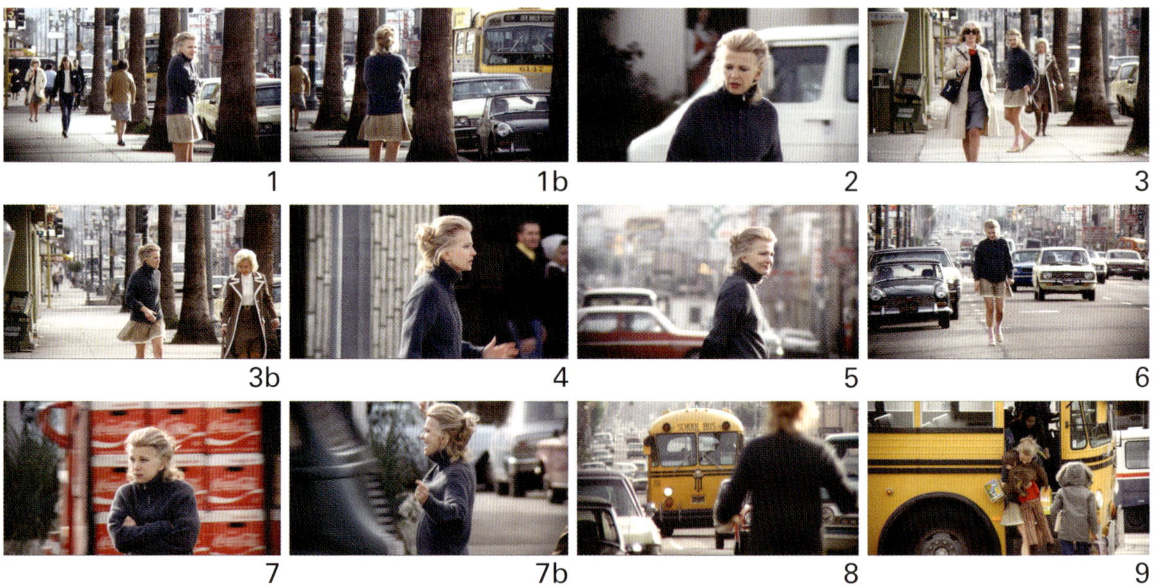

Figure 7.1
A Woman Under the Influence (1974). Director: John Cassavetes. Cinematographers: Mitch Breit and Al Ruban.

of a razor to cut her hand. Nick tries to tame her, as the children run in her direction, frightened by the blood on her hand. He resolves to get the children to bed, which they resist. Tension abounds.

In the scene depicted in Figure 7.2, the camera is obliged to cover a greater number of characters, in particular Mabel and her husband, Nick. The explosive nature of the scene creates a wider range of motion in the blocking and staging. Nevertheless, the handheld camera has relinquished all effort to center characters in the frame, with some shots limited to a limb or torso (Shots 4, 5, 11, and 15). Additionally, the space around Mabel has collapsed, and the coverage does not privilege one character over another. Time is divided equally, shot to shot, between Nick and Mabel.

A Woman Under the Influence includes a transition in the handheld coverage across the timeline of the film, in sympathy with the atmosphere in a household dependent on Mabel's psychological state. The camera coverage is in sync with the character's impact on environment. As such, the camera work has narrative progression, and this progression informs its visual coherence. The movie begins with more static handheld shots that allow Mabel's movements to create the dynamic within the frame. These shots give way to handheld camera movement, Mabel occupying the center of the frame with significant space around her. As the film progresses and family life closes in on her, the handheld camera becomes more erratic, at times, nearly frenetic, while also framing her with much less physical space. These medium close-ups and close-ups, and quick pans to track her lurching toward and away from her husband and her children, dash our hopes that Mabel will have grown the capacity to resist the tide of her internal turbulence.

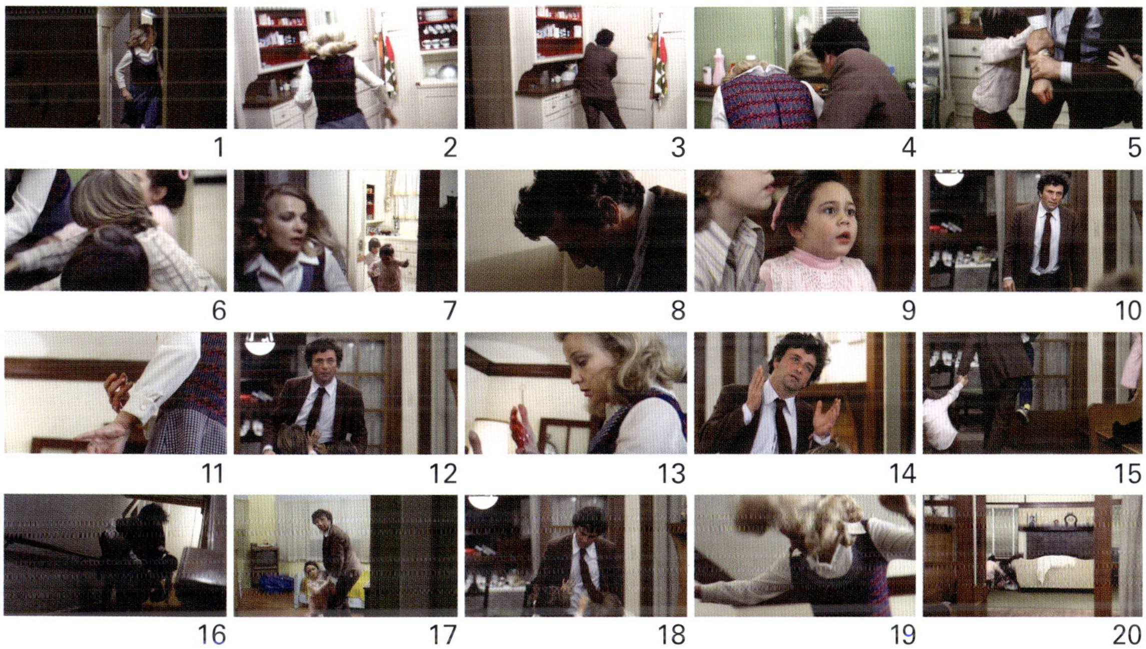

Figure 7.2
A Woman Under the Influence (1974). Director: John Cassavetes. Cinematographers: Mitch Breit and Al Ruban.

Lyrical and authentic

Regarded as one of the pioneers of independent film in America, John Cassavetes began making feature length films as early as 1959. Working with a small crew, and a handful of actors cast in repeated films, Cassavetes was able to uncap on screen a surfeit of emotional intensity and intimate human exchange.[4]

Following in his path is Charles Burnett, director of the 1978 fiction film, *Killer of Sheep*.[5] The film served as Burnett's thesis film at the UCLA School of Film where he received a Masters of Fine Arts degree. The reality of place, circumstance, the use of non-actors, along with handheld coverage, insure the film's authenticity. Shot in black and white near Burnett's family home in the Watts region of Los Angeles, the movie is comprised of a series of vignettes. At the center is Stan, a young African-American man who works at a local slaughterhouse to support his wife and children. Stan spends much of this spare time battling inertia from too few opportunities other than those offered by friends wanting to lure him into shady activities of one kind or another. The movie intersperses the non-events of Stan's life with scenes of children: bicycling in the streets, playing in the rubble, sitting idle on curbs in the neighborhood. The cost to the children of adult impotence and malaise is high and functions as an active theme in the film. Burnett exploits camera coverage in combination with editing as a means for associating the slaughtered lambs with these young lives.

Much of the film's coverage employs handheld camera technique. True to the impulse of handheld's legacy, the film gains authenticity with found locations, as well as casting non-actors, and activities consistent with daily life. A handheld montage of Stan's shift at the slaughterhouse demonstrates immense shot variety, tilts, pans, and swish pans held together by cuts and dissolves.

In a later scene, pictured below, Stan assists a friend in carrying a massive motor down several flights of stairs. You can see, even from the still frames, that the handheld shots go a long way in conveying the weight and labor of their effort. While it encourages our sense of real life in real time, this handheld camera is not haphazard. We can see three main aspects inform the handheld camera movement. First, positioned close to the two men for much of the scene, we're pressed inside the circle of action for every instance of setting the heavy motor down and lifting it again. Second, adding to the tension, Burnett has the camera situated *below* the men as they descend the stairs. This increases our fear that they will stumble, fall, or drop the motor. Finally, punctuating the handheld close-ups intermittently (three times) are wide, static shots. The effect: visual scope and dramatic release. The wide shots also chart the scene's development. We have seen a close-up function as dramatic action. Here, the third wide shot invokes a ready sense of the inevitable. Once we see the two men climb into the truck, the motor perched close to the edge of the truck's bed, we know, even as we dread it, the outcome.

The men leap out of the truck (Figure 7.3, Shot 14)—the two close-ups chart the aftermath in the faces of Stan and his friend. Resigned, as if such disappointments are commonplace, they get back in the truck. In the next shot a child gazes through the truck's back window. And then, a final wide shot, though not static. Here, from her point of view, the heavy motor carried with immense labor and effort down flights of stairs is remaindered as refuse, an abandoned carapace that diminishes from view—hers, ours—as the truck pulls away.

This final two shots echo a lyricism found throughout *Killer of Sheep*. This particular scene creates visual coherence by limiting the types of shots (close-ups, wide shots, and shots from below the men). But the coverage of the scene conforms to the visual style of the entire film with imagery of children juxtaposed with the failed efforts of adults.

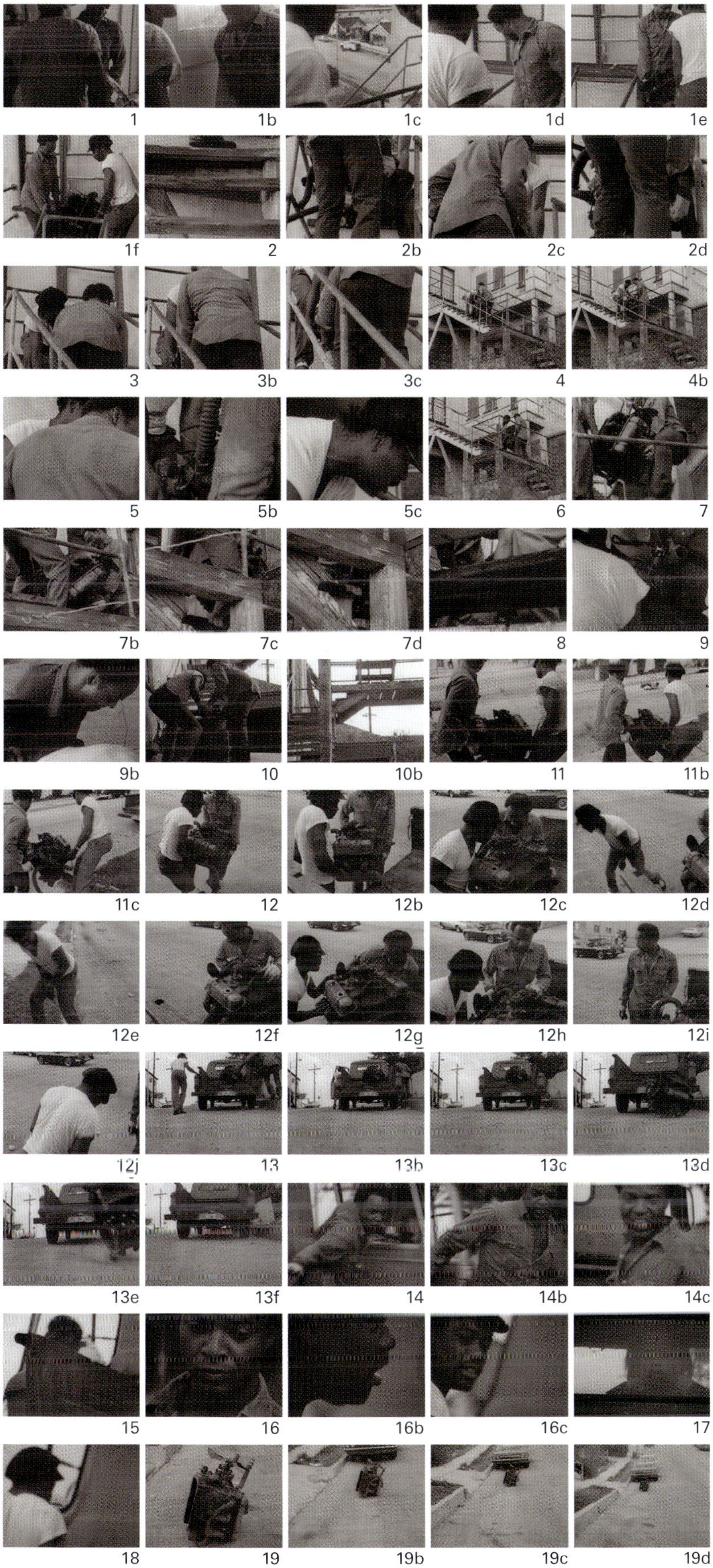

Figure 7.3
Killer of Sheep (1978). Director: Charles Burnett. Cinematographer: Charles Burnett.

Identity

The handheld camera with its capacity to follow and hover at close range through all kinds of character behavior can work to marry the viewer to a character's experience. One such record of character subjectivity occurs in *Corpo Celeste*, the first fiction film by Italian director, Alice Rohrwacher. The director began her work in film as a documentary filmmaker, and even as her films have increasingly courted allegory in their narrative parameters, the realism of setting and tone pervades. *Corpo Celeste* (*Heavenly Bodies*) is decidedly marked by circumstances grounded in reality.

Coming of age is Marta, who has moved with her family back to a small town in Calabria after years in Switzerland. The strangeness of place and local habits are part of what is documented in the film, but within the first twenty minutes, the story zeros in on Marta. At the center of this focus, Marta struggles to reconcile herself with a changing body on the cusp of puberty, and also to find her place in a community governed by Catholic rituals and events. Chief among the church offerings are classes in which Marta is enrolled, leading to her first catechism, an event that becomes the climax of the film's loose plot.

From the first frames, the camera portrays environment, locating the viewer in place, casting about with handheld technique to record the dawn ritual of honoring the Madonna that begins the film. Soon enough, however, the focus turns to Marta and fixes on her, keeping the viewer wedded to her experience as she navigates all of that which is strange to her.

This subjectivity can be felt in the still frames of the scene pictured in Figure 7.4. Marta has sequestered herself in the bathroom to rinse her feet and also, more importantly, to retrieve a padded bra, hidden in the curtains, and put it on. Outside the bathroom, her sister bangs on the door. In a later scene, we discover that the bra belongs to her sister. The first shot of the scene (Figure 7.4, Shots 1–1f) commits the viewer to Marta, with telling handheld close-ups of her behavior. We are driven by her small actions through her intensity and focus. One can also see the control of color palette and graphic elements that inform the mise en scene throughout the sequence. It is also useful to note how subjectivity can be conveyed even in a wider shot. Marta leaves the bathroom and takes off on her own, across an overpass that passes over a vacant industrial highway, alone with her thoughts, walking with intention away from the house and the viewer (Figure 7.4, Shot 3) and then toward the viewer, as the camera repositions (Figure 7.4, Shot 3c).

Tracking a character's experience is more than a sufficient measure for yoking handheld images toward coherence. The close watch of Marta also elevates the importance of casting. Yle Vanello's portrait of Marta endows the role with cherub-round cheeks, blue eyes, and blonde hair, a look that resembles somehow both angel and animal. But given the close watch afforded by the handheld camera, the real impact occurs through the actor's emotionally transparent face. Her capacity to register every nuance or shift of feeling gives each incidental moment dramatic weight.

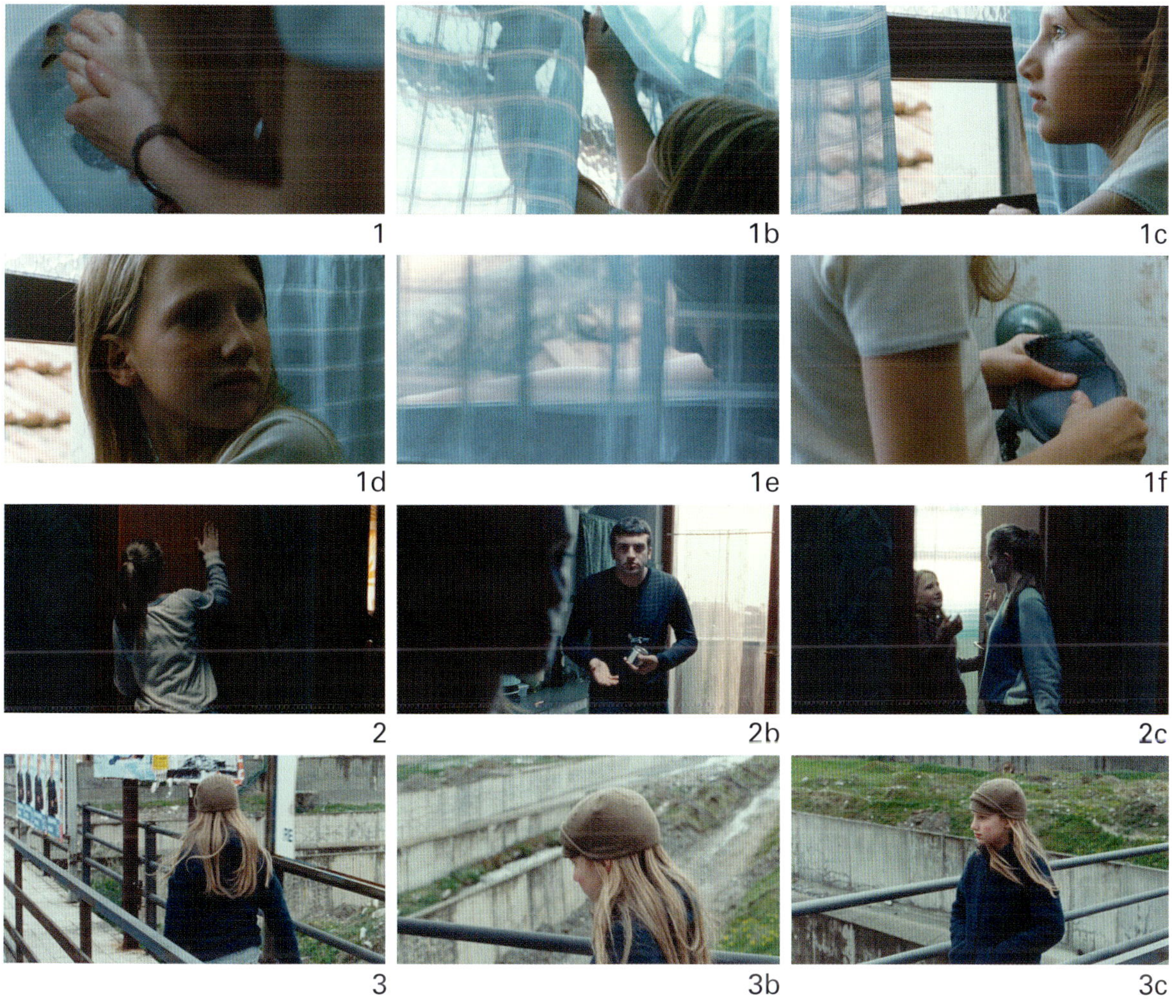

Figure 7.4 *Corpo Celeste* (*Heavenly Bodies*) (2011). Director: Alice Rohrwacher. Cinematographer: Hélène Louvart.

Creating form

Using handheld technique in a film with more than one protagonist increases the challenges of creating visual coherence. Also a first feature film, *Mustang*, directed by Deniz Gamza Ergüven, is set in a northern coastal town of Turkey. The film dramatizes the life of five orphaned sisters whose spirited sensuality incites the grandmother, their caretaker, to exercise extreme measures to keep the girls from violating the strictures and values of conservative society. Her solution: she imprisons the granddaughters in their home. When this proves unsuccessful in keeping them from escapades in the outside world, they are married off, one at a time.

Working with found locations and a cast of predominantly non-actors (four of the five women cast as the sisters had no professional acting experience), Ergüven holds true to the aesthetic of handheld camera as a means for connecting story material to real circumstances. Several incidents in the film are reported to have come from the director's family history.[6] But even the fabricated story material in the film depends, for maximum impact, upon our registering the dramatic situations and their consequences as probable and true.

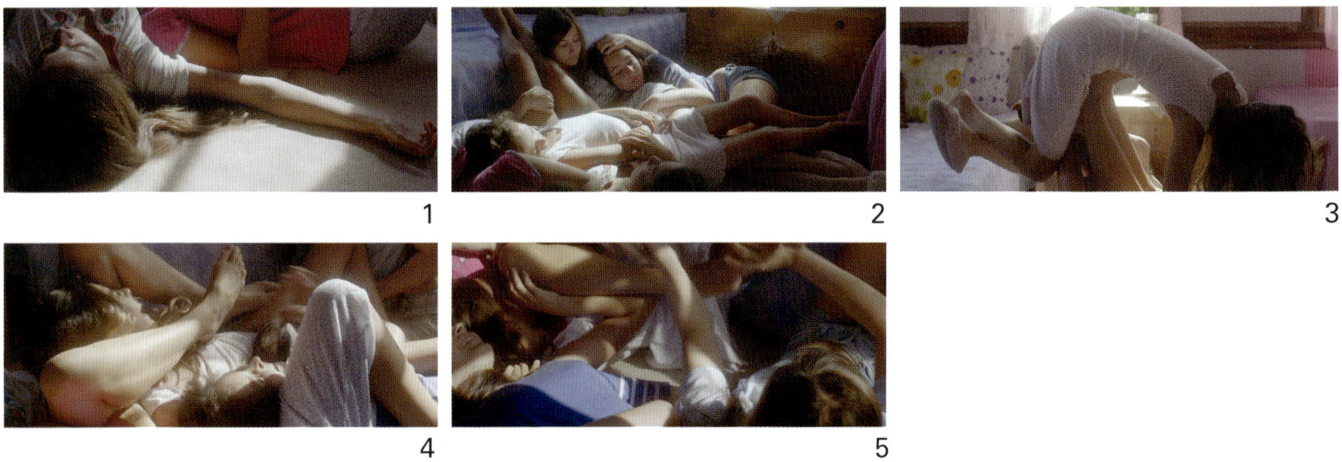

Figure 7.5
Mustang (2015). Director: Deniz Gamza Ergüven. Cinematographers: David Chizallet and Ersin Gok.

In *Mustang*, truthfulness is not the only value claimed by the handheld camera. The camera advantages the sensuality of their young bodies. In Figure 7.5 the sisters, quarantined in the bedroom, lie about in slips and gowns, entwined with one another. The viewer can barely discern whose legs belong to whom, so wrapped up are they in each other. The camera continues to chart their physical affection and closeness, making a point of their camaraderie and seductiveness with shot design (privileging 2, 3, 4, and 5 shots over singles). The number of sisters diminishes as each sister in turn is married.

The filmmaker also exploits the movie's title thematically, correlating the young girls with mustangs, which, in the lore of the American West, are very difficult to tame. This correlation is reinforced by the long mane of hair on each of the five young women. The handheld camera returns again and again to their thick brown hair, each in turn, as a repeated motif, sacrificing at times characters' faces in favor of the back of their heads. This strategy is evident in the scene (Figure 7.6, Shots 1,1d, 1e, 1f, 2b, and 2c), which can be tracked throughout the film.

Interviews with the director convey the practical challenges in shooting *Mustang*, especially insofar as permission to photograph in certain public places.[7] But the cinematography in the film is solving more than practical problems. While handheld coverage often includes improvised movement, the aspects of the story that are given emphasis can lasso that movement toward consistencies that may not be observed during a first viewing when one is caught up with the exigencies of plot. On closer inspection, one begins to see the patterns in the coverage that give the seeming randomness its purposefulness and form.

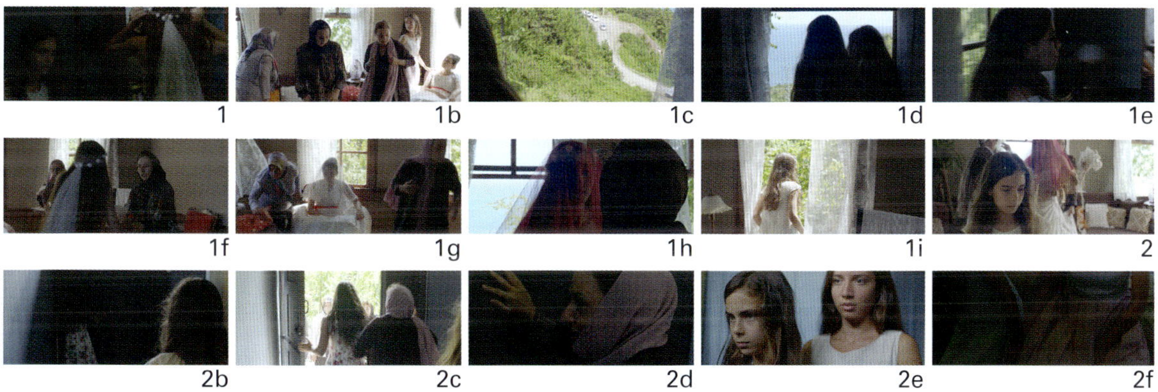

Figure 7.6
Mustang (2015). Director: Deniz Gamza Ergüven. Cinematographers: David Chizallet and Ersin Gok.

One take

Director Andrea Arnold has made repeated use of the handheld camera technique, extending her collaboration with cinematographer Robbie Ryan across each of four feature films. *American Honey* is their fourth effort together and the narrative parameters of the project placed considerable demands on any notion of visual coherence.

Like several other films exampled in this chapter, *American Honey* has story roots in real circumstance. Arnold, after reading about a subculture of magazine sellers going door-to-door across America, drafted a script based on this community.[8] Working with predominantly non-actors, Arnold cast young women and men whose lives resemble the outsiders portrayed in the film. These are characters with little or no promise of a bright future. They sustain their high spirits with music, drugs, and a YOLO mindset ("you only live once"). At the center of the story is Star, a runaway teenager, who joins the sales team to escape abuse in her job as a live-in nanny. Star falls for another member of the sales crew, Jake, played by the one professional actor in the film, Shia LaBoeuf. Their love story works a through-line through the episodic door-to-door, town-to-town road movie, a narrative tracking 12,000 miles of America's Midwest, with stops in cheap hotels.

The ever-changing locations present one challenge to visual unity. The large ensemble cast, another. Interviews with the director and cinematographer report that each scene was covered in but one take, in a style Ryan calls "free-form; we have rules but they're chaotic."[9] And yet, even with the challenges and the purposeful chaos, patterns emerge, the coverage in combination with the editing yielding a number of consistencies. Warm light, for example, pervades the imagery of the film, day and night, and in particular in the love scenes staged between Star and Jake (Figure 7.7). While the film makes graphically clear that this group of young, traveling magazine sellers live at the margins, the light cast on them serves to upend assumptions we might make about their status as outsiders. For those inside the frame, this is very much life and not without vitality or pleasures.

Figure 7.7
American Honey (2016). Director: Andrea Arnold. Cinematographer: Robbie Ryan.

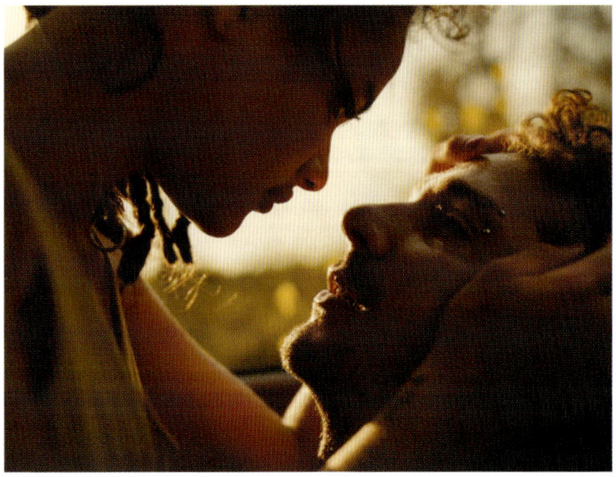

1

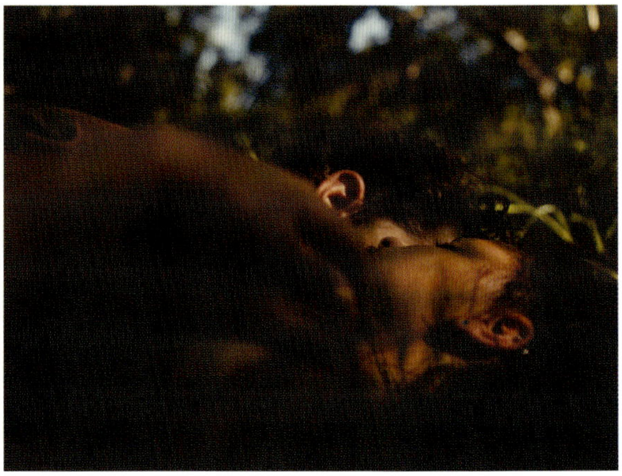

2

Another aspect repeated in the handheld camera coverage is the intermittent departure from character dynamics or interactions to capture telling visual details. For example, look at the scene pictured in Figure 7.8. Star, in the company of the two children in her care, forages through a dumpster for food, jamming her finds in a backpack. In the first shot she discovers a frozen turkey, which she tosses to the young boy. She and the girl child continue rummaging (Shots 2–4).

A cut creates a leap in time to the three of them working the road in an effort to hitchhike a ride. Several cars pass. No luck. In the midst of this effort, the sequence cuts to a shot of the backpack lying on the roadside and next to it the turkey, defrosting (Shot 9). The camera coverage, in tandem with editing, projects, at moments like this, an objective stance. "Look now at this," the camera seems to say. We feel the director's point of view. There will be a more thorough discussion of director's stance in chapter eight. Suffice it to say that the insertion of telling details in *American Honey* asks the viewer, in given moments, to take notice of the particulars of the world. It also adds to coverage grounded in realism, a lyrical quality. This is particularly evidenced when Star returns to the household of her charges. The camera goes on a tour, providing the viewer a visual record of her world. This record can be seen in Figure 7.9.

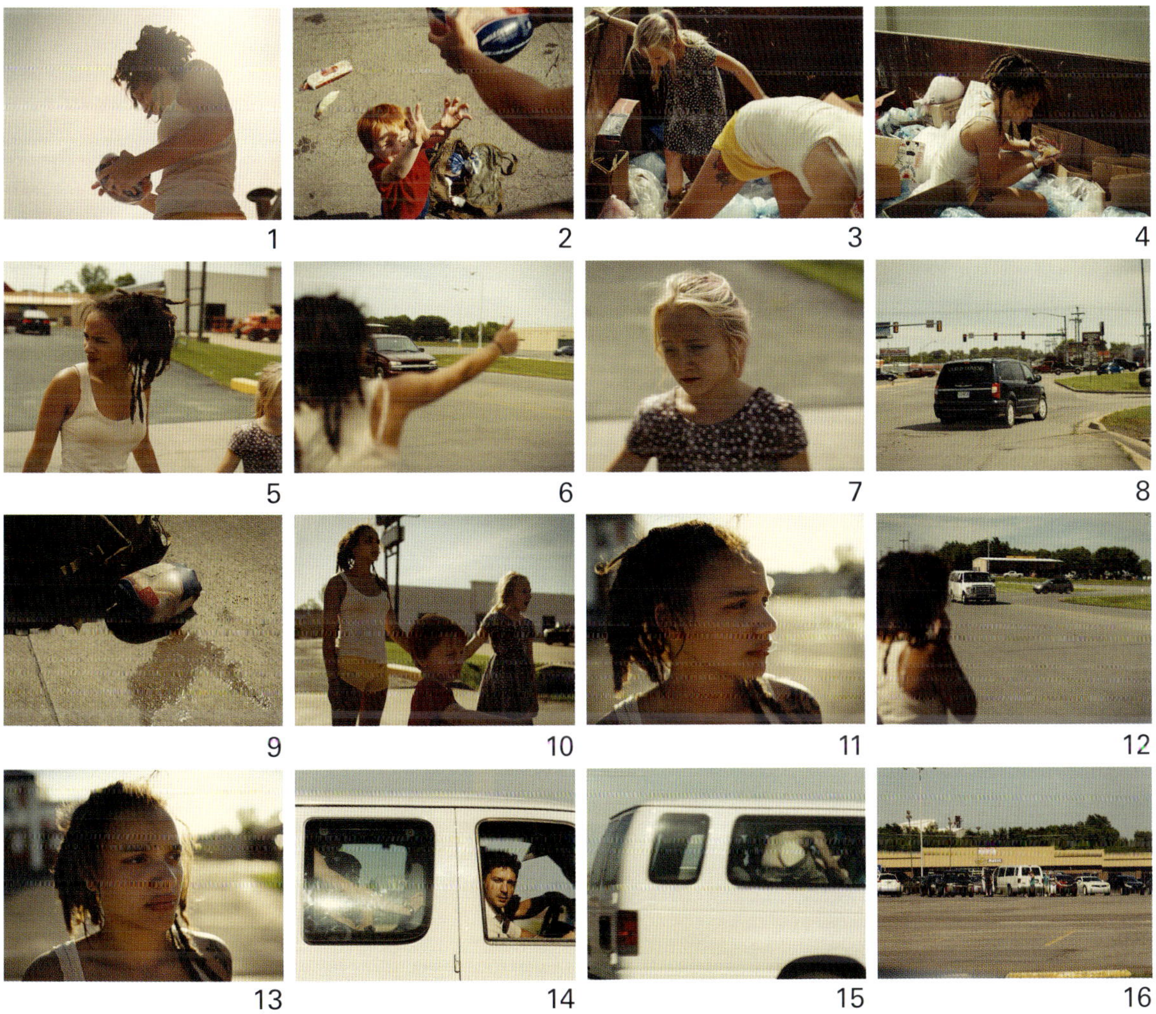

Figure 7.8 *American Honey* (2016). Director: Andrea Arnold. Cinematographer: Robbie Ryan.

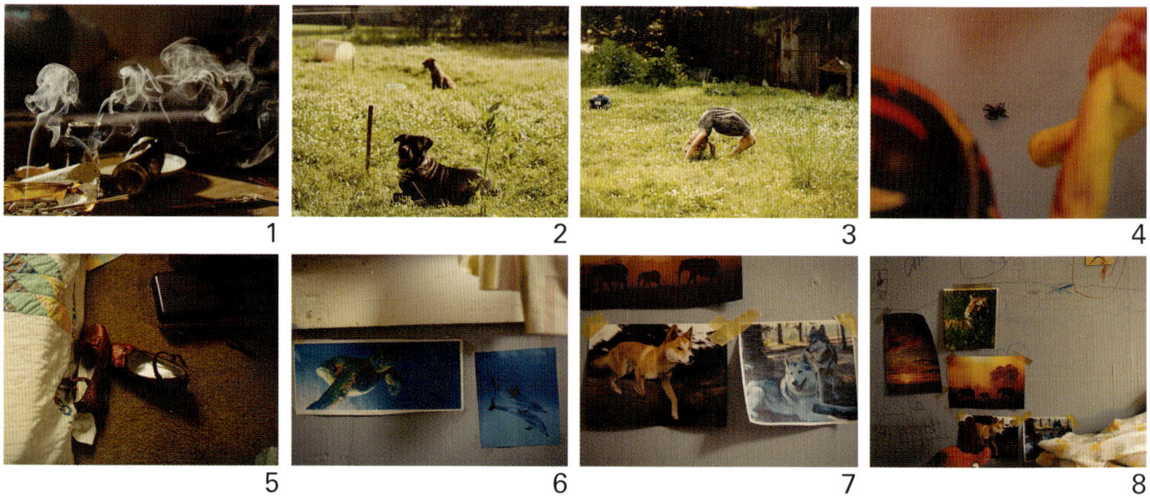

Figure 7.9 *American Honey* (2016). Director: Andrea Arnold. Cinematographer: Robbie Ryan.

Finally, the film achieves additional visual coherence with the continued return to images of Star, the protagonist. This is most noticeable during scenes in which Star appears with her fellow travelers. Figure 7.10 represents one such scene. The magazine crew is on the road in the van. The emphasis given to Star's point of view is made more emphatic by the scene's many cuts away from her. But, like a gravitational pull it returns to her, reminding the viewer that the film belongs, foremost, to her perspective. (Shots 1, 3, 5, 9, 12, 14, and 16)

What I find is that the actors who are more established have to readjust to my style, where a non-actor doesn't have to adjust to anything. There's a more documentary feel to things. Andrea [Arnold] would call it poetic realism. You're trying to be lyrical with something that's real.

—Robbie Ryan. Jenkins, David, "Robbie Ryan on New Andrea Arnold and Ken Loach Movies." *Little White Lies*. September 29, 2015.

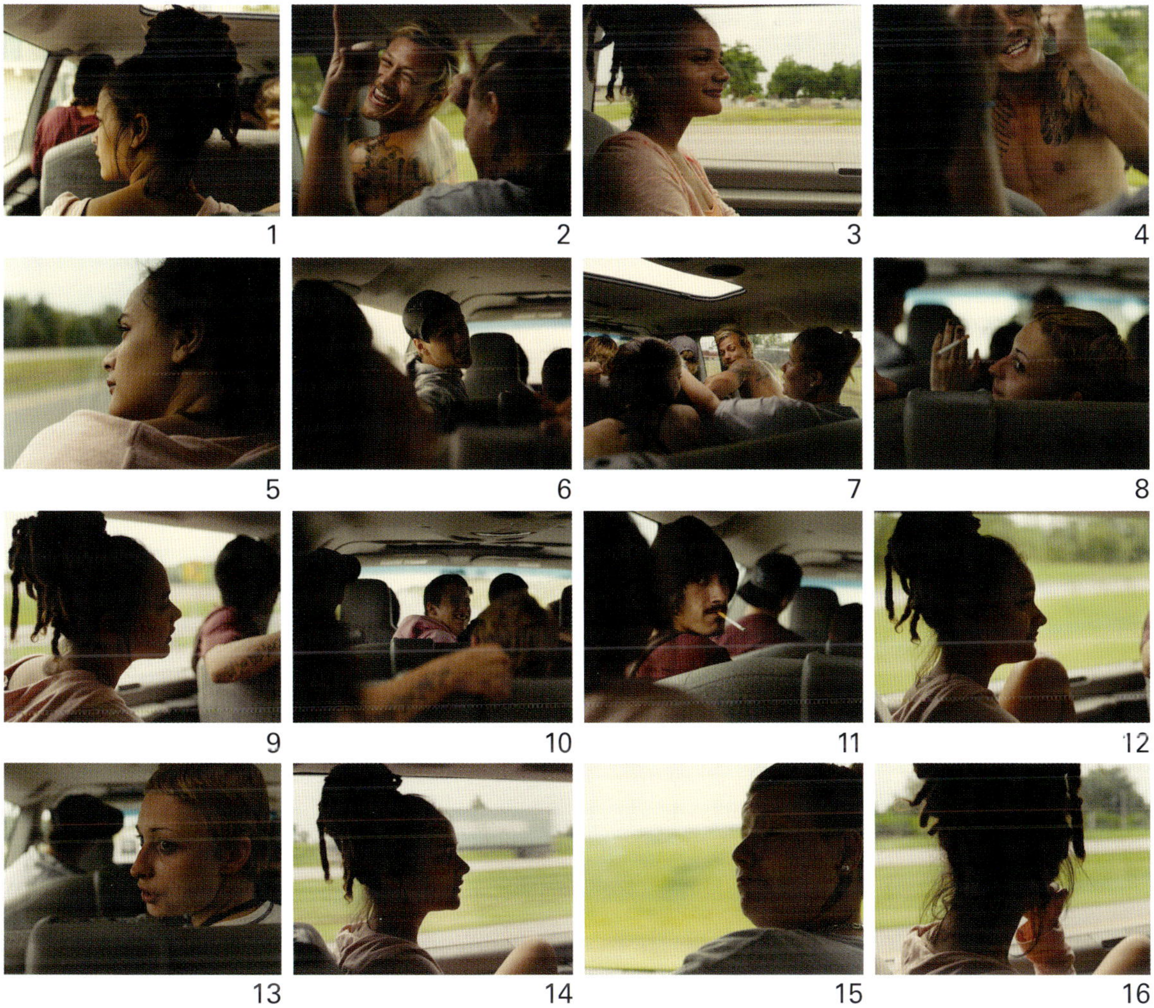

Figure 7.10 *American Honey* (2016). Director: Andrea Arnold. Cinematographer: Robbie Ryan.

Visual dynamics

American Honey anticipates content in the next chapter with camera work that serves a clear point of view, or stance. The camera strategy in Kirill Mikhanovsky's feature film, *Give Me Liberty*, makes a case for visual dynamics, another topic covered in chapter eight. But, looking at the two movies through the lens of handheld technique allows for an exploration of their similarities and their distinctions. There are a number of shared attributes. Each film finds its story material in real-life circumstances, focusing on characters living at the margins. In *Give Me Liberty*, this includes first generation immigrants and members of a disabled community. In both films, non-actors share the screen with experienced actors, culminating in a sizeable ensemble cast. And while *Give me Liberty* limits its locations to the city of Milwaukee, it is also a road movie, given how much screen time is spent on the streets of this Midwestern city, making of it an entire country. For this reason the interior of a transport van also serves as a primary and repeated location. An evocative musical score enlivens each of the films and both employ handheld camera technique, shot by veteran cinematographers accustomed to working in dramatic situations where the boundary between fiction and documentary blur.[10] Despite all of these similarities, the handheld technique in the two films creates vastly different effects. This is worth examining.

Some of the difference in effect will be accounted for by the story parameters. *Give Me Liberty* follows Vic, a Russian émigré and medical transport driver. The long "day in the life" depicted on screen becomes ever more complicated when Vic's grandfather, and his Russian friends and relatives, oblige Vic to transport them to a close friend's funeral. Vic acquiesces and this causes a cascade of delays in the pick-ups and drop-offs associated with his day job, infuriating the disabled riders stalled toward their destination, and his supervisor, who rails at Vic in repeated telephone calls. Among the frustrated riders is Tracy, wheelchair bound, whose wit and savvy become audible in her protests and directives, and who emerges as an equal match for Vic. The story spirals into chaos in the final scene when a rowdy street protest outside the Milwaukee police station obstructs Tracy's efforts to help her brother, held inside.

The most essential element to impact the variation in visual style involves the story's use of time. The story told in *American Honey* stretches across weeks on the road, where many of the most compelling events occur in downtime. The narrative structure of *Give Me Liberty* depends on urgency created by deadlines and the race to meet given demands that are time sensitive. The visual style of the film conveys this urgency. How?

Editing drives the pace but also tames the narrative chaos into a visual form. In the more dramatic action sequences, the camera whips from character to character, tracking the dialogue or action. But there is a stricter oversight that governs coverage. One can discern from just looking at the images in Figure 7.11 that coverage employed more than one take. The scene occurs moments after Vic, racing through side streets to get family members to the funeral, hits another car. The driver, outraged, attempts to exact compensation from Vic, who offers his maxed-out credit cards. Dima, a boxer from the Bronx (who claims to be the nephew of the deceased) tries to intervene with threats (Shot 16). Tracy shouts from the back of the van repeatedly in a litany of commands, urging Vic to leave. And so a getaway ensues. The scene returns several times to images of Tracy (Shots 9, 12, 14, 17, 20, and 22), but this repetition also, and perhaps more importantly, includes framing. Consistent framing can be found in shots 18 and 21; 10 and 15; as well as shots 1, 3b, 5, 5c, and 5d. The camera is democratic, given the variety of characters that appear, including a group shot of the riders framed together (Shot 24) in the penultimate shot. But it is the repeated frames that embed order into the variety, giving the scene coherence despite the wide net of inclusion and high stake theatrics.

This kind of narrative escalation occurs more than once in *Give Me Liberty*. The interaction between camera and editing persists, eventually

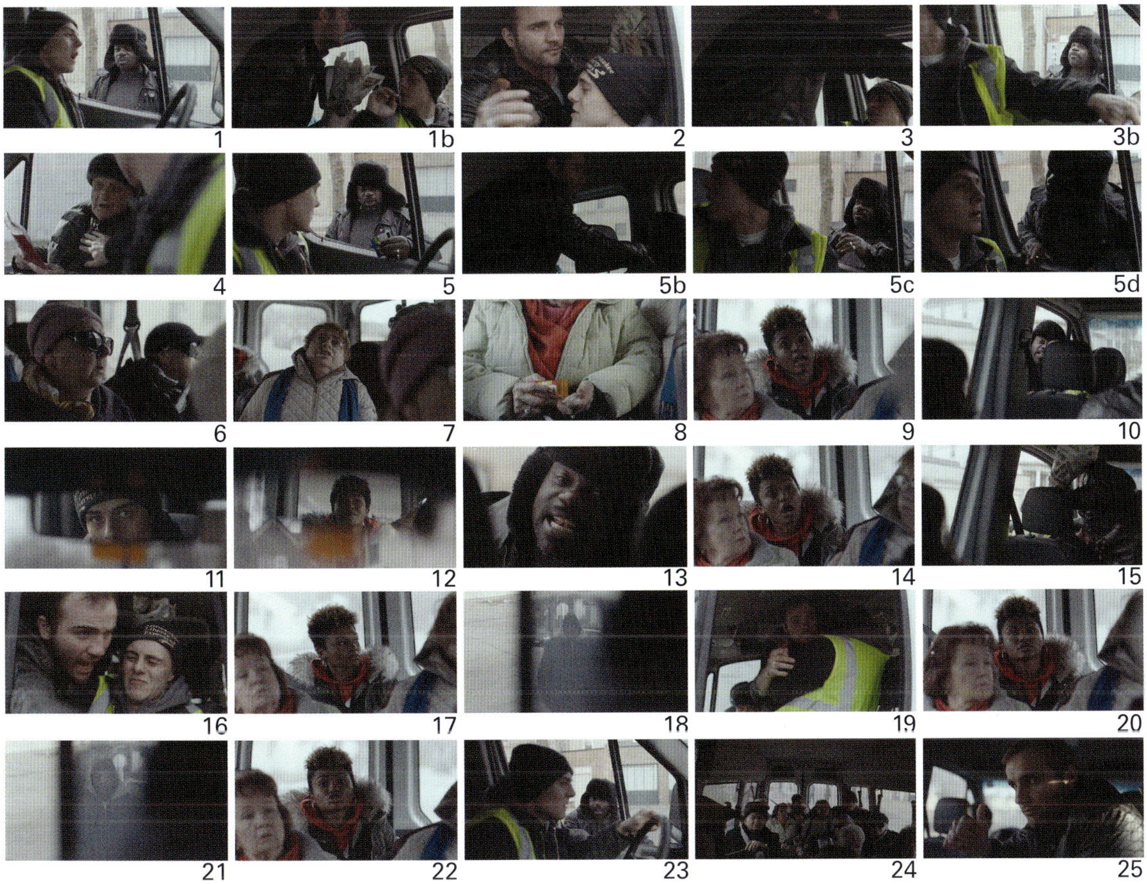

Figure 7.11 *Give Me Liberty* (2019). Director: Kirill Mikhanovsky. Cinematographer: Wyatt Garfield.

shaping scenes so that visual coherence and narrative epiphanies converge. See, for example, the still frames in Figure 7.12. This scene occurs toward the end of the film, when viewers will have already seen the movie transition from color to black-and-white footage, and back to color. Here, in black and white, a protest becomes riotous outside the police station. Dima, and his new love interest, Vic's sister, Sasha, along with Tracy and Vic, become separated from one another. The scene's primary purpose, both dramatically and visually, is to reunite the two couples: Dima and Sasha; Tracy and Vic. Shots 1–5, 10, 11, 15, 16, 18, and 22 reveal Tracy trying to break through the barricade toward the station to rescue her brother. This is cut against shots of Vic following after her (Shots 7, 12, 17, 19, 21, and 23). Dima, also in the crowd, ends up in a punching match (Shots 26 and 27) before being rescued and reunited with Sasha (Shots 28–31b), the two of them joining the protest. The scene concludes with Tracy spilled from her wheelchair onto the ground where Vic hovers above her, protecting.

Finally, while much of the film occurs at a breakneck speed, *Give Me Liberty* includes sequences in which the action slows or stalls, as when Vic—with his passengers in tow—visits Tracy's home, or during a dance sequence that takes place at the disability center. In these interludes, the handheld work becomes graceful, poetic, and even impressionistic.

One such scene is depicted in Figure 7.13. The day has careened to an end. Night has fallen. Tracy, the sole passenger now, sleeps in the van. Vic lights a cigarette. Eyeing Tracy through the rearview mirror, Vic recalls a time earlier in the day when the two shared a moment together (Shots 4 and 4b).

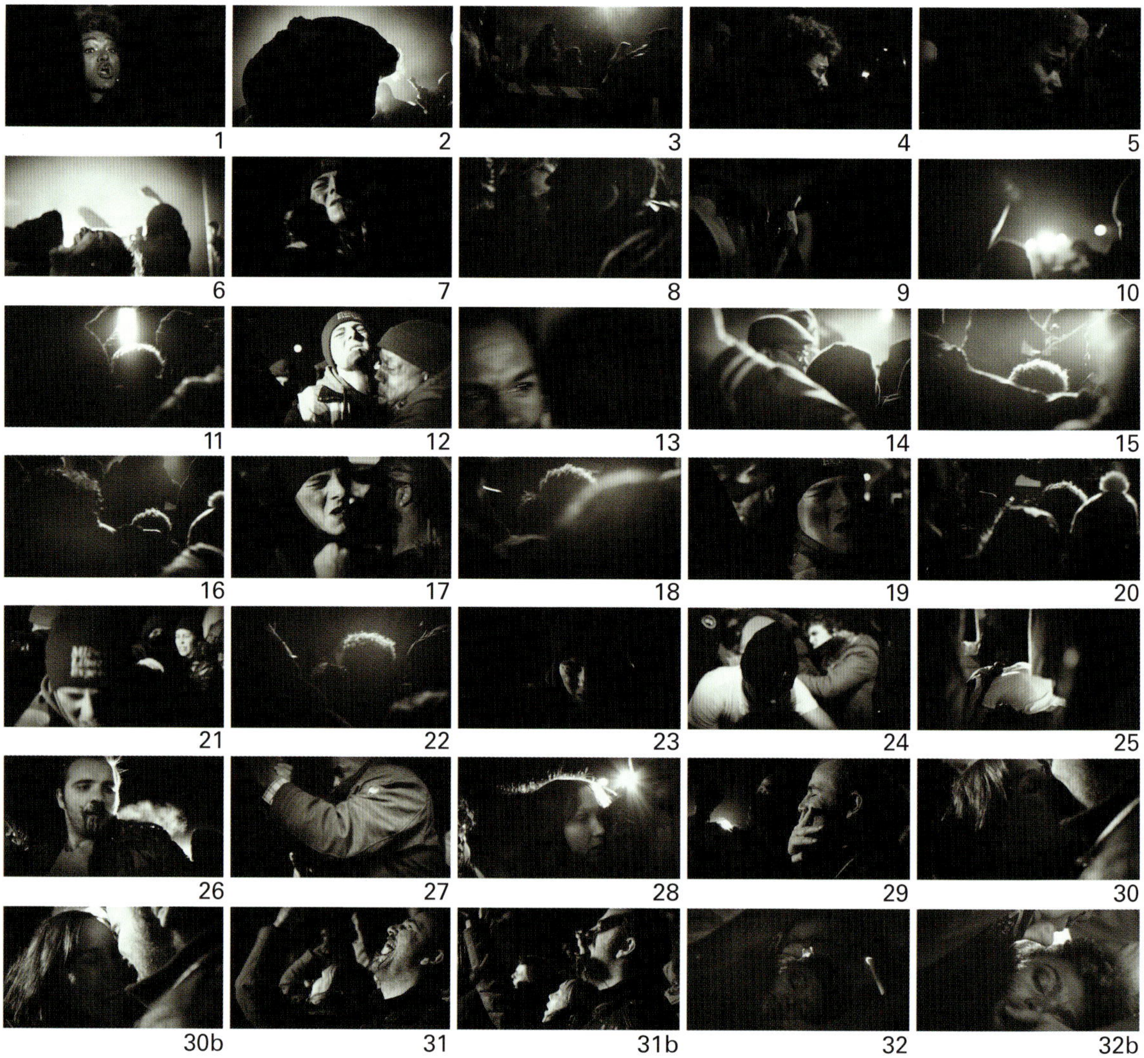

Figure 7.12 *Give Me Liberty* (2019). Director: Kirill Mikhanovsky. Cinematographer: Wyatt Garfield.

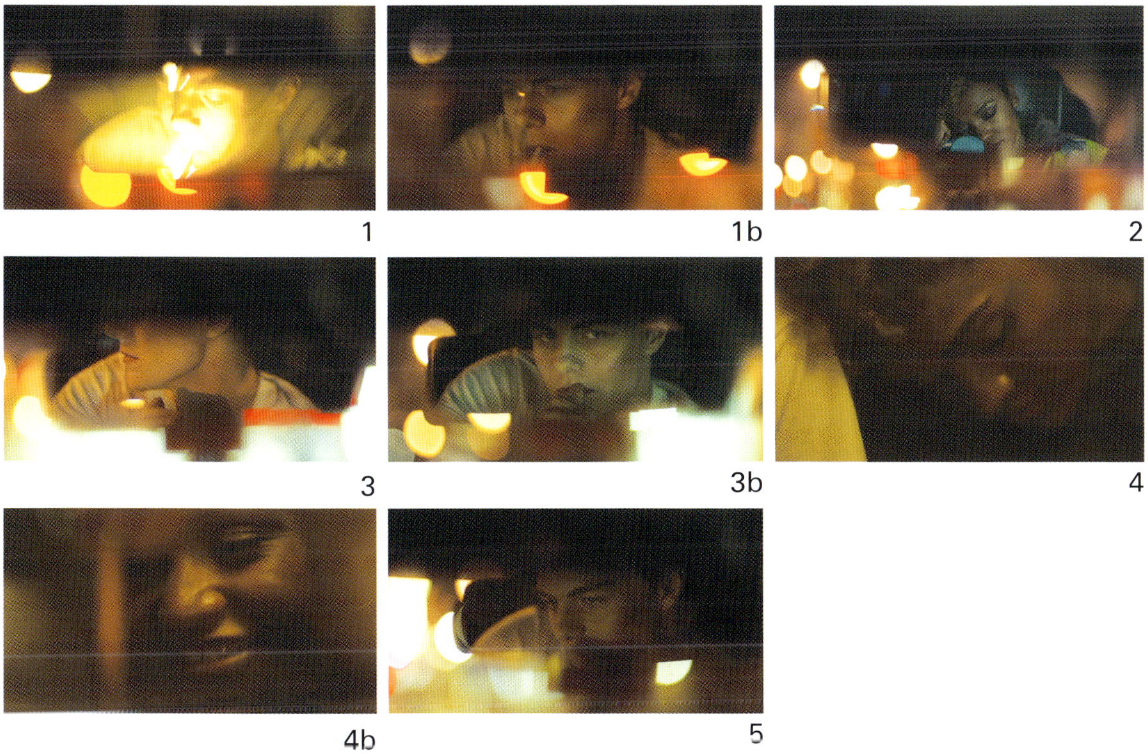

Figure 7.13 *Give Me Liberty* (2019). Director: Kirill Mikhanovsky. Cinematographer: Wyatt Garfield.

Again, the film repeats certain frames. In fact, only three frames dominate the scene's coverage. Without the dynamism of character interaction or narrative urgency, what gives the simple shot construction its charge?

To begin, flares of reflected light from the street, from the lit match, paint a sharp contrast in the shot compositions (Shots 1–3b, and 5). In these shots the mirror within the frame cuts off portions of each face. Added to this, we see Tracy (Shot 2) asleep *before* we see Vic take notice of her (Shot 3b). When he does, two actions converge: Vic looks up at her reflection, which given the eyeline, has him also looking directly at us, his viewer. This prompts the flashback. It is as if Vic looks up to say to us, "Remember this." The scene's treatment abandons the alliance between handheld coverage and real-life occurrence in favor of abstracting shape, color, and light toward more lyrical effect. After the flashback, the scene resumes, Vic with his eyes on the road.

Rehearsed camerawork

Luc and Jean Pierre Dardenne solve the issue of visual coherence by designing the choreography of handheld movements, shot to shot, and scheduling into preproduction a rehearsal period specifically for camera. Handheld technique has long been their camera strategy, having started as directors of documentary film. When they began writing and directing a fiction film in the 1980s, the story content conveyed their sustained interest in the social and economic conditions of Belgium's working class. Even the later films—*La Promesse*, *Rosetta*, *The Son*, *L'enfant*, *Lorna's Silence*, *The Kid with a Bike*, *Two Days, One Night*, and *The Unknown Girl*—employ a handheld camera in exploring lives stripped down to human basics. All of these films reflect the collaboration between the Dardenne Brothers and Belgium cinematographer, Alain Marcoen.[11] To their credit, each of the films, driven by particular narrative exigencies, achieves a distinct style. One obvious aspect of this "distinctness" is the distance between the handheld camera and the subject: from film to film the distance changes. The compelling but guarded vision of reality captured with the handheld camera in *La Promesse* becomes a stalking camera in *Rosetta*, tracking several feet behind the protagonist. In *The Son*, the stalking turns to an intimately close hovering, the camera virtually a burden on the back of the protagonist's neck (Figure 7.14, Shots 1n and 1o).

Use of handheld camera in these films, each in its distinct way, creates immediacy in the worlds that are conveyed. The action looks as if it has been covered coincidentally, betraying the fact that the directors rehearse the camera movements extensively with their technical crew and cast for weeks before principal photography begins. In the film *The Son*, the strategy of combining handheld camera with tight framing of the protagonist required that every physical movement or gesture of Olivier be choreographed in tandem with the camera's movement.[12]

Olivier teaches carpentry at a rehabilitation school and is unsettled by the arrival of a new student, Francis. Olivier approaches and avoids Francis. This leads to the revelation that a terrible bond exists between them, a bond that has emotional and moral consequences. In the scene pictured here, we're introduced to Olivier in the work environment of the carpentry shop. A woman approaches him about the new student (Figure 7.14, Shots 1i–2). The movement of camera is attached Olivier's movement; hovering behind or in front and occasionally sweeping over to ground that reflects his point of view. In the shop, he rescues the efforts of one student (Shots 1b–1g) and helps another finish a window cornice (Shots 3a–3i). Because of the close proximity to subject, we're never afforded an establishing shot, never allowed to see the character in a wide context, situated in his environment. As such, the revelation of space occurs in snatches, glimpses stolen as Oliver moves, or in the rare moments when he stands still. His neck, his profile, the brown leather belt supporting his back, the cigarettes he smokes, and the details of his person are what we see.

The camera's constriction of space around Olivier re-enforces the experience of his tense mood and irritability. Even when almost still—smoking a cigarette, washing a dish in the sink, eating a sandwich—his physical presence strains to contain disturbance. This is what we are pressed up against with little or no relief or escape.

If the readable frame in *The Son* is confined to the back of Olivier's neck—and other details related to his habits and person—is this imagery sufficient to accumulate toward narrative coherence? Of course. The movie is admirably faithful to the axiom of visual storytelling: "show me don't tell me," even while relevant knowledge about the character's circumstances is delayed. Not unlike the strategy of tight frames in *The Holy Girl* explored in chapter three, the hovering handheld camera, in combination with movement, sacrifices wider perspective and orientation in favor of direct, immediate experience.

Eventually, the source of Oliver's intensity emerges. We learn of the opposing forces tugging at him—vengeance and forgiveness. The camera's insistence plants us squarely in the frame of Olivier's moral dilemma. The combination of handheld camera with a tight frame works like a vise from Olivier's workbench, pressing us close to him, like it or not.[13]

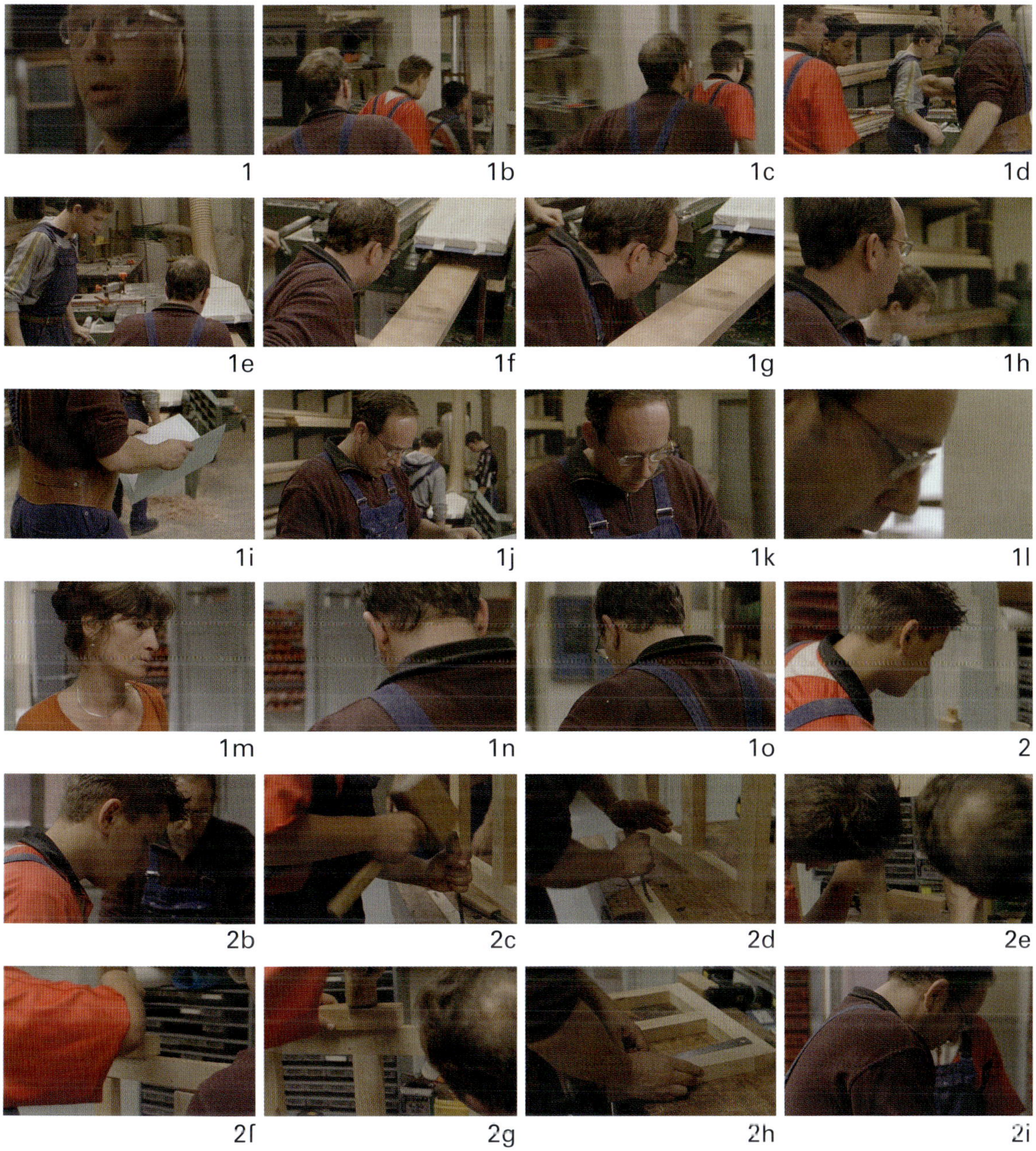

Figure 7.14
The Son (2002). Directors: Jean-Pierre and Luc Dardenne. Cinematographer: Alain Marcoen.

The handheld camera in combination with stasis

Pawel Pawlikowski's finesse in navigating the interaction between camera and story was schooled, to some extent, by his early work in documentary film. In these early films, the director is not satisfied entirely with the "fly on the wall" style of direct observation, and so brings to it lyrical or formal qualities that add dimension or impact to dramatic effects. When Pawlikowski makes the transition in the year 2000 to narrative film, there is already a confidence and muscularity in the execution of handheld coverage. *Last Resort* skillfully combines the handheld camera *with* camera stasis. In doing so, the movie earns immediacy invoked by handheld shots as well as the narrative heft and formal framing of static shots. The result: a dynamic between the two styles of coverage that invigorates story and reinforces tone.

At the story's center are Tanya, a single mother and her son, Artyom. They arrive in the UK from Russia to make a life with Tanya's English fiancée. When the fiancée doesn't show up at the airport, they're left stranded, prompting Tanya to take matters in hand, declaring political asylum. They're transported to a "holding area," an apartment complex in the forsaken Stonehaven, a coastal town whose time has long since passed. While they wait for their application for asylum to be processed, they are taken under the wing of enterprising Alfie, manager of the local amusement arcade.

In the scene pictured in Figure 7.15, Tanya and her son wait in the airport while her fiancée is paged over the loudspeaker. This waiting is captured in two static shots of extended duration (Shots 2 and 3). The second of the two represents a shift in location, shot size, and staging that mark a leap in time, prolonging their wait. Head in hands, Tanya weeps, unsure, with only eighty-seven dollars in her possession, what to do next (Shot 3). Artyom tries to console her and then, annoyed by the intrusive stare of a nearby woman, barks, "What are you looking at?" (Shot 3b). This sets off a succession of handheld images

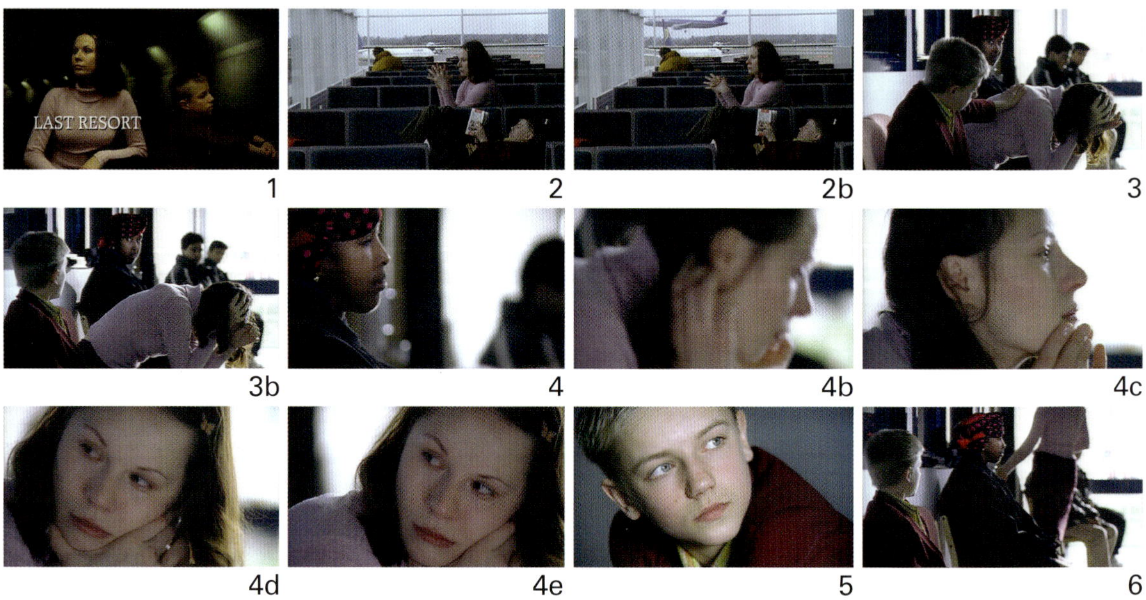

Figure 7.15 *Last Resort* (2000). Director: Pawel Pawlikowski. Cinematographer: Ryszard Lenczewski.

that move from the close-up of the intruding woman to Tanya and then a cut, still handheld, to the close-up of Artyom—as the idea comes to her, as she measures it against responsibility to her son: political asylum. The final image, a static shot, resumes the framing, picturing her moment of action (Shot 6).

In *Last Resort*, there is a dance of sorts between the two different styles of coverage: handheld and stasis. The transitions between them occur organically, in response to drama unfolding in the scene so that we experience no disturbance in viewing. Any given scene is advantaged by the variation the two styles create in dramatic effects. Stasis allows for more objective witness of Tanya and her son, while the handheld affords the viewer an opportunity to draw close, to be given proximity to their experience. In the scene pictured in Figure 7.15, we observe Tanya and her son, and then are brought close, with handheld movements, to her subjective experience (despair, bewilderment, and then resolve) as she mulls over what to do next. Once the decision has been made, an objective stance returns.

We see the two styles again in the sequence pictured in Figure 7.16. The handheld camera covers Tanya and Artyom checking into the holding area. Physical movement and activity characterize the scene with handheld coverage keeping us, again, inside the experience through proximity to character and the camera's quick reflexes and eye for composition. The handheld sequence is punctuated with static shots. These allow for moments of reflection, stalling the action. While handheld coverage enlivens pace, the static shots quiet the narrative, occasionally slowing it to a halt as when the two arrive in the desolate apartment with it's palm tree poster peeling off the wall. The measure of Tanya's decision gains weight as Artyom takes in the view (Shots 7 and 9). Below him, pictured in an extreme wide static shot, the abandoned beach park bears the name *Dreamland* (Shot 8).

One last observation about the relationship between shot size and camera style in *Last Resort*: the handheld coverage privileges medium shots and close-ups, recording moments of emotional intensity or scenes in which the staging is, by necessity, more naturalistic. These shots cover daily activity and character movement, often with groups of characters. Stasis is often reserved for wider shots, or extreme wide shots. When extreme wide shots are delivered, the effect is dramatic emphasis, moments endowed with visual authority through photographic stillness, the grammatical equivalent of an exclamation point at the end of a sentence (Figure 7.16, Shots 8 and 10).

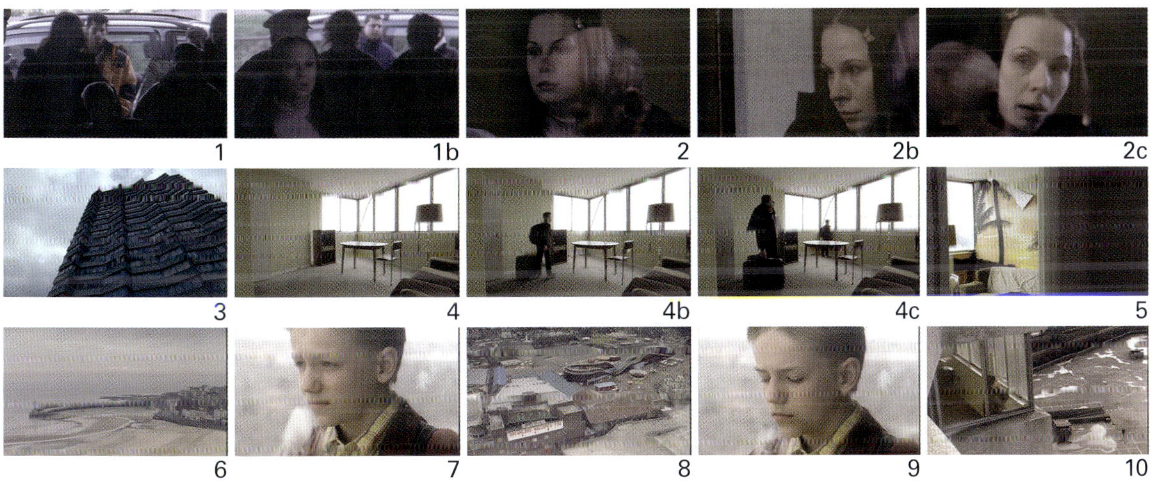

Figure 7.16 *Last Resort* (2000). Director: Pawel Pawlikowski. Cinematographer: Ryszard Lenczewski.

Dogme

Any discussion of handheld camera work requires mention of the Dogme doctrine. In 1995, Lars Von Trier, Thomas Vinterberg, Soren Kragh-Jacobsen, and Kristian Levring signed into law *The Vow of Chastity*, ten rules to challenge conventional, big-budget filmmaking and reassert what they regarded as film truth: movies unencumbered by dictates of genre, special effects, grand design in sound, lighting, art direction, costume, make up, or even mise en scene.[14] Their intention has been an anti-aesthetic stripping down of the act of filmmaking from its concern with effects, thus allowing stories to be told through performance, with more direct access to human realities and human emotions. Exclusive use of the handheld camera (one of the ten criteria) is at the service of character movement. With no "marks" to hit, or frames to limit figure movement or control staging, the actors are said to have greater room for improvisation, adding immediacy and spontaneity to the quality of recorded performance.

Dogme 95

This was a cinematic movement that created a set of filmmaking rules that aimed to "purify" films, removing predictability, complacency, and distraction, forcing filmmakers to focus on the story, actors, and their skills as a director, with the hope that this would increase the chance of creating something with greater "truth." In 1995, Lars Von Trier, Thomas Vinterberg, Soren Kragh-Jacobsen, and Kristian Levring signed into law *The Vow of Chastity*—ten rules to challenge conventional, big-budget filmmaking and reassert what they regarded as film truth.

Vinterberg's 1998 film, *The Celebration*, demonstrates that the application of Dogme rules does not preclude the basic tools of visual storytelling. Photographed by Anthony Dod Mantle, the camera is careful to provide establishing shots—wide shots of a given location as the action moves from place to place. There is also variety in the shot size and plenty of alternating movement and stasis. Movement or stasis is determined to some extent, though not always, by character movement or stasis. The handheld camera of the Dogme project does not, in the case of *The Celebration*, rule out the possibility of shots with interesting formal construction. There is also the method of treating, for example, three sequences recorded as parallel action with three different handheld camera styles, each appropriate to the temperament and action of the characters in the scene. Do these attributes accumulate toward an overall camera style? Vinterberg is clearly not a novice in the craft of making film. But following the principles of Dogme-esque reform, the film style is dedicated—first and foremost—to performance. Film style as a systematic conception and application of technique toward multi-dimensioned visual storytelling is not the priority. Value is given above all else to eliminating any element that challenges the portrayal of human realities and the accompanying emotional life of characters on the screen. Technically speaking, the principal instrument of this reform is the handheld camera.

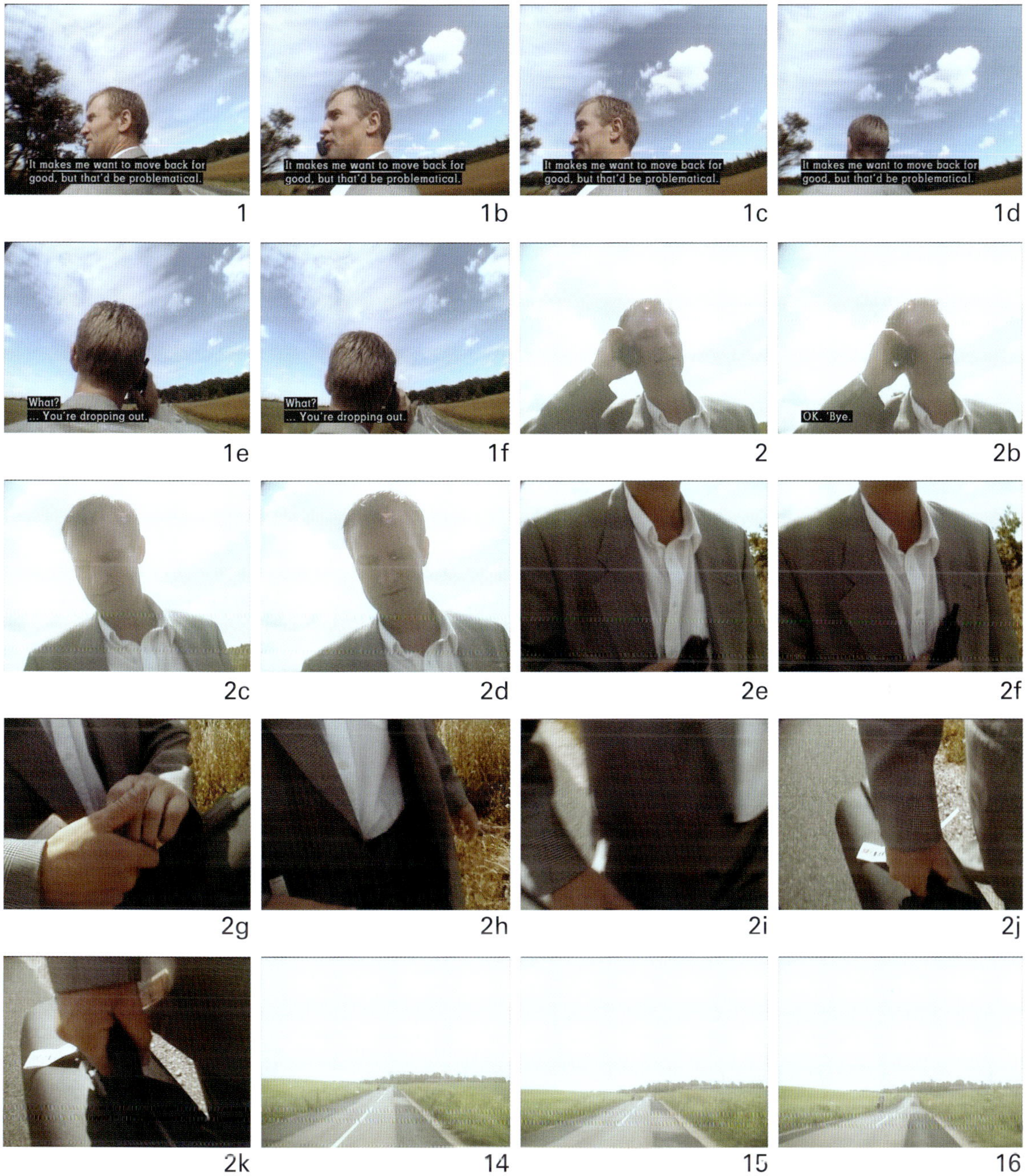

Figure 7.17 *The Celebration* (1998). Director: Thomas Vinterberg. Cinematographer: Anthony Dod Mantle.

Abstracting images

Wong Kar-Wai's 1995 collaboration with cinematographer Christopher Doyle, makes use of a handheld camera that bears no relation whatsoever to the strictures of Dogme or the influence of documentary's verité, with realistic depiction of location and events. And yet visual coherence prevails. While an urban grittiness pervades the geography of each frame, the treatment is futuristic, abstract, and nearly virtual (when virtual implies a computer-generated image environment that seems real). The locations *are* real, but the camera's treatment strategy (of real locations and the characters populating them) shows no deference to moviemaking's conventional storytelling imperatives. The film is intensely visual, and yet the images are neither staged (composed and framed) nor connected (by way of editing) to facilitate story knowledge or narrative development. The camera movement itself—its direction, pace, position, and style—is as much an essential characteristic of the movie world as the image content rendered by the camera's seemingly impulsive gander.

Figure 7.18 depicts a series of shots joined by jump cuts as the female figure makes her way through a deserted subway station. The shots are sequential, but camera positions, various and irregular, seem chosen not for their value in creating continuity of action but for declaring the nature of this urban underworld, and enlarging the effect of the woman's diminished size in relation to it. Added to this is the futuristic design made by striking colors and shapes, with her form, distorted by the wide-angle lens, set against them. It is as if the viewer is peering not into a fish bowl, but from one.

She arrives at a location adjacent to the subway tracks. She sets up the location for her partner, a hit man who is the object of her longing and affection. The camera is handheld and mobile, the lens wide angle, but it is the framing that startles, detached, as it is, from the boundaries of field and ground, from the customary ploy of presenting imagery that accumulates toward narrative development. We are a long way from the shot-to-shot revelation of story as in the prelude of *KAOS*. Here, the camera floats, tilts, slants, circles, darts toward or around an object, dances away. And while motion is often inspired by figure movement it is not precisely synchronized with figure movement, complicating further the dissonance of time and space. In one instance, the woman dresses the bed (Shot 9). The camera, squeezed in front of her, moves back as she moves forward, and forward as she moves back. At other moments it takes distance from her, framing her in the context of other elements in the environment. Another shot depicts her setting the clock in the narrow apartment that she arranges for her partner (Shots 13–14). The motion of the camera—tilted and then upright as it makes a clockwise circle round the clock—follows the movement of her hand as it adjusts the long hand to the correct time. The camera traces the arc of her movement but not at the same pace: the motion is delayed, even if by seconds, and not in sync with her gesture. Not only is the effect disorienting, but the image captured is not tethered to conventional narrative strategies. Showing is not a substitute for telling.

The last series of still frames show the woman, lovelorn, at the jukebox of a local bar (Figure 7.19). Here, the images have all but sacrificed representation for abstraction: planes of color, repetition of shape, and light that seems to effervesce and liquefy on the screen. As elsewhere, the images created by the camera argue on behalf of the camera's play, emphasis given to the evocation of mood and more than mood, state of mind, state of world. Yes, the camera is voyeuristic. Yes, the camera shows particles of a world that reflect characters in motion, but these are characters who manage, altogether, very little dramatic action of the kind referred to in Aristotle's classic text on drama, *The Poetics*. So what kind of world is this in which the camera misbehaves so openly in its participation as the tool of storytelling?

In *Fallen Angels*, images accumulate as bits and pieces of a thoroughly imagined whole. We are shown: characters moving about, performing tasks, going through rituals of work and leisure

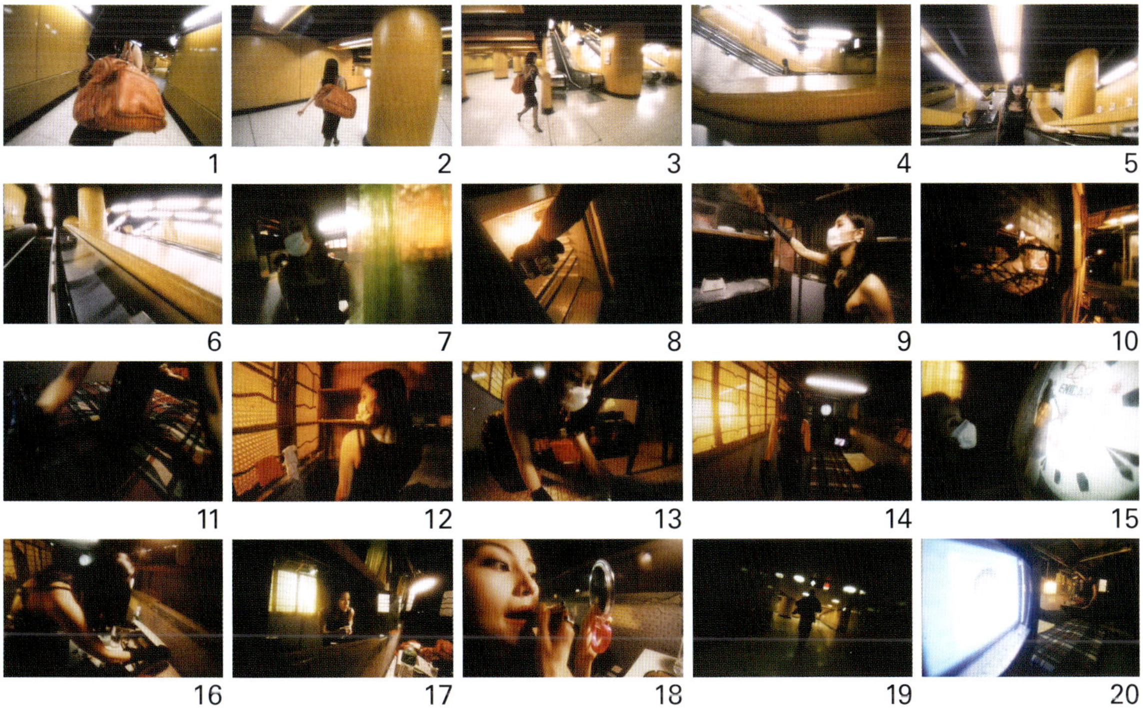

Figure 7.18 *Fallen Angels* (1995). Director: Wong Kar-Wai. Cinematographer: Christopher Doyle.

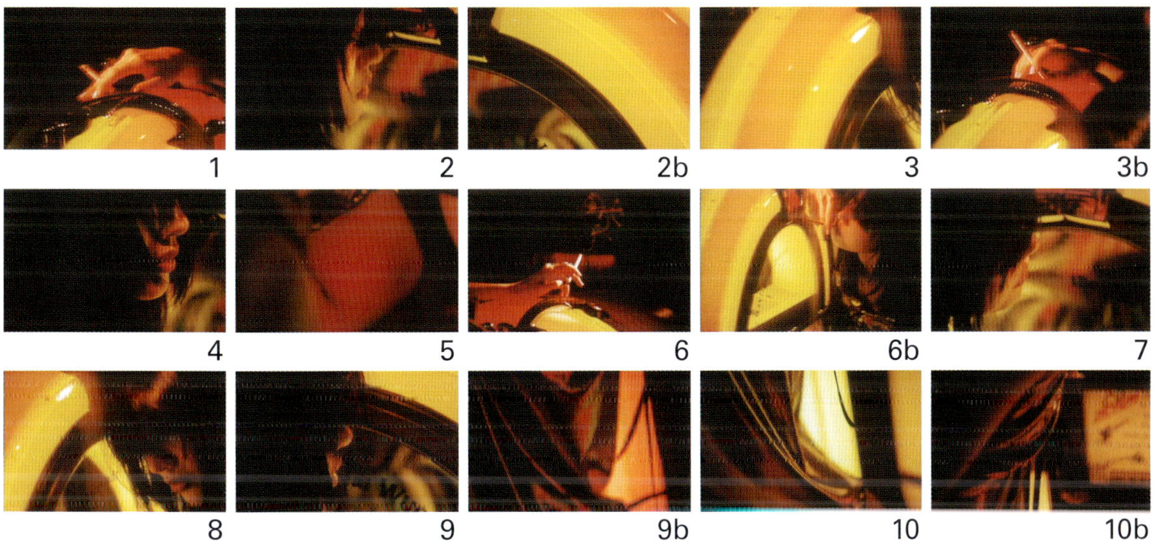

Figure 7.19 *Fallen Angels* (1995). Director: Wong Kar-Wai. Cinematographer: Christopher Doyle.

and heartbreak against the backdrop of a neon-lit city at night (the underworld of Hong Kong). And while we may recognize objects or places ("that's a subway" or "this is a fast food shop"), the style in which they are shown, treated by the camera, dislocates them from the plastic, sensate world. It evokes instead, and powerfully, compromising nothing, *a state of the world* known all too well by anyone who has ever had a cell phone ring during a night at the movies: time and space fractured by technology, the world mapped as an integrated circuit where everything pulses, rarely lingers, and never quiets. It renders intangible or vaporous any sustained presence in place and time, leaving to theory or chance a durable connection between two people.

Discussion questions

1. *American Honey* and *Give Me Liberty* each stage sequences in a van. These are depicted in Figure 7.10 and Figure 7.11. In studying the two contact sheets, can you identify similarities or differences?
2. What focal planes dominate the handheld images in this chapter?
3. In addition to agility, what additional characteristics are associated with handheld sequences?

Notes

1. *Cinema Vérité in America: Studies in Uncontrolled Documentary* (The MIT Press). 1976. p. 1–4.
2. *Ibid*. p. 1.
3. *The work of John Cassavetes: Script, Performance Style, and Improvisation*. Maria Viera. Journal of Film and Video. Vol 42. No 3. Problems in Screenwriting (Fall 1990) pp. 34–40.
4. *Cassavetes on Cassavetes*. Ray Carney. Faber and Faber, Ltd. (London, 2001).
5. *Killer of Sheep* fulfilled the director's thesis requirement in the graduate film program at UCLA. The film was shot over two years, finished in 1979 but not released theatrically until 2008 due to cost of music rights for twenty-two songs in the film.
6. Denis Gamze Ergüven on Her Stunning New Movie, 'Mustang'. Vogue Magazine, November 13, 2015. Julia Felsenthal. https://www.vogue.com/article/mustang-deniz-gamze-erguven-interview.
7. *Mustang: A Feminist Fairy Tale Sticks it to the Turkish Patriarchy*. Feb. 12, 2016. Kate Kilkenny in conversation with the director. Pacific Standard.
8. Andrea Arnold interview: *American Honey, chasing people in Walmart, and the power of Rihanna*. *Independent Online Magazine*. October 12, 2016. Clarisse Loughrey.
9. https://nofilmschool.com/2016/05/andrea-arnold-american-honey-press-conference-cannes-2016.
10. Wyatt Garfield served as the director of photography for *Give Me Liberty*, and also for *Mediterranea*, the film directed by Jonas Carpignano, discussed in Chapter 6.
11. Marcoen is reported to have gone to great lengths and with remarkable imagination in creating the effect of natural light in *The Son*. The workspace in particular was lit with ceiling spotlights, floor lamps, light from the outside, to establish this natural effect.
12. From an interview with the actor Olivier Gourmet on the DVD release of *The Son* by New Yorker Video. "A good take which is synchronized takes many rehearsals. It's difficult to capture something on film, especially when you want to tell a story through someone's body. It's like ballet—everything choreographed and it has to look natural as if it was filmed coincidentally." In fact *The Son* was filmed over a period of thirteen weeks with extensive rehearsals, first with actors prior to each shot, and thereafter, with camera and sound.
13. *A film is a story of how it's been shot*. From the interview with the Dardenne Brothers on the DVD release of *The Son* by New Yorker Films. They also report during this interview of shooting several takes of each shot, varying the pace of performance so that they might have greater control over the rhythm and pace of the film in editing.

14. Dogme 95's Vow of Chastity
    1. Shooting must be done on location. Props and sets must not be brought in.
    2. The sound must never be produced apart from the images or vice versa.
    3. The camera must be handheld.
    4. The film must be in color. Special lighting is not acceptable.
    5. Optical work and filters are forbidden.
    6. The film must not contain superficial action.
    7. Temporal and geographical alienation are forbidden.
    8. Genre movies are not acceptable.
    9. The film format must be Academy 35mm.
    10. The director must not be credited.

8

Visual dynamics and tone

By now you are expert in understanding the dramatic effects created by various camera techniques. These include the static camera, a moving camera, the close-up, wide shot, the long take, and the handheld camera. In this chapter we begin with a focus on films characterized by a strong visual style, often combining many of the techniques we have explored in previous chapters, using, as well, mise en scene and shot duration through editing. We will look closely to assess the specific attributes that give a visual treatment its force. You will quickly discover, in the close look at scenes characterized by strong visual dynamics, the frequent use of converging elements to generate the energy within the frame or shot.

Working in tandem with story necessities to realize specific dramatic effects, the visual style will impact the film's tone, or point of view. Tone is simply an attitude toward the story content and its characters, a mood or atmosphere, and in some instances, a way of seeing the world. There are certainly movies in which the sole purpose is to make a claim or amplify a particular viewpoint. Many of these films fit conveniently into the genre of documentary. In fiction film, which has been the focus of this book, the mere choice of story content can begin to suggest a point of view, enhanced by the stylistic treatment.

This chapter also explores the interaction between visual style and its impact on point of view. We will be analyzing the specific elements that contribute to the film's dynamism and in what way the elements combine to suggest the tone. We will also be attempting to understand how visual treatment works to centralize the story with a specific atmosphere or mood, even as it supports the plot.

Of course, many films cited in earlier chapters demonstrate impressive visual dynamics. Here, we study a few more from which we can discern some basic criteria for animating a film's imagery. We will also notice that with each film, the tone is implicated by camera treatment. While tone can be imprinted through story content, its effect will be dependent upon a treatment strategy that relies on technique, supported by the camera.[1] Many examples of tone conveyed through precise management of technique can be found in the films cited in previous chapters.

We have discovered by now, and repeatedly, the way in which camera treatment will impact and depend on other techniques—production design, editing, sound design, etc. This, of course, continues to be true in our investigation of any kind of visual dynamic and its interaction with a film's tone. We begin the chapter looking at films characterized by an emphatic visual style, looking closely to assess the specific attributes that give the visual treatment its energy or force.

I remember a quote by Akira Kurosawa, something he said at maybe his 70th birthday. Someone asked him, does he know everything about cinema. And Kurosawa said—and I'm paraphrasing here—there's a whole universe of cinema I have yet to learn. So one of my favorite filmmakers, one of the great masters of all time, who had made so many great films, says there's a universe he has still yet to learn.

—Spike Lee, *DGA Quarterly*, Spring 2008

Tone: culture and society, political slant

A film's visual treatment can support commentary or underscore point of view integral to a film's story. And yet, it is not the project of drama to resolve society's issues so much as to place social, cultural, and/or political issues in a context of appropriate complexity. We have seen how affecting screen images can be. When used in service of cultural commentary or political reflection, a film becomes, at the very least, a great way to start conversations. Film narration is known to be the process through which plot conveys or withholds story information. In the stories told in the five films discussed first in this chapter, we see discernible cultural, if not political, information.

We have explored at length the use of camera to convey time, place, and character, acknowledging that each have their own identity within the film and within the world itself. So a natural next step would be to embrace narrative films as cultural artifacts that can take on social and political issues, issues that drive a story's characters in making choices.

Convergence

The Conformist, a 1970 film by Bernardo Bertolucci, exemplifies a concept for visual treatment driving the images on screen. Rendered with precision, the film's visual style creates a wide range of visceral effects. Movies have demonstrated the capacity to excite visceral reactions since the early days of silent film. Think of the panicked audiences fleeing the theater in 1896 during the screening of the Lumiere Brothers' short film, *The Arrival of a Train at La Ciotat*.[2] This may have to do with the way in which moving images approximate reality. It can be more affecting still when projected on a large screen before which we sit in the dark. But it may also have to do with film as a sensual medium. *The Conformist* definitely engages our senses, yes, but also our nervous systems—exciting our pleasures and repulsions, even our sense of taboo.

The Conformist conjures image after image characterized by visual energy. In certain instances a convergence of light, space, and dimension creates the energy. Occasionally, it is managed through mise en scene: a dynamic between camera and the various fields within the composition. In still other instances, the energy comes from sensual beauty. All the while, a story unfolds.

The Conformist, based on a 1951 novel, tracks the life of Marcello Clerici, a young man, eager, after traumatic experiences in childhood, to have a normal life. This desire for belonging, for normalcy, prompts him to enlist as a member of the secret police during Mussolini's Fascist rule of Italy. It also inspires him to marry. He travels to Paris with his new wife, Guilia, under the guise of a honeymoon where he plans, on order from the secret police, to assassinate his former college professor, Luca. The professor, living in exile, is a renowned and vocal anti-Fascist. Plans go awry when Marcello meets the professor's wife, Anna, who tests the limits of his new marriage and his newly felt love for her.

The story does not unfold in chronological time. The film begins during Marcello's honeymoon in Paris. It will travel back to visualize his enlistment in the secret police, his courtship with Guilia, and even further back to the traumatic experiences of his young life. The film's timeline also revisits occasions in which Marcello is called on to provide care for his upscale mother, doped, living alone, and complicit when taken advantage of by her chauffeur.

The absence of chronology does not lessen the impact of the plot on our growing sense of dread over Marcello's life choices and the odds of a disturbing outcome. And yet, scenes persist, one after the next, as riveting. What accounts for this? We can glean certain insights by looking at the images in Figure 8.1. These wide shots have been taken from various scenes across the film.

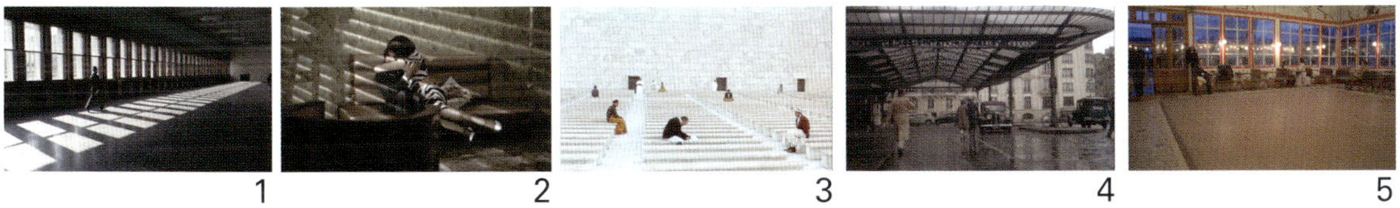

Figure 8.1 *The Conformist* (1970). Director: Bernardo Bertolucci. Cinematographer: Vittorio Storaro.

Readily, we notice a prevalence of formal patterns. Each image features a repeated element and, in each case, the repetition involves grids or striation. Even the stage-like mise en scene in shot 3, picturing Marcello's visit to his father in the sanatorium, includes rows and rows of benches vanishing toward a horizon dividing the benches from a wall of white bricks. In shots 1 and 2, a pattern is created through windows and light. In shots 4 and 5, the patterns emerge from architectural elements. In four of the five shots, image depth acts as an essential element. The application of formal properties pulls away from the documentary aesthetic found so often in films explored in chapter seven, shot with a handheld camera. While the scenes in *The Conformist* are staged in real locations, and story events have real world correlatives and gravity, the visual treatment creates an added dimension, and one might say, a layer of detachment, allowing, as we discussed in chapter two, for narrative complexity. Story turns, even if treacherous or painful or tender, cannot be sentimentalized. In shot 2, for example, the fiancée seduces Marcello on the sofa in her family home. Stripes of light splayed across the two of them work as counterpoint to the sexiness of the action on the sofa, acting almost as commentary, definitely serving the scene's atmosphere and tone. So it is with the formal repetitions in the other four wide shots. Although the narrative particulars are based on an existing world, the film becomes a world artfully fashioned, not a world which exists. And so it is a world we watch, more than a world we enter. Bertolucci keeps us watching through a feast of visual and sensual pleasures that accompany our interest in Marcello and his fate.

Looking at the images in Figure 8.2, one sees further evidence of formal treatment and further examples of converging elements. The images represent a segment of a longer scene, which occurs as a flashback early in the film, while Marcello rides in a car toward the destination that will shape his future (Shot 1). In the flashback, Marcello visits a close friend, the blind Italo, at a radio station where Italo waits to go on air. Both men support the Fascist regimes currently in power. Italo has arranged

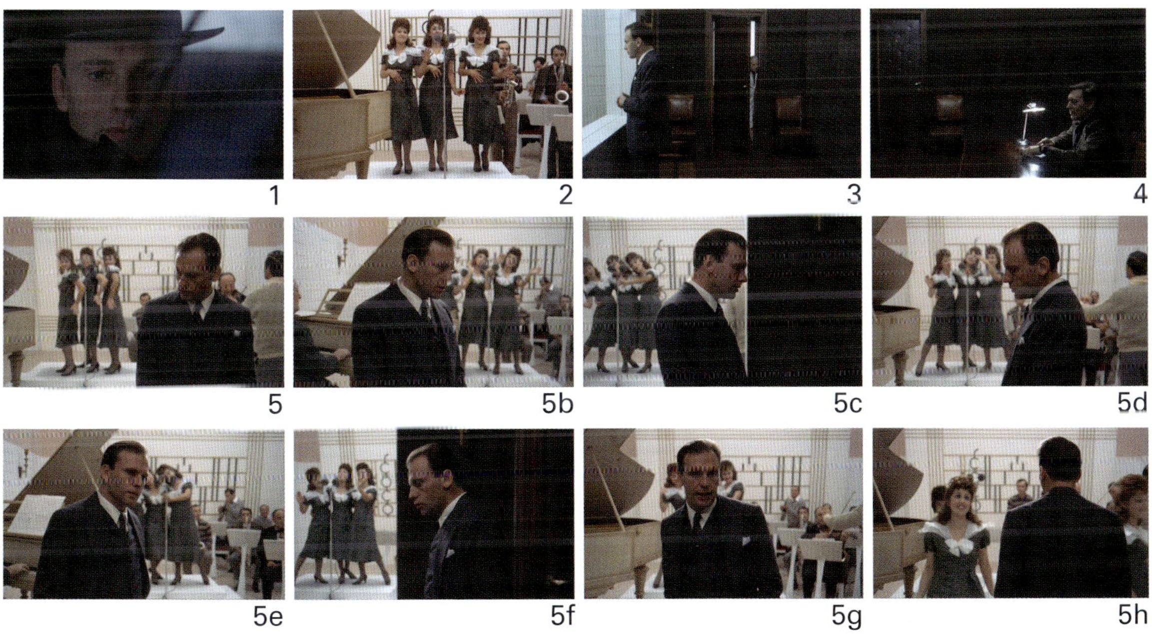

Figure 8.2 *The Conformist* (1970). Director: Bernardo Bertolucci. Cinematographer: Vittorio Storaro.

for a meeting between Marcello and a colonel to further discussions of possible employment with the secret police. It is in this scene that Marcello declares his want for "stability, security." Italo counters him by saying, "Everyone would like to be different from the others and yet you want to be the same as everyone else."

Shots 2, 3, and 4 separate the three areas of activity within the scene: the trio of vocalists, Marcello, and Italo. The dominant frame (Shot 5) includes activity in both the foreground and background, adding depth to the frame. Marcello paces back and forth in action covered with a long take passing in front of the glass that separates him from the trio (Shots 5–5h). Consider which elements are repeated: the young women, their dresses, lineation, and geometric shapes, as well as frames within the long take (Shots 5 and 5d, 5b and 5e, 5c, and 5f). This strategy of placing Marcello in foreground with activity in the background occurs again in the film, also as a long take, during a confrontation with special agent Manganiello in the back room of a restaurant (Figure 8.3).

In each of the two scenes, mise en scene, camera movement in long takes, and the background activity working as counterpoint to foreground action conspire to create enormous visual vitality. Added to this are the formal repetitions. In each of these examples, including shots 2 and 3 in Figure 8.1, this accumulation of elements works to offset or challenge the sincerity of character speech and action, establishing and reinforcing the movie's tone.

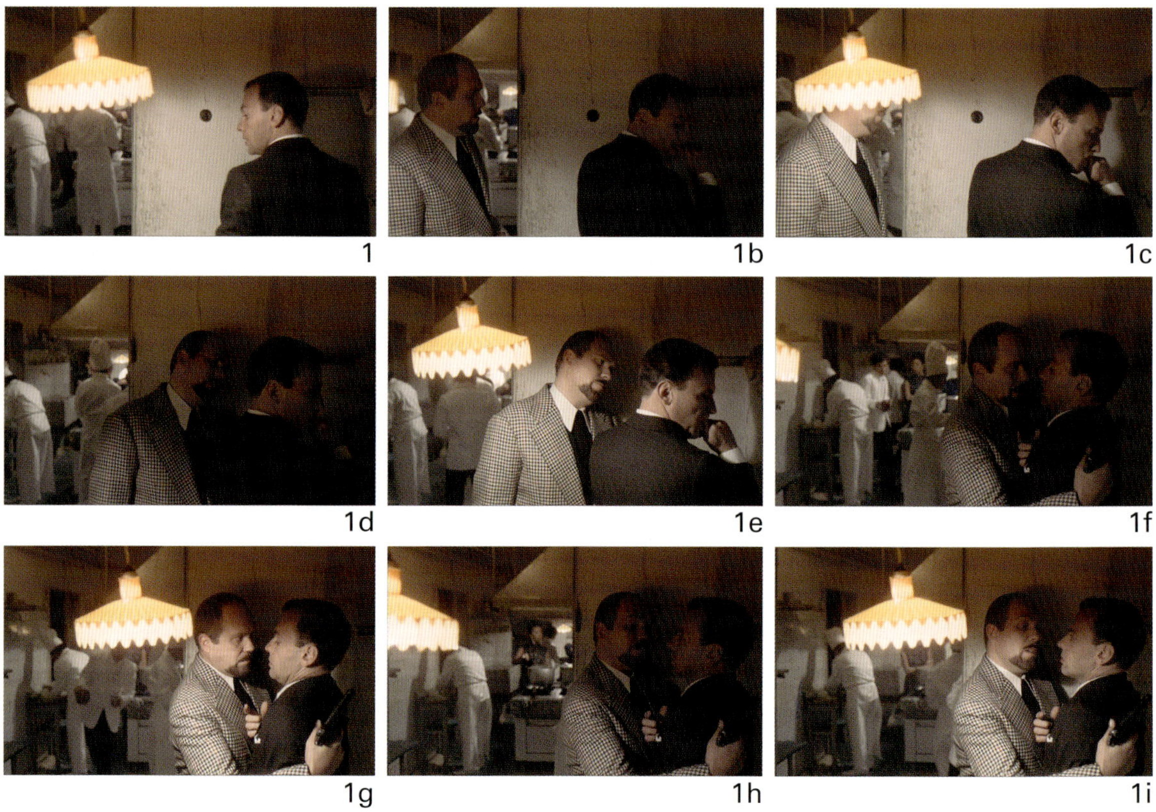

Figure 8.3 *The Conformist* (1970). Director: Bernardo Bertolucci. Cinematographer: Vittorio Storaro.

> When he [Bertolucci] was telling me this story, I thought of one specific painting, which was made by Caravaggio, *The Calling of St. Matthew*, particularly in the [painting's] delineation between light and darkness. This specific relation in the painting was for me the symbol of exactly what I was trying to do in lighting, not only in character, but in the entire principle of *The Conformist*.
>
> —Vittorio Storaro. *Eyes on Cinema*. September 15, 2015.

Sensuous aesthetic

The Conformist uses the contours of a man's life to reflect on the relationship between the need to conform and Mussolini's Fascist Italy. *The Great Beauty* brings to light the decadence and chaos of Berlusconi's Italy through the life of Jep Gambardella. Living in a fabulous terraced apartment overlooking the Colosseum in Rome, Jep is a writer, though he writes little since the publication of his one novel years earlier, reputed to be a "masterpiece." Mostly, Jep is a sybarite; devouring the pleasures life has to offer as defense against an overriding emptiness and moral vacuity.

The first ten minutes of *The Great Beauty* is a visual and aural tour de force. Many elements conspire to create this effect, but camera work persists among them with its energetic persona. Throughout the film, beauty and death spar with one another and at times, converge. This marriage is established visually in the first ten minutes of the film, delivering one of the film's thematic preoccupations.

The film opens with a canon exploding along Rome's Appian Way, followed by a set of elegant, daytime images through a nearby park and then, on location at Fontana dell'Acqua Paola, where a group of Japanese tourists mill about the water pool as a female choral group sings *a cappella* on a terrace of the upper floor. One of the tourists wanders off to take a photograph, when he collapses on the pavement and dies. Much of this is covered in swooping crane shots of a Steadicam, which move laterally, alternating with intermittent shots that stall and move in—from wide to medium-wide to medium close-up to close-up. The camera, itself, becomes a wide-eyed tourist—or a first-time visitor to Rome—studying, surveying the city of arrival.

A woman screams, unleashing the second scene: a frenzy of night shots that reveal an outdoor party set on a rooftop adjacent to the Colosseum. At the center of the party is Jep, on the occasion of his sixty-fifth birthday, though we do not meet him, or discover the party's purpose, until long after the celebration has been active on screen. Many of the shots are one second in duration or less. Here, again, as in the daytime sequence, there are intermittent shots that hover in one place, changing angle or moving in. The camera with its feverish attention darts to one party-goer or set of party-goers, stalls, or moves in, then cut: another set of party-goers, reveling in the decadence and excess. Certain characters are repeated. As the sequence builds toward the introduction of Jep, a few sets of shots become mini-scenes allowing for modest development of characters who will reappear with more significance later.

The party sequence, leading up to the introduction of Jep, lasts for precisely five minutes and includes over seventy shots. Figures 8.4–8.6 represent the party scene, culminating with the introduction of Jep. In looking at the still frames, one can begin to discern the coverage strategy (and also a pattern in the editing). Convergences occur more often as an interaction between shots, given their short duration: crowd shots alternate with single shots, isolated or foregrounded. There are exceptions, in particular shots of the glass case with its use of striking black and white, which punctuate the party scene. Inside, two women dance in an enclosed space that seems to become a cage (Shots 98–98d).

One can also see the immense variation in shot size, angle, movement, and depth of field, along with proximity to character and the number of characters in the frame. And yet this baroque image field is managed with repetitions, familiar images or characters, and the continuous soundtrack of techno music, upstaged

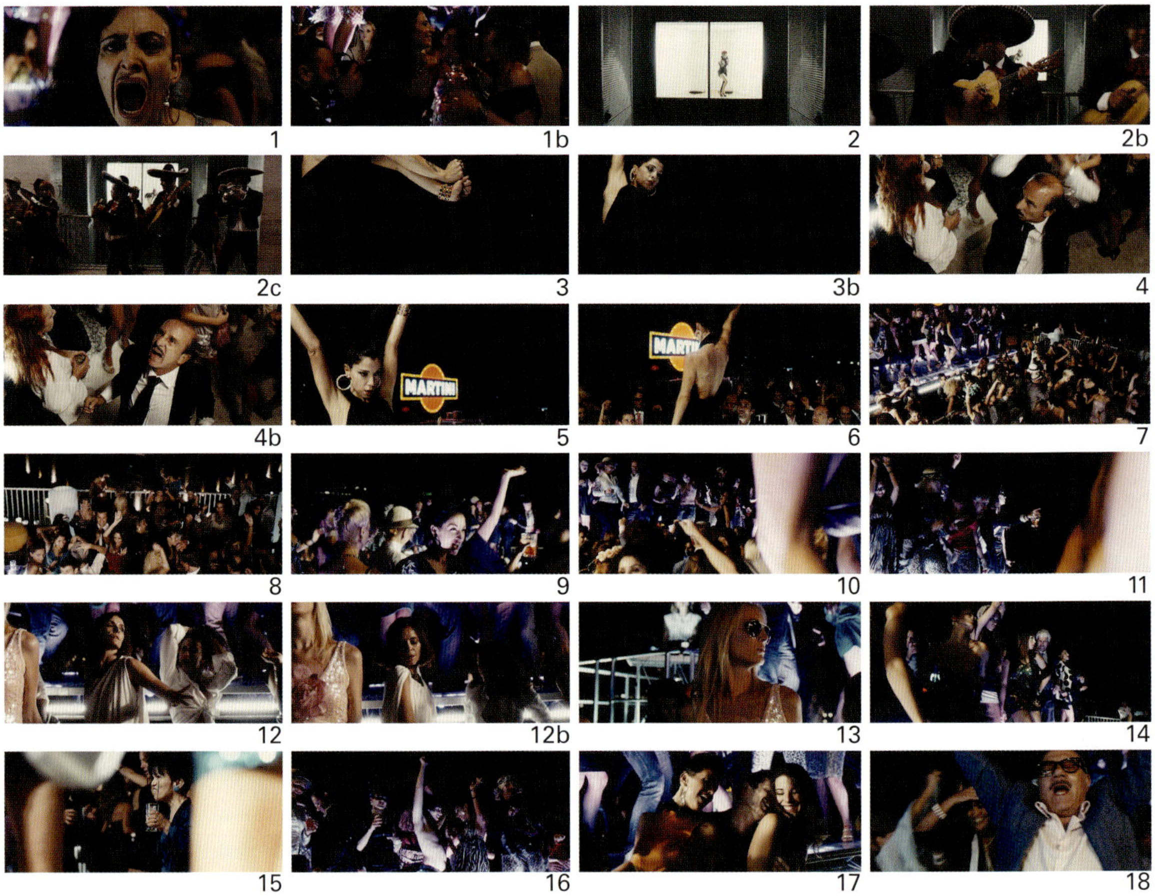

Figure 8.4 *The Great Beauty* (2013). Director: Paolo Sorrentino. Cinematographer: Luca Bigazzi.

temporarily by a Mariachi band moving through the crowd. (Notice, for example, how many screen shots picture a character with both arms raised in the air.) The repetitions create a visual field that is coherent, pulsing with vitality.

Despite this vitality, or the occasion (a birthday party), the tone does not feel entirely celebratory. A sadness hovers over the party scene that adds to its dimension, like another layer of color in a Rothko painting. During the scene, lovers quarrel, characters stand alone in the crowd, friends sink to silly gossip—even Jep's editor falls asleep, forgotten like the women encased in the white room. It is almost as if the excess struggles to overcome the weight of life's gravity but finally, does not. Even the performance of the voluptuous, aging showgirl coming out of the birthday cake seems strained or exaggerated (Figure 8.6, Shots 68b–72b). Into this, Jep appears (Shot 73c).

Jep will soon discover that his first love from many years ago has died. The combined effect of the loss with feelings of purposeless spin him into a search for meaning that takes up the screen time to follow. The camera persists in creating visual wonder while Jep continues his quest, taking long walks along the Tiber, hosting nightly salons, and visiting old friends. "Can you make me disappear?" he'll ask his good friend, the magician, as Jep works to reconcile himself with life's strict terms in a culture hollowed-out by excess, against the beauty that is Rome.

Realism and spectacle

Many of the gestures that create the visual dynamics in Zhangke Jia's film, *Still Life*, occur through a moving camera, a slow-moving camera panning across the many nameless faces populating the film, or various aspects of the landscape. The setting: a waterfront in and

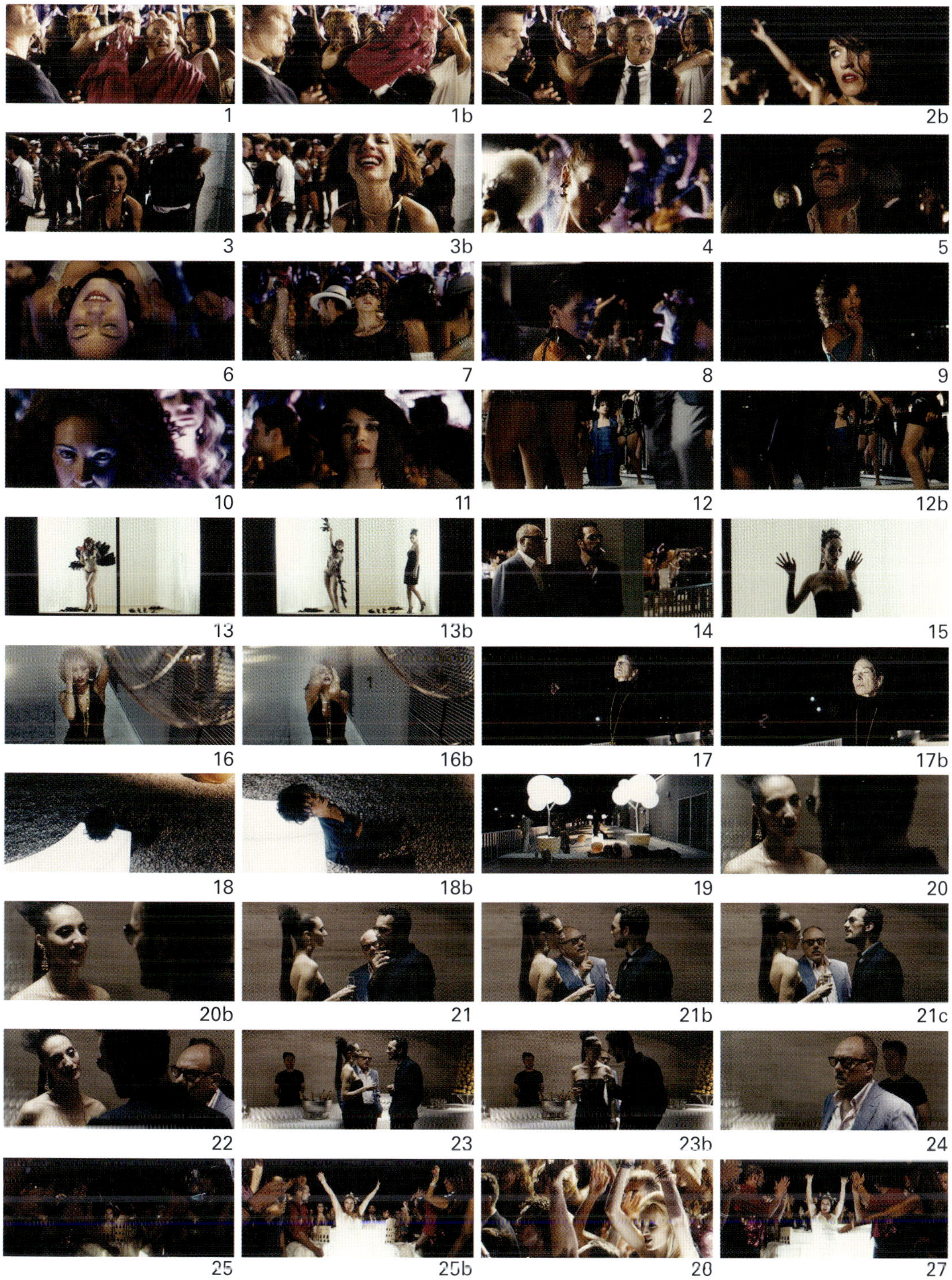

Figure 8.5 *The Great Beauty* (2013). Director: Paolo Sorrentino. Cinematographer: Luca Bigazzi.

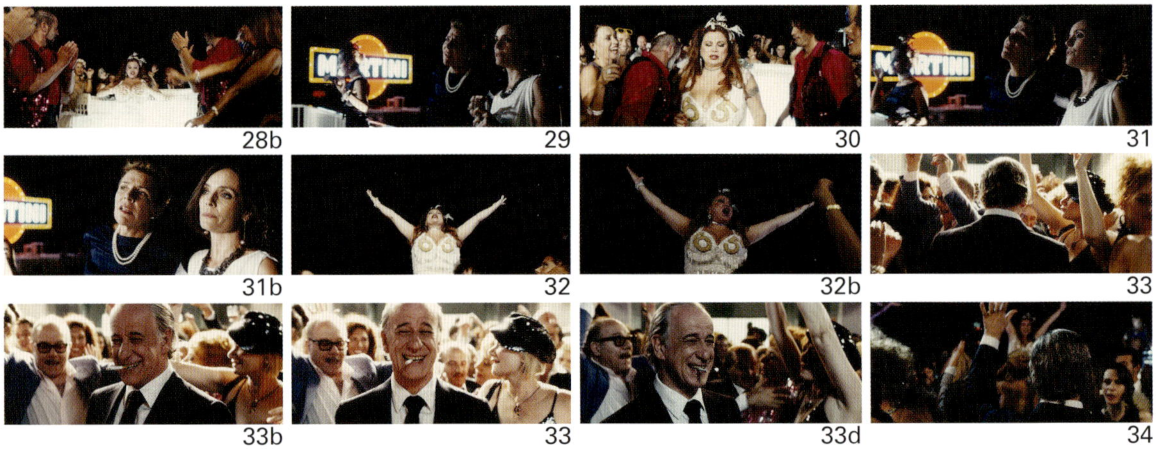

Figure 8.6
The Great Beauty (2013). Director: Paolo Sorrentino. Cinematographer: Luca Bigazzi.

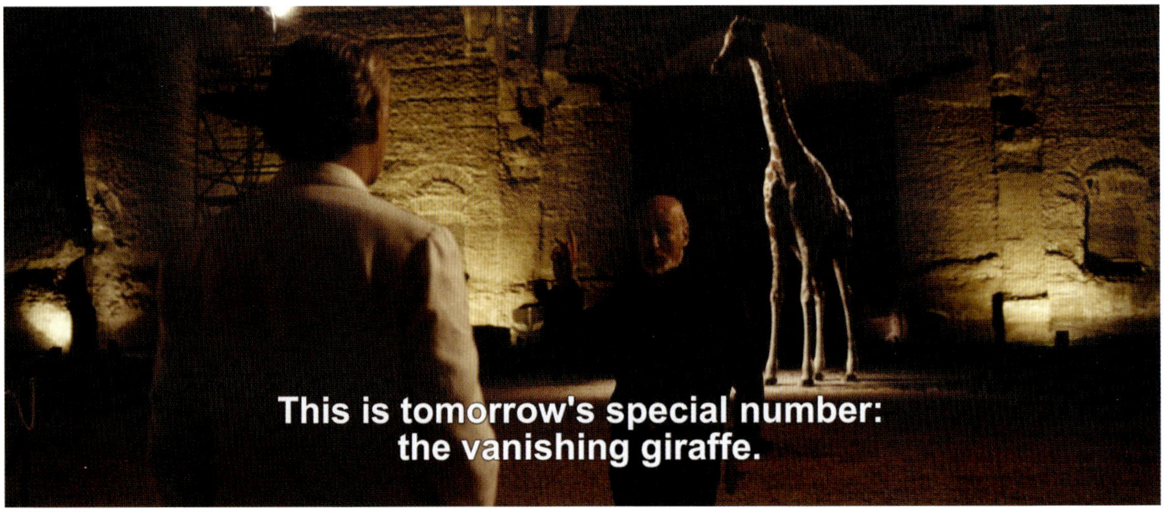

Figure 8.7
The Great Beauty (2013). Director: Paolo Sorrentino. Cinematographer: Luca Bigazzi.

around Fengjie, a village on the Yangzte River undergoing demolition due to flooding after the building of the Three Gorges Dam. In addition to the slow-moving camera, performative elements are woven into the film, a film otherwise tethered to physical reality, paced in real time, with existing locations. Finally, the film—despite its documentary feel—ventures into the fantastic with images of men in white protective suits, a UFO, a building structure transformed into a rocket, and a tightrope walker at great height. These intrude into the everyday life pictured on screen as matter of fact, without commentary, intensifying their effect.

It is difficult to convey movement in still images, but Figure 8.8 represents a very early scene that introduces the visual treatment, as well as one of the two main characters in the film: Han. A coal miner from Shanxi, Han travels by ferry to Fengjie in search of his wife, who left with their infant daughter sixteen years earlier.

In the scene depicted, the camera pans across the ferry travelers, screen left to right, portraying the riders in close-up. A dissolve transitions to the next shot, also a pan, which continues at the same pace left to right, though framing the riders in a medium shot. The ferry, now discernible, travels in the water of the Three Gorges Dam. It moves slowly up river, screen right to left, opposing the direction of the pan. When the second tracking shot finishes, it tilts up to find Han, seated, duffle bag in his lap, looking down. Drawn to something off screen, he looks up and turns. A cut: the Wushan Bridge with its pink/red arch as the ferry horn

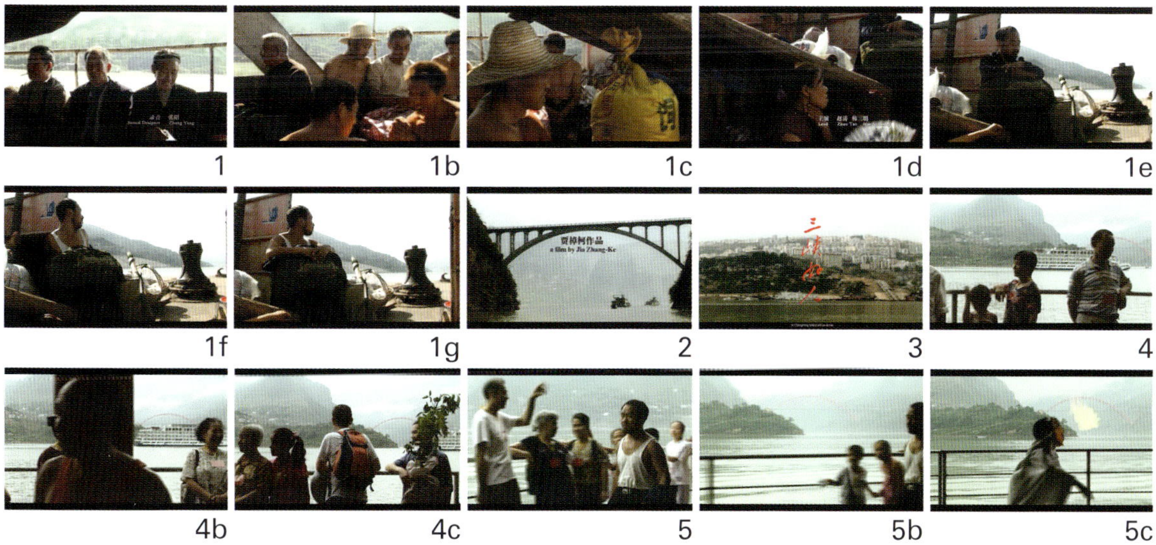

Figure 8.8 *Still Life* (2006). Director: Jia Zhangke. Cinematographer: Nelson Lik-wai Yu.

sounds and the boat slides toward it. A third pan begins, also right to left, now at a brisker pace, with wider framing. Added to the dynamic created by opposing directions is staging in the background with the impressive red arch of the Wushan Bridge, and in front of it, bringing middle ground into the mise en scene, a cruise ship traveling also screen left to right but at a quicker pace than the camera. At one moment in the pan there are passengers stacked in front of one another creating five different layers to the image. Into this last shot walks Han, entering from screen right as the pan moves ahead him framing just the bridge, empty of all ferry passengers, before a masked man steps into the shot, breathing fire. Cut.

Figure 8.9 reveals another kind convergence, which characterizes the film. Han, having met many obstacles in his efforts to locate his wife, takes a temporary job on a construction crew, or more aptly, a destruction crew. Axing old metal and rock, he looks up, compelled by what he sees. This strategy repeats throughout the film: Han's fixed fascination as a prompt for what follows. We have seen it in the earlier scene with his notice of the Wushan Bridge.

Finally, images in Figure 8.10 convey another visual and aural interlude, not unlike the fire breather on the ferry. Here, the story transitions from its focus on Han to our second protagonist, Shen Hong, a nurse traveling on the ferry in search of her husband (Shots 1 and 1b). The camera pans again, left to right to follow a boy who sits at the end of the boat, belting out a song.

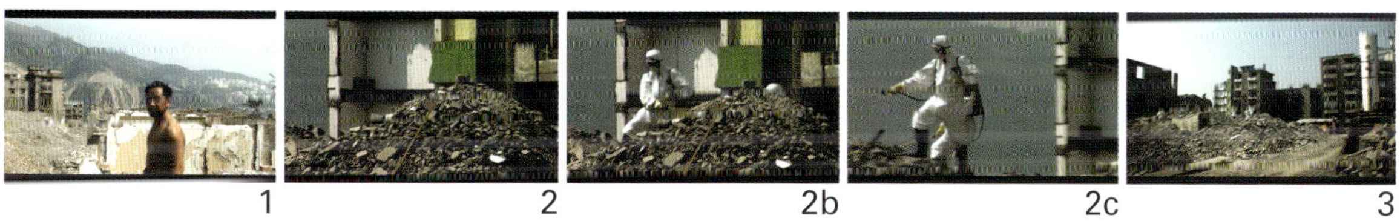

Figure 8.9 *Still Life* (2006). Director: Jia Zhangke. Cinematographer: Nelson Lik-wai Yu.

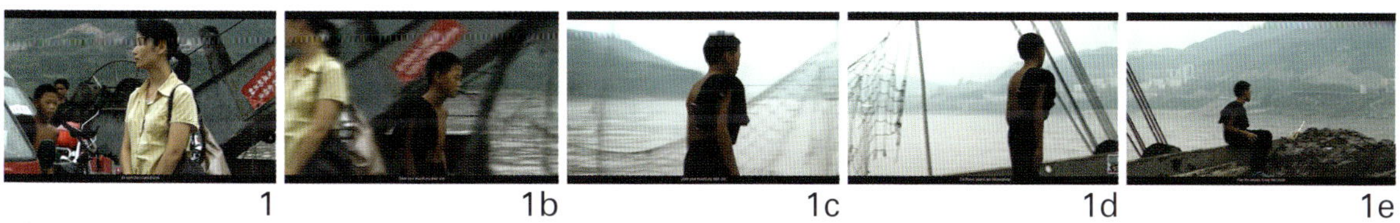

Figure 8.10 *Still Life* (2006). Director: Jia Zhangke. Cinematographer: Nelson Lik-wai Yu.

We have dwelled here on the visual dynamics in *Still Life* as a way of teasing out the tone, which must now seem evident. In this slog of real life in which political initiatives (the Three Gorges Dam project) have social consequences (a village demolished, people rendered helpless, separated from loved ones), characters own their will and resilience. Even amidst the chaos and loss, or perhaps because of it, the spectacular occurs, awakening the capacity to marvel. This is, after all, "still life," and so better than the alternative.

Breaking the rules

Daisies, the 1966 dramatic farce directed by Věra Chytilová is among the most visually dynamic films to have been made. Considered a landmark of the Czech New Wave (Nová Vina), the film, while financed by a state-sponsored movie studio, was banned by Czech authorities after its release and Chytilová was forbidden from working at the studio in Prague until 1975.[3]

Working cultural commentary into metaphor, *Daisies* begins and ends with atomic bomb imagery. In between, the film follows, episodically, the daily escapades of two young women: Marie I and Marie II. Having seen that the world has been spoiled, they decide to be spoiled, too. Their naughty antics escalate to wild proportions, concluding with what might be the most imaginative free-for-all food fight in the history of cinema. There is no real plot to speak of, just this narrative progression—the stakes rise as the young women create havoc with greater and greater consequences, for which they seem to escape all accountability.

Stylistically, the film boldly breaks with a number of conventions. It moves between black-and-white, color, and filter-colored footage. Spatial continuity is sabotaged frequently with editorial license yoking incongruous physical spaces through character behavior or dialogue. And the performance style is theatrical, not naturalistic.

The sequence from the film's beginning depicted in Figure 8.11 sets the movie in motion with the young women bemoaning a world gone bad. It occurs to Marie I (the blonde) that if the world has gone bad, why don't they go bad, too? Marie II (the brunette) affirms her enthusiasm for the idea by slapping Marie I in an otherwise

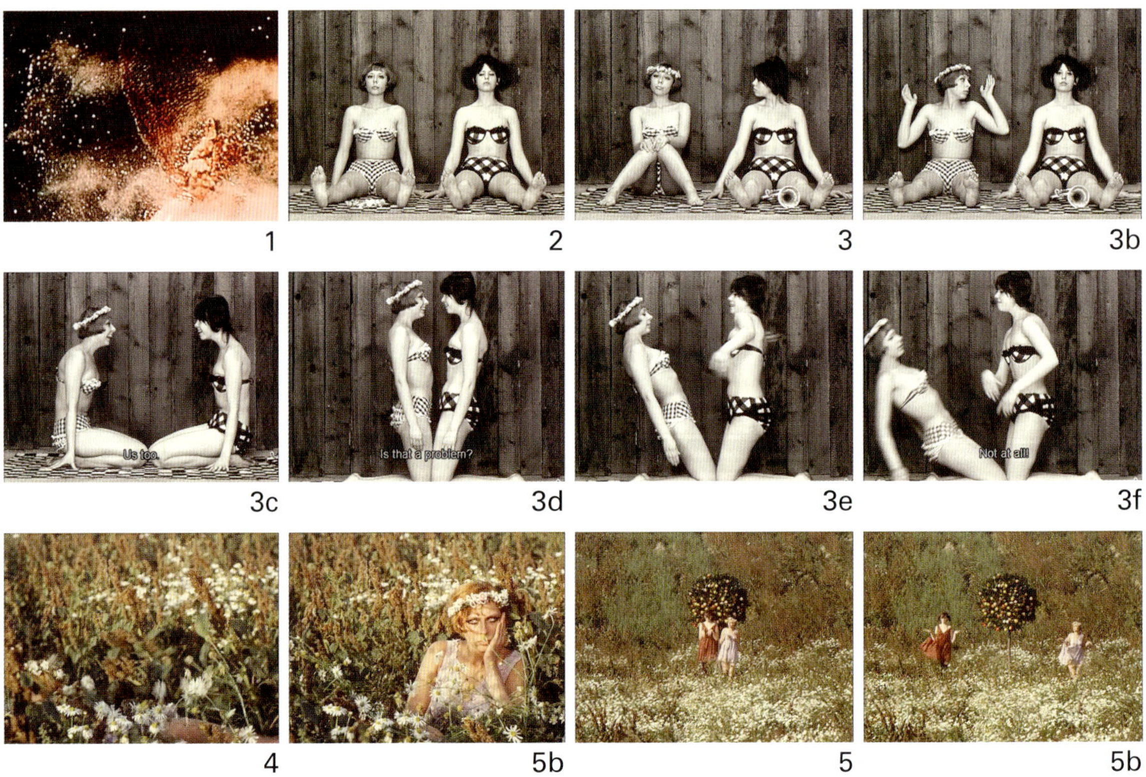

Figure 8.11 *Daisies* (1966). Director: Věra Chytilová. Cinematographer: Jaroslav Kucera.

unmotivated gesture (Shot 3e). Marie II lands in a daisy field, wearing different clothes, rubbing her sore cheek. The use of spatial discontinuity with story continuity persists as a technique throughout the film. Marie II will toss, for example, a piece of fruit plucked from the tree in shot 5, which will land on the floor of the apartment they share, with the two of them present there, Marie II lounging on the bed.

Figure 8.12 depicts the first portion of the ten-minute scene that becomes the film's climax. One can readily identify a certain effect in play with the change from black-and-white to color imagery. Glancing across the still frames, one can also detect the muscular nature of the visual style with its shot variety, staging, and the use of a mirrored wall behind the buffet tables (Shots 4c and 4d).

Hungry, and now thoroughly spoiled, the young women break into a hotel looking for food, and, inside the hotel, duck into a dumbwaiter that leads to a room set for what seems to be a lavish feast. Three buffet tables against the wall are filled with a cornucopia of delicious offerings, and the long table in the center of the hall is elegantly dressed for diners.

At first, Marie I and II nibble at the offerings. It occurs to Marie I that they should set the table, sit down, and have a proper feast. Seated, Marie I reaches across the table and topples a goblet. This incites the shift to color photography, which begins with a fast motion, jump cut collage of the feast table, ending with shots of Marie II seated

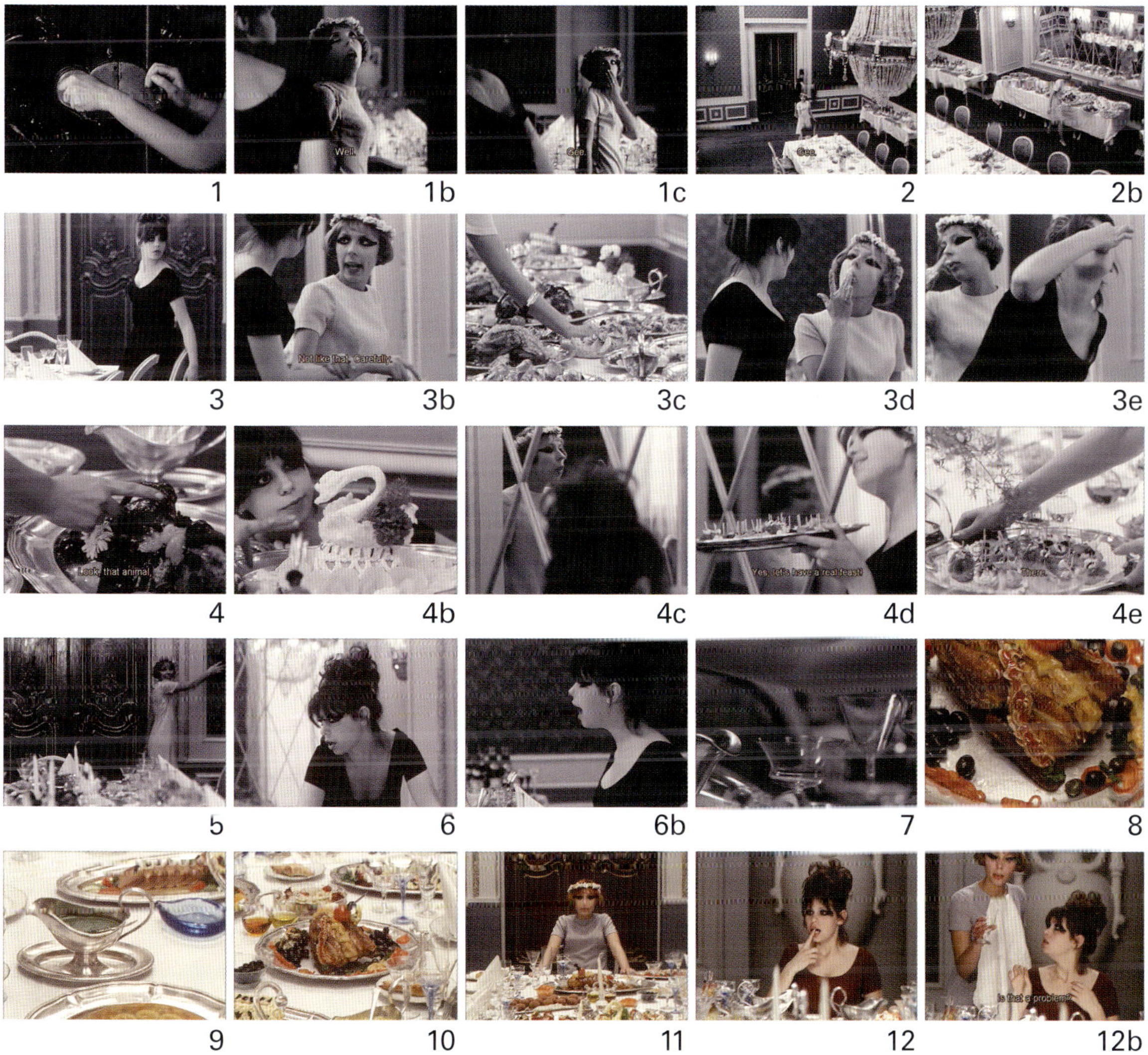

Figure 8.12 *Daisies* (1966). Director: Věra Chytilová. Cinematographer: Jaroslav Kucera.

at the head of the table. Afterward, overhead shots combine with eye-level footage to chart the young women as they go around the table, seat by seat, feasting from any platter in reach (Shots 12–12b). Then, cakes are brought to the table. Marie II marvels, "this is what I call cake," before hoisting a fat slab of it into the face of Marie I (Figure 8.13, Shot 4). A food fight ensues, goblets smashed in the cross fire, along with bottles of liquor and wine. Some combination of striptease and floorshow begins with the young girls on top of the table, prancing through platters of food, before they discover the chandelier.

While the antics of the young women create much of the dynamism in the scene, the camera's coverage is key. It is both moving and static, varied in shot size and angle. In particular, the scene represents masterful shot design, as well as shot order, with compositions set to create the maximum dramatic effect, i.e., close-ups of a face covered with cake or heeled shoes walking through paté, or Marie I in a wide shot dangling from the chandelier (Figure 8.13, Shots 6, 11, 15, 22, etc.). The scene concludes with another gesture of spatial discontinuity, as the young women swing from the chandelier to. . . a different location.

So what of the tone? What kind of world is it, inhabited by these two young, zany women? The convergence of H-bomb imagery at the outset with the wind-up doll actions of Marie I and II suggests a disjointed, dark, but comedic world. The camera, throughout the film, supports this atmosphere, at times creates it, with its kinetic

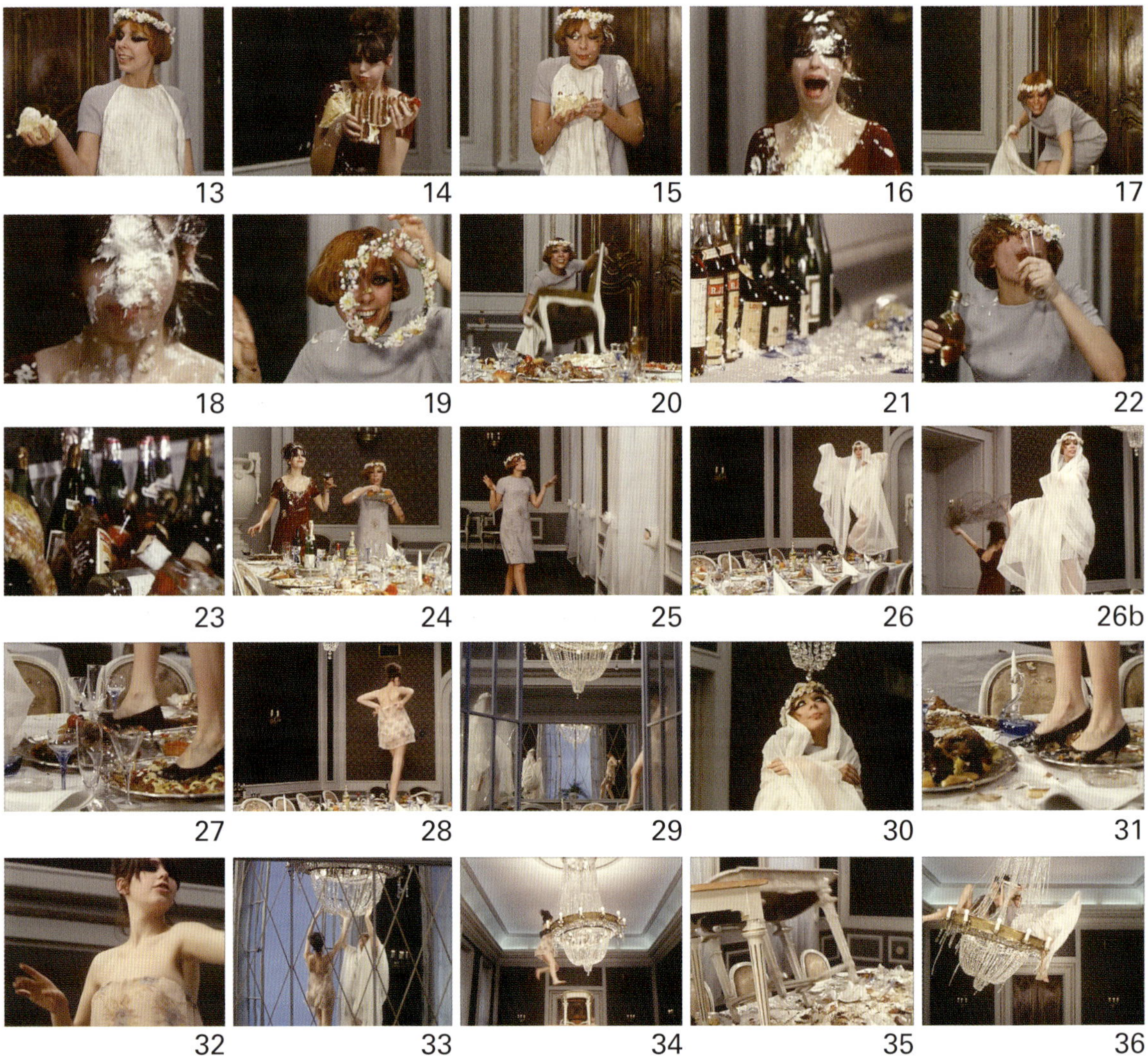

Figure 8.13 *Daisies* (1966). Director: Věra Chytilová. Cinematographer: Jaroslav Kucera.

energy of changing color filters, shifts from black and white to color, collage effects, spatial incongruities, and dynamic shot design. The conclusion of the film is, perhaps, more disturbing than its beginning, with efforts made by the young women to set things right falling into the category of "too little, too late."

Variation in scale

One could make the case that all cinema is political, given the power dynamics so often explored in drama and the worldview suggested by a film's stance. But there are certain films that target significant moments in political history as a means of bringing into focus specific issues or concerns. *Malcolm X* is such a film.

The making of this biographical drama, including the choice of Spike Lee to direct the film, along with preproduction obstacles and budget issues, imbued the project with political capital from the beginning.[4] Added to this, the choice of subject matter: Malcolm X was, during his lifetime, an influential but controversial black leader and activist in the American civil rights movement. His affiliation with the Nation of Islam, and then his repudiation a decade later, stirred intense conflict with the organization, resulting in his death. He was assassinated at the age of 39.[5]

In a long career as a filmmaker, Spike Lee has made political and cultural commentary his divining rod. He has never shown any reluctance to bring to the screen challenging issues, nor is any film directed by him coy conveying a particular stance. And yet, the films continue to privilege the movie going experience as a medium for dramatic storytelling. Charged visual dynamic, original and inventive sound design, and narrative epiphany persists as a priority. His direction of *Malcolm X* is no exception.

Look at images from the film's credit sequence (Figure 8.14). One can discern the unapologetic venture into point of view right from the beginning. An American flag is cross-cut with images of brutality by police to a black man. The flag begins to burn as the brutality continues, ending in the shape of an "X." But the sequencing of shots as purely visual also creates a dynamic—the alternating frames of vivid red, white, and blue, with the darker frame of nighttime street violence. The final shot of the flag reduced to an "X" next to the shot of police interaction begin to mirror one another as compositions, with an increasing portion of the frame occupied by darkness. This is also a story, even as it is a point of view.

The collaboration between Spike Lee and cinematographer, Ernest Dickerson, in creating the film's visual style is on record.[6] But viewing the film makes record enough. The film uses a distinct visual style as treatment for each period in the protagonist's life, née Malcolm Little. Notice the two scenes pictured in Figures 8.15 and 8.16, which are separated by an hour of screen time. Figure 8.15 represents the first shot of *Malcolm X*, and coincides, as the intertitle suggests, with Malcolm Little's life in Boston during the war years. The images are marked by warm colors of red and brown with golden light. Alternatively, the scene depicted in Figure 8.16 takes place during Malcolm's ten-year jail sentence, where he acquires the name Malcolm X, and is characterized by austere compositions with high contrast and a dominance of steely blues and greens.

But added to the variety of visual styles as treatment for the various phases of his life, is the dynamism within the shot, or the sequence of shots. For example, the first shot of the film, depicted in Figure 8.15, demonstrates the energetic camera. The shot, a long take, begins as a wide shot of a billboard on an elevated subway platform at the Dudley Street Station. A subway train cruises through the station as the camera cranes down slowly to the bustling, 1940s street below where it cranes forward toward a sassy pair of men's shoes, shined by a young black boy in front of a Woolworth's store. Continuing, the camera tilts up to the man, wearing a plaid suit (Shorty), who pays the boy

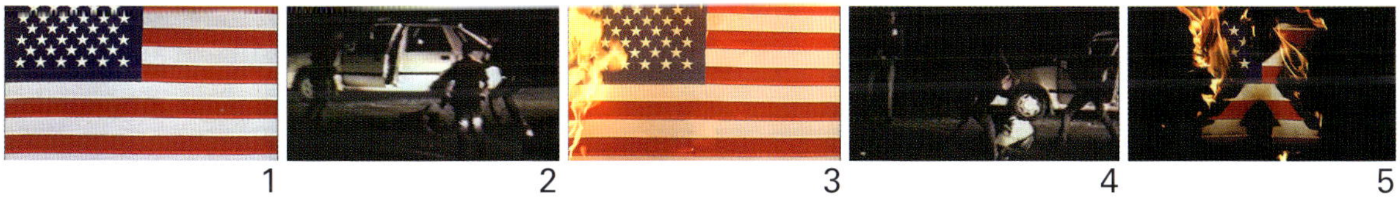

Figure 8.14
Malcolm X (1992). Director: Spike Lee. Cinematographer: Ernest Dickerson.

and takes off into the street where the camera, continuing the take, is positioned in front of him, as he jaunts toward it, and then as he walks past, the camera capturing him in profile, before tracking behind him as Shorty enters the local barber shop, where the shot ends.

There is energy enough in the camera's movement, which varies in direction through the take (down, forward, backward, tracking alongside, and then forward again) and also in the framing. The shot employs an extreme wide shot, a close-up and every shot size in between. The camera is bold enough to call attention to itself. Added to this, however, is the more subtle chemistry between camera and design elements, to include the billboard advertisement: five white men in navy uniform surround a blonde white woman holding a tray of Coca-Colas. All this whiteness disappears as soon as the camera lands on Dudley Street where the entire population circulating up and down the street is black.

Malcolm, prodded by his best friend, Shorty, develops wild, illegal schemes which they enact together. Both are caught and sentenced to years in prison. The decade of prison life for Malcolm is rendered in the film with a much cooler color palette and more formal compositions as would suit the institutional environment of a prison. Power struggles land Malcolm in solitary confinement, a scene pictured in Figure 8.16, where a visit from the prison chaplain stirs his wrath (Shots 4–6). After, he writhes in his cell like a caged animal (Shots 7–7b) until passing out. This is how he is found by a guard and dragged from the cell.

The decision to stage most of the scene in the dark interior of the cell intensifies the visual dynamic with frames of black abstracted by a thin spill of light coming from the slit in the door. Even in the shot of the chaplain emphasis is given to the interaction between light and shade. Narratively, this is the moment that marks Malcolm's rebirth as a character. His endurance has been tested so that conversion to Malcolm X becomes his path to liberation. The shot design elevates this moment, with its stark compositions, dramatizing the internal conflict between darkness and light.

And what about the tone, the film's point of view? From the opening credit sequence the life of Malcolm X is framed in a particular context, as a response to a dark, persistent history of racial prejudice and violence against black people in America. Character drives the storytelling, serving the biographical details. The performance by Denzel Washington becomes a polestar in bringing to light the complexity of Malcolm X—his shortfalls and his genius. Nevertheless, the director interjects into this fabric of character biography, moments that recharge the film's point of view.

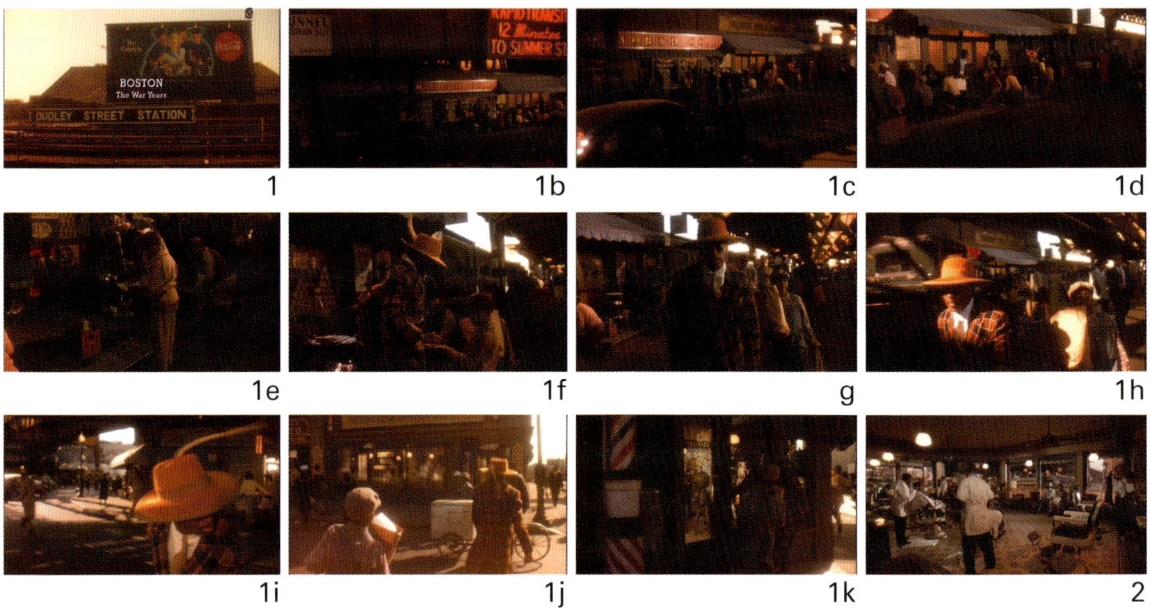

Figure 8.15 *Malcolm X* (1992). Director: Spike Lee. Cinematographer: Ernest Dickerson.

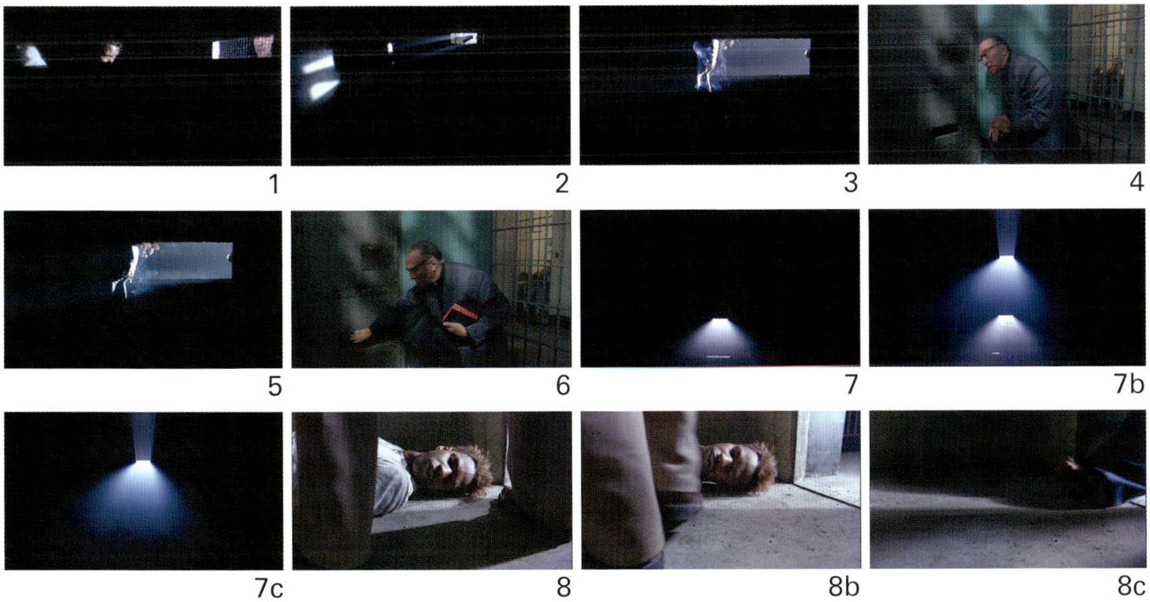

Figure 8.16 *Malcolm X* (1992). Director: Spike Lee. Cinematographer: Ernest Dickerson.

In one such moment, during the prison term of Malcolm X, a number of prisoners stand, side-by-side, in the yard as the camera pans, left to right, framing the men in continuous close-ups (Figure 8.17). Nothing of consequence is happening, just this tracking across the men, all brown and black skinned, and their singular faces. It is as if the movie stops its forward motion of plot to give each of these men a self, an identity. This is point of view.

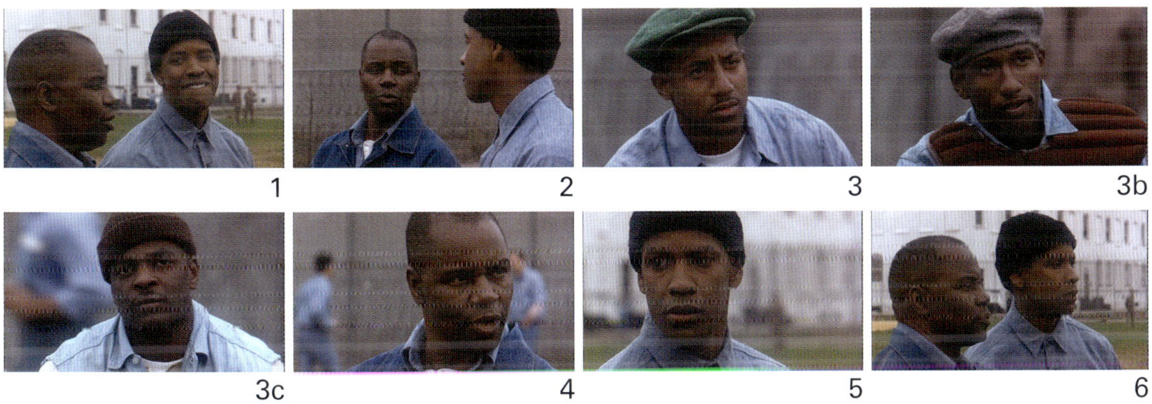

Figure 8.17 *Malcolm X* (1992). Director: Spike Lee. Cinematographer: Ernest Dickerson.

Tone: forces in family life

Family life has been a focus of storytelling for centuries, and any value in adding to it comes from the particulars. The films discussed here forge drama from very specific characters, navigating distinct situations. Of them, three build stories around a single mother and yet the films, as you will discover, differ significantly—in story content, visual style, and tone. In still another film, a vagabond family of siblings moves at the center of a farm film set in the early 1900s, while a fifth film looks at contemporary family life when the wife and husband cannot reconcile a dispute. The last movie in this section explores the life of an aging father against the indifference and opportunism of his son and daughter-in-law. In each film, storytelling particulars inspire a visual treatment, which, along with narrative events, influence the tone.

Aspect ratio

The particular territory staked out by Xavier Dolan in his fifth feature film, *Mommy*, is the chemistry between a mother and a teenage son. Their combustible personalities fuel the conflict as much as, if not more than, the circumstances in which they find themselves. Among these circumstances Diane, or "Die" as everyone calls her, is a widow. With the death of her husband and father of her teenage son, Steve, she's obliged to manage their home with limited resources and limited prospects. Additionally, Steve has ADHD, which includes easy lapses into violence to himself and others. Diane is no "shrinking violet," given her own fierce temperament and tendency for blunt discourse. Despite these complications, or perhaps because of them, they are devoted to one another. Their intimacy, albeit combustible, is part of what the visual treatment aims to convey.

One striking technique used for rendering this intimate portrait is the movie's **aspect ratio**. An aspect ratio is the proportional relationship between the width of the image and its height. Historically, for movies shot on film, the aspect ratio was standard and limited to the area of the film strip between sprocket perforations. These standard ratios were applied worldwide, and impacted, of course, film projectors in commercial venues. But exceptions were also created, driven to some extent by Hollywood studios interested in widescreen formats.[7]

Digital filmmaking offers much greater variety in aspect ratio. Examples of various aspect ratios can be found in Figure 8.18. For each of these films, the proportion governing the frame was an intentional aesthetic choice. Wes

Figure 8.18
Aspect ratios.

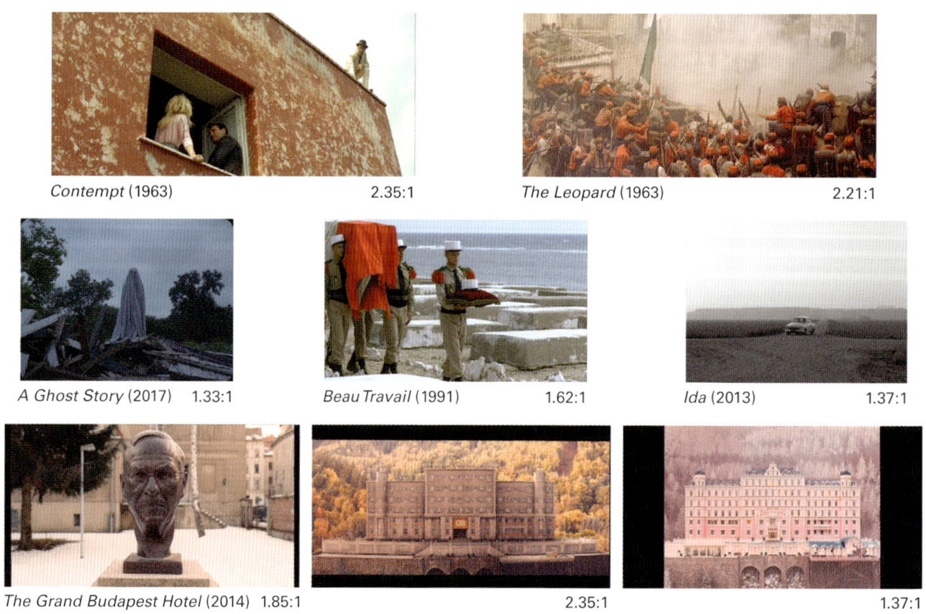

Anderson's *The Grand Budapest Hotel* makes use of three different aspect ratios, relative to time periods portrayed in the film. With the wide and ready use of cell phone cameras, **vertical cinema**, a platform that captures images in portrait mode, has earned status as an option for the aspect ratio of a film[8]

Mommy uses the aspect ratio of 1:1, which, of course, influences shot design. While there are many shots that feature characters seen at a distance, in the 1:1 aspect ratio a character's face in close-up becomes more like portraiture. The square frame also reduces the impact of environment or landscape. It can deprive an image of context or breathing room offered by a frame with greater width. It provides, instead, a sense of drawing close to characters, of staying close to them. Volatile behavior by son, and at times, the mother, can make this proximity difficult for the viewer, invoking a feeling of being trapped. But moments of sweetness and connection compensate by drawing the viewer close.

The scene pictured in Figure 8.19 is one such moment. The closeness we witness occurs between Steve and his late father. He's just returned home, having been expelled from a detention center for setting a fire that put another young man in the hospital. Settling in, he asks to see photographs of his father.

Figure 8.19 *Mommy* (2014). Director: Xavier Dolan. Cinematographer: André Turpin.

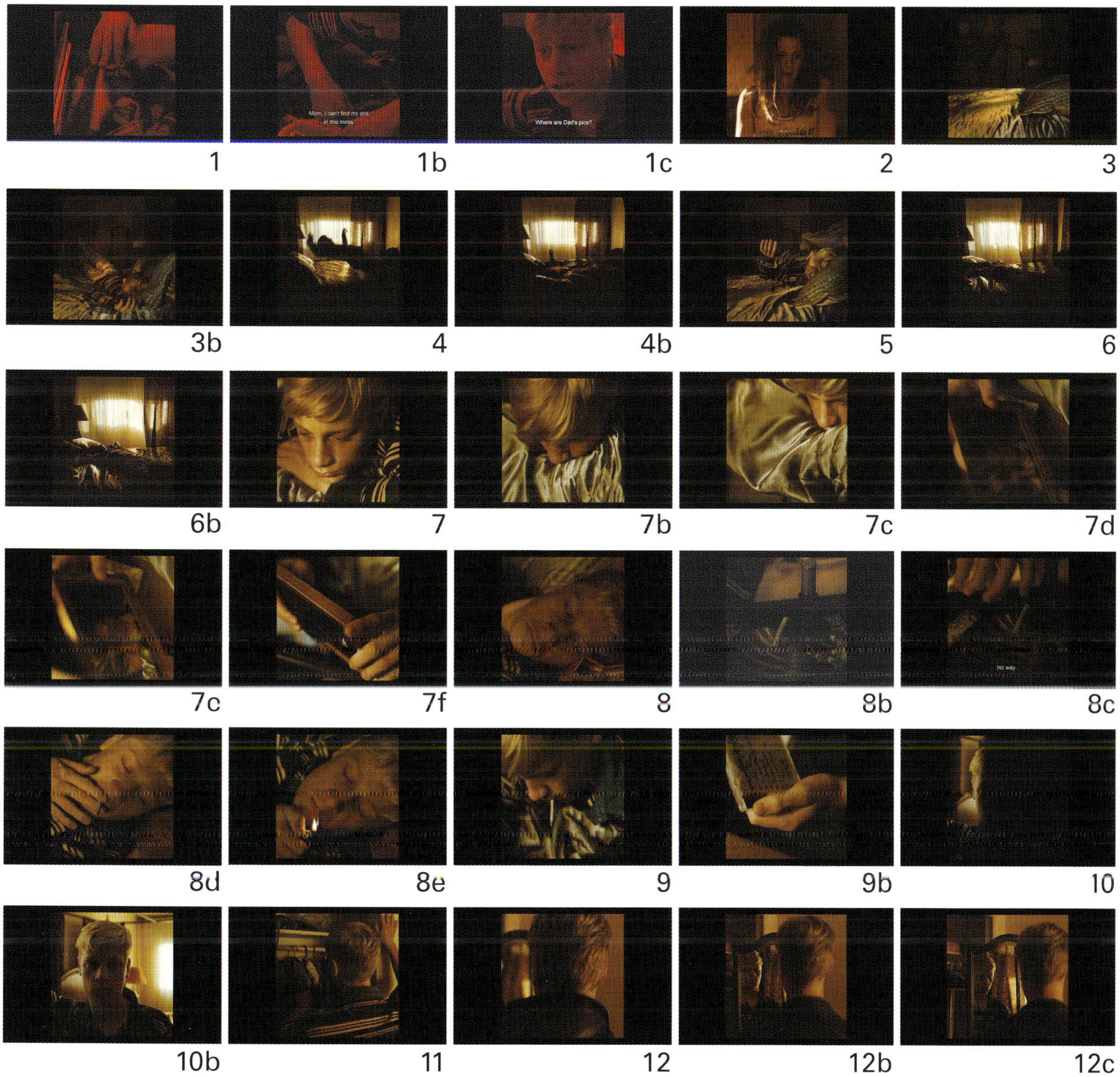

With the exception of crosscutting to his mother in the kitchen (Figure 8.19, Shot 2), the frame size confines our view to him, to his actions, allowing us to enter this space of his reverie. The scene benefits from a lyrical treatment, with the triple cutting of him falling onto the bed, light pouring through the curtains, a play of sunlight across Steve in close-up, the camera framing him from behind as he sports his father's leather jacket, and then slowly panning to capture his face in the mirror. We could be with him like this forever.

A little over an hour into the film, the director makes another bold move with the aspect ratio (Figure 8.20). Optimism is within reach for Steve and his mother, in no small part due to their neighbor, Kyla, who has been tutoring Steve, and whose personal troubles have been soothed by her time with Steve and his mother. Steve zips up the street on a skateboard. Diane and Kyla pedal behind him on bicycles out of view. Violating filmmaking conventions that sublimate technique to story, Steve brings his hands in front of his face and pushes the borders of the frame, stretching it to wide screen. This visual epiphany, timed as it was with well-being for these three characters, evokes supreme delight. And this is how the frame remains until three minutes later, when bad news reaches their doorstep, restricting the frame once again to 1:1.[9]

We have dwelled on aspect ratio as a factor in the visual dynamics of *Mommy*, when, of course, there are other techniques in play. Nevertheless, one can begin to imagine what the tone might be when combining this *particular* mother and son, with a frame size of 1:1 aspect ratio. The moment-to-moment intensity goes without saying, but the characters as seen in these square frames are also relatable, if not lovable. The film's point of view: tenderness and rancor, comedy and pathos are inextricable from one another.

Focal plane

If aspect ratio works as a fundamental strategy for shaping the visual dynamics of *Mommy*, shifts in the focal plane within a single shot charge the imagery in *Madeline's Madeline*, the 2018 feature film directed by Josephine Decker.

For much of film history, the accepted convention relegates some portion of the frame to imagery in focus. With the influence of documentary's handheld camera, one can often see an image come into focus as the camera repositions itself toward a new subject. More recently, de-focusing an entire frame has become a narrative tool in fiction film.

Focus refers, of course, to the range required to depict the image clearly with a given lens. In the 1924 silent film, *The Last Laugh*, for example, one can see a commitment to a depth of field that keeps the entire image in focus—foreground, middle ground, and background. This technique, known as **deep focus**, can also be seen in wide shots exampled earlier from *Yi Yi*, a movie in which the story's progression depends upon the dynamic between different planes of seeable action in the frame. Deep focus works to integrate the narrative content with the various elements in each focal plane.

Shallow focus, on the other hand, emphasizes one plane of the image over another. This can be used to striking effect in isolating characters (or objects) from background (or foreground). Photographers refer to the blurred portion of the frame as **bokeh**. Examples of shallow focus can be found repeatedly in *Lost in Translation*, the 2003 film by Sofia Coppola, her story of displaced travelers. The film charts the unlikely friendship between a young woman, idle in Tokyo while her photographer husband attends to his over-busy schedule, and an aging American movie star who has traveled to Tokyo for a TV commercial. Their chance meeting evolves into tender friendship, moments of which are captured in shallow focus, making a visual metaphor of their isolation and loneliness. The background blurs, if not disappears, un-grounding them to anything but one another. Figure 8.21 pictures a selection of shots from their "goodbye" that ends the film.

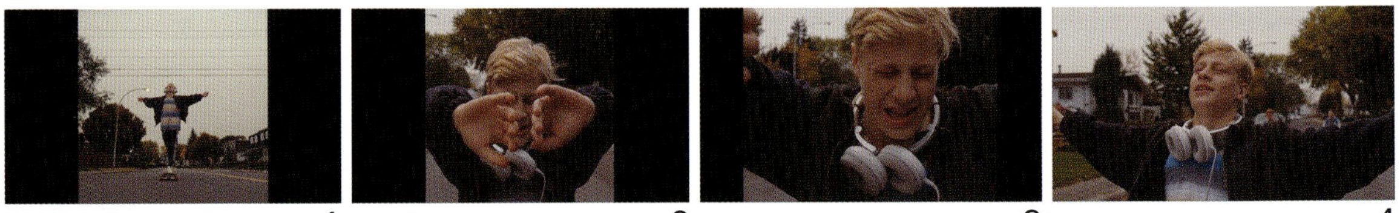

1 2 3 4

Figure 8.20 *Mommy* (2014). Director: Xavier Dolan. Cinematographer: André Turpin.

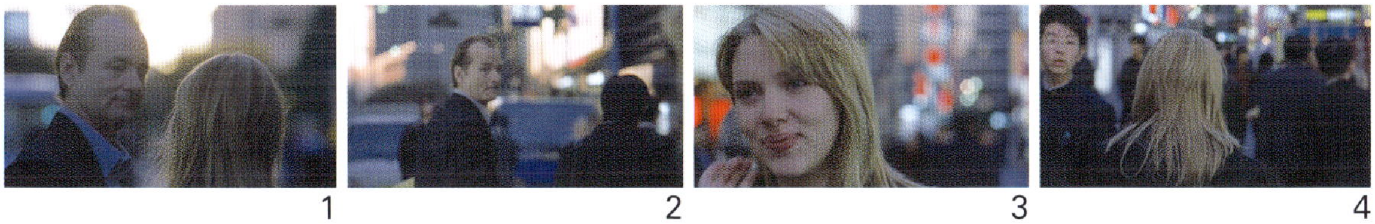

Figure 8.21 *Lost in Translation* (2003). Director: Sofia Coppola. Cinematographer: Lance Acord.

More radically, soft focus defines the frame in the opening scene of *Take This Waltz*. The character, Margot, is a young wife navigating the emptiness that can often emerge after certain life decisions—one's work and/or life partner—have been settled.

When we see her in the first frame of the film—a medium close-up—the shot is out of focus (Figure 8.22, Shot 1). Vivid colors, warm light, and the impression of a woman's head and shoulders are what we can discern. For twenty seconds, we have this blurred image of a woman busy with something. From time to time she raises an arm to wipe her face. After twenty seconds, the camera brings Margot into focus. On screen, her face is concentrating, occupied; a surrender to some task at hand. This repeats throughout the scene: her face in and out of focus, around which other shots occur. The effect: illusiveness, a definition that will not hold, not unlike what we will discover of her character, with its fuzzy margins of self.

More radical still is the way in which Josephine Decker, collaborating with cinematographer, Ashley Connor, makes use of shifts in the focal plane, so that images moving in and out of focus are central to the visual style. The manipulation of focus within a shot is not limited to any one character, or to one scene, but applied expressively across the film. Within sequence after sequence, we see clearly, and then not.

Madeline's Madeline, like *Mommy* is a story with a single mother, but in Decker's film emphasis is given to the daughter, Madeline. A bi-racial teenager, Madeline's relationship with her Caucasian mother is a prime source of frustration and friction. But as the title suggests it may well be Madeline's relationship to self that creates the central conflict. Dividing her is a history of mental instability on the one side and on the other, a desire to fulfill her creative gifts as an actress. She spends her days in training with an improvisational theater troupe led by Evangeline, who serves as a perfect foil to Madeline's mother. Evangeline seizes the idea to build an entire performance around Madeline's issues of identity, attention that excites Madeline but also trips her fears and anxieties.

The camera covering this conflict is handheld and moves toward and away from action in response to staging but more so in response to tension, or to a scene's emotional charge. Out of focus shots are not a consequence of repositioning, as in documentary, but within the shot itself, as if the scene were witnessed by an onlooker who can't quite get close enough, or far enough away, to get a clear view. Perspective is always just out of reach.

Clarity has been a value of storytelling in film from its inception and continues to this day. Sit for any feedback session after a rough cut screening and count the number of times a viewer bemoans story aspects that are not clear.

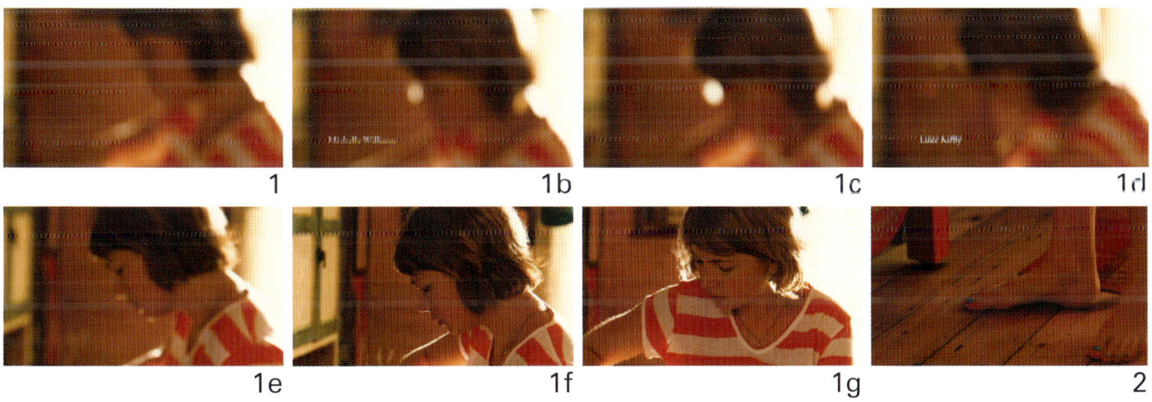

Figure 8.22 *Take This Waltz* (2011). Director: Sarah Polley. Cinematographer: Luc Montpellier.

And yet the history of cinema also includes films in which clarity is upstaged by other values. Some of these values became prevalent in the late 1950s and early 1960s in Europe, Eastern Europe, the USSR, and Asia. From this migration of films into America, US filmmakers took greater risks, and audiences were trained to tolerate less explicit story knowledge or delayed exposition in favor of, well, for one, visual dynamics (except in rough cut screenings).[10] In *Madeline's Madeline*, what competes with clarity is the visceral experience for the viewer. The visual dynamics emerge from techniques applied in service of collapsing any room for viewer detachment, providing instead proximity to the raw experience of characters enduring their predicaments and pleasures, their external and internal frictions. The camera dominates in making this provision.

The first two scenes of the film make scant effort at conventional exposition, yet they are thorough in inducting the viewer into the film's particular narrative strategy and elements of the visual style, including the manipulation of focus. Looking at the film's second scene, a montage depicted in Figure 8.23, we see the great liberty taken with building a storyboard, including spatial and time discontinuities (Shots 12, 14, and 16 are future tense, foreshadowing the scene to follow) and intercutting planes of color empty of narrative content (Shots 6, 9, and 18).

A quarrel escalates between Madeline and her mother, which is pictured in slow motion to the percussive beat of *Hey Na Na*, written and performed by the film's cast. The action is severe: Madeline, picks up an iron we know to be hot (Shot 13) and moves toward her mother's back. The shifting focal planes of Madeline (Shot 7) and her mother (Shot 20) work the counterpoint, the ambivalence in the action, the want without conviction. Counterpoint is one of Decker's basic strategies for keeping the story at dynamic pitch, visual and otherwise, and this counterpoint is central to the film's tone. Vacillations between human cruelty and tenderness pervade the atmosphere of *Madeline's Madeline*, while the film withholds judgment or praise. If there is any insistence in the tone it is simply: live close to this. The camera strategy, holding the viewer in a nether world by allowing a blurred image to dominate the screen, demonstrates a control to which some may not easily submit. If one can relax into the movie's authority over what is seen and what cannot yet be seen, there is an opportunity to be unsettled into immediacy, driving experience toward a present tense that simmers at the heart of the film.

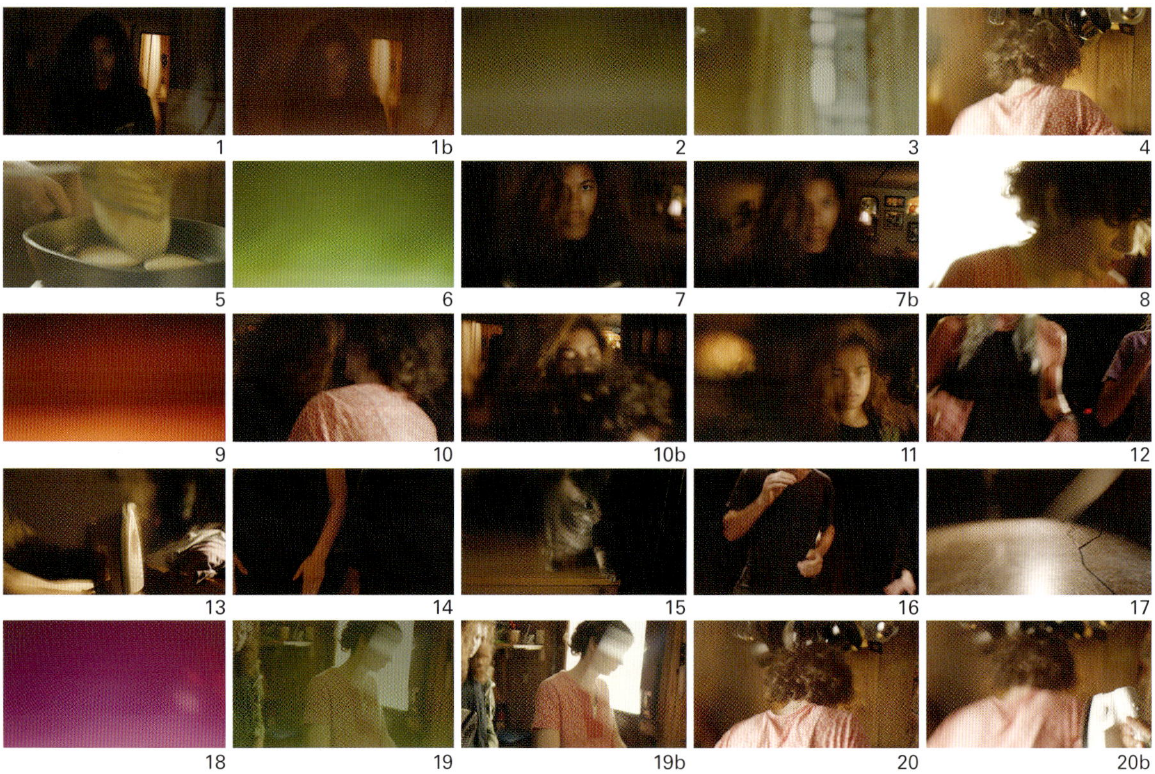

Figure 8.23 *Madeline's Madeline* (2018). Director: Josephine Decker. Cinematographer: Ashley Connor.

I had been developing this way of abstracting the image since the experimental films I made in college and had this idea of a rig I could make. Josephine is a director who really gets excited by experimentation, so she was game to let me do it. At the end of the day, it's how Madeline sees the world, and we wanted the image to reflect that sense of romanticism and fragmentation.

—Ashley Connor. Cadenazzi, Pablo Staricco, "Dancing Through the Unease: An Interview with 'Madeline's Madeline' Cinematographer, Ashley Connor." *Vague Visages*., *World Cinema & Film Criticism*, March 11, 2019.

Magic hour

The quality of light transposed to an image is a fundamental concern for any filmmaker and a definite factor in the visual dynamics of a film. Interior spaces allow for precise control of lighting, given that one can eliminate competition with the sun, or its absence. Exterior spaces require negotiating with the sun—its intensity, its direction—and all kinds of changes in weather. Post-production techniques allow for adjustments in light conditions and color across the image-span of a film but only within a certain range. Much of the effect must be accomplished on location.

Magic hour refers to the daylight hour *before* sunrise and/or *after* sunset when light spreads evenly across a location and colors soften within the frame. Characterized by an amber glow, magic hour can last more or less than an hour, depending on the latitude of the location. It is distinguished from **golden hour**, a term associated with photography but also applied to film, which features heightened colors, especially red and gold, and long shadows through a low sitting sun on the horizon. Golden hour occurs just *after* sunrise and *before* sunset.

Shooting a film, or scenes in a film, during magic hour places immense demands on the crew and cast, given the short duration. But filmmakers compelled to create an atmosphere from the warmth of late day light have found it irresistible. Among them, Terrence Malick, a director whose films are distinguished by exalted exteriors and the lustrous quality of images filmed with natural lighting during magic hour. It contributes to a large extent to the visual dynamics of his films.

Days of Heaven, Malick's 1978 feature, renders the open expanse of farm fields with the lighting and color textures of late day light. Set in 1916, the family at the center of the film is a makeshift one: Bill and his younger sister, Linda, along with Bill's girlfriend, Abby, who poses as a second sister. They are vagabonds, for sure, train hopping out of the slums of Chicago where Bill's temper left consequences too grave for him to stay. They arrive in Texas with a caravan of immigrant farm hands, settling down on the vast property of a wealthy farmer, glad to have work attending the harvest. The farmer's clapboard house sits on a hill, along with a barn and two pillars at the farm's entrance, which pose a rare intrusion into a landscape dominated by sky looming above wheat fields.

If *Madeline's Madeline* accomplishes dramatic effect through proximity—camera to character, character to character—*Days of Heaven* works the terrain of distance, with every plane of the frame in focus. The coverage does not shy away from close-ups (Figure 8.24, Shot 7), but close-ups are sequenced between wide shots, and extreme wide shots. Even the farmer, who throughout the film remains nameless, is introduced in a wide shot (Figure 8.24, Shot 4), preserving the perspective of the arriving farm hands. Characters, or interaction among them, are often abandoned in favor of a herd of buffalo (Figure 8.24, Shot 8), a flock of birds, or a weathervane. The light of magic hour silhouettes characters, casting them against landscape, rather than in or of it. The silhouetting also drains characters of individual identity in favor of other values, one of which is a painterly quality of contrast between light and dark within a composition (Figure 8.24, Shots 10–10b). The visual style of the film also supports other interests.

We shot very often at the "magic hour." We rehearsed with the actors and cameras, and then when the sun set, we started shooting. Of course, we had to work quickly because there was very little time to do the whole sequence.

—Néstor Almendros, *Film Comment*, September–October Issue 1978.

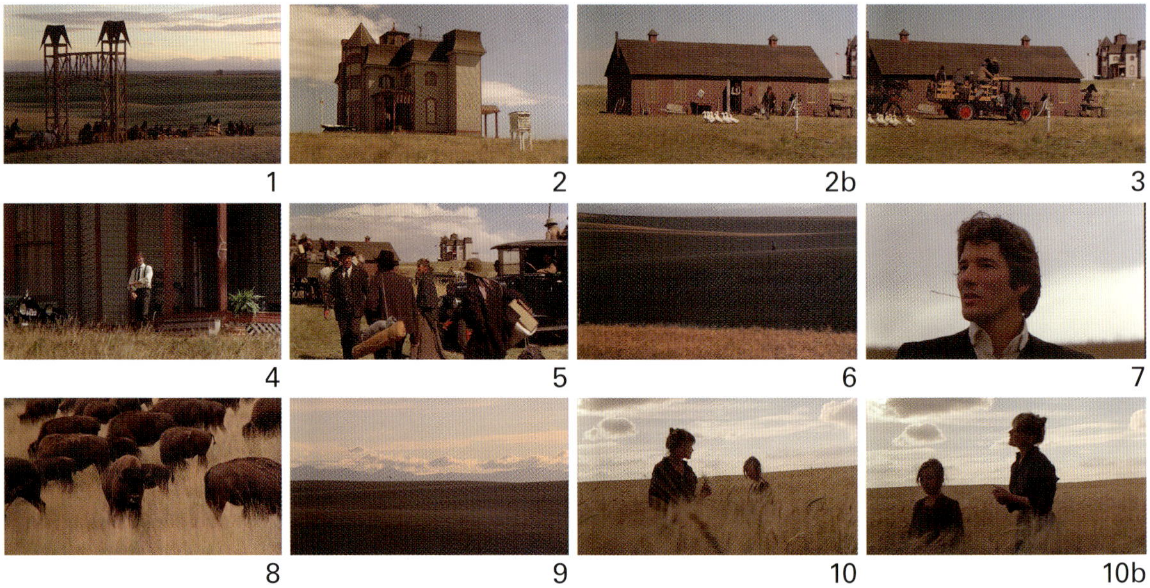

Figure 8.24 *Days of Heaven* (1978). Director: Terrence Malick. Cinematographer: Néstor Almendros.

A loose plot lands Bill in trouble again. Between troubles, there will be "days of heaven" for the three of them, a grace period on the farm that allows the film to do its more pressing work of portraiture. This isn't a portrait of specific people, though we get to know this threesome well enough, but a portrait of rootlessness in America, of isolation and impermanence—even the wheat goes up in flames in an effort to contain the locusts (Figure 8.25, Shots 1 and 3). It is not, however, a portrait of despair. Linda, Bill's younger sister, narrates the film with a raspy voice and fresh outlook: "All three of us been goin' places, lookin' for things, searchin' for things, goin' on adventures." She has already told us of having seen people "sufferin' of hunger and pain," to mean in much worse condition. Homelessness, here, is just possibility.

This scope or perception, this view of the horizon, anchors the film and is reinforced visually. Notice in Figures 8.24 and 8.25 the prevalence of extreme wide shots with the horizon line dividing the sky from land. Notice also how often a character or set of characters exists in isolation within the frame. In this film, with magic hour working its magic, one can glean the tone from the images alone, added to the elegiac score by Ennio Morricone, or Linda's husky voice.

So we developed a technique. Instead of lighting faces with electricity—they usually light with electricity and then they wave things in front of the light to imitate the flickering of the fire—my technique has always been going to the real thing. So I thought, "Why not light with real fire?"

—Néstor Almendros, *Film Comment*, September–October Issue 1978.

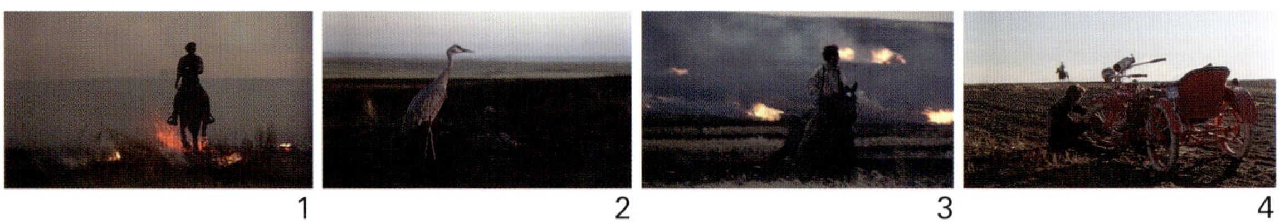

Figure 8.25 *Days of Heaven* (1978). Director: Terrence Malick. Cinematographer: Néstor Almendros.

Static frame

It may seem like a contradiction in terms, the idea of a static frame as visually dynamic, but we have seen in chapter three, the way in which filmmakers employ a variety of techniques to animate a static frame. Even in *Days of Heaven*, the camera quiets somewhat to do its work as landscape painting, allowing the play of light in combination with the frame's composition a greater role in achieving a dynamic visual field. Chantal Akerman's 1975 film, *Jeanne Dielman, 23 quai du Commerce, 1080 Bruxelles*, animates the static frame with a disciplined attention to formal properties. This dramatically impacts the tone, which in turn makes possible certain dramatic effects. In Akerman's film, atmosphere is valued above plot, and when the two converge in the film's unsettling climax, the effect is far more potent.

While the story of *Jeanne Dielman, 23 quai du Commerce, 1080 Bruxelles*, features, like *Mommy*, a single mother and son, most of the screen time is devoted to the mother, Jeanne. The film takes place over three days, during which we see her systematically go about the daily tasks of living: cooking, cleaning, tending to her son, and also accommodating her male clients, who pay her for sex, which finances the life she has with her son.

Jeanne's activities are covered in static shots of medium to wide proportion as seen in Figure 8.26. Any shot variety stems from the various locations, including all of the rooms in the apartment, as well as, later in the film, several locations outside the apartment (i.e., post office, street, tearoom). These shots make a record such that no one activity is privileged over another. Even the act of turning off a light, which Jeanne does fastidiously each time she leaves a room, is given screen time. Every activity receives the same weight or value, and this builds a particular charge on the screen. It is less that her life is monotonous, though one could make that case, but that the tasks are performed without affect, even the sex. The letter she reads to Sylvain from her sister, our only window into the backstory of their lives with its empathy for Jeanne's widowed status, is read without affect. This democratic reverence for each activity endowed by the image works against our assumptions, and this dissonance exaggerates the effect.

Some aspect of the visual dynamic occurs through control exerted over mise en scene, as the camera interacts with the setting and

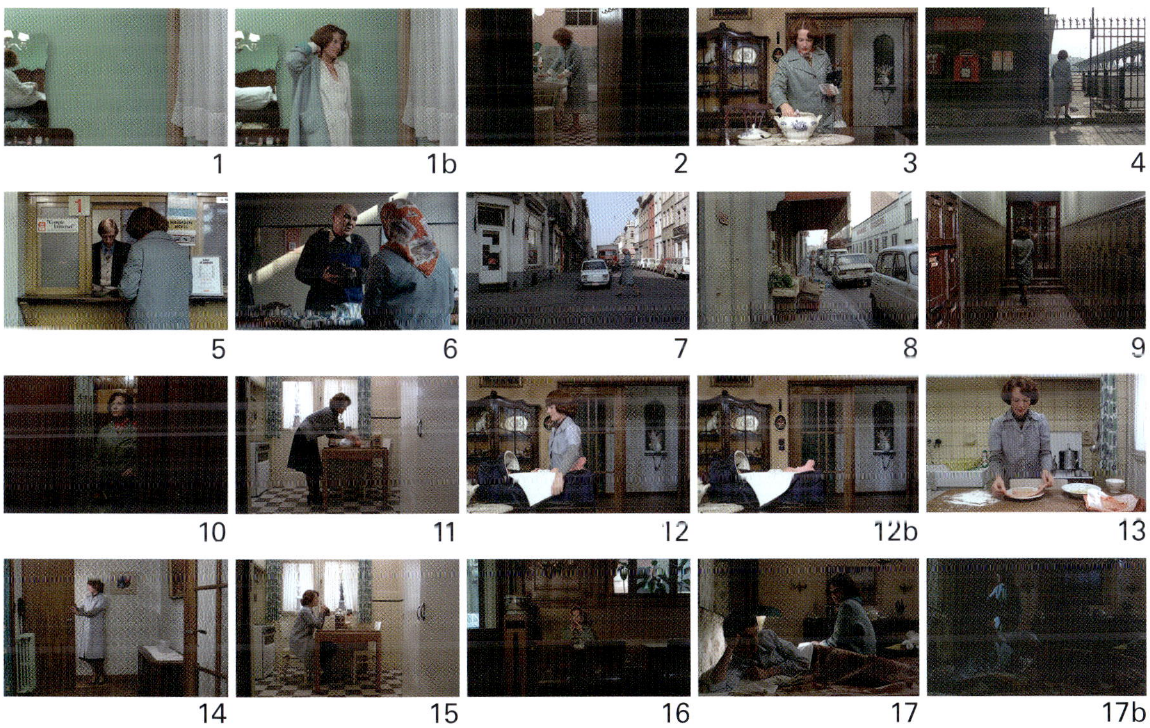

Figure 8.26 *Jeanne Dielman, 23 quai du Commerce, 1080 Bruxelles* (1975). Director: Chantal Akerman. Cinematographer: Babette Mangolte.

staging. In Figure 8.26, shots 1, 5, and 6 repeat the use of a frame within a frame, and shots 11–15 have been staged to increase depth. Look also at Figure 8.27, a scene in which Jeanne interacts with one of her clients, before, during, and after sex. In particular, the shot of Jeanne at her vanity table, the bed behind her, visible through the mirror, allows for the convergence of a number of elements. Not only does the camera capture Jeanne undressing and redressing, but *watching* herself undress and redress, with the photograph of her standing next to her late husband on the table in plain view. Added to this the client, post-sex, sits perched on the bed behind her, but in the image, he is next to her through the mirror. He watches her reflection and then, losing interest, falls back on the bed. All this is reported to us by way of the mirror, her mirror. Production design, in particular the color palette, remain thoroughly consistent in every scene, every shot. Even exteriors are dominated by a particular shade of green and pink, with accents of brown.

Figure 8.28 reveals a static medium-wide shot of Jeanne preparing meatloaf. The long take of this activity endures for four minutes of screen time. Here, the director's point of view digs in, giving witness on behalf of women who sustain a household with a regimen of service. Complicating this witness is the way in which the regimen imbues a life with purposefulness and control, the absence of which may unleash unexpected and unwanted consequences.

Of course, Jeanne is not able to sustain the meticulous control she exerts over every activity and by the third day, vulnerabilities surface. This begins her unraveling, which yields the movie's startling conclusion.

I sometimes think I should have made it (*Jeanne Dielman 23 quai du Commerce, 1080 Bruxelles*) after many other films, at the end of my career. I remember saying to myself, how can I make a better film? But it was also exactly the film I had to make then. It says something about a woman, about a way of living a life, about life after the war. It was the first thing I had to pour out of myself . . . I would have changed nothing about it.

—Chantal Akerman, "Then as Now, the Terrors of the Routine," Dennis Lim, *The New Yorker*, Jan. 16, 2009.

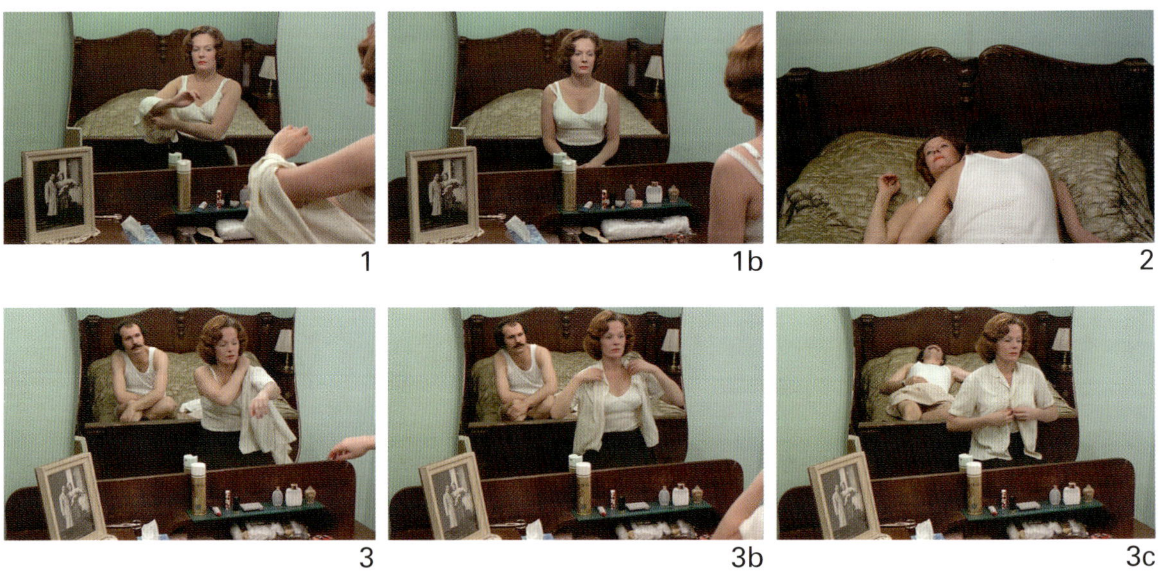

Figure 8.27 *Jeanne Dielman, 23 quai du Commerce, 1080 Bruxelles* (1975). Director: Chantal Akerman. Cinematographer: Babette Mangolte.

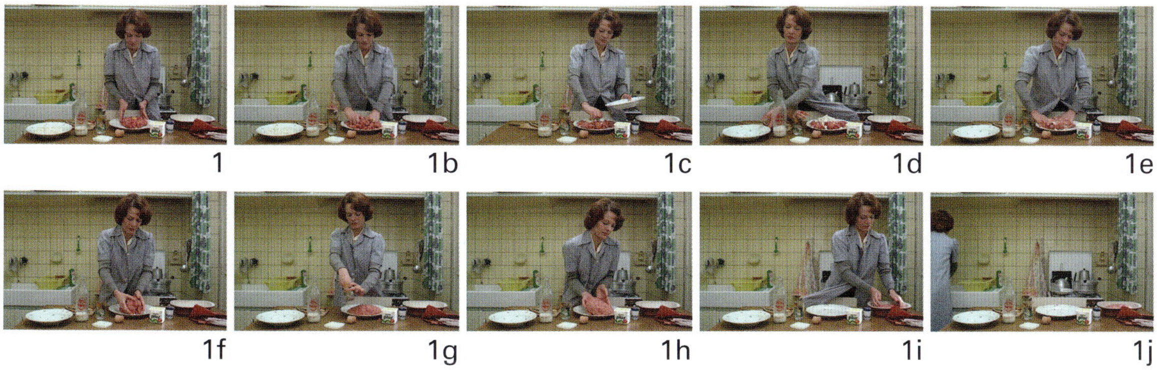

Figure 8.28 *Jeanne Dielman, 23 quai du Commerce, 1080 Bruxelles* (1975). Director: Chantal Akerman. Cinematographer: Babette Mangolte.

Location

Location serves as an essential element in the visual world of a film. As a critical aspect of production design, location interacts with a movie's camera strategy in formidable ways. Locations can be designed and built to accommodate the needs of the story and visual style, but economy and other factors will have filmmakers scouting existing locations. A location that is inherently cinematic can do an enormous amount of work, visually and narratively.

In our discussion of the wide shot in chapter five, many of the films cited made use of cinematic exteriors, which privileged the use of existing locations. Looking again at shots of three exterior spaces from three different films, one recognizes the care in choosing a backdrop for story action to achieve certain effects (Figure 8.29). Even without narrative particulars one can recognize qualities in each location that add to its on-camera value. One can also discern a thoughtfulness regarding camera placement to enhance the value.

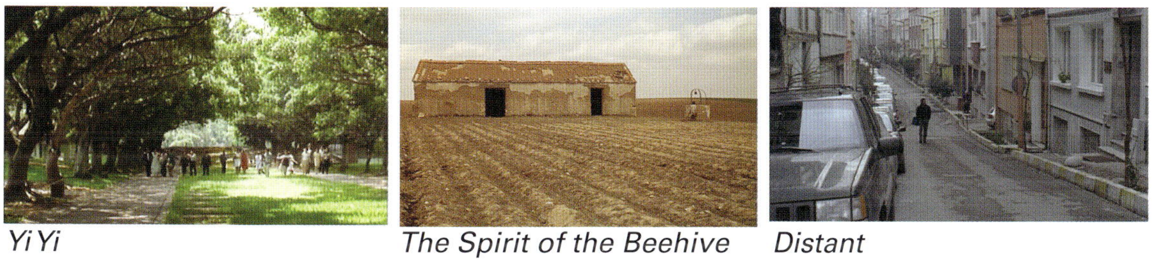

Figure 8.29 Location as critical element in visual storytelling.

Architecture of interior space

Existing interior spaces can also be mined for their visual efficacy and relevance to given story material. *A Separation*, the 2011 film by Asghar Farhadi, makes thorough use of a middle-class apartment in Tehran to charge the dynamics among the family of four who live there. Strife occurs at the outset. Simin, determined to leave Iran, has secured time-limited travel visas for herself, her husband, Nader, and Termeh, their daughter. Nader refuses to abandon his aging father who suffers from dementia, and who lives with them. Simin insists on leaving with their daughter, a plan Nader fiercely rejects. The movie begins with Nader and Simin attempting to settle their dispute in court, but the judge refuses to rule in favor of one or the other. The second scene takes place in the apartment, a section of which is depicted in Figure 8.30. Simin packs her belongings (Shots 2, 6, and 11) for a move into her parent's home while the conflict around Termeh's future is resolved. Razieh is also there (Shot 2b). She has come with her daughter to inquire about paid work providing day care for Nader's father; needed now that Simin will no longer be living in the apartment. These six characters, along with Razieh's husband, drive a plot that dials up intensity at every turn.

In looking at the still frames in Figure 8.30, we can easily discern pertinent characteristics of the interior space. Chief among them for creating visual dynamics is the fact and use of the many windows and doors. Even shot 2 has "faux" windows with the panes of glass on the bookcase. We can also register the camera coverage, which is handheld, working to stage characters in relation to the doors and windows. This works as a metonym for departure but also, and more emphatically, as a means of segregating characters without eliminating their capacity to notice or watch one another. In particular the two children: Termeh (Shots 1, 8, and 10) and Razieh's daughter (Shots2b and 4) are watchful of events unfolding in the apartment, events over which they have no control. Termeh's reflection (Shot 1), has her fixed on her mother cast in the doorway behind her as Simin moves around the apartment packing. Nader is visible at a distance and through a window (Shots 3 and 5), as he shaves the face of his aging father.

The handheld camera coverage has been edited to situate characters next to one another, even as the space separates them. This convergence sums up the narrative plight: irreconcilable differences among people who are inescapably bound together.

Within the story characters confront the large questions: What is fair? What is moral? What is right? The camerawork choreographed as it is with staging and location, with its double exposures and segregated characters, serves the visual dynamic but also the film's tone. It suggests to the viewer a more complex world than one governed by the hard corners of justice or moral virtue, one in which human frailty requires other mediating principles if the bonds are to hold.

In the end, Termeh will be asked by the judge to say where, and with which parent, she would like to live. While we wait for her answer in the hall of the court, we see her mother and father staged once again in proximity to doors and windows, once again separated, even in the same shot, by a wide threshold (Figure 8.31).

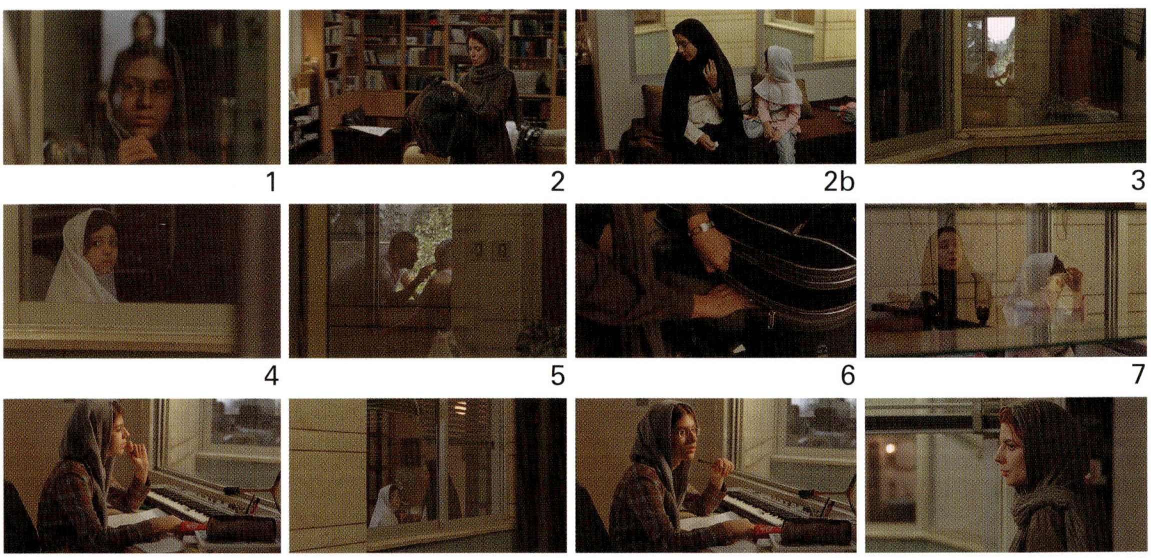

Figure 8.30
A Separation (2011). Director: Asghar Farhadi. Cinematographer: Mahmoud Kalari.

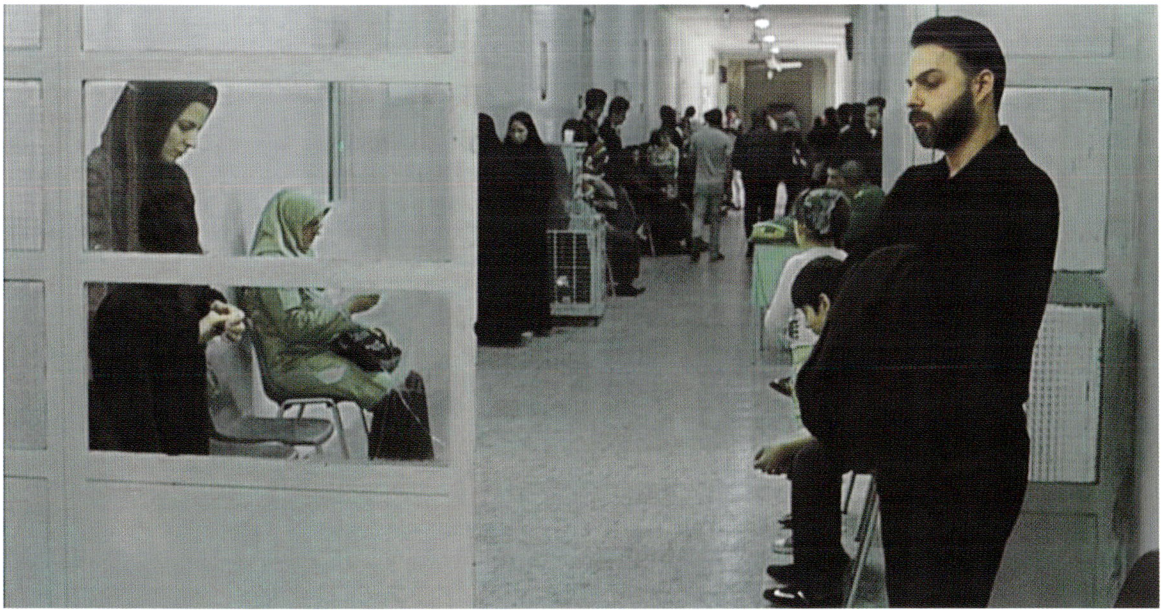

Figure 8.31
A Separation (2011). Director: Asghar Farhadi. Cinematographer: Mahmoud Kalari.

Form and feeling

The handheld nature of the camera in *A Separation* disguises to some extent the repeated use of windows, doors, and thresholds. For certain, the handheld camera de-emphasizes the graphic nature of frame within a frame created by the architectural openings. *Ikiru (To Live)*, the 1952 feature film directed by Akira Kurosawa, takes full advantage of graphic shapes as an essential element of mise en scene, drawing attention to them with the combined effect of camera movement and character movement.

Ikiru (To Live) is the story of Kanji Watanabe, a civil servant who has worked for the same bureaucratic institution for thirty years. He lives with his son and daughter-in-law, though they are clearly more interested in his pension than his well-being. When he learns he has cancer, and only a year to live, Watanabe tells no one, not even his son. Plagued by the lack of meaning in his life, pushing pen and paper all day, he goes on a pleasure spree, indulging in the city's nightlife. When this doesn't bring fulfillment, he takes up with a lively and affectionate young woman. While offering temporary relief, his deeper longing isn't satisfied until she spurs in him the idea that he might make some kind of contribution. He goes back to work and advocates with uncustomary determination and ferocity for a local cesspool to be converted to a children's playground.

The first portion of the story unfolds chronologically, with Watanabe's diagnosis and his spiral into desperation. The second portion of the film is shaped by Watanabe's awakening to service, through a series of flashbacks, prompted by tales from co-workers, friends, his son, and daughter-in-law, gathered to memorialize him after his death. Their recollections shape the second half of the film.

Many scenes in *Ikiru (To Live)* could be exampled for their thoughtful and athletic use of camera. The scene depicted in Figure 8.32 provides an opportunity to analyze the use of camera to create a visually dynamic record of experience that is both poignant and sad. The scene includes the final flashback. It's triggered by the confession of a police officer, arriving late to the gathering of mourners to pay his respects (Shot 1). He brings Watanabe's snow soaked hat, which the son receives from him. He reports of having seen Watanabe swinging in the new park late the night before, during snowfall. Thinking he was some kind of derelict, the officer ignored him. He shares with the mourners his deep regret for not having rescued him, reporting, as well, that Watanabe seemed deeply happy, singing as he was swinging.[11]

Bookending the flashback are two close-ups: the police officer (Shot 1) and the portrait of Watanabe (Shot 5). In between, a variety of elements collide to create visual vitality. To

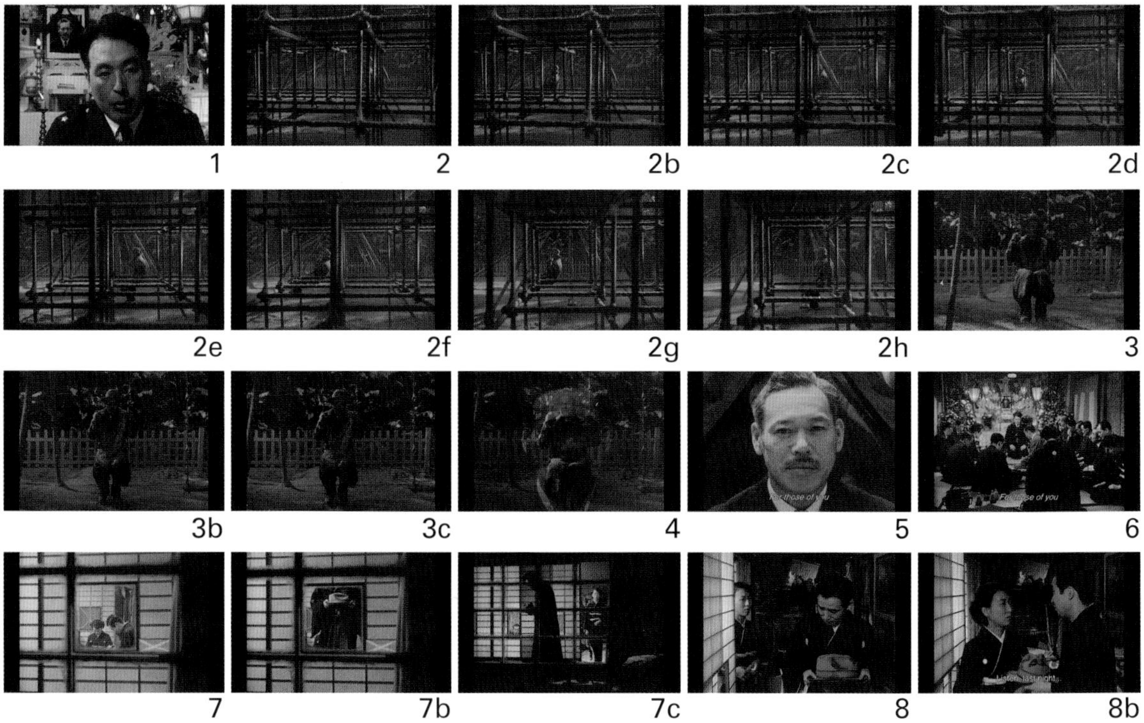

Figure 8.32 *Ikiru (To Live)* (1952). Director: Akira Kurosawa. Cinematographer: Asakazu Nakai.

begin, graphic shapes dominate the frame. Bars of a climbing tower fill the foreground of the children's park, and five bars deep, the middle ground. Behind the climbing tower, a swing occupies the background where Watanabe can be seen swinging right to left to right, and so on. The camera is positioned on the right side of the climbing tower, as if arriving only to discover a man swinging. The camera tracks slowly from the right side of the climbing tower to the left, as if to get a better view, and once centering Watanabe in the repeating "windows" made by the intersection of bars on the climbing tower, the camera dollies toward him, ever so slightly. A cut repositions the camera to face Watanabe, but this also brings him face to face with us, his viewers. Watanabe swings forward and back as the camera moves again almost imperceptibly toward him before the image dissolves into the close-up of Watanabe's portrait, resuming the gathering of mourners in the film's present.

There is already immense pathos gained by witnessing an old man on the cusp of dying sitting in a child's swing, singing a ballad of consolation and warning. The staging works to allow him this moment of reverie at some remove with the climbing tower foregrounding the swing set. But it is the camera that authors the tone of the flashback, tracking slowly in the direction of the man swinging, approaching respectfully, gingerly moving in toward him. When the camera faces him outright, it gives Watanabe both presence and voice. Here, the delicate motion in his direction is a gesture of praise.

The scene doesn't end here, nor the visual athleticism. A wide shot of the mourners follows the close-up of Watanabe's portrait, and then the son seen through a window, holding the father's hat, reckoning with the discovery that his father was sick, and in his dying has left him with all that he owned. Shot 7–7c portrays the son and his wife. We can see that the graphic shapes parallel the playground image. Here, too, the son is seen through a square-shaped window at the center of the frame. The camera, however, instead of moving toward the son, pulls back to make room for him as he rises, slides open the door, and steps outside the mourning room. His wife follows him. A static shot covers the two of them as the son wakes to his own deep regret. While close-ups bookend the flashback, expressions of regret mark the beginning and end of the scene.

Tone: the outsider

The "outsider" as theme and source of story content has deep roots in cinema. Many early silent films capitalized on dramatic values inherent in a central character living outside the social mainstream, among them: Erich von Stroheim's *Greed*, F.W. Murnau's *Last Laugh*, and Alice Guy-Blaché's *The Ocean Waif*. We might consider Watanabe, the protagonist of *Ikiru (To Live)* an outsider, given the separation from peers and family invoked by his cancer diagnosis. This thematic use of the outsider continues into the present. An entire thesis could be written investigating the role of the outsider in narrative film history, including the flood of such stories that came to the screen with Italian Neo-Realism, "kitchen sink" drama in the UK, and the Independent Film movement in the US, but also, in more recent decades, specific films from Mexico, China, and France.

Authority with camera

Set in the banlieues of Paris, two films make striking use of visual dynamics in their treatment of the outsider. The 1995 film, *La Haine*, and 2016 film, *Divines*, draw their story content from young immigrants living on the outskirts of Paris. In each film, characters act out of desperation for more agency in their lives. Also, in each film, the police function as border guards, stationed at the rim of their entry into a larger, more affluent society. And yet the films stake out different territory and themes, which translate into a striking difference in their camera strategies and the tone that the visual style serves.

La Haine, the black-and-white film directed by Mathieu Kassovitz [12] follows three young men, agitated and angered by the recent police shooting of their friend, Abdel, during a neighborhood riot, which has him hospitalized in a coma.[13] This multi-racial trio includes Vinz, a French Jew, revved up by the incident, who seeks revenge; Hubert, Afro-French, who divides his time between boxing and small-time drug deals, keeping a low profile to stay out of trouble; and Saïd, a North African Muslim, spirited and hopeful who tries to keep peace between the two, and stave off any violent confrontations, particularly between Vinz and his target, the police.

For a screen time of one hour and thirty-eight minutes, the dynamic among them stokes scenes with energy despite their aimless wanderings. Casting, performance, and the writing contribute to this in equal part. But the camera drives the film's vitality, with movement staged at every pace, in tracking shots and zooms, slow dollies that eclipse one character in favor of others. Deep focus is often used to give reality to characters in space, and likewise, backgrounds can blur out of focus, giving emphasis to foreground. A theatrical, wide static shot displays Vinz performing and a static close-up has Hubert, breaking the **fourth wall**, eye to eye with the viewer. One scene employs a split screen with ingenious use of a bathroom mirror, and another combines a dolly with a zoom to evoke the characters displacement. Key to what keeps this from seeming like random technique are the repetitions but also the authority and precision with which the shots are executed and actors staged in front of the camera.

While screen shots cannot convey the robust camera movement in *La Haine*, one can discern from them aspects of how the scene is visually constructed that might not be apparent while viewing. Figure 8.33 depicts the three young men during a stretch of idleness, sitting in an abandoned space.[14] Along the wall behind them, graffiti reads *L'avenir c'est nous*, (*The future is us*) cutting a wedge of irony into their idleness. The neighborhood high-rise apartments loom in the near distance. A younger friend holds Vinz captive with an anecdote about a violent interaction between a celebrity and Candid Camera crew. A long take covers this telling, the camera easing in slowly, excluding first Hubert, and then Saïd as the story winds to an end with a two-shot (Shots 2–2d). "Then what?" Vinz wants to know, unimpressed. "'That's all," the young friend says. The scene cuts to an intertitle that reads 14:12, scored with the sound of a ticking clock (Shot 3). When the scene resumes, a 180° jump in perspective has occurred. Framed now from behind, the camera in another long take pushes in slowly as Saïd runs to greet the car of Abdel's brother and the young friend leaves. The shot ends with Hubert framed from behind (Shots 4–4d). A cut to the close-up of his shoes

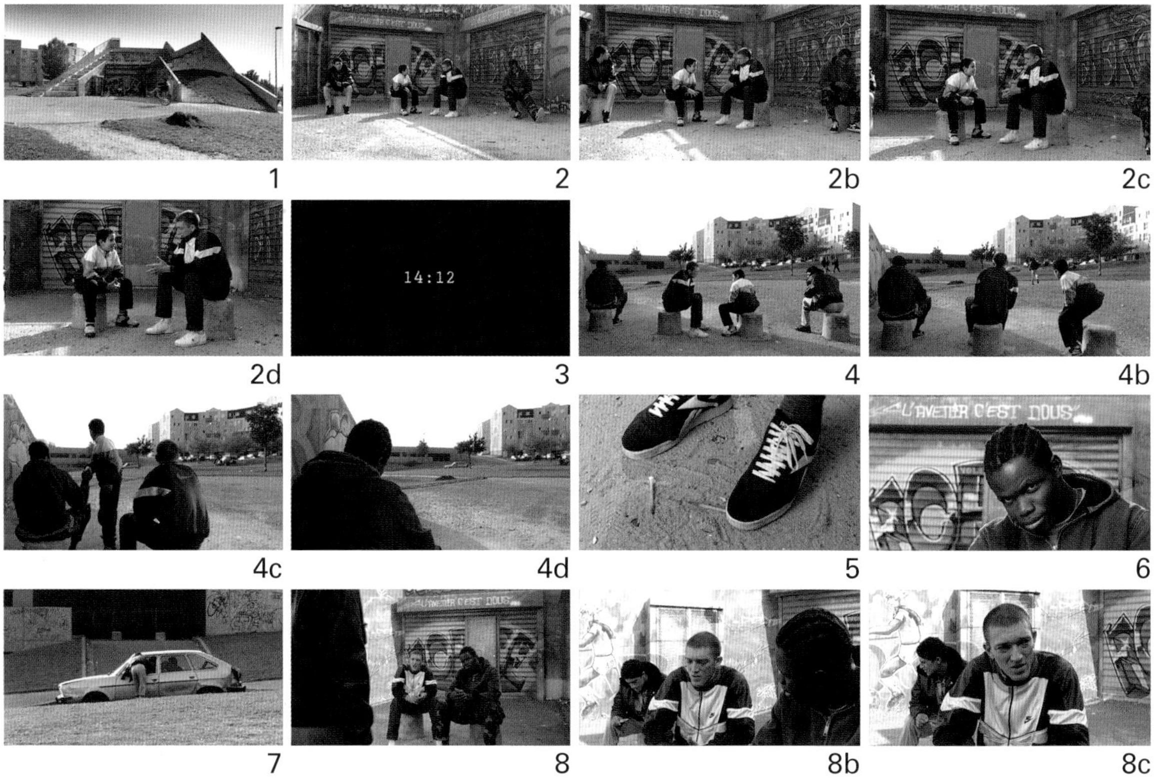

Figure 8.33
La Haine (1995). Director: Mathieu Kassovitz. Cinematographer: Pierre Aïm.

in the dirt, fumbling with empty syringes, brings the camera back to face them, followed by the cut to Hubert in close-up (Shot 6) watching Saïd at the car (Shot 7). The scene ends as Saïd walks back over with news. "He's got a shotgun," he'll tell them. "Party time." Hubert suggests that they visit Abdel in the hospital. The camera closes in on Vinz who reports he has something he wants to show them. The face-off brewing between Hubert and Vinz gets telegraphed in the coverage with their close-ups (Shots 6 and 8c).

The second scene depicted in Figure 8.34 occurs at the mid-point of the film. It follows a hair-raising chase and confrontation with the

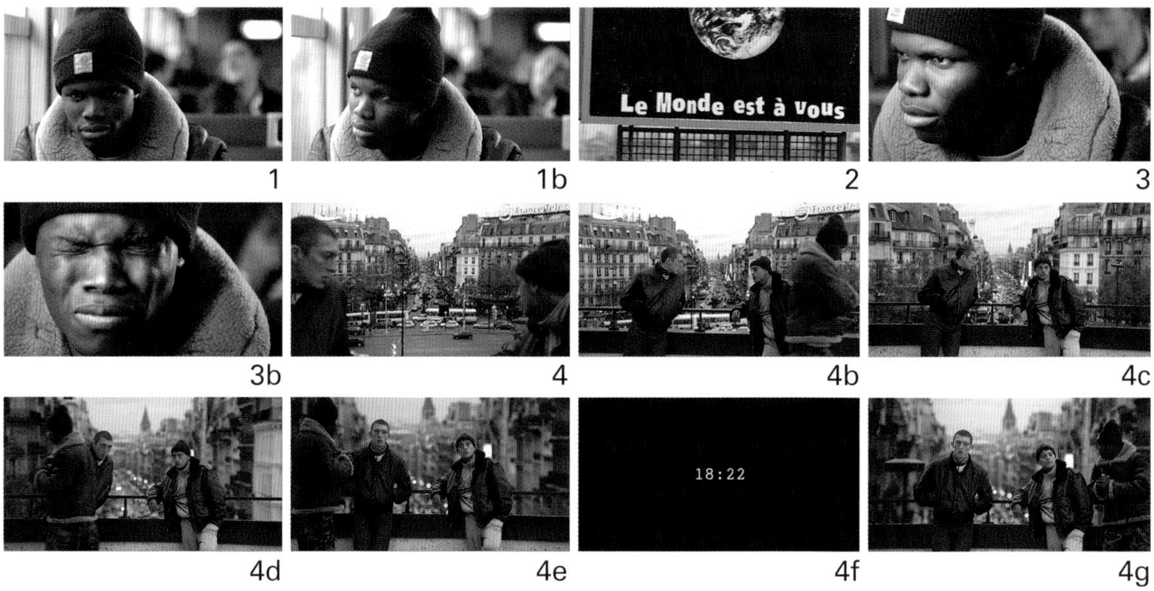

Figure 8.34
La Haine (1995). Director: Mathieu Kassovitz. Cinematographer: Pierre Aïm.

police, a close call for the three young men, ending with Hubert's brisk punch to an officer, saving them from capture. Traveling by Metro above ground, Vinz prattles on endlessly to Saïd of his prowess in the confrontation. He sits, out of focus, behind Hubert, who is framed in close-up. Through the window, something draws his attention. He turns: a billboard fills the screen with signage: *Le Monde est à vous* (*The world is yours*). Cutting back to Hubert, the close-up tightens to picture him, head turning, with piercing gaze, straight into camera. The camera inches in even closer (Shot 3b). He closes his eyes, squeezing tightly. The cut (Shot 4) takes the trio to a ledge overlooking the streets of Paris. Here, a dolly combines with a zoom to de-focus the cityscape while bringing the three young men into view, idle again. Another intertitle appears. "What do we do now?" Vinz wants to know as Hubert paces.

Significant visual information exists in each of the two scenes establishing tone, or point of view. The signage alone, with its stab of irony, underscores a world of contradictions. There is no small trace of fury in the atmosphere, on behalf of the characters, evidenced by the freedom to have the camera meet their gaze, straight on. Too, in each scene, camera conspires with blocking and staging as witness to their inertia. Consider the effect, in the first scene (Figure 8.33) of picturing (and repeatedly) the young men side by side, seated on the concrete pilings. The camera is positioned in front of them, then behind them, and then, in front again, underscoring the nothing they have to do with their time—each of them—strong, energetic, and bright young men. Likewise, in the second scene (Figure 8.34) they lean against a railing, Hubert pacing now, unsettled. The cityscape changes drastically behind them, falling out of focus. They, meanwhile, have no idea what to do next.

Poetry and grit

Divines, the first feature directed by Houda Benyamina, also takes as its subject a community of young people living in the outskirts of Paris.[16] In this film, the protagonists are two teenage girls, Dounia and her best friend, Maimouna, who live in the Romani banlieue. Impatient with the philosophy at school that hard work and good conduct is the best hope for their future, they practice entrepreneurial skills by reselling goods they pilfer at supermarkets. What they don't sell, they hide in the rafters of a local theater where Dounia meets Djigui, an untrained dancer who spends his afternoons rehearsing for a spot in a dance company. The plot thickens with their affection, although Dounia's loyalty to her best friend Maimouna is challenged most by her association with Rebecca, a local drug dealer, who hires the two teenage girls for small-time errands. When Dounia proves worthy of a big score with big payoff, life complicates for her. This leads to tragic consequences after she finds herself caught in regulations of fire and police protection that apply to the banlieues.

Without question, the film's tone and point of view highlight the challenges of young people living in the periphery of Paris, and like *La Haine*, dramatizes the effects of limited personal agency, resources, and power. Here, too, *Divines* implicates the authorities (police, firefighters, and other government officials) who fail these communities. But character, as much as circumstance, drives the story. The guiding values and traits of the individual lead to actions that have consequences. While poverty and powerlessness define the milieu in which Dounia and Maimouna live, they do not define temperament, or dictate choice. Each character is given moments of choice, which combine with circumstance to yield the film's end.

In what way does this implicate the camera technique in *Divines*? First, the movie exudes dramatic energy. A good portion is sparked by the chemistry between Dounia and Maimouna, who radiate exuberance and passion, even when posing as serious Muslim girls, dressed in hijabs and abayas, out for a shoplifting spree.[16] Also, the young duo seem constantly busy, Dounia, in particular, refusing to give in to malaise. The camera supports this liveliness. For example, Figure 8.35 depicts a scene in which the Dounia invites Maimouna to join her in a fantasy of travel to Phuket, Thailand, in their expensive Ferrari. They drink champagne. They pick up a cute blonde guy. They imagine their prowess in having, as they say, *money, money, money*.

The scene follows an exchange with drug dealer, Rebecca, and her crew outside the apartment building. Dounia, ever the optimist,

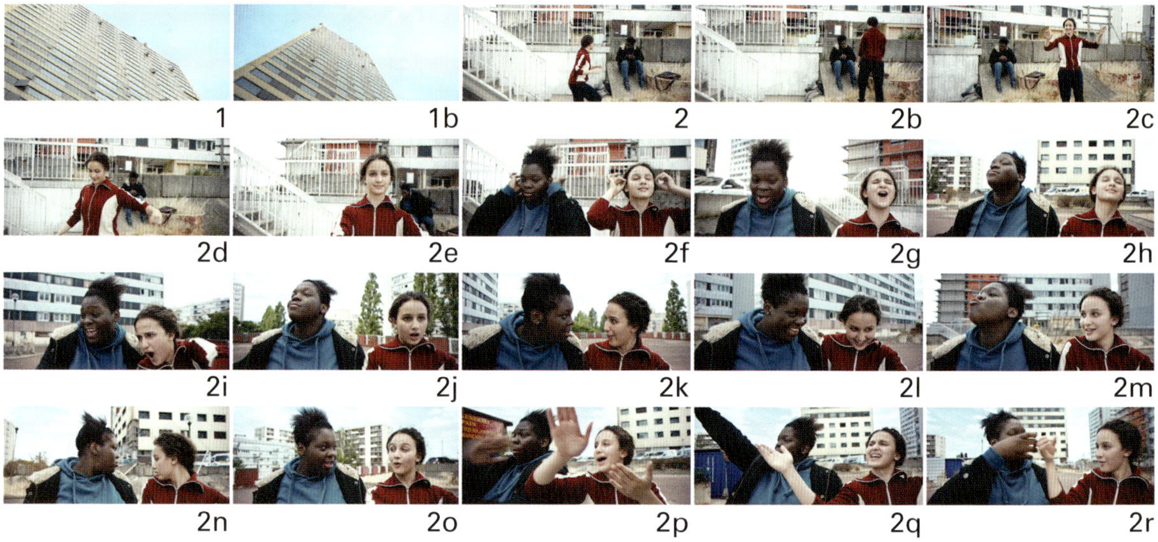

Figure 8.35 *Divines* (2016). Director: Houda Benyamina. Cinematographer: Julien Poupard.

hears Rebecca's words as opportunity. Maimouna is more cautious. The camera zooms back to pitch the apartment building as looming above them, against the sky (Figure 8.35, Shots 1–1b). The second shot begins with Dounia and Maimouna below. It covers the remainder of the scene as a long take, with Dounia imagining her future, climbing into a Ferrari in Thailand (Shot 2c), and Maimouna hesitating, but joining her (Shot 2f). The young women, framed consistently in a medium two shot, scoot around the lot, fantasized as Phuket, hair blowing in the wind, while the background changes, the camera giving in to the fantasy, making it more real. Sound design enhances the scene with traffic noises and effects. Simply put, the camera is complicit with Dounia in her fantasy, bringing it to life, endowing imagination with force, even as hardships prevail.

Many scenes foster a convergence of the tough necessities of life with an operatic camera treatment, often added to by a vivid soundtrack with musical score. Dounia makes a delivery of drugs in a cathedral, kneeling on the prayer pad for the exchange. A liturgical choral music swells to a rousing *Amen* while the camera frames her

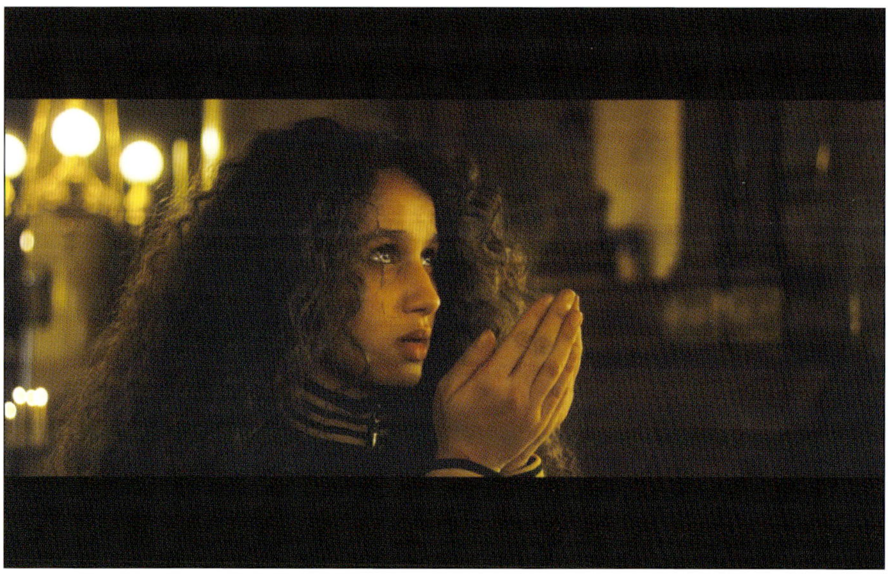

Figure 8.36 *Divines* (2016). Director: Houda Benyamina. Cinematographer: Julien Poupard.

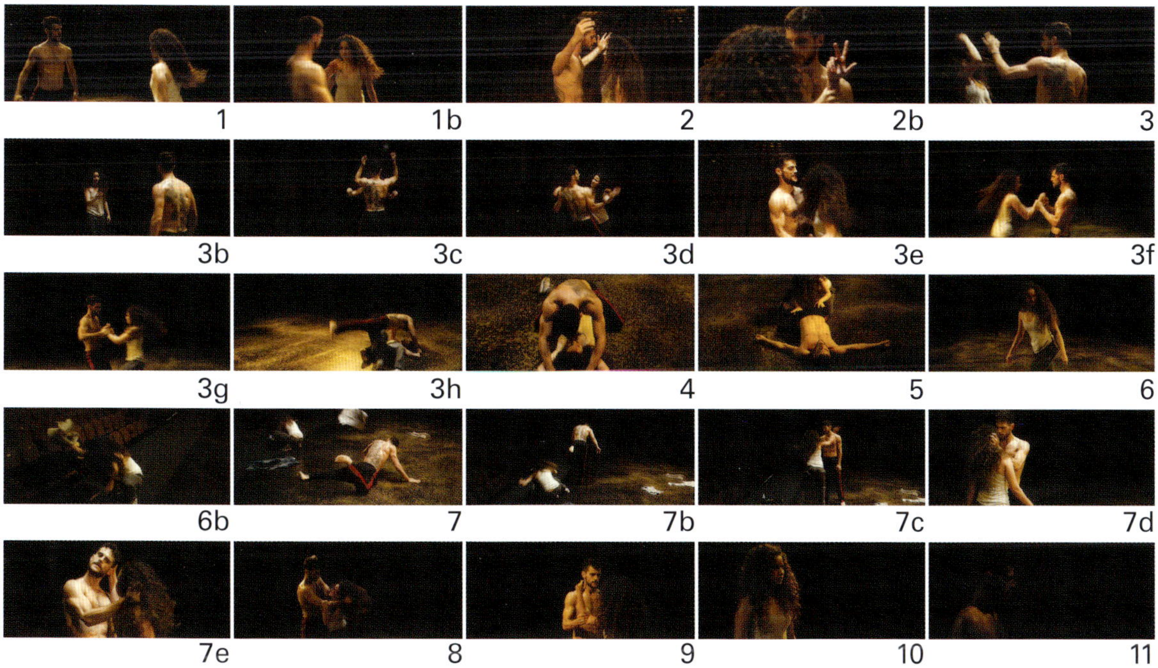

Figure 8.37 *Divines* (2016). Director: Houda Benyamina. Cinematographer: Julien Poupard.

in close-up after the delivery, her hands folded in prayer looking up to the Christ icon painted before her, "Lord, forgive me," she says (Figure 8.36).

In the scene to follow, Dounia discovers cash that she keeps hidden in the theater rafters has gone missing and immediately suspects Djigui. She goes to him, rehearsing in the theater, "Where's my money?" she asks, and a quarrel ensues.

In the still frames pictured in Figure 8.37 the encounter seems like a dance: their golden bodies lit against a black stage. The camera keeps them in the center of the frame even as they move across the stage, making of the scene a dramatic pas de deux, a power struggle that is physicalized between them. The scene ends without resolve, a cut transitions to a daytime interior with Dounia with Maimouna, no mention made of Djigui. There will be another pas de deux between Dounia and Djigui before the film's end, in the aisles of a supermarket, converging again reality with a heightened visual style.

Color

We discussed earlier in this chapter the crucial role that a film location may have in the visual style of a film. For certain filmmakers, the inspiration for story is rooted in place. This inspiration may have to do with a location's photographic value, or historic value, or the cultural milieu associated with a given place. It may be an entirely sentimental attachment. Devotion to a particular place has given rise to many films.

The 2015 feature film *Tangerine*, directed by Sean Baker, hinged on the use of a donut shop situated at the corner of Santa Monica Boulevard and Highland Avenue in Hollywood.[17] But apart from Donut Time, the twenty-four-hour shop known as a haven for transgender workers, the film takes care to reveal a particular version of Hollywood not often portrayed. As in *La Haine*, signage, graffiti, and advertisements become essential elements in visual style. *Tangerine*, as the title suggests, does not portray a world in black and white. Increased color saturation during post production adds to image vitality, which also benefits from the natural lighting of the California sun. This also suits the film's tone, which depends on a blend of comedy with drama.

The camera work contributes to the visual energy and is singular. The film was made using three iPhone 5s cameras, equipped with lens adaptors, a special app for adjusting focus and aperture, and an image stabilizer. An iPhone mounted on a painter's pole served as a crane, a bicycle was used as a dolly, Baker and co-cinematographer, Radium Cheung, improvised as needed.[18]

Figure 8.38 *Tangerine* (2015). Director: Sean Baker. Cinematographers: Sean Baker and Radium Cheung.

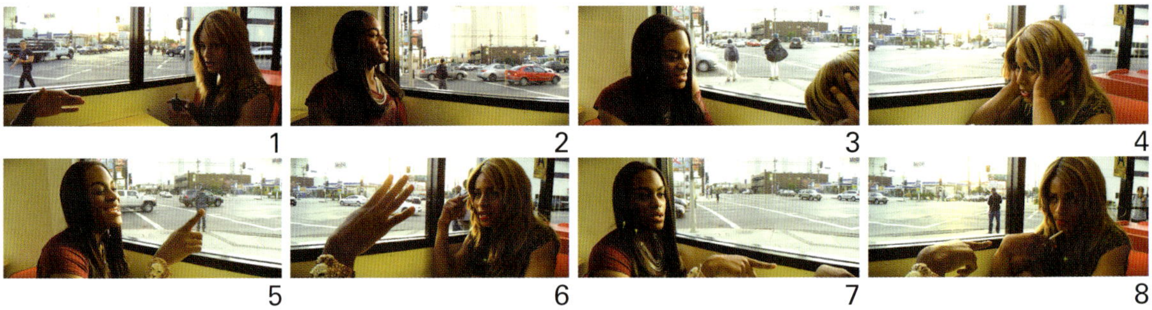

Donut Time is the site of the film's first scene (Figure 8.38). It's Christmas Eve when Sin-dee, a transgender sex worker, fresh from a month in jail, sits down with her best friend, Alexandra, also a trans sex worker, to share a donut. Alexandra, during their reunion, lets it slip that Chester, Sin-dee's boyfriend and pimp, has been dating a cis-gender female. "Chester is cheating on me with a real fish?!!!!" Sin-dee, outraged, goes, on a tear through Hollywood looking for Chester and the girl (Dinah). An Armenian cab driver, and family man, trafficking through the streets with his holiday clientele has a crush on Sin-dee or so Alexandra discovers as she papers the neighborhood with advertisements of a singing gig at a local bar that evening. This collective of characters, including the cab driver's mother-in-law, followed by wife and daughter, come together in the penultimate scene, which takes place in the donut shop. There, a revelation occurs threatening the friendship between Sin-dee and Alexandra, who are left to work it out at Launderland, the local coin laundry.

The coverage in the opening scene makes use of the basic convention of shot/reverse shot: single shots of Sin-dee alternating with single shots of Alexandra. Looking at the individual frames one realizes that the characters take up, at most, only a third of the frame. The other two thirds are given to street life seen through the shop window at the intersection of the two thoroughfares in Hollywood. Taking note of the street life, one does not expect to see Hollywood celebrities. This is not Rodeo Drive. The scene serves to set up, of course, the narrative stakes but also to locate the viewer in the particulars of this world.

Vibrancy, despite the downscale neighborhood and its local bars and eateries, in addition to the adjustments of color, contributes to this. Figure 8.39 depicts a later scene in which Sin-dee, trailed by Alexandra, grills her local trans friends, hoping to learn the name and whereabouts of the girl in Chester's company. Staging the scene in front of a wall painted with a colorful mural animates a situation already lively with Sin-dee's obsessive rant. As the first shot begins (Shot 1) the mural fills the frame. As the camera moves, characters are minimized only to become foregrounded as the first shot ends. In the second shot, they are staged against the mural, with it functioning as background, keeping the frame alive with color.

Notice the interaction between color and composition in the shots depicted in Figure 8.40. Sin-dee, still on the trail of Chester and Dinah, waits for a bus at a bus stop until impatience gets the better of her and she leaves. There are parallel compositions within the sequence (Shots 3 and 7, Shots 4, 4b, and 8). But the composition also makes use of the horizon separating blue sky from the yellow and green below it. Through this frame, the bus arrives; passengers get off, staring at Sin-dee with untoward glances. The shots marginalize Sin-dee within the frame, and yet the world pictured is bright, vivid, and blue-skied.

Figure 8.39 *Tangerine* (2015). Director: Sean Baker. Cinematographers: Sean Baker and Radium Cheung.

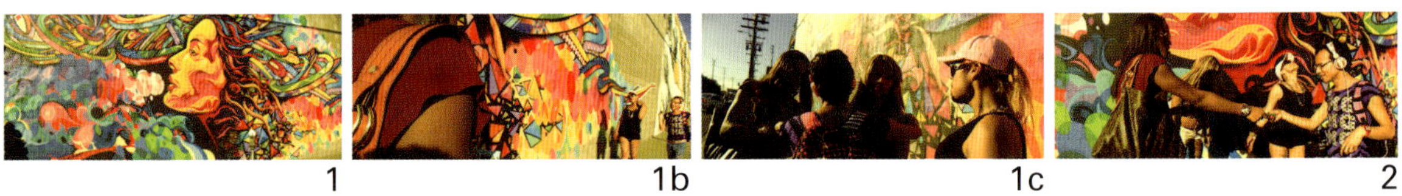

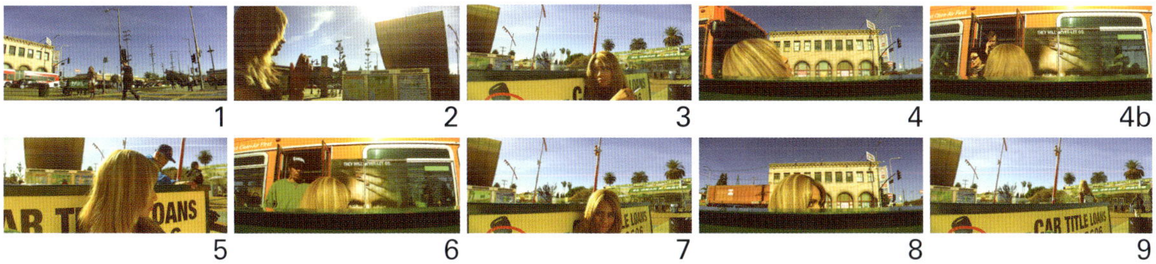

Figure 8.40 *Tangerine* (2015). Director: Sean Baker. Cinematographers: Sean Baker and Radium Cheung.

This is a convergence that occurs repeatedly through the film.

As already mentioned, the film's techniques of camera, location, color palette (and saturation), as well as performance style, add a comedic tone without forfeiting intensity from the dramatic stakes. But there is another aspect of tone in play. For the duration of screen time, the characters—Sin-dee and Alexandra chief among them, but also the taxi driver, Razmik, Chester and Dinah, the entire community of transgender persons depicted and acting in the film—qualify as society's outsiders and are brought inside. Their world, their values, their needs, and their concerns prevail. The movie itself, for its running time, gives over to them supreme authority and value: for an hour and twenty-eight minutes, they have the run of the place.

Expanse vs. confinement

While the history of cinema is flush with stories of the outsider, there is a strand of outsider stories in which individuals or groups prefer living apart from mainstream society, free from the restrictions and demands of conventional life. Likewise, there is an entire sub-genre of films that dramatize life in the wilderness, populated with characters more suited to the natural world than rural, suburban, or city life. *Leave No Trace*, directed by Debra Granik, qualifies loosely in both categories, though in the Thoreau-laced mythology of wilderness living, the film's protagonists, Will and his teenage daughter, Tom, are a long way from Walden Pond.

Debra Granik regards herself as a social realist and the devotion to characters living at the margins found in each of her films validates this claim.[19] The protagonists of *Leave No Trace* are no exception. Will, a widower and war veteran, plagued by post-traumatic stress disorder (PTSD), finds the trials of living in nature—collecting rainwater, protecting against wild animals, building fires with flint, foraging for edibles—easier than the alternatives, though we are left to infer this. The prevailing narrative strategy of the film privileges character behavior over explanation.

The land they inhabit is part of a forested, natural reserve in Oregon and, setting up camp in the reserve to live as they do, illegal. They are discovered by police, despite Will's best efforts to train Tom in camouflage techniques, and remanded into custody until placed in a nearby farm community where Will works as, of all things, a tree-cutter and Tom goes to school. They live together in a boxy, prefab house. Will spends his off hours at the horse stable, consoled by the other confined animal on the property. The larger narrative structure of the film charts the back and forth between their lives in the forest—a relief for what troubles Will, which surfaces in his nightmares—and the more civilized world of school, church, and a day job that answer Tom's need for a wider community of human exchange. Within this structure, the dynamic between father and daughter, their closeness, their competing needs, make up the beating heart of the film.

Will and Tom are humble inhabitants of the natural reserve, living in sympathy with the

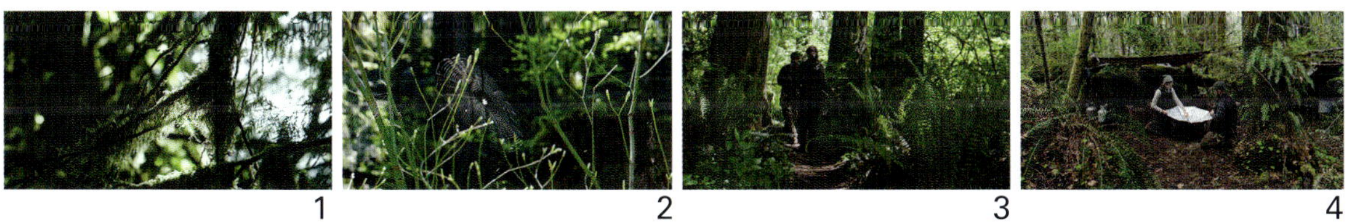

Figure 8.41 *Leave No Trace* (2018). Director: Debra Granik. Cinematographer: Michael McDonough.

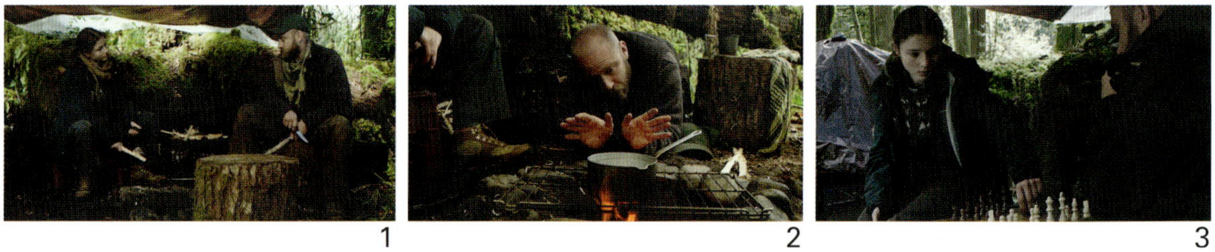

Figure 8.42 *Leave No Trace* (2018). Director: Debra Granik. Cinematographer: Michael McDonough.

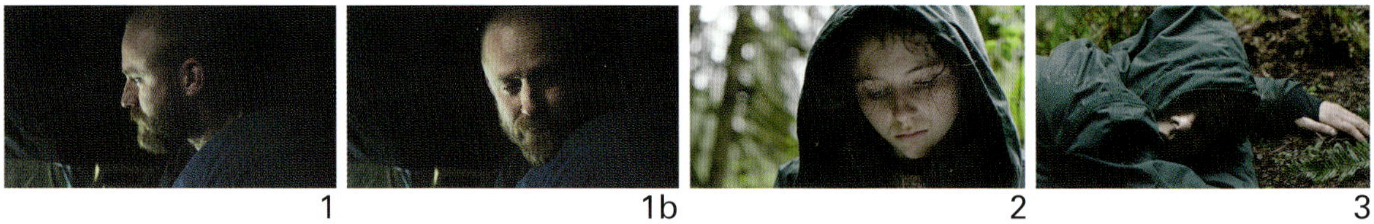

Figure 8.43 *Leave No Trace* (2018). Director: Debra Granik. Cinematographer: Michael McDonough.

land around them, taking just enough from it to survive. They make occasional forays into town to buy supplies, paid for by money Will pockets from selling his PTSD medications to other war veterans. The fact of these illegal transactions, Will's post-war instability, and their trespassing on government property provide the counterpoint to the otherwise idyllic nature of their existence, which includes reading literature, playing chess, and regarding one another with respect and good manners. Their talk seems confined to the essential, but even in the wild of the forest, "please" and "thank you" are common.

Not surprisingly, the visual dynamics in *Leave No Trace* are conjured from the camera's preoccupation with the characters in place. Changes in location prompt shifts in camera style as a way of highlighting the impact of that location on Will and Tom. For example, the visual imagery in early sequences of the film fill the frame with what seems to be every possible hue of green (Figure 8.41). We can see right away what gains emphasis: fern, spiderweb, rain-soaked forest and coverage that features Will and/or Tom in extreme wide shots, enveloping them in green. The natural earth prevails, and they willingly concede.

Reinforcing this idyll, the camera pivots from the extreme wide shots of Will and Tom (Figure 8.41, Shots 3 and 4) to medium shots covering lifestyle (Figure 8.42), to close-ups that resemble portrait painting in the habit of Vermeer (Figure 8.43).

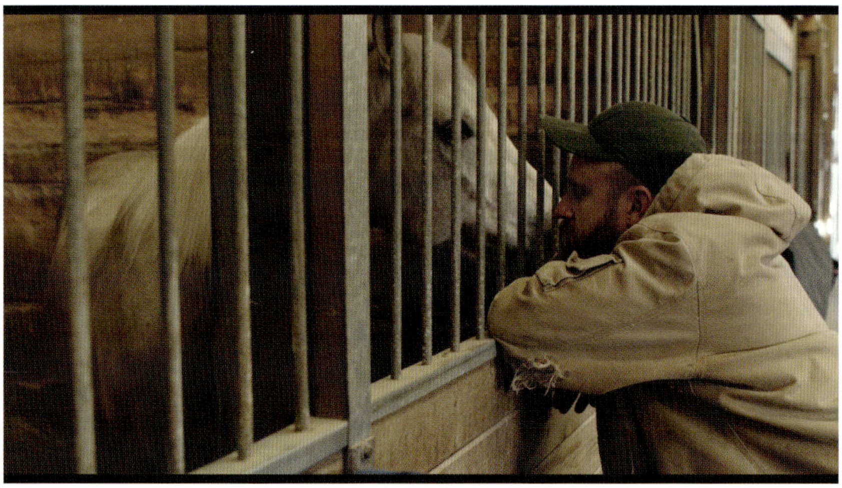

Figure 8.44 *Leave No Trace* (2018). Director: Debra Granik. Cinematographer: Michael McDonough.

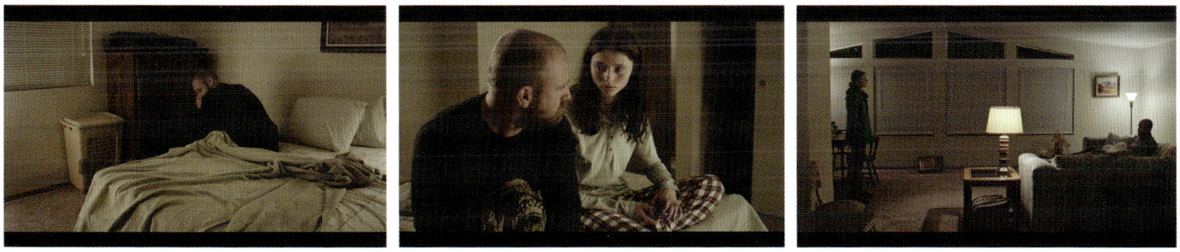

Figure 8.45 *Leave No Trace* (2018). Director: Debra Granik. Cinematographer: Michael McDonough.

No sooner than they are cast out of the Eden, the visual field changes, most noticeably with color palette, reduced to muted colors dominated by beige, brown, green, and blue. Green does not disappear but is tamed by windows, doors, or a manicured lawn. The handheld camera quiets to more static or controlled movements that trap the characters in space. The light flattens compared to the warm highlights of life in the forest. Vertical and horizontal lines, geometric shapes and right angles inform the compositions. Will spends his off hours at the horse stable, consoled by the other confined animal on the property, and here the imagery speaks for itself (Figure 8.44).

Notice also Will and Tom in shot 3 of Figure 8.45, with low ceiling in view, the natural world framed in a small picture on the wall, warmth of a fire replaced by an electric space heater between them. The camera (static) is placed to exaggerate the distance between them, corresponding with the moment of a standoff in their exchange. Will eventually insists that they return to the wilderness, more challenging now with colder temperatures, not to mention Tom's reluctance having experienced other versions of living.

This is how it will go: each change in the general location inspires camera coverage, which registers the influence of place on our two characters. The final location in their sojourn serves as a compromise between indoor and outdoor living. Will incurs an injury in the forest, which lands them in a commune of sorts. A group of people has settled in a campground at the edge of the reserve, living in mobile homes and RVs. They gather in the evenings with their guitars around a metal fire pit. It is not the flint-sparked fire of the wilderness, but it is not a tiny electric heater in a prefab house, either. The capacity for Will and Tom to thrive in this peripheral place drives the movie's ending, though at this point in the story, it may be a question of Will *or* Tom.

> The approach to filming the forest grew out of a respect for the characters' feelings for the forest. When we were in the forest, we tended to be close to the characters, living close to them, within their circle. The camera was handheld; there were wider lenses, and we stood closer to them. When we went to the city, the camera was physically farther away from the characters. That way, you feel separated from them just as they're separated from their comfort and usual surroundings.
>
> —Michael McDonough. *Behind the Lens: Michael McDonough on Leave No Trace*. Elena Lazic, *Seventh Row*. July 9, 2018.

If there is a prevailing tone or point of view, it flows from scene to scene and bends toward tolerance. This tolerance emerges from human need so vividly drawn that each of the two main characters escapes pity, dismissal, or judgment. No one is elevated as heroic. No one cast down as a villain or martyr. Will is a good enough father, and Tom, a good enough daughter, but neither are without the personal limitations that exact a cost for the other. Intact for each of them is the basic human want to flourish, despite severe conditions that occasionally test their survival.

Much of this is in the writing, but the camera confers a clear-eyed, unsentimental view of the characters by keeping our attention focused on their interactions with place and with one another. The visual style of the film also gives the viewer a lens through which to view the lush and soothing properties of the wilderness. In so doing it reminds us of the great gift of the natural world, one Will may not be able to live without.

Off-screen space

We began the discussion in this chapter by high profiling the practice of converging elements as a strategy for creating visual dynamics. It would make a worthwhile exercise to interrogate each of the films discussed here in terms of convergence, assessing which elements collide to give the visual style added energy or dimension. We have seen that much of what converges to engender visually dynamic imagery occurs within the frame, or in the interaction between shots through sequencing. In *The Rider*, the 2017 feature film by Chloé Zhao, visual tension is often conjured through use of elements *omitted* from the frame. In some instances, this is simply breathing room, what with the camera bearing in on a character's face, but occasionally this means the omission of shots that locate the viewer, in space and/or in time, privileging instead the intimate experience of characters.

The Rider is set among the Lakota Sioux of the Pine Ridge Reservation in South Dakota. Brady Blackburn, the film's protagonist, is a twenty-something outsider, twice over. First, his heritage as a Lakota Sioux translates into scarce resources and limited possibilities for his future. He managed to sideline these limitations with success as a bronco rider and gifted horse trainer. This ended when a failed bronco ride at a rodeo competition left him with a crushed skull. When we first meet Brady, staples hold his head together, and we soon learn he is forbidden from riding due to hand trembling and seizures, both effects of the brain injury. This casts him as an outsider even among his cowboy friends, who are clumsy in knowing how to relate to him without hero worship. Brady takes solace from time spent with his closest friend, Lane, also a local rodeo hero but now institutionalized, having suffered paralysis after being tossed by a bull. Reminiscing with Lane, while poignant, doesn't help Brady get on with his life. He gets a part-time job as a checkout clerk at the local grocer, obliged there to interact with customers who want to hold onto his gloried past.

Brady lives in a trailer home with his father and sister. His father cares for him, but the father's drinking and gambling limit the value of that care, never mind bad decisions his father makes related to the drinking and gambling, which effect Brady, and not for good. Brady's sister, Lilly, adores her brother. Her autism doesn't impair her sensitivity to him, or her kindness, but this doesn't equal his misery. Nor does it solve his identity crises. Who is he, who will he become, what can be his future, without mounting or riding a horse?

The film is populated with non-actors in roles that replicate their real circumstances. Lilly is Brady's autistic sister. The man playing

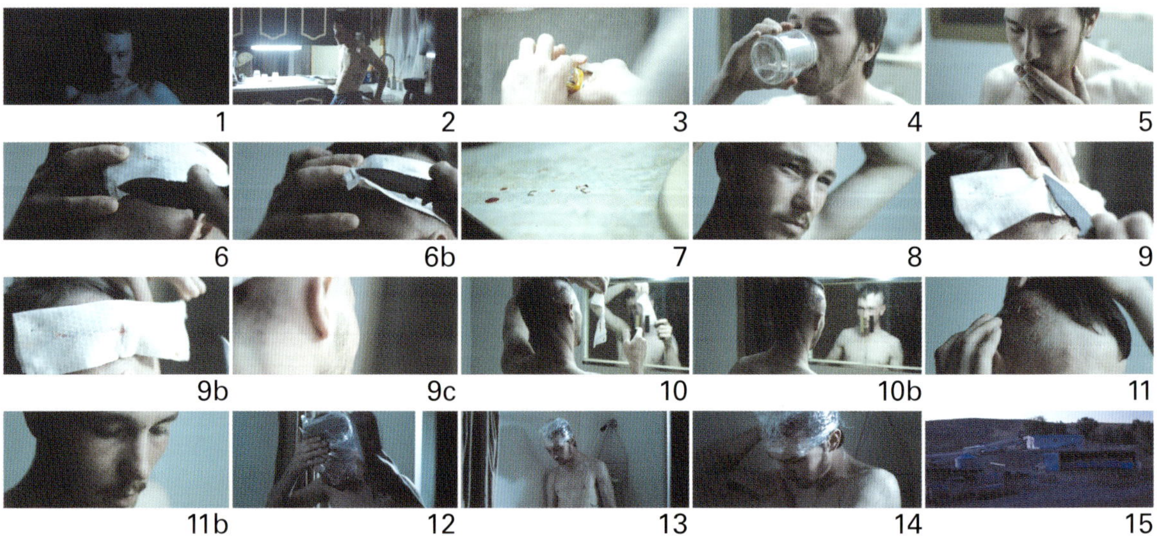

Figure 8.46 *The Rider* (2017). Director: Chloé Zhao. Cinematographer: Joshua James Richards.

the role of Brady's father is actually his father. Lane, genuinely paralyzed from a bull ride, is Brady's best friend. And Brady is a bronco rider and horse trainer. While the film works with these documentary elements, it is very much scripted and staged.[20] More striking, still, is the deliberate shot design. Working with her director of photograph, Joshua James Richards, Zhao dramatizes this story with extreme wide shots and close-ups. The tight shots of characters require not just authenticity, but authentic, sustained performance. Faces don't lie. Too, the images reveal a consistent and dedicated preoccupation with the quality of light, a preoccupation of scripted, fiction filmmaking.

The first scene of the film, after the credits, introduces Brady in close-up, walking into a kitchen (medium wide, Figure 8.46, Shot 2), where he will take a handful of pills and light a joint. The next image (Shot 6) marks a leap in time and space, though we don't know this, given how tight the close-up and the three that follow (Shots 7–9). What is seen: Brady with the blade of a knife as he removes staples that attach a layer of gauze to his head: underneath the bloodied gauze, a zipper of more staples where his head split open. This would not be easy to watch even in a wide shot. In close-ups, it challenges even the heartiest viewer. And yet, the tone is set right away: we learn that the camera will not be squeamish or sentimental, despite what may seem like punishing fate for the characters.

Brady goes on to wrap his head in plastic so that he can shower (Shots 12–14). Between the two activities, lodged within a scene dominated by close-ups, a medium shot reveals Brady looking into a mirror (Shots 10–10b). Now we are located (a bathroom). But more than located, we are given guidance as to *how* to see what we have just seen, and for that matter how to see all that follows. Looking into his bathroom mirror, even Brady grimaces. His psychological and physical discomfort is palpable. The fierce will that took the stapled gauze from his head weakens even him. And yet he carries on, gingerly wrapping his head, giving his small frame over to the shower.

With a cut the scene transitions to a wide shot of the exterior at twilight—a trailer house sits beneath a hill, surrounded by an RV, a silo, vehicles, and a horse standing corralled in the center of the frame (Shot 15). With this we are introduced to a camera strategy that repeats throughout the film: a scene dominated by close-ups punctuated by a wide establishing shot of place (Figure 8.47). In *The Rider*, the punctuating wide shots are inserted as salve or relief, against the harshness or loss often framed in close-up.

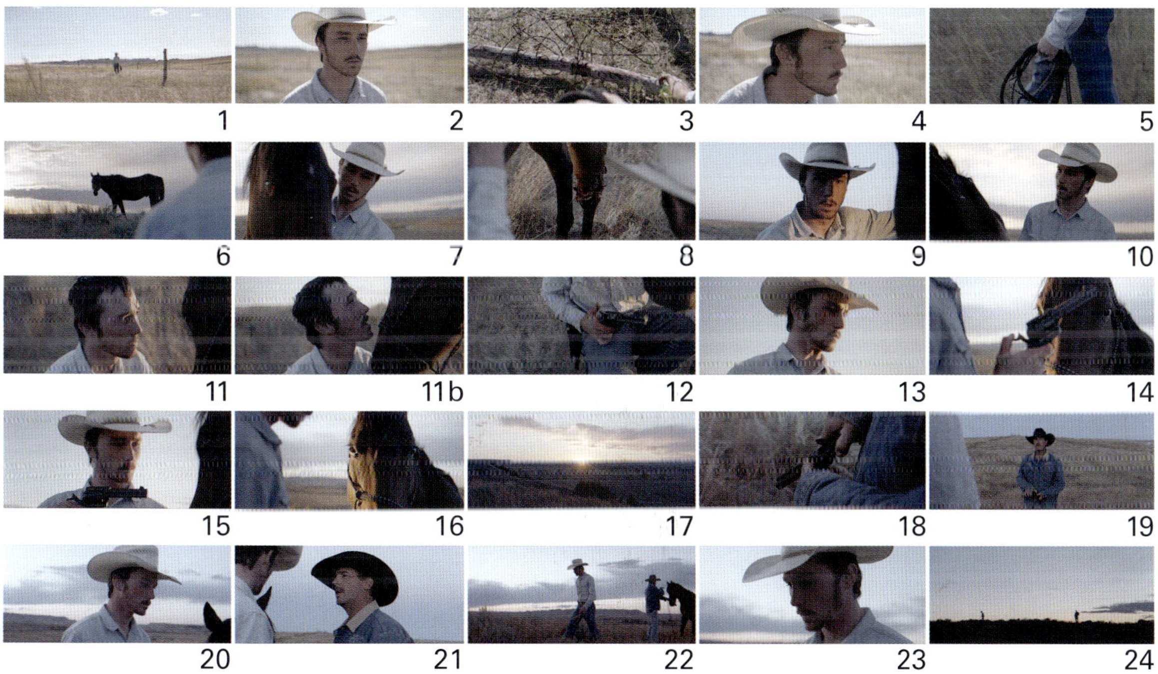

Figure 8.47 *The Rider* (2017). Director: Chloé Zhao. Cinematographer: Joshua James Richards.

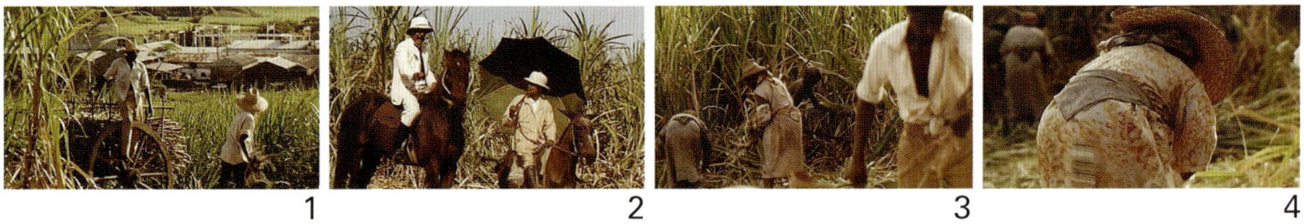

Figure 8.48 *Sugar Cane Alley* (1983). Director: Euzhan Palcy. Cinematographer: Dominique Chapuis.

Almost as a coda, the exterior wide shot (Figure 8.46, Shot 15) is followed in the film by a shot of Brady talking to and caressing the horse (not pictured here). Their exchange reveals a capacity for tenderness that has not been eclipsed by his terrible luck. This excites in the viewer relief but also apprehension, the latter from the recognition of just how much more could be lost to Brady. Will his capacity for affection survive the hour and forty minutes of screen time remaining? As if to taunt us, the scene finishes with the camera panning from a close-up of the horse's eye to Brady, who closes his eyes, as if dizzied, remembering his fate.

Characters empowered by camera

Euzhan Palcy's 1983 film, *Sugar Cane Alley*, is set among the sugarcane plantations of the French West Indian island of Martinique during the 1930s. The story centers around a village of field workers who live in a shantytown known as Black Shack Alley. Narrating the story is Jose, an orphaned, eleven-year-old boy in the care of his grandmother, Ma'Tine. They have next to nothing of material value, but along with other field workers and children, they band together in community, and this is life, despite low pay and abuse from their white colonial bosses. Ma'Tine is loving and stern, while also ambitious on Jose's behalf. He learns to read; he excels at the school. Jose acquires life lessons, as well: Leopold, a mulatto boy, is forbidden by his white father from playing with Jose. The village elder, Medouze, also mentors Jose recanting stories of Africa, imbedding in him a sense of his racial history. When Jose earns the opportunity to study at the high school in Fort-de-France aligned with the French academic system, his grandmother goes to the capital with him. She works as house help

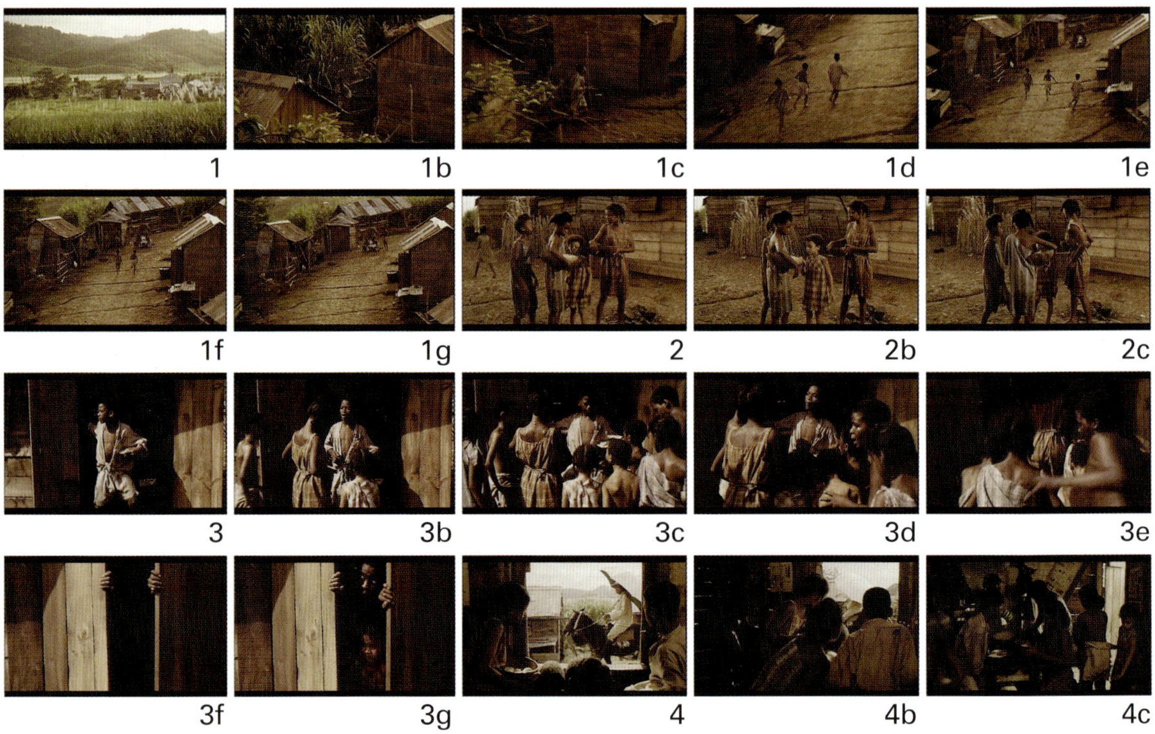

Figure 8.49 *Sugar Cane Alley* (1983). Director: Euzhan Palcy. Cinematographer: Dominique Chapuis.

for a local family so that Jose can afford to stay in school. While the story includes a community of characters, the pathos created by exchanges between Jose and the others lives at the heart of the drama. Chief among these exchanges is his relationship with Ma'Tine.

The camera, unhurried and thorough, portrays their lifestyle in the countryside and in the city, in place and time. Its primary focus is not the French colonial superiors but the locals and their daily routines, their joys and trials. Power dynamics are conveyed, but while the setting includes hardship (Figure 8.49), the abuses and disadvantages endured by the workers do not define them. The children also demonstrate spirited resilience, as yet unfazed by the limits implied by circumstance. One senses a larger project at work: the patient enterprise of dignifying the lives of these colonized people.

This spirit is conveyed in the film's visual style. Early in the film we see children shrieking and laughing as they run through a creek bed and taunt a fenced-in snake. They play in the countryside adjacent to the sugarcane fields. The camera, as depicted in Figure 8.49, follows them, panning from the green fields (Shot 1) to the rows of houses that make up the shantytown where they live (Shots 1b–1g). Camera movement as a technique for revelation is a common strategy in the film. Here, we discover that the path cutting through these houses is no yellow brick road. This is pictured in a wide shot. As such, the camera does not emphasize any particular element. In fact, once the revelation is made, the viewer's attention is commanded to a medium wide shot of a cluster of girls comparing their offerings of food: bananas and codfish. They gather at the entrance of Jose's modest dwelling (Shots 3e–3g) and duck inside as the overseers pass by (Shots 4–4c). For Jose, the greater threat is Ma'Tine—his friends have broken, by accident, one of the only two bowls his grandmother owns.

Figure 8.50 depicts Jose and his grandmother, as Jose waits anxiously for her to discover the fate of the bowl. Jose is framed in repeated close-ups, while Ma'Tine is seen in medium shots, actively preparing their dinner. Looking at this set of images, as well as images in Figure 8.51 and 8.52, we can see readily the coherence in elements of visual style—the repeated use of graphics, emphasis given to windows and window light, frames within the frame, and camera movement in service of narrative revelation.

The sepia-tinted scenes evoke early twentieth-century film and photography. This is reinforced with the opening credit sequence in which a series of still photographs portray life in Martinique in the early 1900s. Rooting the film's imagery so firmly in the past allows for an attitude of detachment; it lends to the camera the vision of an ethnographer, making a record of culture and habits. Both of these techniques influence the film's tone.

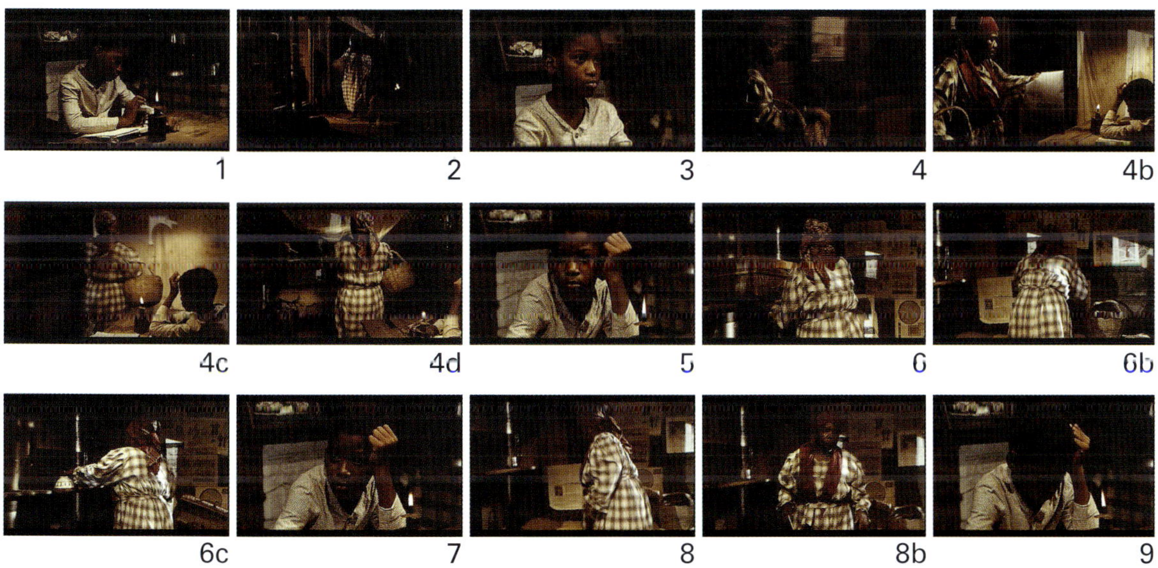

Figure 8.50 *Sugar Cane Alley* (1983). Director: Euzhan Palcy. Cinematographer: Dominique Chapuis.

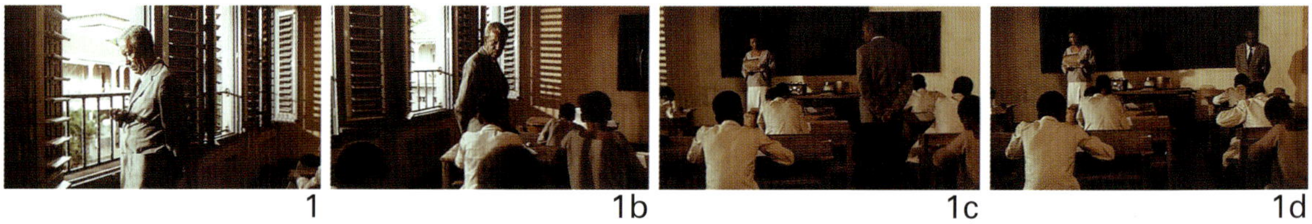

Figure 8.51 *Sugar Cane Alley* (1983). Director: Euzhan Palcy. Cinematographer: Dominique Chapuis.

A scene toward the film's conclusion brings tone and stance into high relief. The film's preoccupation with dignifying the culture becomes foregrounded in an exchange between Jose and Flora, a ticket seller at the local cinema in the capital city of Fort-de-France. Flora loses patience when a black man, a petty thief, vandalizes moviegoers in a line outside the theater. She rants to Jose against black people, her race: "These people are hopeless," she tells him, "I really detest that race." Jose, startled by this, questions her further (Figure 8.52, Shot 4). "My character is white," she retorts. Jose counters her, "I'm sure no white ever yelled, 'I hate my race' when a white stole or even murdered." Flora doesn't relent, "it hurts me to see someone who is already black do something bad." "My impulse is to hurl my race into the

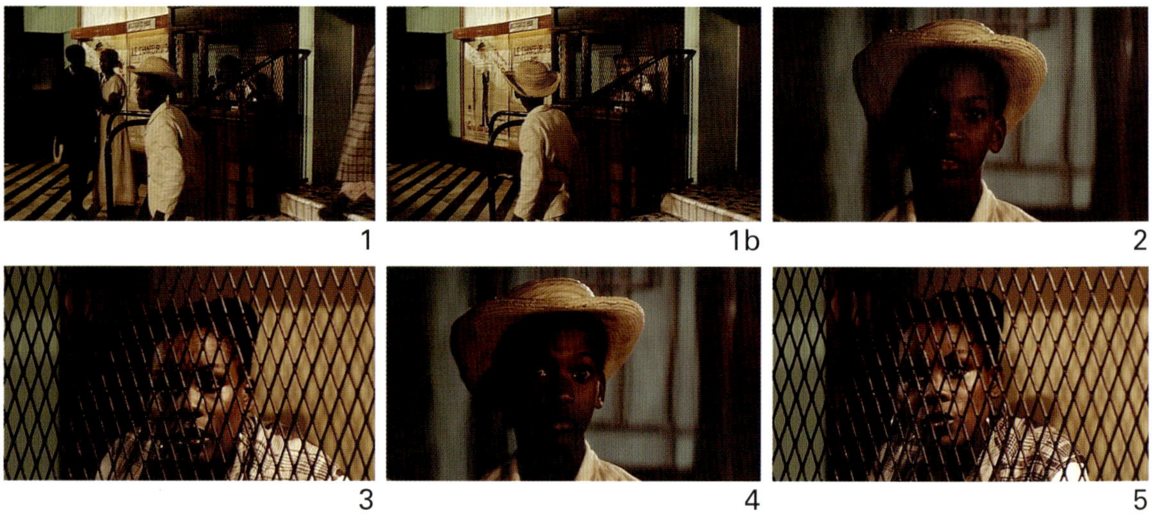

Figure 8.52 *Sugar Cane Alley* (1983). Director: Euzhan Palcy. Cinematographer: Dominique Chapuis.

Great stories can be through comedy, action thriller, suspense thriller etc. Alfred Hitchcock, Costa Gavras and Billy Wilder were all mentors to me. They are very different and that's what I love. What is important to me is to talk about humankind, human things.

—Euzhan Palcy, *Shadow and Act*, April 20, 2017.

fire." Jose, saddened by her declaration, goes off to meet his grandmother. "Goodbye, Miss Flora," he says with a mix of kindness and resignation.

The film is rigorous in its effort to portray the particulars of place: the small boat puttering along the waterway from the countryside to capital, the city streets, the farm fields, the local and city schools, homes of the well-to-do white colonials, and the shantytown shacks in sugar cane alley. It is equally meticulous in detailing the contours of life for Jose and his grandmother: low wages, backbreaking work, and the strife that Jose endures—bigotry, loss, false accusations—all of which seems to foster his coming of age. Here, at the end of the film, Jose is asked to confront outright the value of blackness, and we, the viewer, are invited to witness it. In close-ups of equal size, Flora is sequestered within the gated window of her ticket booth and Jose, clear-eyed, stands unfettered, in front of the bars shadowed on the wall behind him (Figure 8.52, Shots 3 and 4).

Visual dynamics and stance

With one final example, we bring our conversation full circle in exploring a scene from Hal Ashby's 1971 cult classic, *Harold and Maude*. Like *Buffalo 66* and *Ordinary People* in chapter one, the scene exploits the interaction of camera and editing to achieve certain visual dynamics that support dramatic effects. Like *Sugar Cane Alley*, experiences accumulate for the main character toward his coming of age. This scene from *Harold and Maude* seems perfectly suited to end our conversation given its charismatic evocation of the director's stance through a precise management of technique and too, because it never fails to provide pleasure—through repeated viewings, after over thirty years since its original release. The scene employs many of the techniques that have occupied our conversation for the last eight chapters: static camera, moving camera, close-up, wide shot, and the long take. Only the handheld camera is not in use.

The movie chronicles the love story between two outsiders: a twenty-something-year-old boy and a seventy-nine-year-old woman. Harold, a rebellious malcontent meets Maude at a graveside funeral service. Along with driving a hearse and playing suicide pranks on his socialite mother, attending funerals is among Harold's favorite pastimes. The two become fast friends

> **Stance**
>
> This refers to the point of view, attitude toward the story content and its characters, or a way of seeing the world portrayed.

and Harold surrenders gladly to the instructive charm of Maude's eccentric lifestyle and habits. In fact, it seems that Maude is forever teaching Harold one life lesson after the next. In the scene pictured below, Maude, after lunching with Harold at his cherished demolition site, challenges his taste for destruction, "I ask you Harold, is it enough?"

We assume they are still at the demolition site when Maude declares in a close-up: "I love to watch things grow." The close-up, as transition, works to withhold the re-location until the cut (Shot 3). Harold and Maude are now in a greenhouse. This is followed by eight shots that yoke five different locations with a continuous stream of monologue. The continuous time and spatial discontinuity animate the scene as Maude makes her case with Harold for the uniqueness of every living thing. The film gives her assertion counterpoint in compositions filled with sameness—rows of potted plants, then full-grown plants, followed by a massive field of a trillion daisies where Harold and Maude are tiny specks in the upper left corner of the frame. Working with leaps in physical space, the dialogue and repeated elements in the frame exemplify a strategy we now recognize as convergence.

In response to Harold's assertion that all the daisies are alike, the camera pans across the daisy field in a medium shot, for a closer look at each one. The pan comes to rest on Harold in another close-up as Maude counters him by claiming "all kinds of observable differences" (Figure 8.53, Shot 8c). The "lesson" culminates in a two shot of Harold and Maude for the delivery of Maude's last line: "You see, Harold, I feel that much of the world's sorrow comes from people who are this. . . (she holds up the one-of-a-kind daisy) yet allow themselves to be treated as that." She gestures across the mass of daisies in the field. This is already a potent summation given the permanent numbers on Maude's arm signaling a past outside the film's time frame.

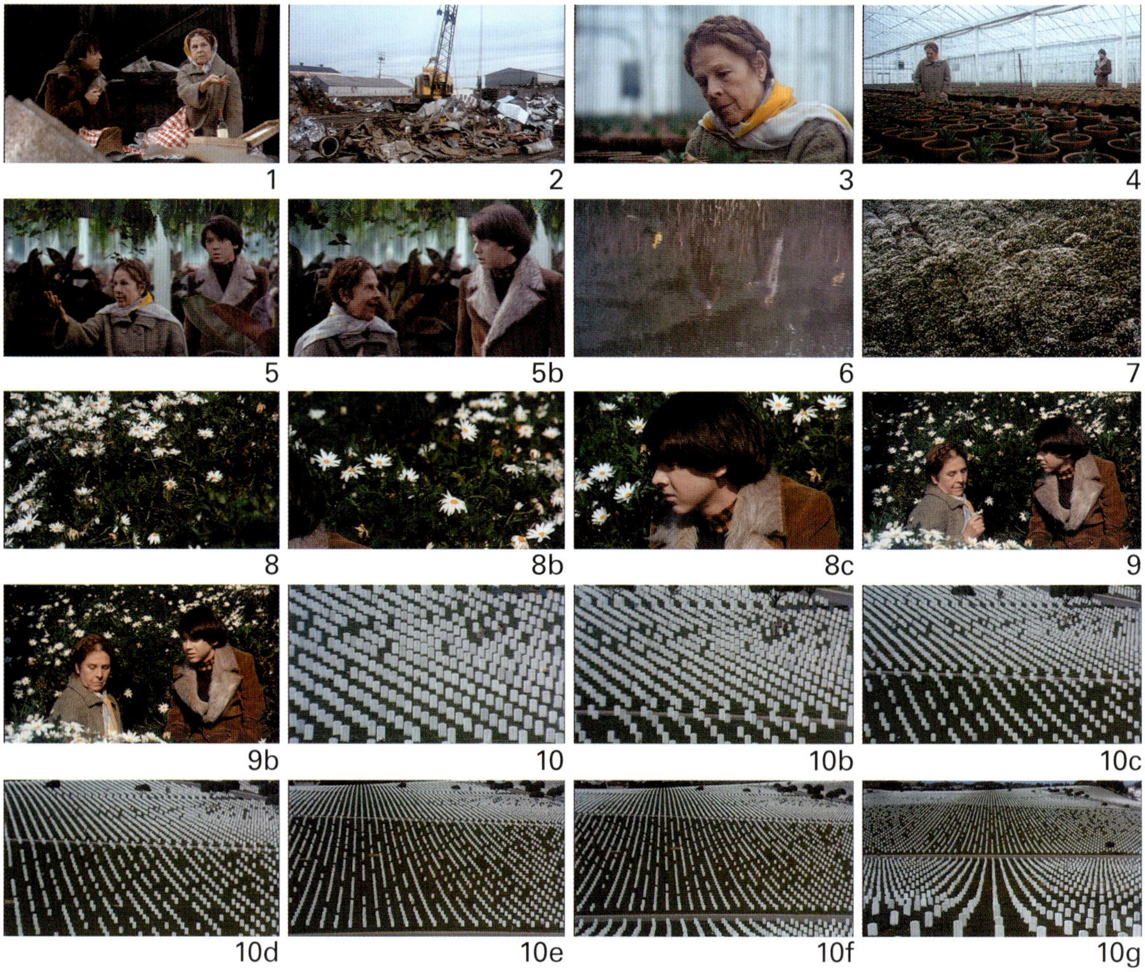

Figure 8.53 *Harold and Maude* (1971). Director: Hal Ashby. Cinematographer: John A. Alonzo.

But when Ashby cuts to a wide shot, transposing Harold and Maude to a cemetery, the story is thrown outside the film's present to a cause of national and international consequence in 1971: the Vietnam War. It is almost as if the director is in conversation with Věra Chytilová's 1966 film, *Daisies*, discussed earlier in the chapter, which begins and ends with images of war and makes bold use, as we have seen, of lifting the two girls from one location to another with no spatial logic or continuity. In the military cemetery of Ashby's film, Harold and Maude—tiny figures in the distance—stand to leave. The shot widens and widens with the voice of Cat Stevens singing "Where do the Children Play" as rows and rows of white tombstones crowd into the frame.

The sequence satisfies the story's immediate concern—Maude's lesson in a movie-long series of lessons that bring Harold to life and to living, or more generically, that advance his "coming of age." This lesson—growth versus destruction, uniqueness versus sameness—is stretched beyond the scene's dramatic intention and movie's overall narrative development to a wider framework. The widening framework demonstrates an exercise of tone, which also manifests the film's point of view or stance. Stance, as we have seen, need not always take the form of commentary, as it does in *Harold and Maude*. A film's point of view can reside simply in the way characters are framed. But whether as commentary, tone, or by way of a particular style, any story rendered with carefully conceived technical strategies advantages the movie toward a specific vision and amplified voice. By "advantage" I mean also to emphasize again the deeper reservoir of pleasure for the viewer, who lends to the enterprise of making movies its full meaning and purpose.

Discussion questions

1. Are there other aspects of filmmaking, not discussed here, that influence visual dynamics? Give a specific example from a film.
2. When evaluating the tone or mood of a film, what do you see as the role of the location? Give an example.
3. What draws you most to a film by a particular director: the style, story, or stance?

Notes

1. There are many directors who have become known for muscular attention to film images across an entire body of work. One can look at any movie, for example, by Martin Scorsese, Lucretia Martel, Spike Lee, Andrei Tarkovsky, Roy Andersson, or Claire Denis to find memorable, charged imagery, regardless of the camera style or storytelling strategy. This list includes, of course, many directors omitted from this book due its necessary limits.
2. "Did a Silent Film about a Train Really Cause Audiences to Stampede: A closer look at an enduring tale of movie-induced panic." Eric Grundhauser, *Atlas Obscura*. November 3, 2016.
3. Věra Chytilova was able to make a film during this period but was refused support by the Barrandov studios in Prague. https://www.nytimes.com/2012/07/01/movies/daisies-from-the-czech-director-vera-chytilova-at-bam.html.
4. DVD commentary but also history of making of Malcolm X. *A Movie Producer Remembers the Human Side of Malcolm X*. Weintraub, Bernard. "Don't Mess Malcolm Up." Omar Moore, https://www.rogerebert.com/far-flung-correspondents/dont-mess malcolm-up; https://film.avclub.com/malcolm-x-1798171853.
5. *Malcolm X: A Life of Reinvention*. Manning Marable, pp. 20–30. Penguin Books. Reprint Edition, 2011.
6. DVD commentary. *Malcolm X*, Spike Lee and Ernest Dickerson. Warner Brothers, February 8, 2005, release.
7. Directors more recently have taken this liberty in hand, adjusting frame size for aesthetic purpose and also applying ratio as one more technique that can add dimension to the narrative. Additional information about aspect ratios can be found in *A Brief History of Aspect Ratios, aka Screen Proportions*. David Pogue, *Scientific American*. February 20, 2018.
8. Director Damien Chazelle created a short film (*The Stunt Double*) as a promotion for Apple, with the 9:16 aspect ratio. It can be accessed here https://www.youtube.com/watch?v=xqiPZBZgW9c. A discussion of the use of aspect ratio in *The Grand Budapest Hotel* can be found at Slate.com/culture/2014/03. Pawel Pawlikowski on the aspect ratio in *Ida* can be found in the *L.A. Times*. Feb. 12, 2015 edition.
9. It is interesting to note the way in which Dolan returns from wide screen to 1:1. Diane is served notice by the court of a judgment against her son for injuries incurred by the young man burned at the retention center. The judgment includes a payout of damages for $250,000. Cutting between Diane and the document, all in wider screen, the scene lands finally on her face while she absorbs this news. As she does, the wall paper and stained glass behind her, screen left and screen right, are overcome by black, the frame pressing in on her, as it returns to 1:1.
10. David Bordwell explores film form in his text, *The Classical Hollywood Cinema: Film Style & Mode of Production to 1960*. Columbia University Press. (New York, 1987).
11. Watanabe sings a Japanese ballad, *Gondola no Uta*, the lyrics of which caution the young of wasting passion and missing opportunities while they are young. .
12. *La Haine* was shot in color and printed in black-and-white for theatrical distribution, https://www.theguardian.com/film/2020/may/23/how-la-haine-lit-a-fire-under-french-society.
13. The Paris shooting in 1993 of young immigrant Makome M'Bowole while in police custody is said to have inspired the script, https://www.criterion.com/current/posts/642-la-haine-and-after-arts-politics-and-the-banlieue. Also *La Haine: French Film Guide* (2005) Ginette Vincendeau. *Cine-File French Film Guides*.

14. Locations throughout *La Haine* serve the visual style. Locations will often include graffiti and signage reinforcing theme with points and counterpoints.
15. Benyamina grew up as one of twelve siblings in a suburb of Paris, raised by her immigrant parents. She reports first-hand experience with the sense of limited opportunity and resources, and the failure of the French government to respond to the needs of immigrant communities, https://www.newyorker.com/culture/persons-of-interest/houda-benyamina-the-french-filmmaker-who-brought-the-banlieues-to-hollywood
16. *Houda Benyamina, The French Filmmaker Who Brought the Banlieues to Hollywood*. Negar Azimi, *The New Yorker*. April 9, 2017.
17. Sean Baker has earned a reputation for the role location plays in his feature films. He admits that a particular place will often serve as a starting point for a film, https://www.filmcomment.com/blog/interview-sean-baker/. Sean Baker talks about the location Donut Time in *Tangerine*, https://vimeo.com/132656196.
18. https://www.macworld.com/article/2971675/how-to-make-a-movie-with-an-iphone-an-interview-with-tangerine-director-sean-baker.html.
19. Interview with Debra Granik, https://seventh-row.com/ebooks/leave-no-trace-debra-granik-book/.
20. Chloé Zhao describes her writing process in this interview, https://www.tracking-board.com/the-rider-filmmaker-chloe-zhao-on-writing-for-and-working-with-non-actors-interview/.

Conclusion

In over twenty years of training young directors, we have heard it suggested more than once that filmmakers most need immediate solutions to practical problems. This is only partially true. The films exampled in this text are proof of what is also true: story translated into a strategy of thoughtful technical choices can layer even a simple narrative with dramatic complexity and create a wide range of dramatic effects.

The legendary film, *Arrival of a Train at La Ciotat*, made in 1895 by Auguste and Louis Lumiere, stirred rumors of audiences running out of the theater as the train approached the station on screen. The fact or fiction of this rumor has been debated. What we can be sure of is that the filmmakers chose to place the camera on the station platform so that the train arriving is seen barreling into the foreground toward the viewer. And this, we know, charges its dramatic effect.

Returning to the two basic questions posed at the beginning of this book, ones that were meant to assist in unpacking the elements of a scene, we suggest entering into the space of any film by asking: 1) What dramatic effects are in play? and 2) What combination of techniques have been used to create them? We trust that a reminder of the questions will register the insight you have gained, and the ready toolkit acquired for deciphering the engaging and arresting elements of any movie. We hope that this dive into dramatic effects conjured with a movie camera will have deepened your reach as a filmmaker and filmgoer. We would not have undertaken this endeavor had we not been nearly certain that while analytic skills applied to film may make you a more discerning viewer, the insight into the mechanics and aesthetics of a well-made movie will only enhance your viewing pleasure.

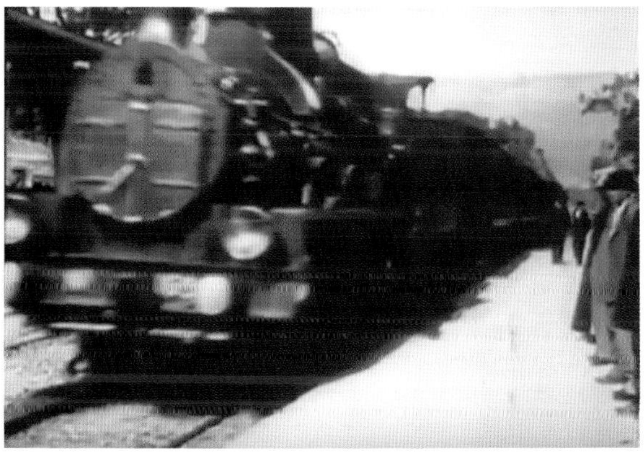

Figure 9.1
The Arrival of a Train at La Ciotat. (1895) Directors: Auguste and Louis Lumiere. Cinematographers: Auguste and Louis Lumiere.

These techniques serve the storyteller in laying claim to our attention and also, to our emotions. They help to map the emotional space in a film and guide us, as viewers, in making sense of that geography, inhabited by characters. These techniques command our response and offer us the opportunity to co-author the film world flickering on the screen in real time.

With the collaborative nature of moviemaking and the need to enlist large creative teams and a wide variety of technologies to create a finished film, many more artists are involved than could be credited or listed for the films analyzed on previous pages. Our project has been to focus on the power of camera unleashed by the collaboration between a director and cinematographer in service of a vision for telling a particular story. The films explored here make clear that while each of the filmmakers have their own particular style, stance, or artistic DNA, the available tools and techniques are the same. This becomes the shared visual language of film.

Glossary

Aspect ratio—The image frame's width in relation to its height.

Background—The details that appear behind the main action of the shot or scene.

Beauty shot—An image, usually a close-up, which emphasizes the attractive qualities of an actress or actor.

Birds-eye-view—A shot from a high angle that lends a bird's perspective on the scene.

Blocking—The coordination of movement between characters in the space of a shot or scene.

Bokeh—The unfocused area of the image produced when using a camera lens that keeps only one plane of the image in focus.

Camera—A device, either analog or digital, that records images by capturing reflected light.

Camera angle—The height of the camera's placement and the resulting angle of the action in the shot or scene (high angle, eye level, or low angle).

Camera height—The placement of the camera in relation to its distance from the ground.

Camera level—See *camera angle*.

Camera movement—The direction and speed of the camera's motion in a shot or scene.

Camera placement—The location of the camera in relation to the character(s) actions or interactions taking place in the shot or scene.

Camera set-up—The arrangement of the camera and lighting equipment by the DP.

Camerawork—The physical movement of the camera and lens during a shot or scene.

Casting—The selection of actors or actresses for specific roles in a film.

Centers of action—Movement of the camera and its focus on the area of action from one shot or scene to another in continuous space and time.

Change in perspective—The shifting of point of view, especially in a long take that simulates editing by changing the viewer's focus.

Character—The specific role an actor or actress embodies in the film/story.

Cinéma vérité—Knows as the French style of documentary where the camera can be more intrusive, and may provoke or drive events and responses, also, usually focuses on a particular "character" or person.

Close-up—A shot that shows a part of the body (usually a face) or object filling up most of the screen.

Coherence—The organization of the narrative elements in the exposition as the film/story unfolds.

Composition—The organization and framing of the characters and objects in the physical space of the shot or scene.

Continuous shot feature film—Also known as a one-shot feature, describes a movie filmed in one long take with a single camera, or constructed to convey that impression.

Coverage—The use of different perspectives and camera angles on the same shot or scene.

Crane shot—the making of a shot by the placing of a camera on a moving crane.

Cross-cutting—An editing process that moves between different scenes in the narrative suggesting concurrent moments in time.

Cut(s)—Term originally devised in the celluloid film editing process where moving from one shot or scene meant that the film was literally cut and then joined to another piece of film. Currently, refers to a transition from one shot to another.

Cutaway—The diverting of the main action taking place to another shot or scene.

Deep focus—Creating an image with the use of a camera lens that keeps objects and characters in focus whether near or far.

Depth of field—Creating an image that has a specific distance range from the camera lens that is in sharp focus.

Depth of space—See *depth of field*.

Direct cinema—A US style of documentary that gives the feeling that we are in the event(s) as they are taking place. An observational style where we see in a more objective way and there are usually no reconstructions of events in this form.

Direction—Can refer to the guidance/instructions given to the actors and actresses by a director or the trajectory of movement of the camera.

Distribution—Refers to the physical or digital circulation of a completed film.

Dogme doctrine—A list of ten rules or principles referred to as *A Vow of Chastity* that governed the making of films.

Dolly—A large, mobile flatbed that can carry a variety of film equipment and crew.

Dolly shot—A shot created by using a mobile flatbed (dolly).

Dramatic effect—The response elicited by what is seen on and heard from the screen, or resulting from an accumulation of techniques.

Drone shot—The making of a shot by placing the camera on a drone, a small aerial device that can be operated remotely.

Dutch tilt—Also known as a canted angle, where the image is not level or horizontal

Establishing shot—A shot wide enough to encompass all the pertinent information about the location of the scene, the characters involved and their proximity to one another.

Expressive value—A shot that has pertinence to the overall story and not necessarily devoted to plot advance.

Extreme close-up—A shot that shows a part of the body (usually a face) or object very close, filling up the entire screen.

Extreme wide shot—A shot that encompasses a vast distance in the scene extending beyond the characters.

Eye line—A shot that follows an actor or actresses gaze with what they are looking at.

Figure movement—Refers to the guidance or instructions regarding the actors and actresses movements within the shot or scene.

Film technique—Refers to the cinematic tools used to create a particular desired effect.

First person camera—A shot that reveals the character's point of view.

Focal length—The distance from the lens to all points in focus.

Focal plane—An image that has a specific distance where images are in focus.

Focal point—The exact distance at which all details are in sharp focus.

Focus—The area of the image created by light passing through the lens that is seen in sharp, clear details.

Foreground—The area in the shot or scene that is closest to the audience.

Fourth wall—The presumed wall or separation between the cinematic space and its audience.

Framing—The use of the boundaries of the image to organize and orchestrate all the details therein.

Golden hour—The time of day where a low-sitting sun on the horizon produces heightened colors.

Image depth—Creating an image that has a specific distance range from the camera lens that is in focus.

Lighting—The use of portable electrical lights to brighten an interior shot or scene to desired effect or the intentional use natural light outdoors.

Location—The physical spaces selected for a film, scene, or shot.

Location shooting—Shooting that occurs in a real-world setting rather than on a sound stage or studio lot. This can include an exterior or interior location, often referred to as a found location.

Long shot—A shot where an object or figure is seen in its entirety but does not exceed the height of the frame.

Long take—A shot that continues without disruption for more time than usual.

Low angle—A shot or scene where the camera is placed close to the ground and appears to be looking up at the action taking place.

Magic hour—The time of day before sunrise or after sunset when light spreads evenly and produces softened colors.

Manner—How elements of a shot, scene, or film are arranged.

Medium close-up—A shot that shows a part of the body or object appearing relatively large in the frame.

Medium shot—A shot that shows a body from waist up on the screen.

Medium wide shot—A shot that presents character(s) in their environment and preferences interaction between characters in their setting.

Method of arrangement—The goal/intention with which a particular director arranges elements in the shot, scene, or film.

Metonymic—The use of one concept or object in place of another.

Mise en scene—All of the visual material included in a given shot or scene including lighting and character choreography.

Montage—A style of editing credited to Soviet Filmmakers of 1920s where the relationship is rather between the shots presented and not overtly tied to any one of them.

Mood—An atmosphere or tone set by elements within mise en scene such as colors, lighting, etc.

Moving camera—A camera that is mobile in a variety of ways such as hand hold, dolly, steadicam apparatus, etc.

Moving image—A paced succession of pictures that simulates movement.

Narrative coherence—The way(s) the plot and story are held together.

Observational cinema—A form of storytelling that renders events from their midst, acting as witness and presenting an objective representation of people and events.

Off-screen space—All of the spaces surrounding the visible narrative space including spaces above and below.

On-screen space—All of the spaces visible in the scenes and shots.

180 degree rule—Also known as 180 degree line or axis of action which calls for the cameras position to remain on one side of the narrative activity to keep left and right spaces in consistent relation throughout shooting of the film.

Pan—Short for panorama, and refers to a camera movement left or right on the horizontal line.

Pattern—The organization of visual elements within the frame.

Pattern of technique—The sequence and frequency of cinematic tools employed.

Performance—The embodiment of a film character's role by an actor or actress.

Perspective—How the three-dimensional world is presented on a two-dimensional surface, most essential is to create a sense of depth in the pictured space. This can also change the size of objects or subjects.

Plot—The presented events that are seen and heard in the progression of the narrative.

Point of view—The place in the film's narrative from which the camera reveals the plot and story.

Pre-production—The first of three steps in the filmmaking process where all the production (second step where the film is shot) plans are put in place.

Prop(s)—Short for property and is any tangible object connected to a character or placed in the character's setting.

Proximity—Refers to either the camera or audience distance from the dramatic action taking place in the film or to one character in relation to another or their environment.

Quick cutting—A style of editing that moves rapidly from one shot or scene to the next.

Realism—A kind of filmmaking that aspires to represent people, places, and events without blatant and visible efforts of distortion.

Repetition—When elements are used repeatedly in the exposition of the narrative.

Rhythm of action—Refers to how often an element is repeated and the space between those moments.

Scene—A portion of the film narrative's time that takes place in one or more locations.

Shallow focus—Creating an image with the use of a camera lens that keeps only one plane of the image in focus.

Shape—To create a recognizable form.

Shooting script—A version of the screenplay with all of the details and instructions needed for the production process.

Shot—A continuous image without cuts or edits in a film that represents one of the many segments of a scene or the overall film.

Shot duration—The length of continuous time of a shot in seconds or minutes.

Shot size—The relative size of the object or subject(s) within the frame, such as close-up, medium shot, or long shot.

Shot tightening—The closing in of space in a given shot.

Shot widening—The expansion of space in a given shot.

Staging—Also known as blocking, is the coordination of character movement with the shot or scene.

Stance—The point of view, attitude toward the story content and its characters, or a way of seeing the world portrayed.

Static camera—A stationary and unchanged camera image during a given shot.

Static shot—A stationary and unchanged camera image during the shot.

Steadicam—A mechanism worn by a camera operator that insures image stabilization for the handheld camera.

Strategy—The emotional intention of the combination of techniques used to devise a shot or scene.

Style—The particular ways in which elements are combined that are unique to an artist and reveals their particular creative DNA.

Subjective camera—A shot that reveals the character's point of view.

Subtext—The secondary message or a less obvious conveyance.

Swish pan—A rapid pan left or right that can appear blurry due to the speed of the motion.

Technique(s)—The use of a particular cinematic tool or combination of cinematic tools used to create a desired effect.

Theme—The specific focus or topic of the film's narrative.

Three shot—One of the basic shot compositions where three characters appear prominent in the frame.

Tilt—The movement of the camera up or down from a fixed mounted position.

Tone—The mood or emotional atmosphere created in a shot, scene, or film.

Tracking shot—A shot that moves in a variety of ways while the scene transpires to reveal the center of action, into or away from the action, or along side or above.

Transition shot—The manner in which we move from the end of one shot to the beginning of the next.

Traveling shot—*See tracking shot.*

Two shot—One of the basic shot compositions where two characters appear prominent in the frame.

Variation of shot size—Refers to changes in the size of objects or figures relative to the image frame.

Vertical cinema (or vertical video)—a mode of moviemaking that privileges portrait framing, giving the image an aspect ratio in which height is nearly double the width.

Visual dynamics—The grouping of elements that converge to generate strong energy in the frame, shot, or scene.

Voice-over—One of the non-diegetic elements in a film where a voice from outside the film's world becomes an added element of the film's soundtrack to enhance or narrate the story.

Wide shot—Also referred to as a long shot and shows character(s) in full view in the environment and preferences interaction between characters in their setting.

Zoom—Accomplished with the use of a lens that allows for a stationary camera to affect movement towards or away from a subject or object.

Filmography

A Ghost Story. Directed by David Lowery. 2017. USA.
A Separation. Directed by Asghar Farhadi. 2011. Iran.
A Woman Under the Influence. Directed by John Cassavetes. 1974. USA.
American Honey. Directed by Andrea Arnold. 2016. UK.
An Autumn Afternoon. Directed by Yasujirō Ozu. 1962. Japan.
Archipelago. Directed by Joanna Hogg. 2010. UK.
Arrival of a Train at La Ciotat. Directed by Auguste and Louis Lumiere. 1895. France
Baby's First Steps. Directed by Auguste and Louis Lumiere. 1897. France.
Beau Travail. Directed by Claire Denis. 1999. France.
Black Girl. Directed by Ousmane Sembène. 1966. Senegal/France.
Blue Is the Warmest Color. Directed by Abdellatif Kechiche. 2013. France.
Body and Soul. Directed by Oscar Micheaux. 1925. USA.
Broken Blossoms. Directed by D.W. Griffith. 1919. USA.
Buffalo 66. Directed by Vincent Gallo. 1998. USA.
Caché. Directed by Michael Haneke. 2005. France, Austria, Germany, Italy.
Certain Women. Directed by Kelly Reichardt. 2016. USA.
Cleo from 5 to 7. Directed by Agnès Varda. 1962. France.
Climates. Directed by Nuri Bilge Ceylan. 2006. Turkey.
Corpo Celeste. Directed by Alice Rohrwacher. 2011. Italy.
Daisies. Directed by Věra Chytilová. 1966. Czechoslovakia.
Days of Heaven. Directed by Terrence Malick. 1978. USA.
Distant. Directed by Nuri Bilge Ceylan. 2002. Turkey.
Divines. Directed by Houda Benyamina. 2016. France, Qatar.
8½. Directed by Federico Fellini. 1963. Italy.
Elephant. Directed by Gus Van Sant. 2003. USA.
Erin Brockovich. Directed by Steven Soderbergh. 2000. USA.
Fallen Angels. Directed by Wong Kar-Wai. 1995. Hong Kong.
4 Months, 3 Weeks and 2 Days. Directed by Cristian Mungiu. 2007. Romania.
Get Out. Directed by Jordan Peele. 2017. USA.
Girlhood. Directed by Céline Sciamma. 2014. France.
Give Me Liberty. Directed by Kirill Mikhanovsky. 2019. USA.
Goodfellas. Directed by Martin Scorsese. 1990. USA.
Harold and Maude. Directed by Hal Ashby. 1971. USA.
Humanité. Directed by Bruno Dumont. 1999. France.
Ikiru (To Live). Directed by Akira Kurosawa. 1952. Japan.
In the Mood for Love. Directed by Wong Kar-Wai. 2000.
Inglourious Basterds. Directed by Quentin Tarantino. 2009. USA.
Jeanne Dielman, 23 Quai du Commerce, 1080 Bruxelles. Directed by Chantal Ackerman. 1975. France.
KAOS. Directed by Paolo and Vittorio Taviani. 1984. Italy.
Killer of Sheep. Directed by Charles Burnett. 1978. USA.
La Haine. Directed by Mathieu Kassovitz. 1995. France.
Last Resort. Directed by Pawel Pawlikowski. 2000. UK.
L'Avventura. Directed by Michaelangelo Antonioni. 1960. USA.
Leave No Trace. Directed by Debra Granik. 2018. USA.
Lost in Translation. Directed by Sofia Coppola. 2003. USA.
Love. Directed by Károly Makk. 1971. Hungary.
Madeline's Madeline. Directed by Josephine Decker. 2018. USA.
Malcolm X. Directed by Spike Lee. 1992. USA.
Massive Attack: Protection. Directed by Michel Gondry. 1995. USA.
Mediterranea. Directed by Jonas Carpignano. 2015. Italy, Africa.
Middle of Nowhere. Directed by Ava DuVernay. 2012. USA.
Mommy. Directed by Xavier Dolan. 2014. Canada.
Mustang. Directed by Deniz Gamze Ergüven. 2015. Turkey.
Mystery Train. Directed by Jim Jarmusch. 1989. USA.
Notorious. Directed by Alfred Hitchcock. 1946. USA.
Ordinary People. Directed by Robert Redford. 1980. USA.
Pather Panchali. Directed by Satyajit Ray. 1955. India.
Paths of Glory. Directed by Stanley Kubrick. 1957. West Germany.
Psycho. Directed by Alfred Hitchcock. 1960. USA.
Punch Drunk Love. Directed by Paul Thomas Anderson. 2002. USA.
Ratcatcher. Directed by Lynne Ramsey. 1999. Scotland.
Red Desert. Directed by Michaelangelo Antonioni. 1964. Italy.
Roma. Directed by Alfonso Cuarón. 2018. Mexico.
Safe. Directed by Todd Haynes. 1995. USA.
Son of Saul. Directed by Lázló Nemes. 2005. Hungary.
Songs from the Second Floor. Directed by Roy Andersson. 2000. Sweden.
Spa Night. Directed by Andrew Ahn. 2016. USA.
Stalker. Directed by Andrei Tarkovsky. 1979. USSR.
Still Life. Directed by Jia Zhangke. 2006. Hong Kong.
Sugar Cane Alley. Directed by Euzhan Palcy. 1983. France.
Take This Waltz. Directed by Sarah Polley. 2011. Canada, Spain, Japan.
Tangerine. Directed by Sean Baker. 2015. USA.
The Body Remembers When the World Broke Open. Directed by Kathleen Hepburn and Elle-Máijá Tailfeathers. 2019. Canada, Norway.
The Celebration. Directed by Thomas Vinterberg. 1998. Denmark.
The Conformist. Directed by Bernardo Bertolucci. 1970. Italy.
The Gold Rush. Directed by Charlie Chaplin. 1925. USA.
The Graduate. Directed by Mike Nichols. 1967. USA.
The Grand Illusion. Directed by Jean Renior. 1937. France.
The Great Beauty. Directed by Paolo Sorrentino. 2013. Italy, France.
The Harvesters. Directed by Etienne Kallos. 2018. South Africa.

The Holy Girl. Directed by Lucretia Martel. 2004. Argentina.
The Last Laugh. Directed by F. W. Murnau. 1924. Germany.
The Man Without a Past. Directed by Aki Kaurismäki. 2002. Finland.
The Match Factory Girl. Directed by Aki Kaurismaki. 1990. Finland.
The Milk of Sorrow. Directed by Claudia Llosa. 2009. Peru.
The Mirror. Directed by Andrei Tarkovsky. 1975. USSR.
The Passion of Joan of Arc. Directed by Carl Dryer. 1928. Denmark.
The Red and The White. Directed by Miklós Jancsó. 1967. Hungary.
The Rider. Directed by Chloé Zhao. 2017. USA.
The Son. Directed by Jean-Pierre and Luc Dardenne. 2002. Belgium.
The Spirit of the Beehive. Directed by Victor Erice. 1973 Spain.
The Sweet Hereafter. Directed by Atom Egoyan. 1997. Canada.
Through the Olive Trees. Directed by Abbas Kiarostami. 1994. Iran.
Timbuktu. Directed by Abderrahmane Sissako. 2014. France/Senegal.
Touch of Evil. Directed by Orson Welles. 1958. USA.
Under the Skin. Directed by Jonathan Glazer. 2013. UK.
Weekend. Directed by Andrew Haigh. 2011. UK.
Werckmeister Harmonies. Directed by Béla Tarr. 2000. Hungary.
What Time Is It There? Directed by Tsai Ming-Liang. Taiwan.
Woman Is the Future of Man. Directed by Sang-soo Hong. 2004. South Korea.
YiYi. Directed by Edward Yang. 2000. Taiwan.

Index